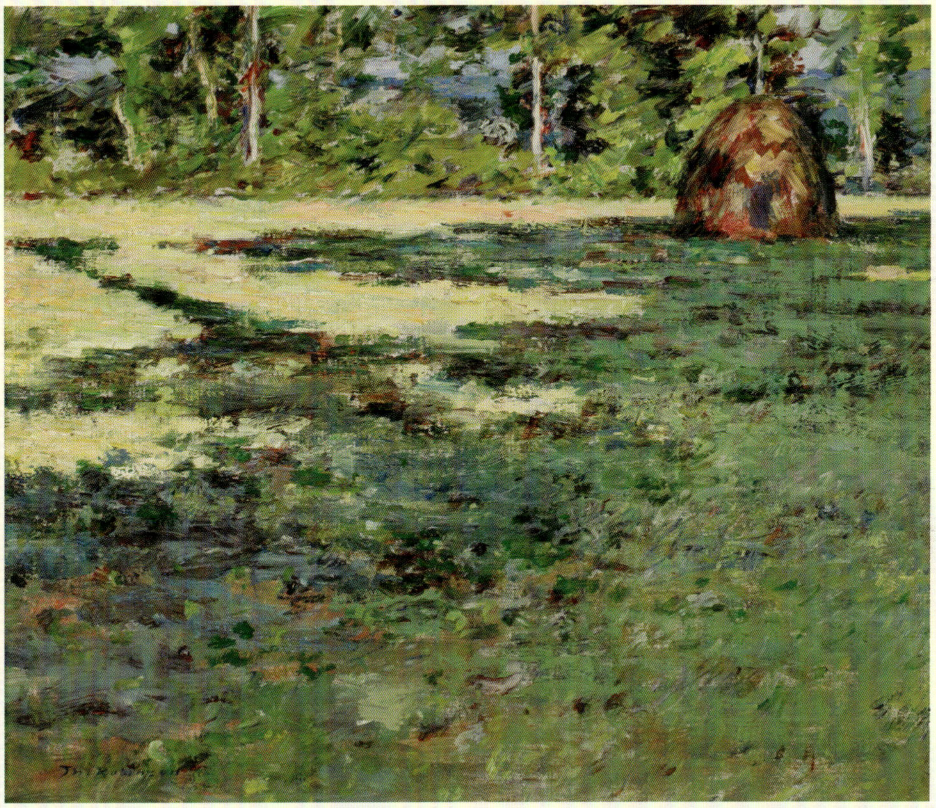

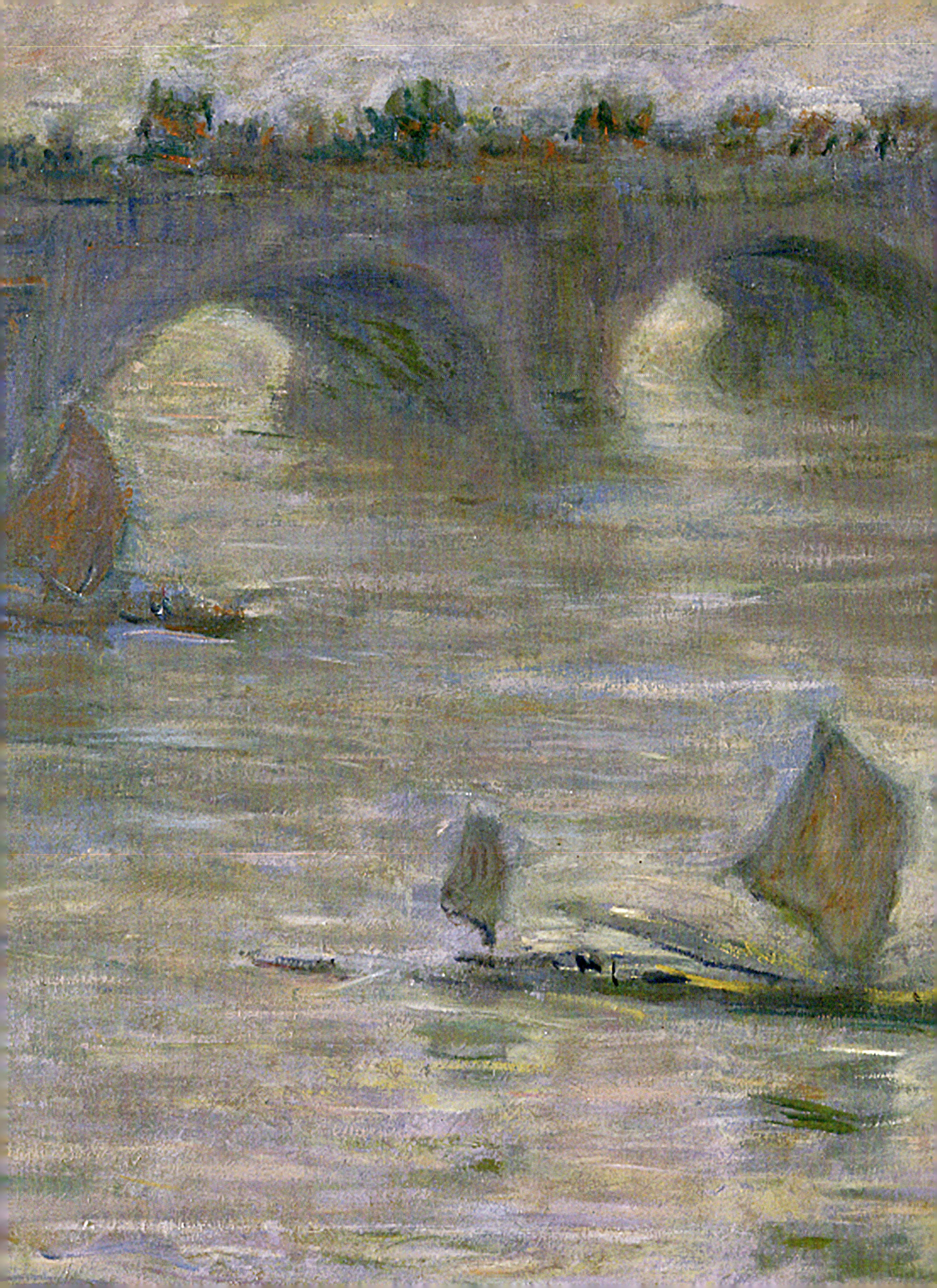

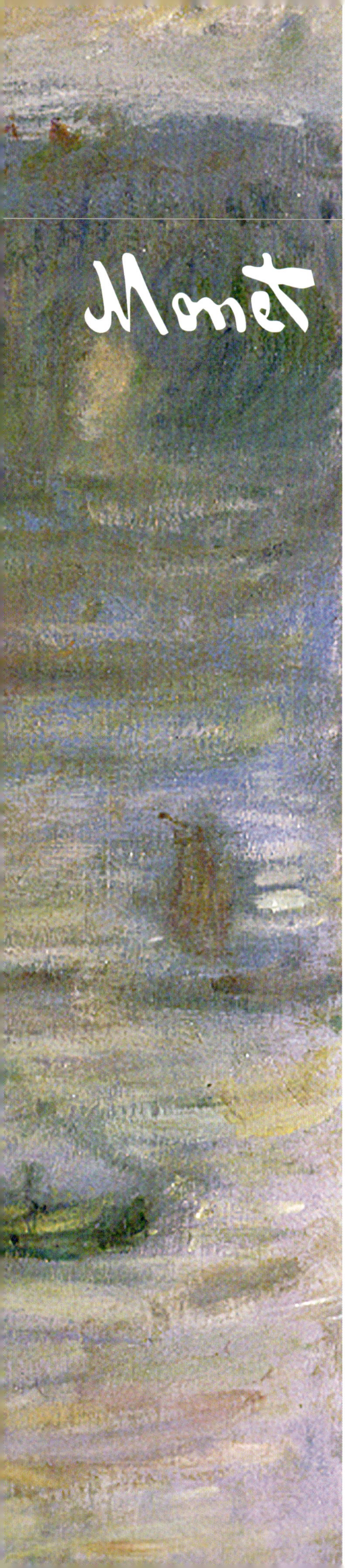

Monet and American Impressionism

DULCE M. ROMÁN

WITH AN ESSAY BY NANCY MOWLL MATHEWS

and contributions by

Sophia Krzys Acord

Sean Patrick Adams

Melissa Lee Hyde & Eric J. Segal

Courtney A. McNeil

Carol J. Murphy

Louise M. Newman

Stephanie A. Smith

Gayle Zachmann

Samuel P. Harn Museum of Art

UNIVERSITY OF FLORIDA, GAINESVILLE

Cover, front: Claude Monet, *Champ d'avoine (Oat Field)* (detail, pl. 3), 1890

Frontispiece: Theodore Robinson, *Afternoon Shadows* (pl. 5), 1891

Title page: Claude Monet, *Waterloo Bridge* (detail, pl. 40), 1903

Contents page: Guy Wiggins, *Columbus Circle, Winter* (detail, pl. 33), 1911

This publication is made possible by Michael A. and Donna Singer, with additional support from the University of Florida Office of Research, Bill and Hazel Hough, and the John Early Publication Endowment.

Printed in Canada on acid-free paper

20 19 18 17 16 15 6 5 4 3 2 1

Library of Congress Cataloging-in-Publication Data
Monet and American impressionism / Dulce M. Román ; with an essay by Nancy Mowll Mathews ; and contributions by Sophia Krzys Acord, Sean Patrick Adams, Melissa Lee Hyde and Eric J. Segal, Courtney A. McNeil, Carol J. Murphy, Louise M. Newman, Stephanie A. Smith, Gayle Zachmann.
pages cm
"Published in conjunction with the exhibition Monet and American Impressionism, organized by the Samuel P. Harn Museum of Art, University of Florida, in partnership with Telfair Museums and Hunter Museum of American Art."
Includes bibliographical references.
ISBN 978-0-9833085-1-5
1. Painting, American—19th century—Exhibitions. 2. Painting, American—20th century—Exhibitions. 3. Impressionism (Art)—United States—Exhibitions. 4. Monet, Claude, 1840–1926—Influence—Exhibitions. I. Román, Dulce María, writer of introduction. II. Mathews, Nancy Mowll. Monet and the Americans. III. Samuel P. Harn Museum of Art. IV. Telfair Museums (Savannah, Ga.) V. Hunter Museum of American Art.
ND210.5.I4M66 2015
759.13074'75979—dc23 2014039645

UF | UNIVERSITY of FLORIDA

Produced by the University Press of Florida · Design and composition by Louise OFarrell

HARN MUSEUM OF ART
UNIVERSITY OF FLORIDA

Published by the Samuel P. Harn Museum of Art
University of Florida
3259 Hull Road
Gainesville, Florida 32611-2700
www.harn.ufl.edu

This catalogue was published in conjunction with the exhibition *Monet and American Impressionism*, organized by the Samuel P. Harn Museum of Art, University of Florida, in partnership with the Telfair Museums and the Hunter Museum of American Art.

Samuel P. Harn Museum of Art, University of Florida, Gainesville
February 3, 2015–May 24, 2015

Hunter Museum of American Art, Chattanooga, Tennessee
June 25, 2015–September 20, 2015

Telfair Museums, Savannah, Georgia
October 16, 2015–January 24, 2016

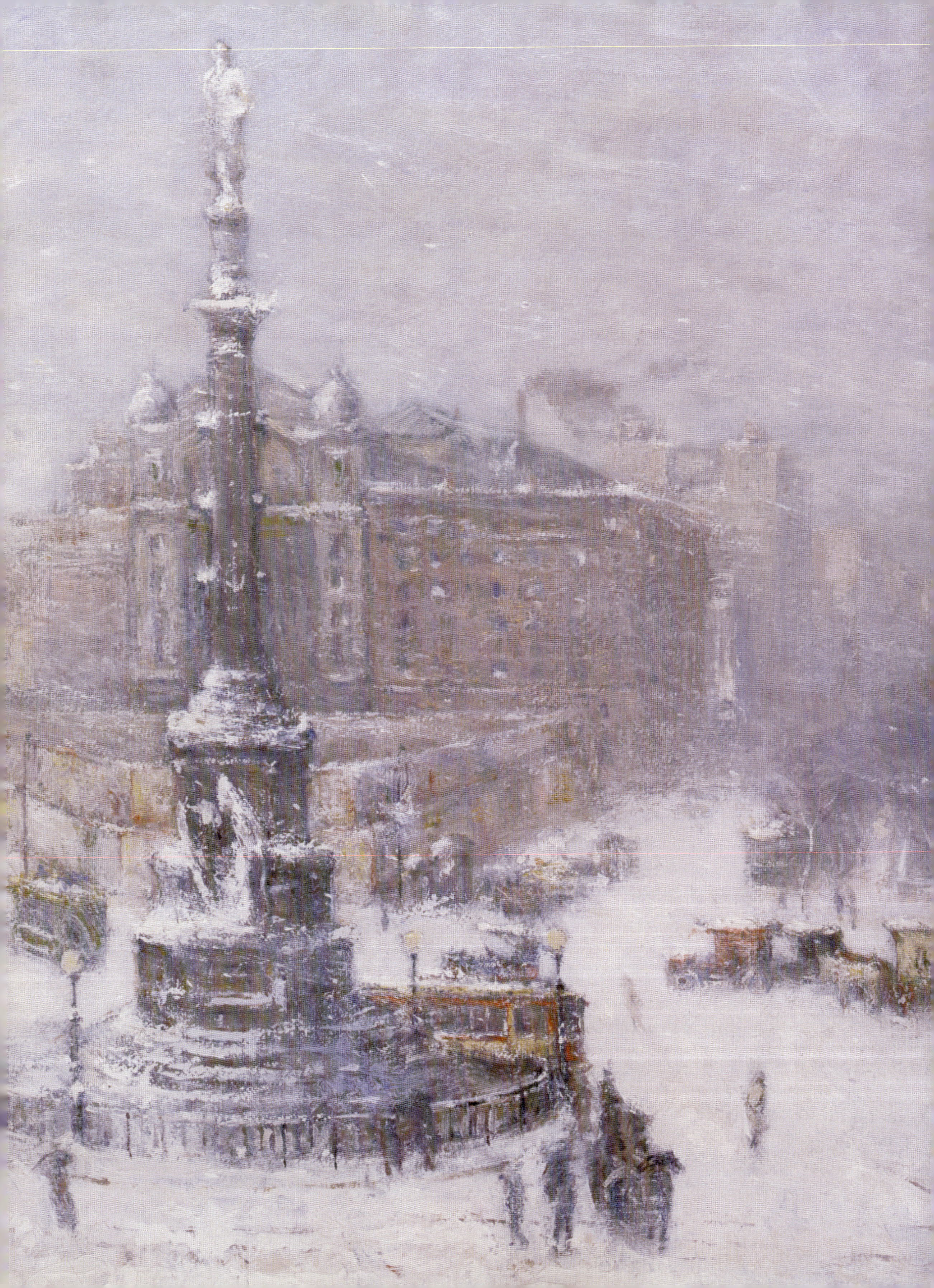

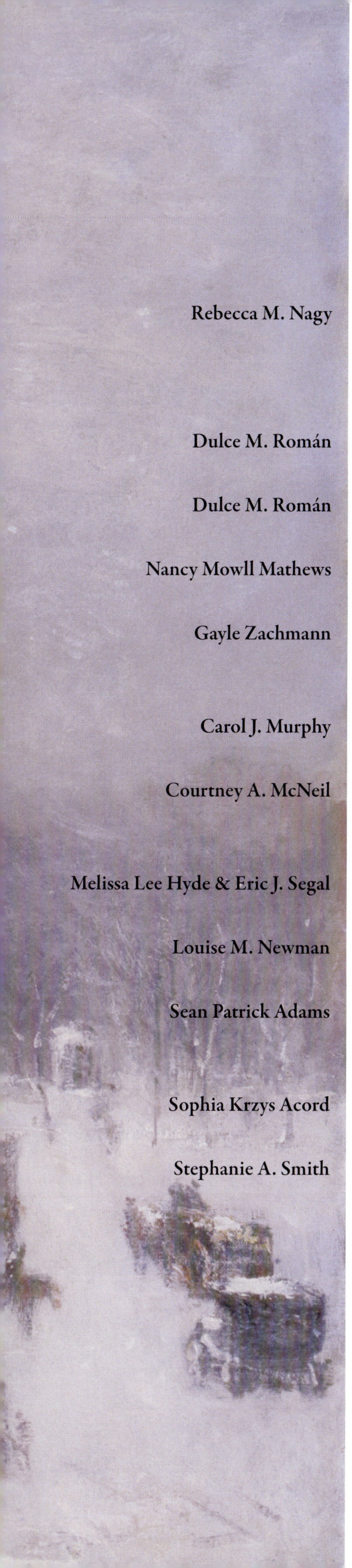

Contents

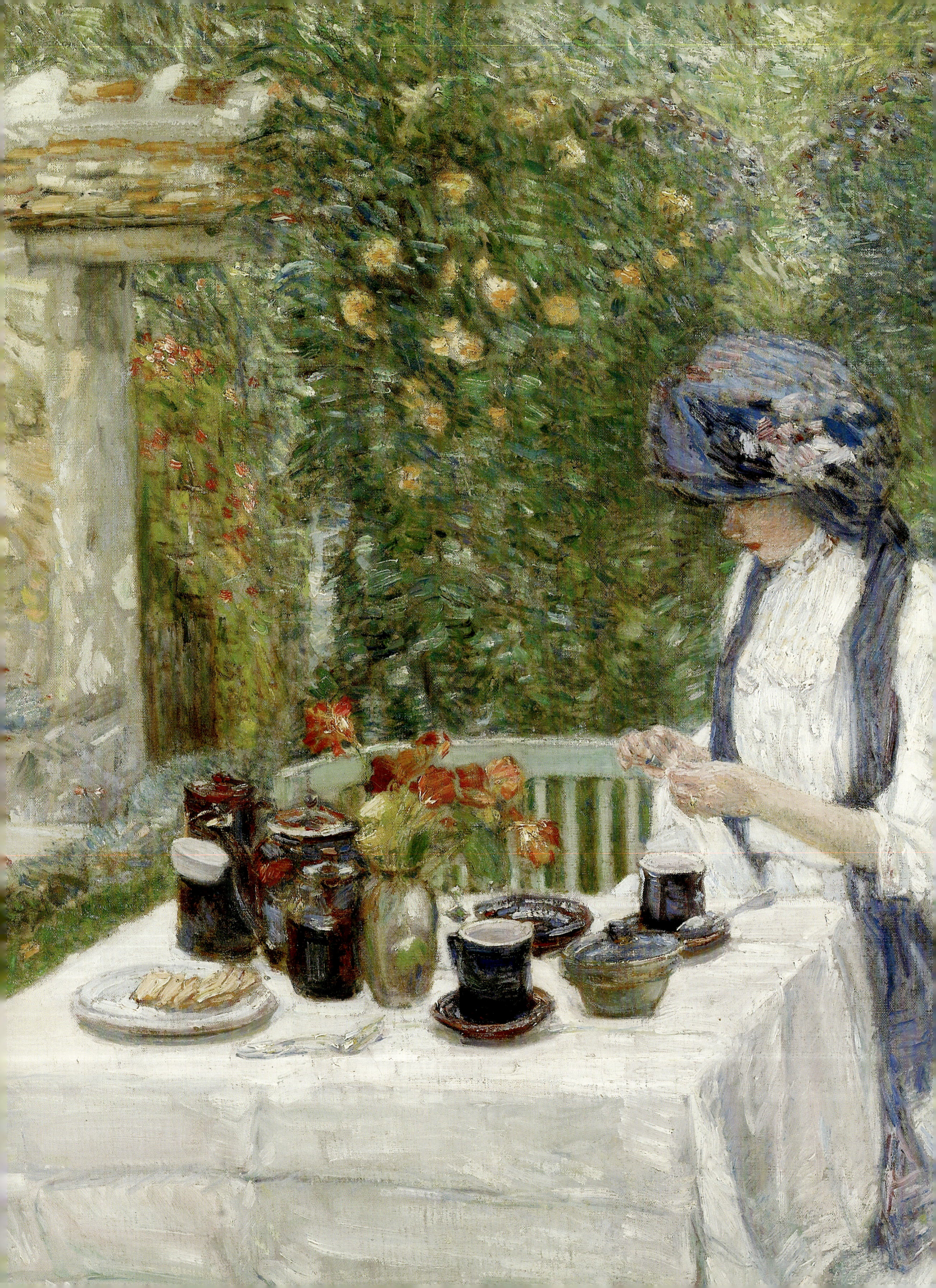

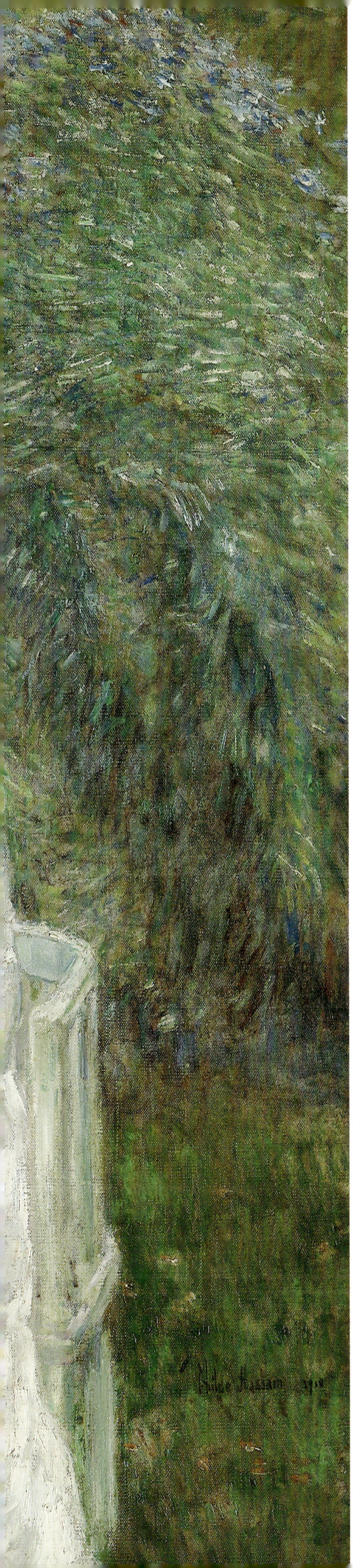

Foreword

REBECCA M. NAGY

Director, Harn Museum of Art

In 1999, when the Harn Museum of Art was only nine years old, the director received a surprising call. A friend and donor of the museum inquired if the museum would be receptive to the gift of a landscape painting by Monet, his splendid *Champ d'avoine* of 1890. Although the strength of the Harn's collection at that time was American art, the museum did not hesitate to accept this transformative gift from donor Michael A. Singer and his wife, Donna. Quickly the Monet was embraced by the community as a local treasure. Years later another faithful supporter of the Harn, Ruth Phillips, included in her bequest to the museum Rodin's lovely bronze *Faunesse debout*, and thus gradually the addition of French art to the galleries broadened our offerings. Meanwhile, Curator of Modern Art Dulce Román made the acquisition of works by American Impressionists a priority so that a strong connection could be made between the Harn's Monet and the American collection. Today the collection includes paintings by Frederick Childe Hassam, Theodore Robinson, J. Alden Weir, and Maurice Brazil Prendergast and prints by Hassam and Frank Benson.

The growing strength of Impressionist works in the collection inspired Ms. Román to build an exhibition around them, focusing on the influence of Monet and his fellow French Impressionists on their American contemporaries. As she began to explore possibilities for loans, she found the curators of two other southeastern museums to be kindred spirits. Building on these new friendships, I had fruitful conversations with Daniel Stetson, director of the Hunter Museum of American Art in

Frederick Childe Hassam (American, 1859–1935), *French Tea Garden* (also known as *The Terre-Cuite Tea Set*) (detail, pl. 35), 1910

Chattanooga, and Lisa Grove, director of the Telfair Museums in Savannah. These talks led to a partnership among the three museums, each of which has contributed a number of major works of art to the exhibition. In addition, the Telfair's curator of fine arts and exhibitions Courtney A. McNeil agreed to contribute an essay on Impressionist prints to the exhibition catalogue. I am grateful to our colleagues in Chattanooga and Savannah for embracing the project at an early stage of its development and for their strong support through planning and implementation. It is a joy to work with congenial colleagues to produce an Impressionism show that offers fresh scholarship and new perspectives on the artists and their work while also holding strong appeal for audiences in our home cities and surrounding regions.

At the University of Florida, numerous faculty members have contributed to the success of the exhibition and accompanying publication through participation on the exhibition advisory committee and the contribution of essays for the catalogue. In addition, Nancy Mowll Mathews provided an insightful and informative lead essay, setting the context for these contributions from University of Florida scholars. Community members who served on the advisory committee also shared their expertise and ideas to make the installation of the show and the interpretive programs dynamic and exciting. I thank each of them most sincerely for these generous contributions.

I congratulate Ms. Román on the realization of her vision of a major Impressionism exhibition. In her acknowledgments she recognizes and thanks each of the institutions and private collectors who loaned works to the exhibition, despite the fact that it is very hard to part with one's Impressionist treasures! She thanks the many generous donors who made the exhibition and catalogue possible. And she recognizes the contributions of many members of the Harn staff who have worked collaboratively as an effective team to organize and install a stunning exhibition as well as to plan an array of stimulating and rewarding programs around the show. I add my heartfelt thanks to hers.

Lenders to the Exhibition

Adelson Galleries, Inc., New York
The Art Museum at the University of Kentucky, Lexington
The Baltimore Museum of Art, Maryland
Brooklyn Museum, New York
Chrysler Museum of Art, Norfolk, Virginia
The Columbus Museum, Georgia
Cornell Fine Arts Museum, Rollins College, Winter Park, Florida
The Cummer Museum of Art & Gardens, Jacksonville, Florida
Gari Melchers Home and Studio, University of Mary Washington, Fredericksburg, Virginia
Georgia Museum of Art, University of Georgia, Athens
High Museum of Art, Atlanta, Georgia
Hunter Museum of American Art, Chattanooga, Tennessee
Library of Congress, Washington, D.C.
Lowe Art Museum, University of Miami, Florida
The Metropolitan Museum of Art, New York
National Gallery of Art, Washington, D.C.
The Newark Museum, New Jersey
The New York Public Library, Astor, Lenox and Tilden Foundations
North Carolina Museum of Art, Raleigh
Pennsylvania Academy of the Fine Arts, Philadelphia
Philadelphia Museum of Art, Pennsylvania
Reynolda House Museum of American Art, Winston-Salem, North Carolina
Samuel P. Harn Museum of Art, University of Florida, Gainesville
Smithsonian American Art Museum, Washington, D.C.
Telfair Museums, Savannah, Georgia
Terra Foundation for American Art, Daniel J. Terra Collection, Chicago, Illinois
Virginia Museum of Fine Arts, Richmond
Williams College Museum of Art, Williamstown, Massachusetts

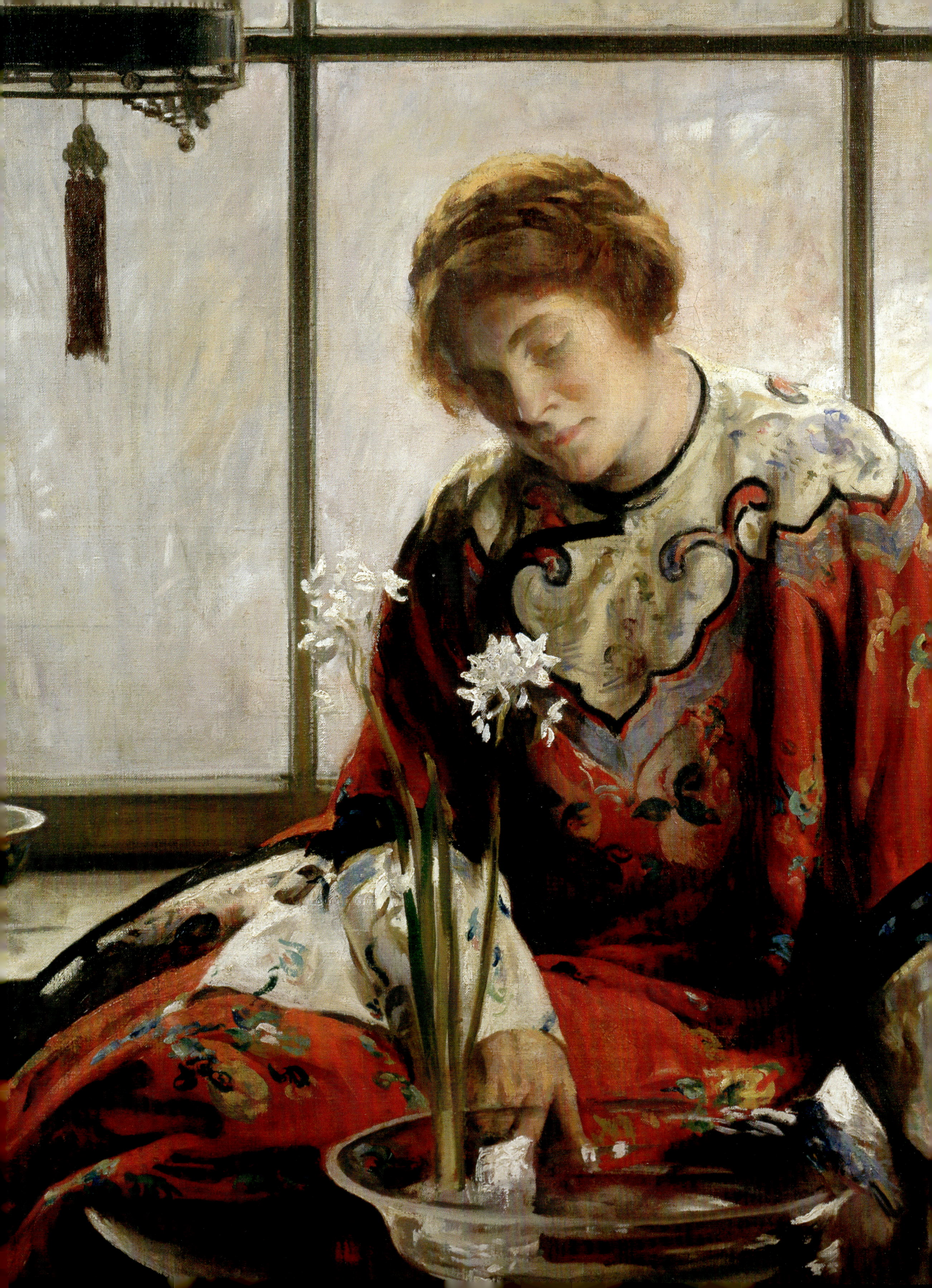

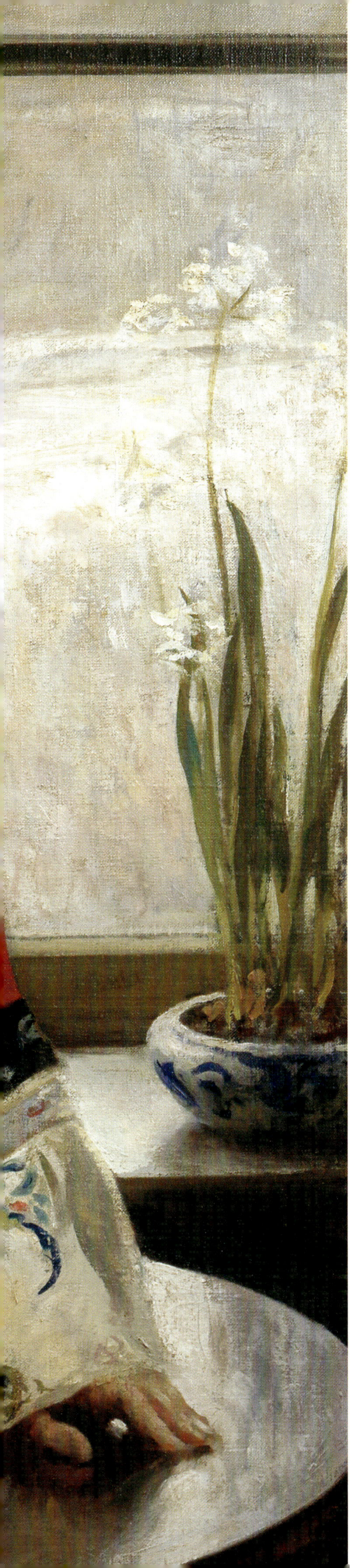

Acknowledgments

DULCE M. ROMÁN

Curator of Modern Art, Harn Museum of Art

THIS EXHIBITION and its catalogue reflect the contributions and support of many individuals and institutions who have given of their time, expertise, and resources. I have been honored to work with so many talented and generous people.

I am deeply grateful to those who have so generously provided financial support for this exhibition and accompanying publication. In particular, I wish to acknowledge Michael A. and Donna Singer, the University of Florida Office of Research, Bill and Hazel Hough, and the John Early Publication Endowment, whose contributions have made this handsome catalogue possible. The exhibition received generous support from the AEC Trust, the University of Florida Office of the Provost, the C. Frederick and Aase B. Thompson Foundation, Dr. Robert Thoburn, the Harn Museum 20th Anniversary Fund, the John V. and Patricia M. Carlson Program Endowment, the Londono Family Endowment, the Eloise R. Chandler Program Endowment, and the Harold Walton and Margaret Harn Goforth Endowment. I would also like to acknowledge the Alachua County Visitors and Convention Bureau who provided funds to promote the exhibition to out-of-county areas through the Tourism Product Development Grant.

A symposium, "America and France: New Perspectives on Transatlantic Visual Culture," has been organized in conjunction with the exhibition and will be supported in part by the Harn Eminent Scholar Chair in Art History Program, School of Art and Art History.

Joseph Rodefer De Camp (American, 1858–1923), *The Red Kimono* (detail, pl. 43), c. 1919

It has been a pleasure to work with our partners on this exhibition and tour, the Telfair Museums and Hunter Museum of American Art, and their directors, Lisa Grove and Daniel Stetson, respectively. I thank them for their enthusiasm and commitment to the project and for their loans, which formed the initial core of the project. Staff members at each institution deserve thanks for their kind assistance. In particular, I would like to thank Courtney A. McNeil, curator of fine arts and exhibitions, and Jessica Mumford Estes, registrar, at the Telfair Museums; Nandini Makrandi, chief curator, and Elizabeth Le and Theresa Slowikowski, registrars, at the Hunter Museum of American Art; and Ellen Simak, former chief curator at the Hunter Museum of American Art.

The inclusion of singular works of art is pivotal to the success of this exhibition and tour. Heartfelt thanks are extended to the many lenders to the exhibition for their willingness to part with treasures for the year required to complete the tour. Their names appear preceding these acknowledgments.

I also wish to thank the authors who contributed their scholarship to this publication. Nancy Mowll Mathews deserves special recognition. I have benefited greatly from her knowledge and invaluable advice in selecting works of art for the exhibition and refining exhibition themes. In addition to contributing an insightful essay on Impressionist prints, Courtney A. McNeil provided guidance on locating prints for the exhibition. Collegial support was provided by Eric Segal, the Harn's education curator of academic programs. His efforts resulted in identifying University of Florida faculty contributors whose expertise has enriched the catalogue: Sophia Krzys Acord, Sean Patrick Adams, Melissa Lee Hyde, Carol J. Murphy, Louise M. Newman, Stephanie A. Smith, and Gayle Zachmann. Emeritus professor of musicology David Z. Kushner contributed an essay on Impressionism and American music for the related exhibition website.

I also am indebted to Michele Fiyak-Burkley, editorial, design, and production manager at University Press of Florida, for her expertise in catalogue production. I am especially grateful for Louise OFarrell's elegant design and for copy editor Jonathan Lawrence's and proofreader Jennifer Boynton's scrupulous attention to detail.

Special thanks are due to the faculty, community members, docents, and students who volunteered their time to serve on an advisory committee and who shared their knowledge and ideas regarding exhibition interpretation, collaborative opportunities, and stimulating educational programs. They include Karla Aguayo, Hélène Blondeau, Alexandra Braddy, Jennifer L. Gillett-Kaufman, Tina Gurucharri, Amandine Hom, Bobby Hom, Melissa Lee Hyde, Sheryl Kroen, Andrea Lucky, Annie Pais, Susan Robell, Alioune Sow, Michele Gonzales Talmor, and Keith D. White. I also benefited from the help of exceptional interns, many of them University of

Florida students: Amy Brown, Carolina Chavez, Kimberly Gross, Bethany Guglielmino, Rachel Shroats, Sarah Soltis, Anna Toptchi, Gianina Valle, and Emily Wood. Each assisted with administrative tasks, research, gallery interpretation strategies, and other important aspects of exhibition planning.

Organizing and implementing an exhibition of this size and complexity is a team effort. I am sincerely grateful for the opportunity to work with the dedicated staff of the Harn, whose talents comprise a major resource for the museum. I am especially indebted to the registration and preparation department, led by registrar Laura Nemmers, who worked with enthusiasm in support of the exhibition from the planning stages through its implementation. Special thanks go to Jessica Uelsmann, associate registrar, who expertly managed the day-to-day oversight of exhibition contracts and loan agreements, packing and coordination of shipping, and oversight of the exhibition installation. Assistant registrar Elizabeth Bemis provided crucial assistance with record keeping, condition reporting and installation while registration assistant Alyssa Magnone provided much needed help with administrative tasks and condition reporting. I also wish to recognize chief preparator Michael Peyton and preparator Tim Joiner, who did an extraordinary job of installing the exhibition. Their astute observations regarding installation design were much appreciated.

A special note of appreciation goes to Megan Pugh, coordinator of marketing and public relations, who obtained photography and managed rights and reproductions permissions for the catalogue. Tami Wroath, director of marketing and public relations, worked with Resnicow Schroeder Associates and the Alachua County Visitors and Convention Bureau to market and promote the exhibition and catalogue. I also wish to express my thanks to departmental colleagues Ivy Chen, curatorial program coordinator, and curators Susan Cooksey, Carol McCusker, Kerry Oliver-Smith, and Jason Steuber for proofing gallery interpretation and sharing their insights throughout the project. I am also grateful to Eric Segal, Brandi Breslin, and Elizabeth King for devising and managing the engaging educational programming in support of the exhibition; to Phyllis DeLaney for her expertise in fund-raising for the exhibition; and to Mary Yawn for overseeing budgetary aspects of the project. I am especially grateful to Harn director Rebecca Nagy, whose encouragement and enthusiastic commitment to this project made the exhibition and catalogue possible.

Finally, I thank my wonderful family, especially my husband, Tim, and our son, Timothy, who provided enduring devotion and support throughout this project.

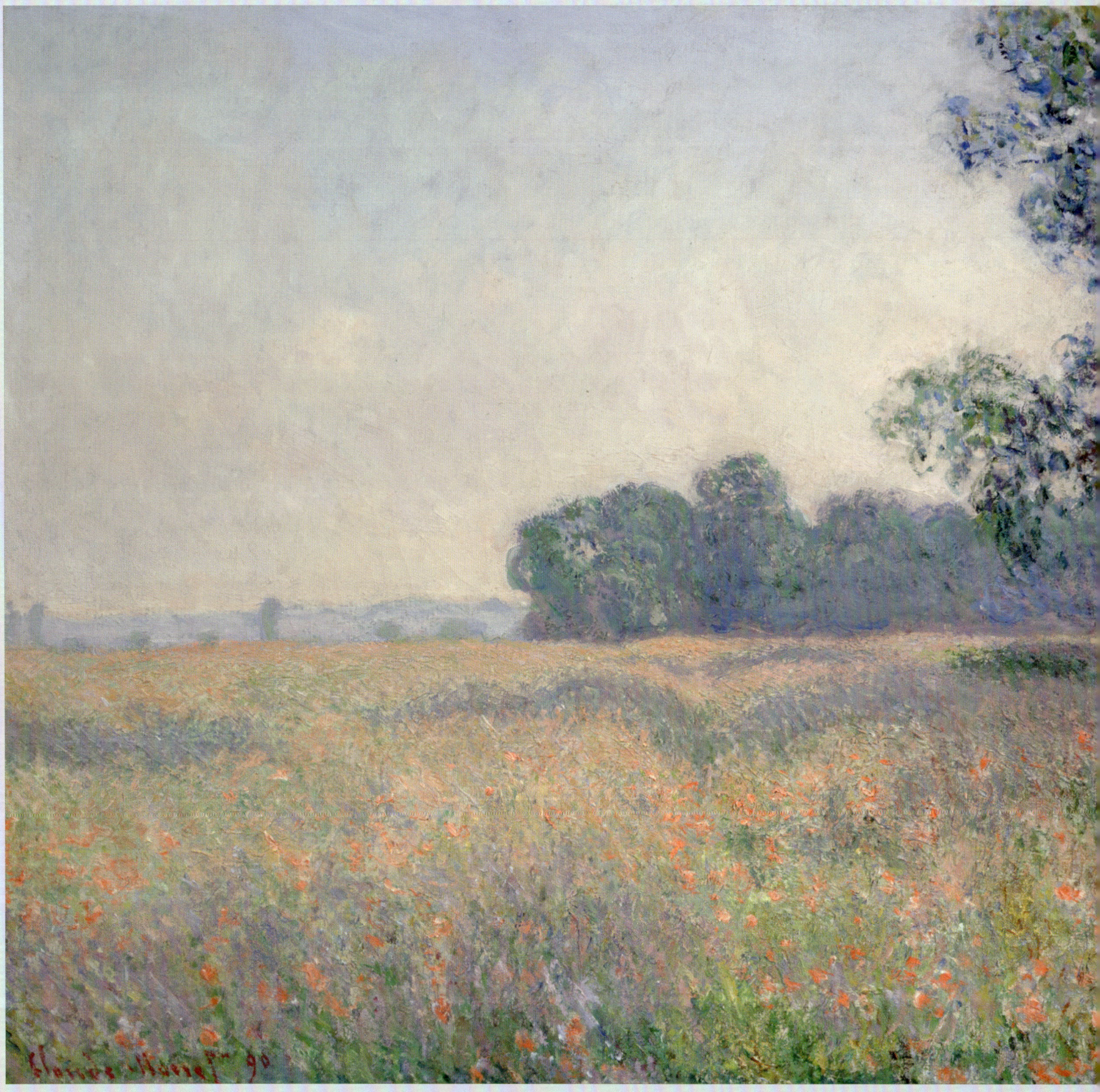

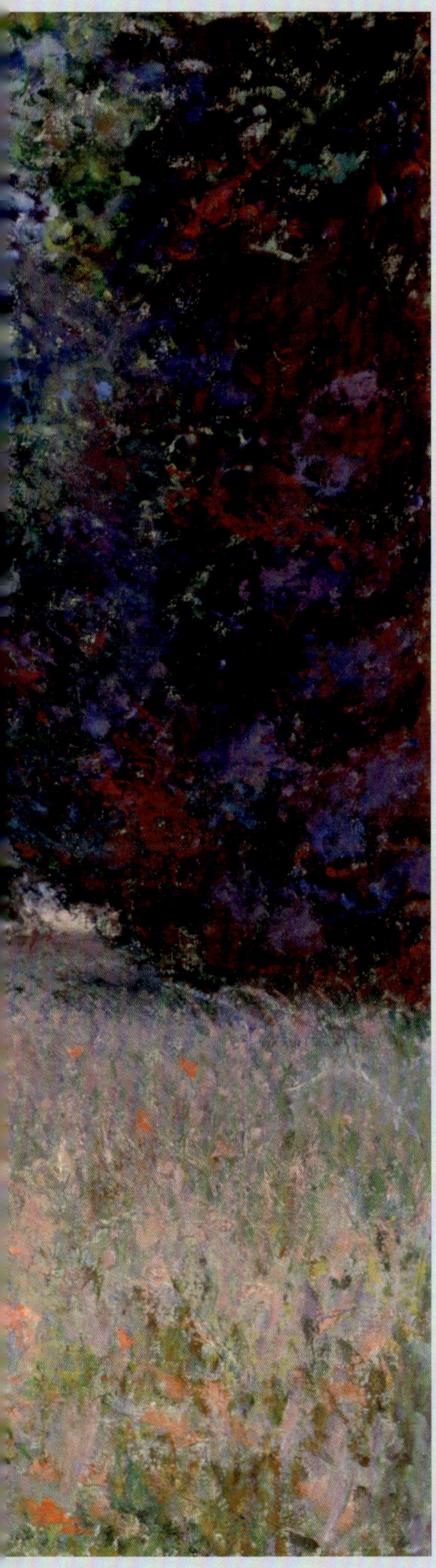

Introduction

Monet and American Impressionism

DULCE M. ROMÁN

MONET AND AMERICAN IMPRESSIONISM highlights the work of American artists who launched a new way of painting in the late nineteenth century in response to the innovations of Claude Monet (1840–1926) and his French contemporaries. This focus on Monet is inspired by the Harn Museum's landscape, *Champ d'avoine (Oat Field)* (Fig. 1, Pl. 3). Painted in Giverny in 1890, this landscape is a superb example of Monet's exploration of momentary effects of light on one's perception of color and form. Following the example of Monet, the artists surveyed in this exhibition rejected the established academic tradition of painting idealized historical subjects, allegories, and portraits with carefully blended brushstrokes and restrained color. Instead, they favored pictures that emphasized the transience of everyday reality and utilized spontaneous methods involving quick, visible brushstrokes, a bright palette, and an emphasis on light and its changing qualities.

Strictly speaking, the term *Impressionists* refers to the group of French artists who showed their work in eight exhibitions held in Paris between 1874 and 1886. The most recognizable names include Edgar Degas, Camille Pissarro, Pierre-Auguste Renoir, Alfred Sisley, and Claude Monet, whose painting *Impression, soleil levant* (*Impression, Sunrise*), 1873 (Musée Marmottan, Paris), led an art critic to coin the group's name.[1] Although Edouard Manet is often credited as their leader, he consistently refused his colleagues' invitations to exhibit with them, preferring instead to submit his paintings to the Paris Salon. In the late nineteenth and early twentieth

FIGURE 1, PLATE 3. Claude Monet (French, 1840–1926), *Champ d'avoine (Oat Field)*, 1890, oil on canvas, 26 × 36 7/16 in. (66 × 92.6 cm), Samuel P. Harn Museum of Art, University of Florida, Gainesville, Gift of Michael A. Singer, 1999.6

centuries, Monet was the acknowledged "father" and "high priest" of Impressionism, and his seemingly spontaneous, rapidly executed landscapes, city views, and domestic subjects painted in a light palette were emulated by artists on both sides of the Atlantic.[2] It is generally recognized that American Impressionism owes more to this taste for Monet than to any other painter.[3] Although the style and techniques used by American Impressionists varied widely, each of these artists shared an interest in treating subjects drawn from modern life and capturing fleeting atmospheric light effects through loosely painted daubs of broken color.

The works presented in the exhibition offer a broad survey of American Impressionism as practiced by many of its leading figures: Mary Cassatt, William Merritt Chase, Frederick Childe Hassam, Willard Metcalf, Theodore Robinson, John Henry Twachtman, and J. Alden Weir.[4] In the late nineteenth century, they adapted the innovations of French Impressionism and ultimately paved the way to its place as one of the most enduring styles in American painting. Some of these artists had direct knowledge of Monet's theories and techniques through extended stays in Giverny, where Monet had established his home and studio in 1883. Others were exposed to his style through exhibitions of his art or through the filter of important teachers such as Robinson and Metcalf. The oil paintings, watercolors, pastels, and prints in the exhibition are grouped along five themes that parallel many of the subjects found in Monet's oeuvre. These thematic sections are "The Allure of Giverny," "A Country Retreat," "The Vibrance of Urbanism," "The Comfort of Home," and "A Graphic Legacy." These examples indicate an awareness of Monet's innovations. Yet, as is evident in the works on display, American artists responded to Monet in different ways and to varying degrees.

The American paintings presented in *Monet and American Impressionism* span the years between 1887 and 1920. These dates mark the beginning of Monet's influence on American artists and the end of Impressionism as a popular style in American art. Although Impressionist techniques and subjects continued to attract American artists well into the 1920s, the Impressionist aesthetic had diminished in popularity by the mid-1910s in the wake of competing art movements. The most significant event in its decline was the 1913 International Exhibition of Modern Art, also known as the Armory Show, which introduced American audiences to the avant-garde styles of Pablo Picasso's Cubism, Henri Matisse's Fauvism, and Marcel Duchamp's Futurism.

The period covered by the present exhibition involved immense changes and upheaval that informed artistic production. These years witnessed new inventions (automobiles, electric lights, telephones, moving pictures, cameras), political changes (social reform, child-labor laws, women's suffrage), and social changes (more educational and work opportunities for women). This catalogue includes eight essays representing the fields of art history, American history, French literature, and sociology that shed light on these developments and contribute to the dialogue on how American artists applied the style and themes of French Impressionism to their depictions of contemporary life in the United States. In her essay "Monet and the Americans: Whose Impressionism?" Nancy Mowll Mathews focuses on the appeal of Impressionism for American artists and the role played by nationalistic concerns in artists' acceptance of the new imported painting style. Gayle Zachmann's essay, "Framing Impressionisms: Mirrors of Dissonance and Realism in Literature and the Visual Arts," provides insight into the early critical response to French Impressionism through the lens of the French poet-critic Stéphane Mallarmé, who sought to situate the new movement historically, aesthetically, and ideologically. In "Seeing Nature, Poetically: Proust and Impressionism," Carol J. Murphy discusses scientific discoveries and technological advances that revolutionized existing theories of sight and presented new ways of seeing that paralleled the basic tenets of Impressionism.

Courtney A. McNeil's essay, "Imprinting Impressionism: The Graphic Work of Mary Cassatt, Frank Benson, and Childe Hassam," addresses the challenges of translating Impressionist ways of seeing into the graphic media of etching, drypoint, aquatint, and lithography. In their essay "Women and the Nature of Impressionism," Melissa Lee Hyde and Eric J. Segal examine the role of gender in paintings by male and female artists and what these images tell us about cultural understandings of women in the period. This subject is also addressed by Louise M. Newman in "The 'Woman Question' in American Impressionist Painting, 1880–1920." Newman provides insights into the social changes affecting American women's lives in the Victorian era and how these cultural concerns inform our understanding of depictions of the intimate lives of women. In "Constructing Landscapes: Impressionism, Urban Parks, and the City Beautiful Movement," Sean Patrick Adams describes a set of reform policies that established the foundations of urban planning and development at the turn of the twentieth century. Our understanding of a number of paintings in the exhibition is enhanced by Adams's discussion of these policies, which were aimed at improving urban living conditions in the United States.

In "A Taste for What 'Moves' Us: The Audiences of American Impressionism," Sophia Krzys Acord engages sociological themes in her discussion of the roles played by patrons, artists, and museums in the creation of a taste for American Impressionism in the United States. Complementing these essays is a fictional account that focuses on Childe Hassam and his influence on the formation of a young female artist. Stephanie A. Smith's "Winter Studio, 1901 (A Short Story)" reflects many of the exhibition's themes, especially the subjects of modernity and changing social roles of women in the period.

Impressionism and the American Audience

By the late nineteenth century, American artists studying in Paris academies were learning about French Impressionism through the group's eight exhibitions as well as through exhibitions of Impressionist art at the École des Beaux-Arts, Galerie Durand-Ruel, Galerie Bernheim-Jeune, and other venues. The initial response among many American artists in France, however, was lukewarm. In a letter to his parents about the experience of viewing the third Impressionist exhibition in 1877, J. Alden Weir wrote: "I went across the river the other day to see an exhibition of the work of a new school which call themselves 'Impressionalists,' I never in my life saw more horrible things. . . . It was worse than the Chamber of Horrors."[5] As a student of the French academic painter Jean-Léon Gérôme in Paris, Weir still adhered to academic principles such as highly finished surfaces and figures conceived in the round; he was not yet ready for the revolutionary new approach to painting represented by Monet and his contemporaries.

American audiences began to warm up to Impressionism after several important exhibitions in New York and Boston. The Foreign Exhibition, held in Boston in 1883, included paintings by Monet, Pissarro, Renoir, and Sisley. An exhibition at New York's American Art Association in 1886, organized by Paris art dealer Paul Durand-Ruel, featured nearly three hundred French works, including forty-eight by Monet.[6] Other exhibitions of Monet's work were held at the Union League Club in New York (1891), St. Botolph Club in Boston (1892 and 1899), and the World's Columbian Exposition in Chicago (1893), thus expanding the American public's knowledge of Monet and sparking critical interest in French Impressionism. American collectors soon began to make important purchases of Impressionist paintings, thus providing additional examples for artists to discover when they toured important private collections.[7] By the mid-1880s, Americans were among Monet's top customers, so much so that in 1886 Monet lamented to his dealer, Paul Durand-Ruel: "After all that you have sent to America, what remains in France?"[8] The Harn's *Champ d'avoine* was purchased in 1891 by one of these early collectors, John Nicholas Brown of Rhode Island, and was included in the 1892 and 1899 Monet exhibitions at St. Botolph Club in Boston. On April 7, 1891, the art dealer Desmond Fitzgerald wrote to Brown urging him to purchase the painting: "It is the most complete picture that I have ever seen of Monet's and a masterpiece. . . . It will be worth $10,000 some day."[9]

Beginning in the 1880s, many American artists who were attending Paris art academies spent their summer breaks in Giverny, the small village in Normandy that Monet called home. Attracted by Monet's presence, they hoped to gain informal guidance and to paint *en plein air*, outdoors, in the company of like-minded artists.

This first generation of American artists in Giverny included Robinson, Metcalf, and Lilla Cabot Perry, among others. These early converts to Impressionism returned to the States and shared their enthusiasm for the innovations of Monet with their American colleagues. In addition, the success of expatriate artists who had become associated with Impressionism helped smooth the way for other artists to experiment in the new style. Three in particular—James Abbott McNeill Whistler (1834–1903), John Singer Sargent (1856–1925) and Mary Cassatt (1844–1926)—served as early models for artists back home. Americans viewed Whistler's atmospheric and loosely painted landscapes as radical, and associated him with the new Impressionist style. Inspired by his friendship with Monet, whom he visited in Giverny between 1887 and 1891, Sargent painted his own landscapes *en plein air* with a loose brush technique during a brief Impressionist period that lasted from 1883 to 1889.[10] The fact that Cassatt was the only American to exhibit with the French Impressionists did not go unnoticed back home. Much of the critical attention surrounding her exhibition in New York in 1895 centered on her American nationality.[11]

By the mid-1890s, American artists had become enthralled with the new style and had begun to show their Impressionist paintings to a wide audience. Important venues included the 1893 World's Columbian Exposition in Chicago, group exhibitions organized by the Society of American Artists, and, beginning in 1898, exhibitions of the newly formed "Ten American Painters." Most members of "The Ten" are represented in this exhibition: Hassam, Metcalf, Weir, Twachtman, Frank Benson, Joseph Rodefer De Camp, and Edmund C. Tarbell, as well as Chase, who joined the group in 1905.[12] As discussed below, other important factors in the spread of Impressionism in America included the formation of art colonies and the teaching activities of leading painters.

The Allure of Giverny

Monet's influence was felt most profoundly among the early pioneers who spent extended periods of time in Giverny. A number of these artists are represented in this section of the exhibition: Metcalf, Robinson, Perry, and Theodore Earl Butler.[13] In Giverny they painted outdoors while enjoying the camaraderie of other artists centered at the Hôtel Baudy, which served as a social nexus offering attractive amenities such as a café, studio spaces, and tennis courts.[14]

Theodore Robinson (1852–1896) was the leader of the first generation of American artists who painted in Giverny.[15] He may have visited the colony as early as 1885 and spent half of each year there between 1887 and 1892. The early 1890s marked the high point of his response to Monet, which involved a fluid handling of paint, luminous and atmospheric color, and an interest in the effects of light on a particular view at specific times of day. Robinson's *House with Scaffolding, Giverny*, 1892 (Pl. 9), demonstrates his ability to capture reflected moonlight on a building and its surround-ings. Here, he used short, quick brushstrokes and a subdued chromatic range to convey a sensual experience that he described as evoking "much mystery."[16] Robinson also was familiar with Monet's taste for asymmetrically balanced compositions and his use of space created through carefully measured intervals—techniques that are present in Monet's *Champ d'avoine.* Robinson used these devices in *Afternoon Shadows* (Pl. 5), painted in Giverny in 1891. This landscape portrays a single stack of grain in a meadow of vivid greens and yellows bordered by a stand of trees. The deep shadows in the foreground recede toward the sunlit boundary of the field, suggesting midday. Robinson borrowed both the theme and the idea for working in series from Monet.

Willard Leroy Metcalf (1858–1925) may have visited Giverny as early as 1885 and certainly by 1886.[17] His *Giverny* landscape of 1887 (Pl. 4) possesses vibrant sunlight and shadows, a high-keyed palette, and a loose handling of paint. It also shows his commitment to representing the essence of a place as opposed to its details. Following his return to the States in 1888, Metcalf built a reputation as a painter of rural landscapes that emphasized the changing seasons and qualities of light (Pl. 18, *The Thawing Brook,* 1917).

Theodore Earl Butler (1861–1936), another early visitor to Giverny, arrived in 1888 and eventually married one of Monet's stepdaughters, Suzanne Hoschedé-Monet, thus becoming a permanent resident of the village.[18] In the 1890s Butler focused his attention on painting his family at their home in Giverny. *Un Jardin, Maison Baptiste* (Pl. 10), painted in the summer of 1895, depicts the family cottage and surrounding garden in a blanket of soft pastels. A sense of immediacy in the brushwork attests to Butler's continued interest in working *en plein air*. The strong diagonal of the composition suggests familiarity with Monet's practice of using the inherent geometry he saw in nature as an organizing principle for his landscapes.

Lilla Cabot Perry (1848–1933), one of the few women artists to spend time in Giverny, made nine visits to the colony between 1889 and 1909 and developed a close friendship with Monet.[19] Her Giverny landscape *A Stream Beneath Poplars*, c. 1890–1900 (Pl. 1), emulates Monet's subject matter and recalls his rural landscapes of fields lined with poplars painted in the 1880s. *A Stream Beneath Poplars* also follows Monet's use of broken color, varied surface texture, and fleeting effects of light. In her "Reminiscences," written shortly after Monet's death in 1926, she explained his method as follows: "Monet's philosophy of painting was to paint what you really see, not what you think you ought to see; not the object isolated as in a test tube, but the object enveloped in sunlight and atmosphere."[20]

FIGURE 2. Claude Monet (French, 1840–1926), *The Artist's Garden at Vétheuil*, 1880, oil on canvas, 59 ⅝ × 47 ⅝ in. (151.5 × 121 cm), Courtesy National Gallery of Art, Washington, D.C., Ailsa Mellon Bruce Collection, 1970.17.45

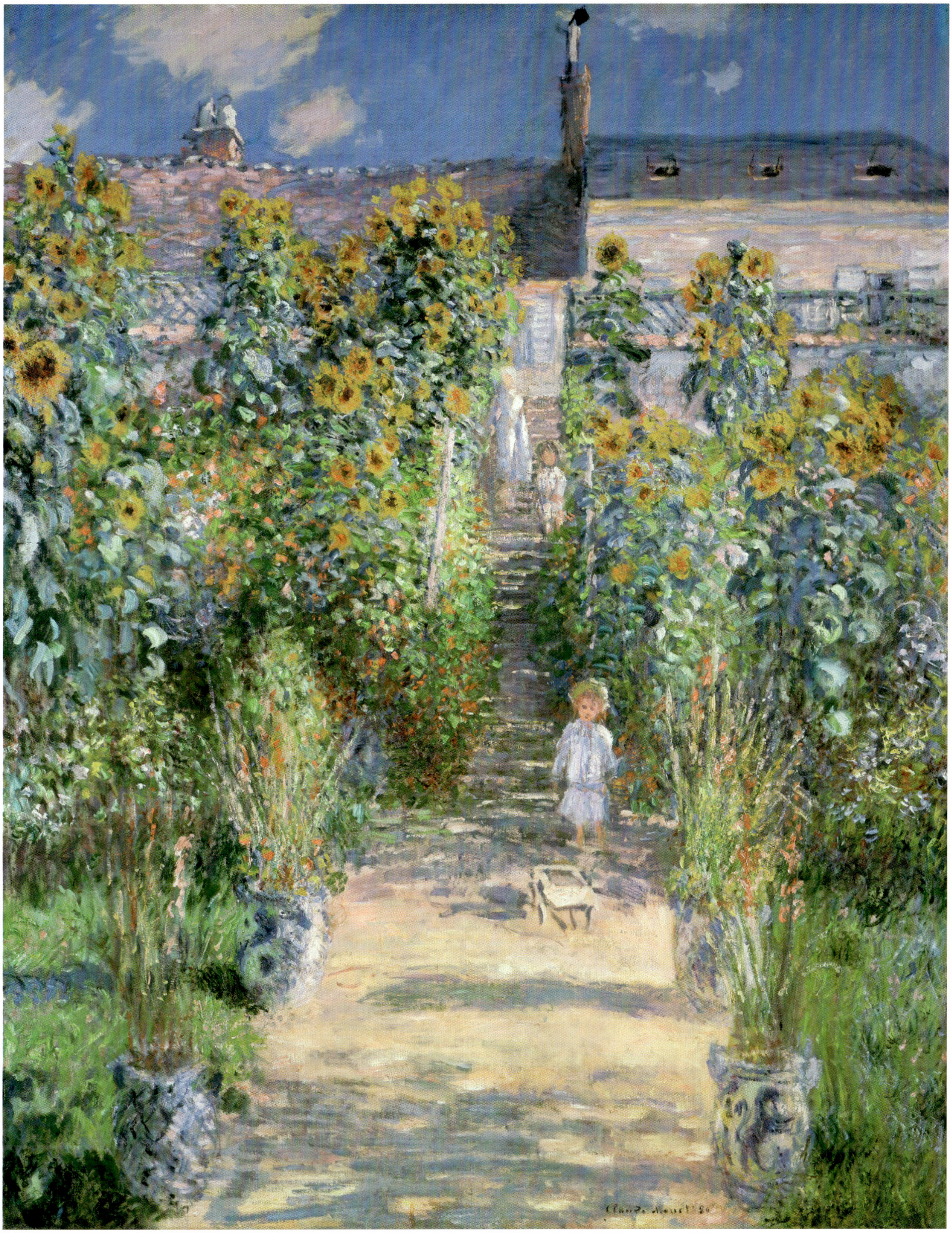

Frederick Carl Frieseke (1874–1939), a key figure among the next generation of artists in Giverny, first visited the colony in the summer of 1900. Beginning in 1906, he rented the house next door to Monet, and he spent his summers there until 1919.[21] Although Renoir's color and figural style have been cited as Frieseke's primary inspiration, a closer look at Frieseke's *The Garden Umbrella* (Pl. 12), painted in Giverny by 1910, reveals affinities with Monet's garden views in terms of subject matter and composition. Consider, for example, Monet's *The Artist's Garden at Vétheuil,* 1880 (Fig. 2), in which the artist's young son and members of his extended household descend the steps leading from the house. Like Monet, Frieseke pictures the garden surrounding his home as the site of informal domestic activity. In both scenes, sunlight casts a dappled play of light and shadow on the path and lawn, and the entire surface is covered in textured color that seems more decorative than descriptive. The high horizon line in both paintings focuses the viewer's attention on the garden and the figural grouping in the center. Frieseke would likely have been familiar with Monet's garden themes. He may even have seen *The Artist's Garden at Vétheuil* in person, since it was in Monet's collection until 1910, when it was acquired from the artist by a Paris collector.[22]

Other American artists to arrive in Giverny beginning in the 1890s included Karl Anderson, Edmund Greacen, Richard E. Miller, Lawton Parker, and Guy Rose. Together with Frieseke they became known as the "Giverny Group" when they exhibited together at New York's Madison Gallery in 1910. With the onset of World War I, it became impossible for Americans to return to Giverny, and its dominance as an American colony in France came to an end.

A Country Retreat

During the summer months, American artists often escaped the city for rural retreats where they concentrated on painting landscapes inspired by their knowledge of Impressionism. Artists gathered at colonies in Connecticut (Cos Cob and Old Lyme), Massachusetts (Gloucester), and New Hampshire (Appledore Island) to paint in the company of other artists. In addition, the summer schools of Twachtman at Cos Cob and Chase at Shinnecock, Long Island, taught Impressionist techniques through *plein air* painting classes. Artists featured in this section of the exhibition include figures who had painted in Giverny—John Leslie Breck, Metcalf, and Robinson—as well as others who had not, such as Chase, Hassam, Twachtman, Edward Redfield, Ernest Lawson, and Maurice Brazil Prendergast.

John Leslie Breck (1860–1899) was one of the few American artists in Giverny to develop a relationship with Monet.[23] During his visits between 1887 and 1891,

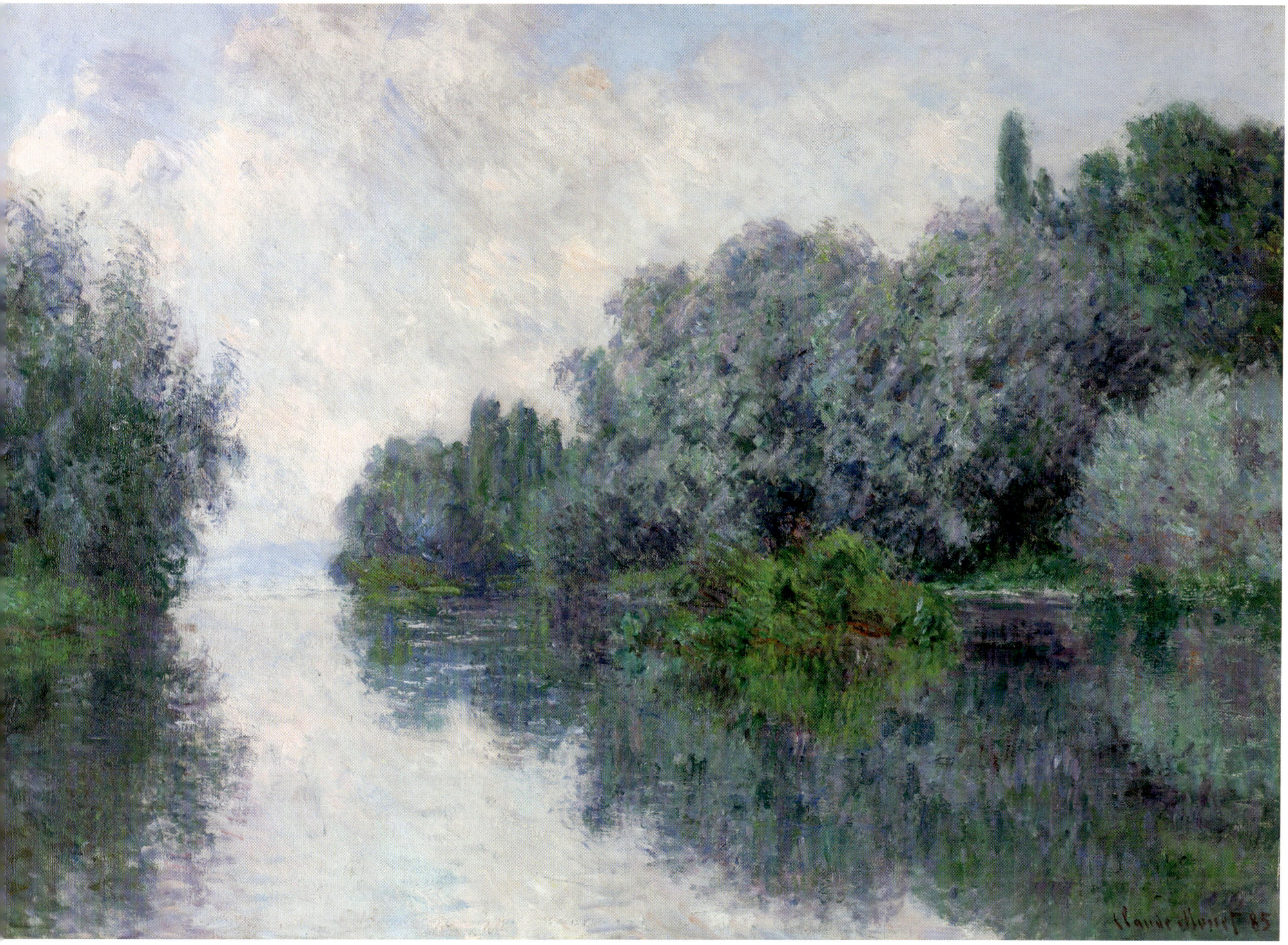

FIGURE 3. Claude Monet (French, 1840–1926), *The Seine at Giverny*, 1885, oil on canvas, 25 ½ × 36 ½ in. (64.8 × 92.7 cm), Museum of Art, Rhode Island School of Design, Providence, Museum Appropriation Fund, by exchange, 44.541

Breck painted Monet's lush gardens and developed an interest in capturing the qualities of moving water. Back home in Boston, he painted *Grey Day on the Charles*, 1894 (Pl. 28), a lyrical view of the Charles River interpreted in terms of color and luminosity. Breck's painting captures the effects of light and shadow on a particular day and under specific weather conditions. Monet gave similar titles to landscapes, such as *Bridge at Argenteuil on a Gray Day*, circa 1876 (Pl. 29). The purplish blue hues, blurred contours, and atmospheric rendering in *Grey Day on the Charles* suggest Breck's familiarity with later landscapes like Monet's *The Seine at Giverny*, 1885, which captures the reflection of trees and sky with extraordinary perception (Fig. 3).

Although William Merritt Chase (1849–1916) admired the work of Monet, he cautioned his students against too much reliance on the example of a single artist.[24] Important influences on his artistic development included French Impressionism, Old Master paintings, and the contemporary artists Whistler and Sargent (Sargent was a lifelong friend). Chase gained a familiarity with Impressionism through travel to Paris between 1881 and 1884 and his work as an organizer for the 1883 Pedestal Fund Art Loan Exhibition held in New York City. Planned in order to raise funds to build a pedestal for the Statue of Liberty, this exhibition included two works by Manet and one by Degas. Chase especially admired the Impressionists' concern with "open-air, light and air" and cited Monet as a specific example.[25] His *Shinnecock Hills* landscape, circa 1892 (Pl. 17), celebrates the harmony of nature and captures the remoteness of its location on eastern Long Island. The summary brushstrokes, high horizon line, use of diagonals as a compositional device, and the suggestion of a fleeting moment—especially in the cloudy sky and shadows on the ground—indicate a response to Impressionist style and techniques.

In 1889, John Henry Twachtman (1853–1902) settled in Connecticut following a period of extended travel in France, Italy, and Holland.[26] In Connecticut he founded the Cos Cob art colony, which attracted other leading Impressionist artists, including Hassam, Robinson, and Weir. Responding to Twachtman's landscapes of the early 1890s, one reviewer remarked that Twachtman came "nearer than any New York artist to solving some of the problems of *plein aire* [*sic*] that Monet has set down."[27] His loose brushwork and concern with painting light and atmosphere are evident in works such as *Horseneck Falls*, circa 1900 (Pl. 21), and *The Little White Bridge*, circa 1896 (Pl. 20), and align him with the Impressionist aesthetic. He painted four views of the white footbridge on his property, suggesting the influence of Monet's tendency to work in series. Yet Twachtman altered the vantage point in each of his bridge pictures, casting doubt on the theory that he conceived them as a series.[28] While Monet returned to the same scene in order to capture changing effects of light at different times of day, Twachtman's aim was more likely "the opposite of seriality: that he sought to capture sites freshly every time he painted them, conveying the feelings that a locale evoked in each of his new encounters with it."[29]

Aside from Mary Cassatt, Frederick Childe Hassam (1859–1935) is the best-known American Impressionist painter. During his lifetime, Hassam was acclaimed in the contemporary press as "the American representative of French Impressionism"[30] and a direct observer of Monet: "Stemming from Monet he has made the formula of Impressionism his own and imbued it with the native tang of our own soil."[31] Yet Hassam never visited Giverny. Instead, he adopted the subjects and basic stylistic elements of Impressionism as a result of his extended stays in Paris between

1886 and 1889 and the exhibitions he saw in New York and Boston in the 1880s. In addition, he visited, along with Twachtman, Weir, and Robinson, private collections and galleries in New York to see works by Monet, Degas, and Renoir.[32] He is renowned today for his varied depictions of New England's contemplative landscapes, quaint villages, bustling harbors, and rugged seascapes.[33] *Ironbound,* 1896 (Pl. 24), is a breathtaking view of the cliffs of Ironbound Island in Frenchman's Bay, Maine, from a high vantage point. The cliffs' rocky surfaces are animated by broken strokes of color and reflected light recalling the dramatic seascapes and plunging perspectives of Monet's Étretat paintings. Hassam could have seen Monet's *The Manneporte near Étretat* of 1886 (Fig. 4) in two exhibitions held in 1895. The first was at Durand-Ruel's gallery in New York, and the second was at St. Botolph Club in Boston.[34]

Hassam continued to explore similar themes for decades, as illustrated in *Northeast Gorge at Appledore,* 1912 (Pl. 23), depicting the rocky ledges, chasms, and roughly piled gorges of Appledore Island, one of the Isles of Shoals off the coast of New Hampshire. From the mid-1880s to 1916, Hassam spent most summers at Appledore, where his friend, the poet Celia Laighton Thaxter (1835–1894), had established an informal salon of writers, musicians, and artists. At Appledore, Hassam explored the full range of his palette, and his paintings became a lush saturation of color and light, resonating with visual energy. Some of his Appledore pictures depict the Northeast headlands from alternate viewpoints and include a solitary clifftop cottage silhouetted against the open sea beyond, thus sharing compositional elements with Monet's paintings such as *Marée montante à Pourville* (*Rising Tide at Pourville*), 1882 (Pl. 22).

The present exhibition also includes landscapes by three individuals belonging to a younger generation of realist artists, known as "The Eight," who emerged as a group in 1908: Maurice Brazil Prendergast (1858–1924), William Glackens (1870–1938), and Ernest Lawson (1873–1939).[35] Although "The Eight" generally preferred a darker palette as opposed to the high-keyed color of Monet, some of these artists responded to Impressionism at some point during their careers. Prendergast's joyous scenes of leisure set in coastal parks near Boston were inspired by French Impressionist views of beaches and cafés. Pictures like *Low Tide*, circa 1895–1897 (Pl. 26), and *Surf, Nantasket*, circa 1900–1905 (Pl. 27), demonstrate his concern with the chromatic range, sunlight effects, and casual subject matter of Impressionism. Lawson's urban and rural landscapes dating to the first few decades of the twentieth century show an interest in brilliant color and light. *Spring Thaw*, painted circa 1910 (Pl. 19), evokes luminous color, vibrating atmosphere, and the sensation of flickering light across the canvas. Lawson's knowledge of the basic features of Impressionism was gained through studies under Twachtman at New York's Art Students League (1891) and at Cos Cob (1892) and through travel in Paris (1893).

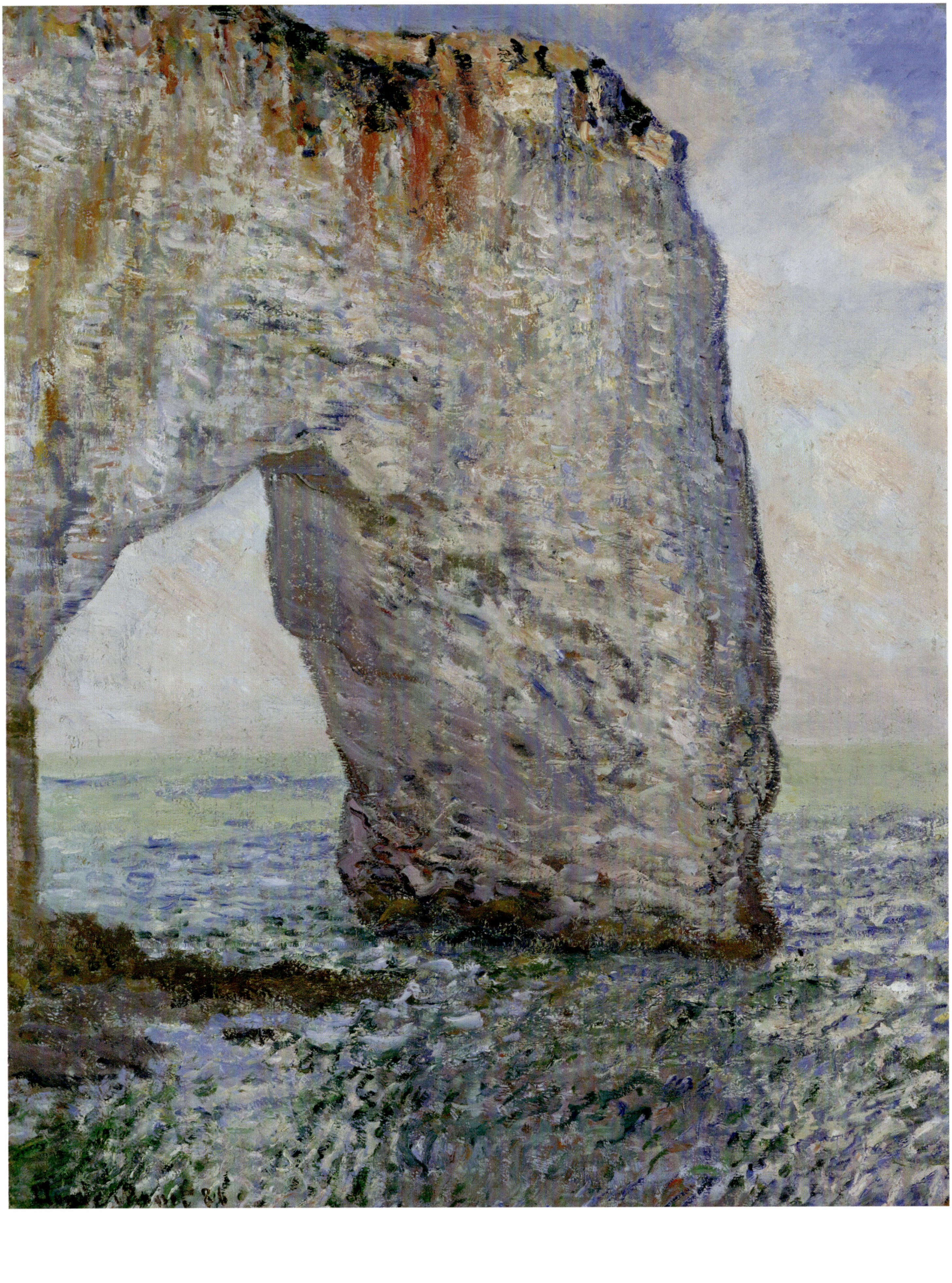

The Vibrance of Urbanism

Contemporary life in the city was a popular subject in American painting of the period. Common themes included views of city streets and harbors, skyscrapers and bridges that celebrated feats of modern engineering, and city parks populated with figures enjoying leisure activities. These evocative pictures parallel themes found in the works of Monet, Degas, Sisley, and Manet. Monet's Thames series (painted between 1899 and 1904), for example, includes more than forty paintings of the river and its famed Waterloo and Charing Cross bridges. As *Waterloo Bridge*, 1903 (Pl. 40), demonstrates, the series focuses on the transformative beauty of fog, its ability to both reveal and obscure the solidity of the bridge and its arches. American artists were similarly drawn to paint famed landmarks such as Central Park and the Hudson River, as well as iconic streets like Broadway and Fifth Avenue. The Norwegian-born American painter Jonas Lie (1880–1940) addresses similar concerns in *Dusk on Lower Broadway*, circa 1910 (Pl. 41). The picture's bravura brushwork and blue hazy atmosphere punctuated by rays of sunshine suggest Lie's familiarity with Monet's urban themes painted around 1900. In his lifetime, Lie's New York cityscapes were celebrated for merging his close observation of subjects with the bright palette and vigorous brushwork of Impressionism: "Light has always fascinated Mr. Lie—and his paintings . . . are notable for their unusual and vivid light effects. He has been influenced profoundly by Claude Monet, who he says 'cleaned the palette of the whole world.'"[36]

Childe Hassam built his reputation as a painter of modern life. He especially admired the skyscrapers and city streets of New York, which inspired many of his best-known works celebrating the energy and spirit of Manhattan. In an article that appeared in the *Commercial Advertiser* in 1898, Hassam wrote: "Toward the late afternoon the big masses of buildings in New York come out in that light with a significance and an effect which makes the Paris kind of thing quite trivial."[37] Hassam treated this theme in his flag series of 1916–1919, which depicted the flags of the Allied nations suspended from buildings along Fifth Avenue. *Avenue of the Allies,* 1917 (Pl. 32), shows Hassam's indebtedness to the example of similar works by French Impressionists, especially in terms of its vibrant color, strong contrasts of light and dark, and the faceless crowd below. Hassam was familiar with such works, especially Monet's *Rue Montorgeuil, Paris, during the Celebrations of June 30, 1878* (Musée d'Orsay, Paris), which he had seen and sketched as a student in Paris.[38] This connection to Monet was noted in the critical response to an exhibition of twenty-four of Hassam's flag paintings at New York's Durand-Ruel Gallery in November 1918. "It will hardly be denied," wrote one reviewer, "that Mr. Hassam is, as far as technique goes, a disciple of Claude Monet."[39]

FIGURE 4. Claude Monet (French, 1840–1926), *The Manneporte near Étretat,* 1886, oil on canvas, 32 × 25 ¾ in. (81.3 × 65.4 cm), The Metropolitan Museum of Art, Bequest of Lillie P. Bliss, 1931, 31.67.11; Image copyright © The Metropolitan Museum of Art. Image source: Art Resource, NY

Hassam also painted smaller urban centers in New England communities in pictures like *Gloucester*, 1919 (Pl. 30). As Monet often did, Hassam allowed the texture of this canvas to show through and used color to link various parts of the scene. Here, the blues and purples of the rocks and boulders in the foreground are echoed in the rooftops of the middle ground and the hills in the distance. Other elements suggesting the influence of Monet include the brilliant colors and lively, open brushwork, the picture's high horizon line, and the sharply tilted picture plane, which permits a sweeping view of the harbor beyond the village. Hassam's *Gloucester* is an idyllic view of the village and its harbor, which was an important hub for fish-packing, ironworking, and shipbuilding industries. Here the church spire is given special importance as it rises above the densely packed buildings of the foreground. Bathed in bright light, it is a symbol of New England's colonial heritage and solid American values. This optimism and idealism was noted in the press, where works by Hassam and other members of "The Ten" were described as images of "hope, of life, of promise" and the audience was encouraged to "fill your soul with color, light and the breeze of promise."[40]

City parks and gardens were also popular subjects during the period. A prime example is Chase's *An Early Stroll in the Park*, 1890, set in New York's Central Park at the site of the Bethesda Terrace and Fountain (see Fig. 2 in Sean Patrick Adams's essay, page 88). In Chase's painting, the park is devoid of crowds and appears as a quiet oasis from the hustle and bustle of city life. Yet this serene and ordered view of city life contrasts sharply with the realities of urban living during the period. As noted in Adams's essay, city parks were planned as part of the City Beautiful movement, an architectural and urban-planning reform movement aimed at addressing the negative consequences of rapid growth, such as pollution and overcrowding, and offering a clean space for restorative leisure. In this context, the choice of setting within Central Park should be noted. The fountain is topped with Emma Stebbins's (1815–1882) bronze sculpture *The Angel of the Waters*, 1873, which was inspired by the biblical story of the Bethesda Pool—a Jerusalem spring with healing powers.[41] Thus the connection between water's healing and restorative powers and the park's role within the life of New York may explain why Chase selected this particular site for *An Early Stroll in the Park*.[42]

Other scenes depicting city parks include Gari Melchers's *Bryant Park (Twilight)*, circa 1906 (Pl. 31), and Glackens's *The Horse Chestnut Tree, Washington Square*, circa 1915–1919 (Pl. 34). In *Bryant Park (Twilight)*, Melchers (1860–1932) explores the effects of snow, moonlight, and streetlights on the park as viewed from a high vantage point. His choice of subjects and his experimentation with Impressionist color, broken brushwork, and hazy atmospheric effects may have been influenced by his knowledge of works by Hassam and Frieseke. For example, as an art adviser to the Telfair Academy as well as a Savannah collector beginning in 1906, Melchers secured major paintings by Hassam (*Avenue of the Allies*) and Frieseke, including three works in the present exhibition: *The Garden Umbrella* (Pl. 12), *Reflections (Marcelle)* (Pl. 50), and *The Hammock* (Pl. 13).[43] In the early 1900s, Melchers was one of the most famous American artists working in the South.[44]

The Horse Chestnut Tree, Washington Square, by William Glackens (1870–1938), is a lively view of an urban park and center of cultural activity in New York City. Probably best known for its monumental arch honoring George Washington, the park was the site of two major demonstrations in the 1910s: the 1912 march of twenty thousand workers commemorating the Triangle Shirtwaist Factory fire, which killed 146 workers in 1911, and the 1915 march of more than twenty-five thousand people demanding women's suffrage. Rather than focusing on its landmark arch or the political significance of the park for city residents, Glackens directs the viewer's attention to the park's idyllic aspects, including its trees, landscaping, and meandering paths. Monet's importance for the development of Glackens's art was recognized by his contemporaries, who noted that he and other members of "The Eight" followed "in the footsteps of the men who were the rage in artistic Paris . . . Manet, Degas, and Monet."[45] At times Glackens's style paid homage to Monet's palette and brush techniques, yet works like *The Horse Chestnut Tree, Washington Square*, with its soft, feathery brushwork and palette of soft pinks, yellows, and greens, reveal Glackens's study of Renoir, whose paintings he would have seen in 1906 during his second trip to Paris.[46]

The Comfort of Home

Domestic interiors and gardens, spaces in which women play a central role, are a major theme in American Impressionist paintings. Whether they depict women in comfortable interiors or outdoors in sheltered gardens, these images represent the domestic tranquillity of middle- and upper-class society. These subjects promoted contemporary ideals and responded to the social norms of the period. In the words of the historian S. J. Kleinberg, "A specific set of economic and demographic circumstances gave rise to the mid-nineteenth century cult of domesticity, accentuating female responsibility for home and family" and turning "the household into a haven from the increasing disorder of the urban, industrial world."[47]

Mary Cassatt is best known for her portraits and intimate scenes of women's daily lives: visiting acquaintances, embroidering, drinking tea, caring for children. Her pictures of mothers and their children, such as *Madame Gaillard and Her Daughter*

Marie-Thérèse, 1897 (Pl. 42), drew praise from her audiences and were popular among collectors. At first glance this double portrait seems quite formal, yet Marie-Thérèse wraps her arm around her mother's shoulders—a gesture that enhances the immediacy of the portrait and adds an air of informality. This work demonstrates Cassatt's experimental approach to color, form, and space in her use of blues and purples to suggest the shadows on the faces of mother and daughter. Cassatt also overlays textured fabrics to create a decorative surface pattern that animates the portrait. Although she did not enjoy the same friendship with Monet that she did with Degas, her mentor, Cassatt was an important promoter of Monet and is known to have purchased at least one of his paintings for her own collection.[48] Long after the eighth and final Impressionist exhibition in Paris, in 1886, Cassatt still saw herself as part of a group of artists that included Monet. For example, in 1903 she wrote excitedly about an upcoming exhibition to be held at Galerie Bernheim-Jeune in Paris "of all our set, including Manet, Degas, Monet, Sisley, Berthe Morisot & myself."[49]

Paintings of women in garden settings offered further opportunities to explore the themes of motherhood and femininity. In Monet's *Camille Monet and a Child in the Artist's Garden at Argenteuil,* 1875 (Fig. 5), the artist's first wife and a small child appear in the garden of their house in Argenteuil, near Paris, where they lived from 1872 to 1877. Reinforcing the informality of this domestic scene, Camille is seated on the ground, her attention focused on her embroidery. American artists painting in France in the late nineteenth century also captured the informality and immediacy of women in outdoor settings. One such artist was Robert Vonnoh (1858–1933), who painted in the French village Grez-sur-Loing. *Jardin de paysanne (Peasant Garden),* 1890 (Pl. 6), shares the informality and subject of Monet's garden scene, yet Vonnoh's mother and child interact in a tender embrace that underscores the maternal role. The painting's spontaneous brushwork, the asymmetry of the composition, and the informality of the setting are trademarks of Impressionism. When Vonnoh returned to Grez-sur-Loing for an extended stay from 1907 to 1911, he was accompanied by his wife, Bessie Potter Vonnoh (1872–1955), a sculptor.[50] Her best-known works are her bronzes of women in the conventional role of mother. Two of her impressionistically modeled bronzes, *Young Mother,* 1896 (Pl. 53), and *Modern Madonna,* 1904 (Pl. 52), are presented in the exhibition in conjunction with paintings of domestic subjects.

Frederick Frieseke's *The Hammock* (Pl. 13) exemplifies the popular theme of middle- and upper-class women at leisure in outdoor settings. Painted by 1915, toward the end of his Giverny period, *The Hammock* reveals Frieseke's concern with formal elements and the decorative possibilities of contrasting patterns. Here, dappled sunlight abstracts the figures, textiles, and the floral tea service, blurring them into a tapestry of flat decorative pattern. The momentary effect of natural light is

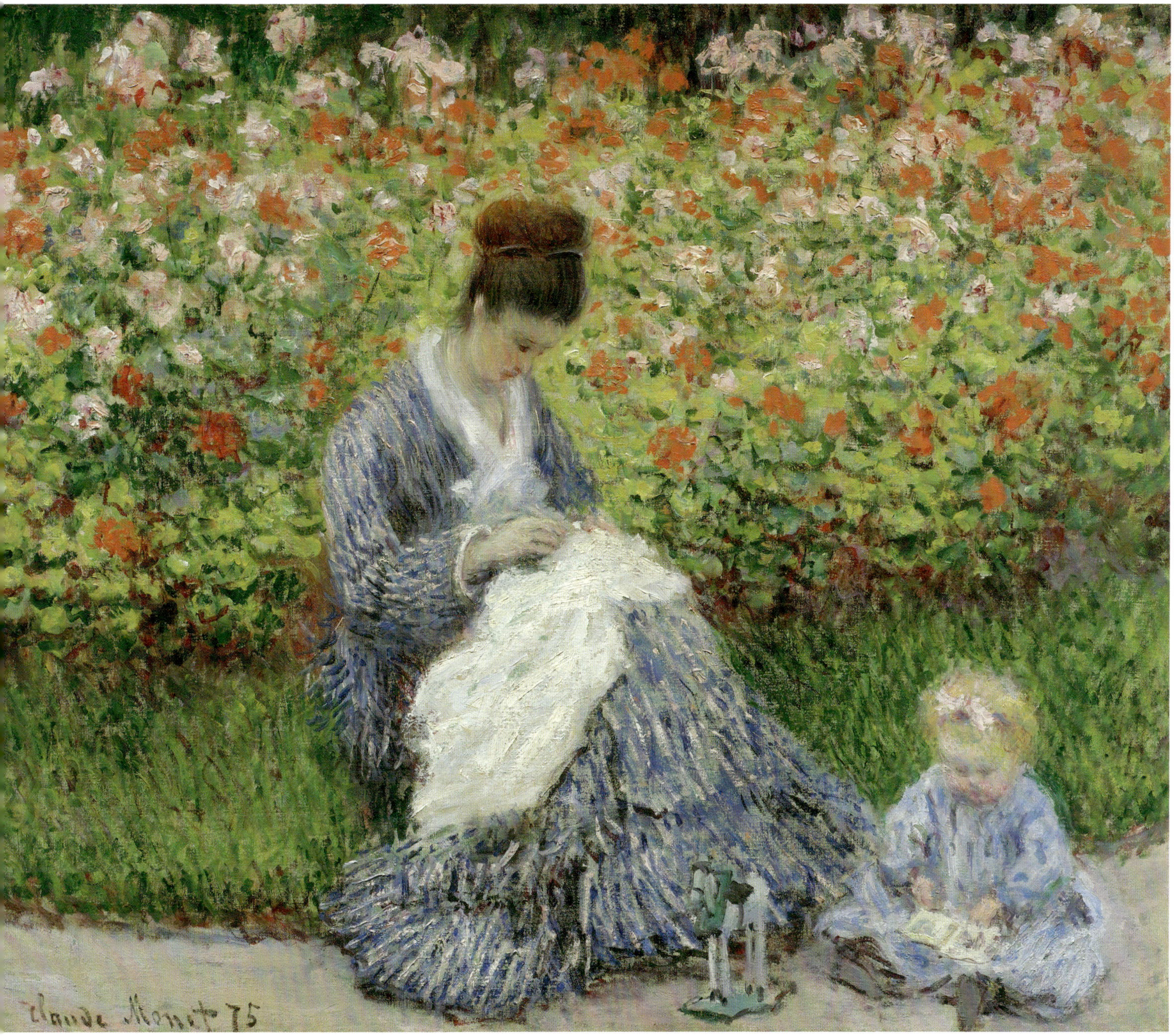

FIGURE 5. Claude Monet (French, 1840–1926), *Camille Monet and a Child in the Artist's Garden at Argenteuil*, 1875, oil on canvas, 21 ¾ × 25 ½ in. (55.3 × 64.7 cm), Museum of Fine Arts, Boston, Anonymous gift in memory of Mr. and Mrs. Edwin S. Webster, 1976.833

also an important theme in Gari Melchers's *Unpretentious Garden* (Pl. 46), painted in Holland around 1903–1909. Melchers situates his wife, Corinne, on a bench in a garden bathed in bright sunlight. Her status as a woman of the privileged class is indicated by the presence of her maid, identified by her attire. The long shadows and dappled light on the house, lawn, and figures suggest Melchers's immersion in the coloristic and light effects of Impressionism.

Edmund C. Tarbell (1862–1938) addressed the theme of light in both outdoor figural scenes and narrative paintings set indoors. In his day, critics cited Monet as one of Tarbell's greatest influences. According to a reviewer for the *Boston Post*, "Mr. Tarbell has been profoundly impressed and greatly helped by the work of Claude Monet."[51] Tarbell's familiarity with Monet's paintings stemmed from his knowledge of exhibitions in which Monet's work figured prominently. For example, in 1892 Tarbell exhibited a painting at the Pennsylvania Academy of the Fine Arts at the same time that the museum was hosting a loan show of works by Monet.[52] Although he built his reputation by 1890 as a painter of fashionably dressed women in sunlit gardens, in the late 1890s he turned his attention to interior scenes with subdued color and soft lighting. Works like *The Breakfast Room*, circa 1903 (Pl. 45), exhibited with "The Ten" at Durand-Ruel Gallery in New York in 1903, combine the atmosphere and broken brushwork of Impressionism with the solidity of figure drawing learned as a student at the Académie Julian.[53]

Another member of "The Ten," Joseph Rodefer De Camp (1858–1923), was best known for his portraits and scenes of women in domestic interiors. In *The Red Kimono*, painted around 1919 (Pl. 43), a pensive solitary figure occupies a shallow space before a window that reveals a hushed light from the outside. The large birdcage suspended from above alludes to the woman's comfortable leisure-class status. It also symbolizes the traditional view of women as objects of beauty and desire. The woman's kimono responds to a growing interest in collecting Japanese art during this period, both among private collectors and museums.[54] Chase, Hassam, and Tarbell painted similar works, and Monet addressed the theme as well. In 1876, Monet portrayed his wife in a fanciful kimono in a large-scale painting that makes an amusing observation on the fad for Japanese art and material culture (*La Japonaise/Camille Monet in Japanese Costume*, Museum of Fine Arts, Boston). Unlike Monet's playful treatment of the subject, De Camp's painting is a melancholy rendering of a woman in deep contemplation.

A few paintings in the exhibition present more intimate glimpses of women's private lives. *La Toilette*, circa 1914 (Pl. 51), by Richard Emil Miller (1875–1943), portrays a beautiful young woman dressed in morning attire. The floral patterns of her robe, the tablecloth, and the teacup are echoed in the colorful blossoms of the garden view through the window—a skillful merging of interior and exterior. Miller's response to French Impressionism is evident in his sensuous, open brushwork and emphasis on natural light and surface texture. He especially admired Monet's taste for bright color and light, as noted by one of Miller's students at the École Colarossi in Paris: "These were the days of impressionism and Monet was their God. Black was taboo and those students who used it were banished from the class."[55]

American Impressionists also painted nude subjects, yet these images represented a minority. Although the theme of the nude was treated more often in the late nineteenth century than ever before, puritanical restrictions persisted, and these subjects were often considered vulgar or coarse by American audiences.[56] For example, upon viewing nudes at an exhibition in Worcester, Massachusetts, in 1902, a reviewer commented that "studies of the nude and semi-nude are in the minority and the lack was not lamented."[57] Frieseke's *Reflections (Marcelle)*, painted by 1909 (Pl. 50), is a sensuous image of a nude rendered in soft hues of lavender, blue, and yellow. The sitter is Frieseke's favorite paid model, Marcelle, who appears seated before a mirror with her back to the viewer, seemingly unaware of the viewer's gaze. In this composition, Frieseke employs the mirror to expand the pictorial space and create a sense of movement in the reflected surface of the glass.

A Graphic Legacy

The French Impressionists are known today primarily as painters, yet they also worked experimentally in printmaking, translating the painterly into an unpainterly medium. Among the best-known examples are Degas's etchings of dancers and female nudes, Renoir's etchings and lithographs of women reclining and bathing, and Pissarro's etchings of city views and peasants in the landscape. These artists also recognized the printmaking media's potential for expanding their audiences to the art-loving middle class. Monet, too, recognized this potential and collaborated with other artists to translate his paintings into the print medium for publication in the press. A number of American artists represented in the exhibition created etchings, drypoints, and lithographs that explored many of the themes found in their paintings. They were also attracted by the opportunities for fresh, creative expression offered by the print medium. These artists include Frank Benson, Mary Cassatt, Childe Hassam, Maurice Brazil Prendergast, and J. Alden Weir.[58] James Abbott McNeill Whistler (Pls. 66 and 67) is included in the exhibition as an example of an artist whose atmospheric and loosely painted landscapes of the 1880s were associated by his American contemporaries as participating in the new Impressionist style.

Among the American Impressionists who experimented in the print medium, the general public is probably most familiar with Cassatt. Her drypoints, aquatints, and etchings repeat many of the themes found in her paintings of women and children in casual domestic settings. *Tea*, 1890 (Pl. 58), and *Woman Bathing*, 1891 (Pl. 61), are superb examples of Cassatt's experimentation with economy of line and abstract pattern, as well as new approaches to perspective that were informed by her study of Japanese woodcuts. J. Alden Weir (1852–1919) experimented with etching, engraving, and lithography, although etching was his preferred medium. Prints such as *My Back Yard no. 2*, 1890 (Pl. 73), and *By Candlelight*, circa 1887–1893 (Pl. 62), explore a common Impressionist theme—the fugitive effects of light both indoors and on the landscape. Hassam also explored this theme in etchings like *Easthampton*, 1917 (Pl. 77), and *Fifth Avenue, Noon*, 1916 (Pl. 71). Both prints are distinguished by their displays of light and shadow and use of shimmering lines to suggest atmosphere. In addition, these two examples refer to specific places and convey the immediacy of sketches created on the spot.

Prendergast's favorite print medium was the monotype, which is created through a transfer process in which the artist paints with ink or oils on a glass or metal plate. The paint is then transferred to a piece of paper by applying pressure with a press or roller. Prendergast's monotypes, such as *Franklin Park* (Pl. 65) and *Marine Park, South Boston* (Pl. 64), both dated circa 1895–1897, parallel themes found in his oils and watercolors. These are happy scenes of fashionable ladies and children in parks and on beaches. Frank Benson (1862–1951) addressed the themes of waterfowl and hunters in a large body of prints. The overwhelming success of his sporting prints helped to establish the theme as a popular American genre. In etchings like [*Dusk*], 1914 (Pl. 79), and [*Second Island Outlet*], 1916 (Pl. 78), Benson captured the atmospheric qualities of the landscapes in which he placed his subjects.

Impressionism: The Denouement

Introduced to a skeptical French public in the 1870s, Impressionism was discovered and promoted by American collectors, art writers, and artists beginning in the 1880s. Its popularity continued for some four decades, making it one of the longest lived and most enthralling artistic expressions in the history of American art. To the American audience, Monet's work best embodied the Impressionist taste for transience, loose brushwork, prismatic color, natural light, and movement. Following decades of soaring popularity in which the paintings of Monet and his French contemporaries were emulated by many artists in the United States, Impressionism's hold on American art began to wane. By the mid-1910s, competing avant-garde styles inspired artists to follow other examples. Nevertheless, a watered-down form of Impressionism that included a general preference for bright color, light, loose brushwork, and spontaneity continued well into the 1920s. Its presence some forty years after the eighth and last Impressionist exhibition, in 1886, makes it "among the most viable modes of artmaking since the Hudson River School artists defined the American landscape."[59] Today, the popularity of the movement endures in the form of major exhibitions organized in the United States, Europe, and Asia, where adoring audiences flock to see original paintings by Monet, Renoir, and Degas. By contrast, the American Impressionists featured here are relatively unknown. In casting light on Monet and American Impressionists, this exhibition allows us to see the unique achievements of individual American artists who encountered Impressionism and made it their own.

Notes

1. For an in-depth overview of French Impressionism, see Robert Herbert, *Impressionism: Art, Leisure, and Parisian Society* (New Haven: Yale University Press, 1988). For an overview of the eight Impressionist exhibitions, see *The New Painting: Impressionism, 1874–1886*, curated by Charles S. Moffett (San Francisco: Fine Arts Museums of San Francisco, 1986).

2. A reviewer of an exhibition of Monet's paintings at the Pennsylvania Academy of the Fine Arts in 1892 called Monet "the high priest of this feature of art." "New Pictures at the Academy," *Philadelphia Inquirer,* January 21, 1892, 5, quoted in Laurene Buckley, *Edmund C. Tarbell: Poet of Domesticity* (New York: Hudson Hills Press, 2001), 45.

3. Kathleen Adler, "'We'll Always Have Paris': Paris as Training Ground and Proving Ground," in *Americans in Paris, 1860–1900,* curated by Kathleen Adler, Erica E. Hirshler, and H. Barbara Weinberg (London: National Gallery, 2006), 46.

4. Overviews of American Impressionism include Richard J. Boyle, *American Impressionism* (Boston: New York Graphic Society, 1982); *American Impressionism and Realism: The Painting of Modern Life, 1885–1915*, curated by H. Barbara Weinberg, Doreen Bolger, and David Park Curry (New York: Metropolitan Museum of Art, 1994); William H. Gerdts, *American Impressionism,* 2nd ed. (1984; New York: Abbeville, 2001); and *American Impressionism: A New Vision, 1880–1900*, curated by Katherine Bourguignon, Frances Fowle, and Richard R. Brettell (New Haven: Yale University Press for Editions Hazan, Paris, 2014).

5. Weir to Mr. and Mrs. Weir, April 15, 1877, in Dorothy Weir Young, *The Life and Letters of J. Alden Weir*, ed. Lawrence W. Chisholm (New Haven: Yale University Press, 1960), 123.

6. Hans Huth, "Impressionism Comes to America," *Gazette des Beaux-Arts* 29 (April 1946): 225–52. For a more recent discussion of Durand-Ruel's 1886 exhibition in New York, see Ann Dumas, "Degas in America," in *Degas and America: The Early Collectors*, ed. Ann Dumas and David A. Brenneman (Atlanta: High Museum of Art in association with the Minneapolis Institute of Arts, 2000), 22–23. Early exhibitions of Impressionist painting in New York and Paris are also discussed in Adler, Hirshler, and Weinberg, *Americans in Paris,* 44–48.

7. Theodore Robinson's diary includes an account of visits taken in the company of Hassam, Twachtman, and Weir to private collections in New York in 1893 to see works by Monet, Degas, and Renoir. Robinson mentions these visits in his diary entries of November 30 and October 31, 1893. The diaries are in the Frick Art Reference Library, New York, and are quoted in Ulrich W. Hiesinger, *Childe Hassam: American Impressionist* (Munich: Prestel, 1999), 70, 106 n. 15.

8. Monet to Durand-Ruel, January 23, 1886, quoted in Paul Hayes Tucker, *Monet in the '90s: The Series Paintings* (New Haven: Yale University Press, 1989), 36.

9. Fitzgerald to Brown, April 7, 1891, handwritten note, transcription in *Christie's Impressionist and Nineteenth Century Art,* sale catalogue, London, Tuesday, December 8, 1998, lot 12, p. 35.

10. Sargent also acquired four of Monet's paintings for his own collection. For a discussion of Sargent's Impressionist period, see William H. Gerdts, *Monet's Giverny: An Impressionist Colony* (New York: Abbeville Press, 1993), 21–23; and Elaine Kilmurray, "Sargent, Monet . . . and Manet," in *Sargent and Impressionism* (New York: Adelson Galleries, 2010).

11. Kevin Sharp, "How Mary Cassatt Became an American Artist," in *Mary Cassatt: Modern Woman*, curated by Judith A. Barter (Chicago: Art Institute of Chicago in association with Harry N. Abrams, 1998), 153.

12. The other three members of "The Ten" were Thomas Dewing, Robert Reid, and Edward Simmons. For a comprehensive discussion of "The Ten," see Ulrich W. Hiesinger, *Impressionism in America: The Ten American Painters* (Munich: Prestel-Verlag, 1991); and William H. Gerdts, "The Ten: A Critical Anthology," in *Ten American Painters* (New York: Spanierman Gallery, 1990), 9–81.

13. For an overview on the American artist colony at Giverny, see Gerdts, *Monet's Giverny*; and Katherine M. Bourguignon, ed., *Impressionist Giverny: A Colony of Artists, 1885–1915* (Chicago: University of Chicago Press, 2007).

14. Mildred Giddings Burrage, "Arts and Artists at Giverny," *The World Today*, March 1911, 351.

15. The most comprehensive discussion of Monet's influence on Robinson is Sona Johnston, "Theodore Robinson and Claude Monet," in *In Monet's Light: Theodore Robinson at Giverny*, curated by Sona Johnston (London: Baltimore Museum of Art and Philip Wilson Publishers, 2004), 47–75.

16. Robinson's diary entry of October 4, 1892, in which he discusses the painting, is quoted in Sona Johnston, "Catalogue of the Exhibition," in Johnston, *In Monet's Light*, 108.

17. On Metcalf in Giverny, see Gerdts, *Monet's Giverny*, 23, 26; Gerdts, *American Impressionism*, 61, 63; and Richard J. Boyle, "The Art," in Elizabeth de Veer and Richard J. Boyle, *Sunlight and Shadow: The Life and Art of Willard L. Metcalf* (New York: Abbeville Press, 1987), 196–203.

18. For Monet's influence on Butler, see Richard H. Love, *Theodore Earl Butler: Emergence from Monet's Shadow* (Chicago: Haase-Mumm, 1985), especially 70–73, 159–60.

19. On Perry, see Meredith Martindale, Pamela Moffatt, and Nancy Mowll Mathews, *Lilla Cabot Perry: An American Impressionist* (Washington, D.C.: National Museum of Women in the Arts, 1990); and Marcia Lynn Soderman-Olson, "Reconstructing Lilla Cabot Perry (1889–1923): A Study in Class and Gender"

(Diss., University of Minnesota, 2000; Ann Arbor: UMI, 2001), especially chapter 12.

20. Lilla Cabot Perry, "Reminiscences of Claude Monet from 1889 to 1909," *American Magazine of Art,* March 1927, reprinted in Martindale, *Lilla Cabot Perry,* 116.

21. For background on Frieseke in Giverny, see David Sellin, "Frieseke in Le Pouldu and Giverny: The Black Gang and the Giverny Group," in *Frederick Carl Frieseke: The Evolution of an American Impressionist,* curated by Nicholas Kilmer (Savannah, Ga.: Telfair Museum of Art in association with Princeton University Press, 2001), 71–97.

22. Daniel Wildenstein, *Claude Monet: Biographie et catalogue raisonné*, 5 vols. (Lausanne and Paris: La Bibliothèque des Arts, 1974–91), vol. 1, no. 685.

23. Margaret Werth, "A Long Entwined Effort: Colonizing Giverny," in Bourguignon, *Impressionist Giverny*, 65.

24. Ronald G. Pisano, *A Leading Spirit in American Art: William Merritt Chase, 1849–1916* (Seattle: Henry Art Gallery, 1983), 89. Another good source on Chase is D. Scott Atkinson and Nicolai Cikovsky Jr., *William Merritt Chase: Summers at Shinnecock, 1891–1902* (Washington, D.C.: National Gallery of Art, 1987).

25. "Address of Mr. William M. Chase before the Buffalo Fine Arts Academy, January 28, 1890," *The Studio* 5, no. 13 (1890): 22, quoted in Pisano, *A Leading Spirit*, 154.

26. For an overview of Twachtman's life and art, see *John Henry Twachtman: An American Impressionist*, curated by Lisa N. Peters (Atlanta: High Museum of Art, 1999). The most comprehensive study of the Cos Cob art colony is Susan G. Larkin's *The Cos Cob Art Colony: Impressionists on the Connecticut Shore* (New York: National Academy of Design in association with Yale University Press, 2001).

27. *New York Sun*, 1893, 6, quoted in H. Barbara Weinberg, "Summers in the Country," in Adler, Hirshler, and Weinberg, *Americans in Paris*, 160.

28. Peters, *John Henry Twachtman,* 113–14.

29. Ibid., 114.

30. Anna Seaton-Schmidt, in *L'Art et les artistes* 6, no. 67 (October 1910): 45, quoted in Hiesinger, *Childe Hassam*, 11 n. 1.

31. Forbes Watson, "Childe Hassam," *New York Evening Post Illustrated Magazine*, February 28, 1914, 11, quoted in H. Barbara Weinberg, Introduction, in *Childe Hassam: American Impressionist*, curated by H. Barbara Weinberg (New York: Metropolitan Museum of Art, 2004), 24 n. 26.

32. See also note 7 above.

33. On Hassam's New England works, see Susan G. Larkin, "Hassam in New England," in Weinberg, *Childe Hassam*, 119–77; and David Park Curry, *Childe Hassam: An Island Garden Revisited* (New York: Denver Art Museum, 1990). For Monet's influence on Hassam, see Curry, 91–108 (Hassam's Appledore poppies paintings), 130–34 (Hassam's scenes of middle-class leisure), and 140–42 (Hassam's Isles of Shoals paintings).

34. Daniel Wildenstein, "1887–1898: Peintures," in *Claude Monet,* 3:66 n. 1278, as included in exhibitions at Durand-Ruel, New York, and St. Botolph Club, Boston, in 1895.

35. On Prendergast, see Nancy Mowll Mathews, *Maurice Prendergast* (Munich: Prestel-Verlag, 1990); and Nancy Mowll Mathews, *The Art of Leisure: Maurice Prendergast in the Williams College Museum of Art* (Williamstown, Mass.: Williams College Museum of Art, 1999). On Lawson's response to Impressionism, see Gerdts, *American Impressionism*, 275–79; William H. Gerdts, "American Art and the French Experience," in *Lasting Impressions: American Painters in France, 1865–1915* (Evanston, Ill.: Terra Foundation for the Arts, 1992), 99–100; and Larkin, *The Cos Cob Art Colony*.

36. "Jonas Lie Sails for Norway," *Art News,* May 1, 1926. For a brief discussion of Lie and bibliography of the artist, see Gerdts, *American Impressionism*, 290, 342 nn. 18–19.

37. Hassam quoted in "New York Beautiful," *Commercial Advertiser*, January 15, 1898, 1, reprinted in Hiesinger, *Childe Hassam*, 181.

38. H. Barbara Weinberg, "Hassam in New York, 1889–1896," in Weinberg, *Childe Hassam*, 217.

39. "'Avenue of the Allies' at Durand-Ruel's," *American Art News,* November 23, 1918, 2, quoted in Weinberg, Introduction, 24 n. 26.

40. James B. Townsend, "Annual Exhibition of the Ten," *American Art News,* March 21, 1908, 4, quoted in David R. Brigham, *American Impressionism: Paintings of Promise* (San Francisco: Pomegranate, 1997), 10. The reviewer's comments were in response to the 1908 exhibition of "The Ten" at Montross Gallery.

41. Margaret Lynn Ausfeld, Charles C. Eldredge, and Mark M. Johnson, *American Paintings from the Montgomery Museum of Fine Arts* (Montgomery, Ala.: Montgomery Museum of Fine Arts, 2006), 82.

42. See Barbara Dyer Gallati, *William Merritt Chase: Modern American Landscapes, 1886–1890* (New York: Brooklyn Museum of Art, 1999), 37–46.

43. Diane Lesko, "Gari Melchers and the Telfair Academy: A Foundation for the Future," in *Collection Highlights: Telfair Museum of Art,* ed. Hollis Koons McCullough (Savannah, Ga.: Telfair Museum of Art, 2005), 25–35.

44. For background on Melchers, see Joseph G. Dreiss, *Gari Melchers: His Works in the Belmont Collection* (Charlottesville: University Press of Virginia, 1984); and *Gari Melchers: A Retrospective Exhibition*, curated by Diane Lesko (St. Petersburg, Fla.: Museum of Fine Arts, 1990).

45. W. B. M'C[ormick], "Art Notes of the Week," *New York Press*, February 9, 1908, 6, quoted in William H. Gerdts, "William Glackens: Life and Work," in William H. Gerdts and Jorge H. Santis, *William Glackens* (New York: Museum of Art Fort Lauderdale in association with Abbeville Press, 1996), 85.

46. On Glackens's stylistic development and the influence of Monet and Renoir, see ibid, 66–98.

47. S. J. Kleinberg, *Women in the United States, 1830–1945* (New Brunswick: Rutgers University Press, 1999), 34.

48. In May 1879 she purchased a painting titled *Springtime*. Sharp, "How Mary Cassatt Became an American Artist," 180.

49. Cassatt to Ada Pope, ca. late March 1903, quoted in ibid., 161.

50. For background on Robert Vonnoh, see May Brawley Hill, *Grez Days: Robert Vonnoh in France* (New York: Berry-Hill Galleries, 1987); and Gerdts, *Lasting Impressions.* On Bessie Potter Vonnoh, see Julie Aronson, *Bessie Potter Vonnoh: Sculptor of Women* (Athens: Ohio University Press, 2008).

51. "Some Remarkable Pictures," *Boston Post,* March 9, 1891, 14, quoted in Buckley, *Edmund C. Tarbell,* 45. The reviewer was commenting on Tarbell's work in an exhibition at Boston's J. Eastman Chase Gallery.

52. Buckley, *Edmund C. Tarbell,* 45. Also in 1892, a group of twenty-one of Monet's landscapes, on loan from local collections, was exhibited at Boston's St. Botolph Club.

53. For a discussion of *The Breakfast Room*'s theme, its possible setting in an artist's studio, and the influence of Old Master Dutch painting, see Erica E. Hirshler, "Good and Beautiful Work: Edmund C. Tarbell and the Arts and Crafts Movement," in *Impressionism Transformed: The Paintings of Edmund C. Tarbell*, curated by Susan Strickler (Manchester, N.H.: Currier Gallery of Art, 2001), 77–80.

54. For Americans' fascination with Japanese art and culture in the period, see William Hosley, *The Japan Idea: Art and Life in Victorian America* (Hartford: Wadsworth Atheneum, 1990).

55. Frederick Knecht Detwiller, "Richard Miller N.A. 1875–1943," Salmagundi Club Papers, quoted in Marie Louise Kane, *A Bright Oasis: The Paintings of Richard E. Miller* (New York: Jordan-Volpe Gallery, 1997), 34–35. On Miller

and his indebtedness to French Impressionism, see Kane, *A Bright Oasis*, especially 26–37; and Gerdts, "American Art and the French Experience," 87–90.

56. William H. Gerdts, *The Great American Nude: A History in Art* (New York: Praeger, 1974), 153.

57. "Private View at Art Museum: Summer Exhibit of Oils Seen by 200 Ticket Holders," *Worcester (Mass.) Daily Telegram*, May 30, 1902, 5, quoted in Brigham, *American Impressionism,* 32.

58. For background on prints by the artists represented in the exhibition, see Elizabeth E. Barker, "'A truly learned weaving of light and dark': Hassam's Prints," in Weinberg, *Childe Hassam*, 267–84; Janet Flint, *J. Alden Weir, An American Printmaker, 1852–1919* (Provo: Brigham Young University Press, 1972); Nancy Mowll Mathews, "The Color Prints in the Context of Mary Cassatt's Art," in *Mary Cassatt: The Color Prints* (Williamstown, Mass.: Williams College Museum of Art, 1989); Mathews, *Maurice Prendergast*, 41–43; John Ordeman, *Frank W. Benson's Etchings, Drypoints and Lithographs: An Illustrated and Descriptive Catalogue* (Summit, N.J.: Hickok-Bockus, 1994).

59. Emily Ballew Neff, "'Europe' or 'Heaven'?: American Painters and European Trends," in Emily Ballew Neff and George T. M. Shackelford, *American Painters in the Age of Impressionism* (Houston: Museum of Fine Arts Houston, 1994), 53.

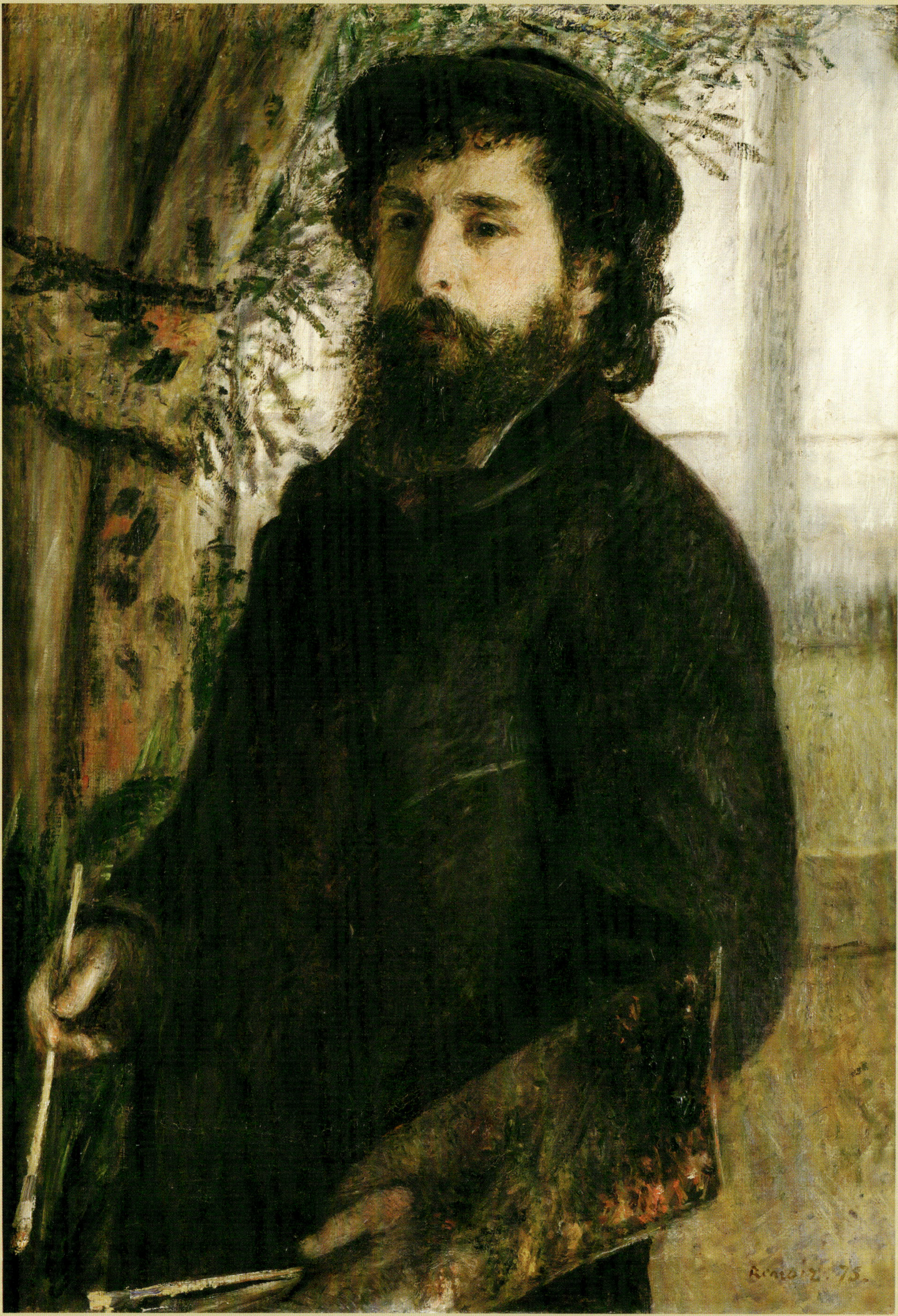
Renoir. 75.

Monet and the Americans

Whose Impressionism?

NANCY MOWLL MATHEWS

FROM THE VERY FIRST, Monet and his painting style (which we would later call Impressionism) attracted the attention of the international art world centered in Paris. The man himself was impressive. Monet was handsome, stylish in a rather bohemian way, and wickedly funny (Fig. 1). As a teenager in the port city of Le Havre, he had made a living as a caricaturist and was taken under the wing of the experimental marine painter Johan Barthold Jongkind. Stories flew around Paris about his unorthodox methods, including sudden shifts of paintings for that most serious of exhibitions, the Salon, and he married the model of his most flamboyant Salon success, *Camille (Woman in a Green Dress)*, 1866.[1]

Loosely brushed, with dramatic, sometimes crude use of color and light, Monet's paintings leapt off the walls of large and small exhibitions. By 1870 Monet had attracted the modern art dealer Paul Durand-Ruel and was buoyed by the formation of a group of equally talented young artists, each experimenting differently with color and light but all achieving what seemed to be a new art for a new age. After Napoleon III's empire collapsed and the Franco-Prussian War ground to a halt (1871), the new republican Paris quickly returned to its former glory as the art capital of the world. And the Impressionists were there to celebrate it.

Also celebrating the return of Paris to the world stage were the Americans. Wealthy and eager, they flooded French museums, exhibitions, and art schools to inhale the essence of great art, something they felt they lacked at home. Astute observers among them, such as Mary Cassatt, had noticed the rumblings in the Paris

FIGURE 1. Pierre-Auguste Renoir (French, 1841–1919), *Portrait of Claude Monet with Palette*, 1875, oil on canvas, 33 × 23 4/5 in. (84 × 60.5 cm), Musée d'Orsay, Paris. Photo credit: Erich Lessing/Art Resource, NY

art world since the 1860s. "The French school is going through a phase. They are leaving the Academy style and each one seeking a new way—consequently just now everything is Chaos. But in the end," wrote Cassatt's friend and fellow art student Eliza Haldeman to her parents in May 1868, "they will be better for the change."[2] These young American artists pined for a distinct identity, one drawn from a European source but representative of the new nation. Thanks to the open-mindedness shown by artists like Cassatt, the new style began to capture the American imagination.

Thirty years after the first Impressionist exhibition (1874), the results were in. American Impressionist painters dominated the exhibitions in New York, Boston, Chicago; they started art schools and *plein air* summer sessions; and they formed their own artists' societies, such as "The Ten." As for Monet, he was surrounded by American followers staying near his home in Giverny, and the largest proportion of Monet paintings sold were in collections in the United States.[3] All the original artists who exhibited in the eight Impressionist exhibitions in Paris found transatlantic success by the end of the century, but none could compare to Monet.

On the face of it, there can be no question that Impressionism's international success was due to its "Frenchness." The dream of leading an artistic life in France in the later nineteenth century was shared from Berlin to Moscow to Tokyo to Lima to St. Louis to New York. Coming home with Impressionist art that depicted Paris streets or Giverny's poplars kept that dream alive for those lucky enough to have traveled there, and it could be a talisman for those who could only hope to go. The vibrant brushstrokes and color, the sense of spontaneity, and the challenge of the technique symbolized France's traditional leadership role in establishing the cutting edge of cultural expression. It also represented that country's allegiance (recently reestablished) to republican ideals and the freedom of the individual.[4]

That French artists felt their leadership responsibilities is undeniable, especially in the face of an increasingly competitive international artistic community in Paris and outlying artistic colonies. Although Monet's cool, flippant manner suggested that he was above such concerns, Paul Tucker has argued that Monet was deeply attached to France's long-standing cultural dominance.[5] Monet's championing of Impressionism and its place in the history of French art can be seen in his leadership of the effort to keep Manet's pivotal work, *Olympia*, in France in 1890. Monet's nationalism can even account for the choice of motifs for his serial paintings, such as Rouen Cathedral, grainstacks, and even the poplars, which, Tucker points out, had a long association with French freedom and "populism" dating back to the Revolution.[6] He cites a contemporary critic's admiration for Monet's paintings of the French poplar, "which summarizes all the grace, all the spirit, all the youth of our land."[7]

The long friendship of France and America, which included their respective revolutions, the War of 1812, and even the American Civil War, made American intellectuals sympathetic to the patriotic content of French art throughout the nineteenth century. As artists and writers turned their attention to Impressionism in general and Monet in particular, their shared political ideals were evoked once again. "The influence of French art upon American [art] . . . would be folly to deny and ungrateful to minimize," argued the writer of an 1888 article in the *Chicago Daily Tribune.* "The moral and material aid which France gave us during the Revolution is matched by her beneficence to Americans in art." Simply put, American painters "go to Paris. There they learn to paint."[8] The American art students who filled Paris's ateliers knew that whatever French styles they learned would find a receptive audience at home.

But a parallel belief in the importance of an original American artistic tradition had already spawned the Hudson River school of landscape painting and motivated such major artists as Winslow Homer and Thomas Eakins to distance themselves from developments in French modern art. The increasingly popular belief that art should be divided into distinct national schools affected European as well as American practices. The Chicago World's Columbian Exposition of 1893, for instance, continued the nineteenth-century practice of organizing art and achievement by separate national sections. The argument was that if we see the characteristic artistic aims and tastes of a country, we may better forgive their faults and foibles, thus promoting world peace.[9] This benign interpretation of the heightened nationalism of the late nineteenth century was the basis for the practice of organizing art history by nationality, much to the chagrin of modern scholars, and for the current divide between French Impressionism and American Impressionism in art historical study.

But despite its impracticalities, late-nineteenth-century cultural nationalism also made it possible for Americans to believe that Impressionism was in essence an American style. Although Impressionism was born in France, many Americans felt that it would not have survived there without American intervention and that the very tenets that Monet proclaimed and successfully brought forth in his painting were American in spirit.

There can be no doubt that American patronage, successfully developed by Monet's dealer, Durand-Ruel, throughout the 1880s made Monet a very wealthy man and largely paid for the extravagant property in Giverny.[10] His association with American artists and collectors did not go unnoticed by disapproving colleagues such as Pissarro, and may be behind Monet's push in the 1890s, as set forth by Tucker, to showcase French national subject matter and to open the doors of French national museums to the modern school. After all, it was rumored that Manet's *Olympia* was about to be purchased by an American collector, and Monet was protecting his

French patrimony by organizing a subscription among artists to keep it from crossing the ocean (as had so many of his own paintings). The subscription to buy Manet's painting did not cost him any lost sales of his own art to American collectors, and it put him in the good graces of the French modern art world.

Mary Cassatt, on the other hand, believing that the *Olympia* could have an equally important role in her own country's cultural history, refused to contribute to the subscription and grumbled to Pissarro, "I wish it had gone to America."[11] Monet and Cassatt were not close, but her contribution to American critical reception, artistic trends, and collecting was enormous and began benefiting Monet early in the history of the Impressionist movement. Even before Cassatt was invited to join the group (1877), she had facilitated the purchase of a Degas dance picture to Louisine Havemeyer (then Elder) and later that year a Monet (1875)—the start of a collection that eventually included thirty Monets.[12] Cassatt, like the rest of the Impressionists, had a sharp tongue, and she used it to make nationalistic comments. In 1878 she wrote to J. Alden Weir about the problems of organizing the Impressionists, "You know how hard it is to inaugurate anything like independent action among French artists." She praised his own efforts to form the Society of American Artists in New York, believing that one day New York would be as much an artistic center as Paris and that Weir and his group would "create an American school."[13]

Even before joining the Impressionists, Cassatt was considered one of the emerging stars among the Americans, so over the years she was a magnet for those interested in studying Impressionism, such as Weir, William Merritt Chase, and Theodore Robinson. She was also known to American critics, who showed special interest in the Impressionists' exhibitions because of her participation in them. The *New York Times* covered its first Impressionist exhibition in 1879 in a review, which, although generally dismissive of the work, singling out Monet, Degas, and Caillebotte for snide comments, expressed special surprise that Cassatt would go in this direction: "I am sorry for Mary Cassatt; she is a Philadelphian, and has had her place in the Salon—a great triumph for a woman and a foreigner; but why has she gone astray?"[14]

As Impressionism gained ground among art critics, Cassatt became a source of information about the movement, and, with her nationalistic agenda, she made a special effort to help American writers communicate the virtues of this style to the audience back home. In 1890, when the Durand-Ruel Gallery launched its brief art journal, *L'Art dans les deux mondes* (referring to the two worlds of France and America), Cassatt was the first artist featured (Fig. 2). As her American Impressionist friends became teachers, she helped to place their students with appropriate artists in and around Paris.[15]

Thanks to Cassatt's firsthand experience with the early history of the French Impressionists as well as other literature widely read in the United States, the story of

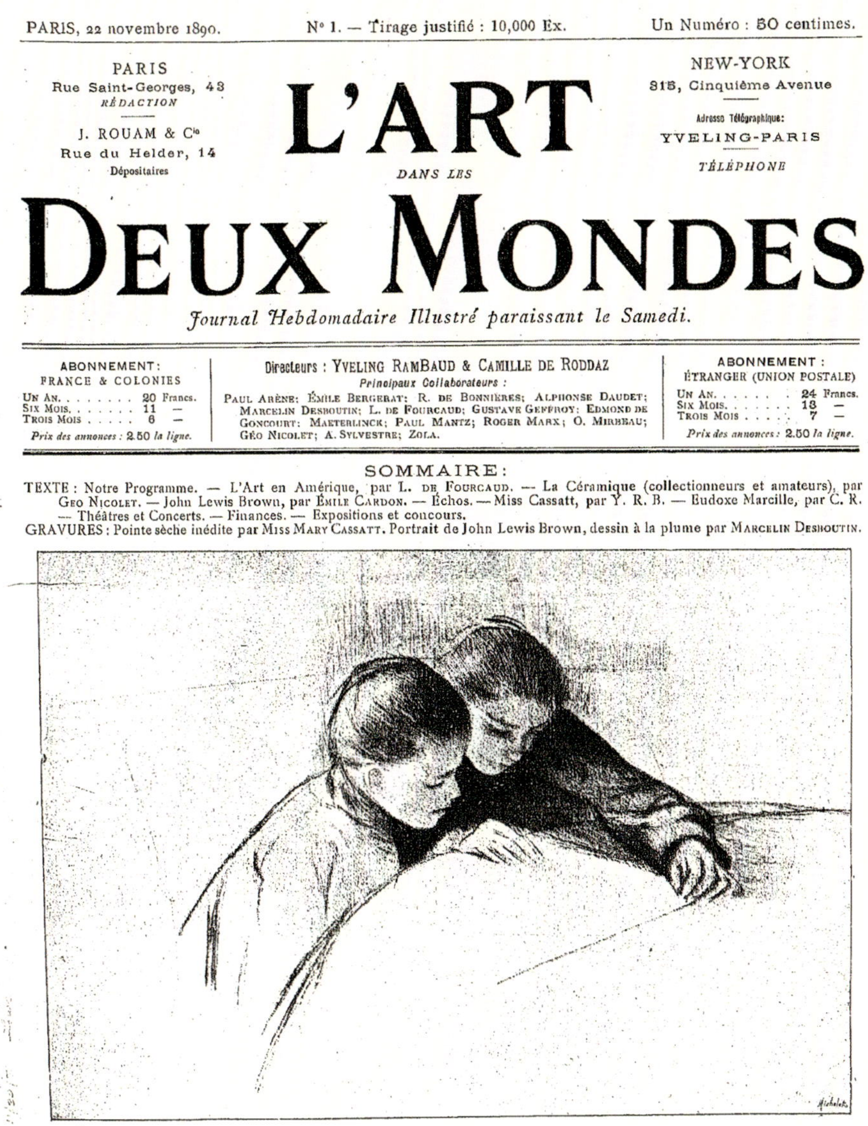

PARIS, 22 novembre 1890. N° 1. — Tirage justifié : 10,000 Ex. Un Numéro : 50 centimes.

PARIS
Rue Saint-Georges, 43
RÉDACTION
J. ROUAM & Cie
Rue du Helder, 14
Dépositaires

L'ART
DANS LES
DEUX MONDES

NEW-YORK
315, Cinquième Avenue
Adresse Télégraphique:
YVELING-PARIS
TÉLÉPHONE

Journal Hebdomadaire Illustré paraissant le Samedi.

ABONNEMENT: FRANCE & COLONIES
Un An . . . . 20 Francs.
Six Mois . . . . 11 —
Trois Mois . . . . . 6 —
Prix des annonces : 2.50 la ligne.

Directeurs : YVELING RAMBAUD & CAMILLE DE RODDAZ
Principaux Collaborateurs :
Paul Arène; Émile Bergerat; R. de Bonnières; Alphonse Daudet; Marcelin Desboutin; L. de Fourcaud; Gustave Geffroy; Edmond de Goncourt; Maeterlinck; Paul Mantz; Roger Marx; O. Mirbeau; Géo Nicolet; A. Sylvestre; Zola.

ABONNEMENT: ÉTRANGER (UNION POSTALE)
Un An . . . . 24 Francs.
Six Mois . . . . . . 13 —
Trois Mois . . . . . 7 —
Prix des annonces : 2.50 la ligne.

SOMMAIRE:
TEXTE : Notre Programme. — L'Art en Amérique, par L. de Fourcaud. — La Céramique (collectionneurs et amateurs), par Geo Nicolet. — John Lewis Brown, par Émile Cardon. — Échos. — Miss Cassatt, par Y. R. B. — Eudoxe Marcille, par C. R. — Théâtres et Concerts. — Finances. — Expositions et concours.
GRAVURES : Pointe sèche inédite par Miss Mary Cassatt. Portrait de John Lewis Brown, dessin à la plume par Marcelin Desboutin.

Pointe sèche de Miss Mary Cassatt.

FIGURE 2. Yveling Rambaud (French, 1843–1899), "Miss Cassatt," in *L'Art dans les deux mondes,* November 22, 1890, Sterling and Francine Clark Art Institute, Williamstown, Massachusetts

the struggles of this group in Paris was often told by the American press. The belief soon arose that since the United States was historically more receptive to new ideas than Europe, Impressionism should find more fertile ground in the new world than the old.[16] And furthermore, because of the large number of Monets in New York, it was posited that Monet in particular had found New York to be his true spiritual home after having been rejected by Paris: "The city has become the Medina toward which flee such apostles in art as are rejected of the haughty sectaries who rule the roost in the Mecca of the Parisians."[17]

Artists, writers, and collectors who began to see Impressionism as more American than French also gravitated to the scientific rationale for such a "new" style.[18] Monet was not a highly theoretical painter, but he understood how his methods exploited advances in recent scientific research on light, color, and movement and encouraged writers, such as his friend Octave Mirbeau, to align him with the modern researchers seeking the scientific basis of nature's mysteries.[19] Monet knew that this would appeal to the "foreign public,"[20] and indeed, Americans particularly saw another way that French and American national interests competed. Since the 1870s, research in photographic methods pitted Eadweard Muybridge against Etienne-Jules Marey in instantaneous motion studies, the Lumière film company against Kodak in advancements in film and handheld cameras, and, by the 1890s, Edison against the Lumières in developing early methods of moving pictures.[21] Photography focused attention on capturing movement and light effects, as well as early experiments in color. Related research into the physics of light, color, and other secrets of nature were carried out in laboratories in both countries, with the Frenchman Michel-Eugène Chevreul and the American Ogden Rood both influencing Impressionism and Neo-Impressionist theory in the 1880s and 1890s. Although the two countries were intertwined in these pursuits, American leadership in science and technology grew as the century wore on.

American artists took up Monet's modern approach to light and color with an impressive zeal. The longtime Giverny resident Will Low remembered that the flood of American students coming in the early 1890s were exclusively preoccupied with Monet and spoke of little else but "color values, vibration, decomposition of tones, the orange light, and the purple shadow."[22] They were particularly influenced by the discovery that all visible light, even if it appears white, contains all the colors of the rainbow. With that in mind, those colors could now be discerned by the eye and revealed by the brush on the canvas. But it was not easy to reach this level of observation, and intense study in front of nature was necessary.[23]

While artists of all nationalities headed to the countryside to observe nature firsthand and suspended their studio and classroom studies for the summer, a particularly American phenomenon was the summer school, which brought students to picturesque locales in the United States and abroad for the practice of *plein air* painting. The competing schools of John Henry Twachtman's Cos Cob art colony in Connecticut and Chase's Shinnecock Hills Summer School on Long Island were only two of many that spread up and down the East Coast. Chase also established summer sessions that took students to locations in France, Spain, and the Low Countries. In Giverny, Frederick MacMonnies and others taught summer classes.[24]

Will Low attributed the flood of American students in Giverny to Theodore Robinson, who became Monet's best American friend in the late 1880s. In a subtle way, Robinson, through his art, his teaching, and his writing, claimed Monet for Americans. Writing in *The Century* (1892), Robinson allowed his intimacy with the artist to flow through his eloquent descriptions of Monet's achievements.[25] As Robinson opened the door to the workings of this artist's mind, the American art world felt it could discuss not only Monet's paintings but Monet's house, the poplars along the river, and the haystacks in his backyard.[26] By 1906, Giverny was a stop on an American tourist's itinerary through Normandy.[27]

Of course, Monet saw this familiarity as annoying, and he refused to take students. But, all things considered, he was extraordinarily tolerant of the American affection for him. It wasn't until about 1910 that he finally closed off his gardens from public access (although they could still be viewed over the low fence);[28] and, even in the height of the invasion, he would good-naturedly look at the suppliants' work. As Americans like the MacMonnies and the Friesekes settled in Giverny and created luxurious country retreats similar to his own, Monet lived in an American colony whether he liked it or not. And he was intimately tied to the American Impressionist Theodore Earl Butler, who had married one of Monet's stepdaughters in 1892 and remained a central figure in American circles in Giverny for the rest of his life.

In his advocacy of Impressionism, Robinson urged artists to see that Monet was returning to what Robinson called "first principles"—"independence of thought and intense love of nature."[29] The deep, "scientific" study of color and light became a new classicism that well-trained artists would use as a foundation for their work no matter what the particular subject matter or technique (Fig. 3, Pl. 5). In that regard, it did not matter that Americans were imitating a French artist or struggling to capture the essence of the French countryside. What was most important was that they learn from their studies, arrive at their own individual understanding, and communicate it in the vibrating colors of modern vision. Yet even Monet saw the paradox of Americans' following this path. To one earnest art student he asked, "This is the way you see nature?" "Oh yes, that is exactly the way I see nature." "Impossible," retorted the master, "for that is the way I see nature *myself*."[30]

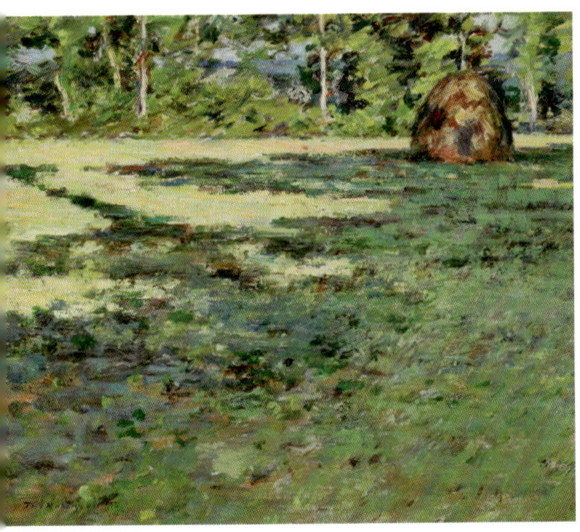

FIGURE 3, PLATE 5.
Theodore Robinson (American, 1852–1896), *Afternoon Shadows*, 1891, oil on canvas, 18 ⅛ × 22 in. (46 × 55.9 cm), Samuel P. Harn Museum of Art, University of Florida, Gainesville, Museum purchase, Funds provided by Michael A. and Donna Singer, 2007.7

Robinson and other American Impressionists understood this dilemma. Independence of thought could be practiced at Giverny, certainly, but personal and national identity were not to be taken lightly. As Monet turned to traditional nationalistic subjects in the 1890s, so too did the Americans. Robinson returned to New York in 1892 with a renewed determination to apply the "first principles" inherent in Impressionism to a new American art. When he exhibited at the Macbeth Gallery in 1895, he separated his paintings into French and American groups, inviting his audience to discern national differences.[31]

Robinson and the other prominent American Impressionists began to dominate group exhibitions in New York and Boston by 1890, and the Chicago World's Columbian Exposition of 1893 was considered a triumph of the style. Since the murals of the buildings of the fair were to be painted exclusively by American artists, such Impressionists as Mary Cassatt, J. Alden Weir, Mary MacMonnies, and Robert Reid were chosen by the administrator of the project, Frank Millet, who was a friend

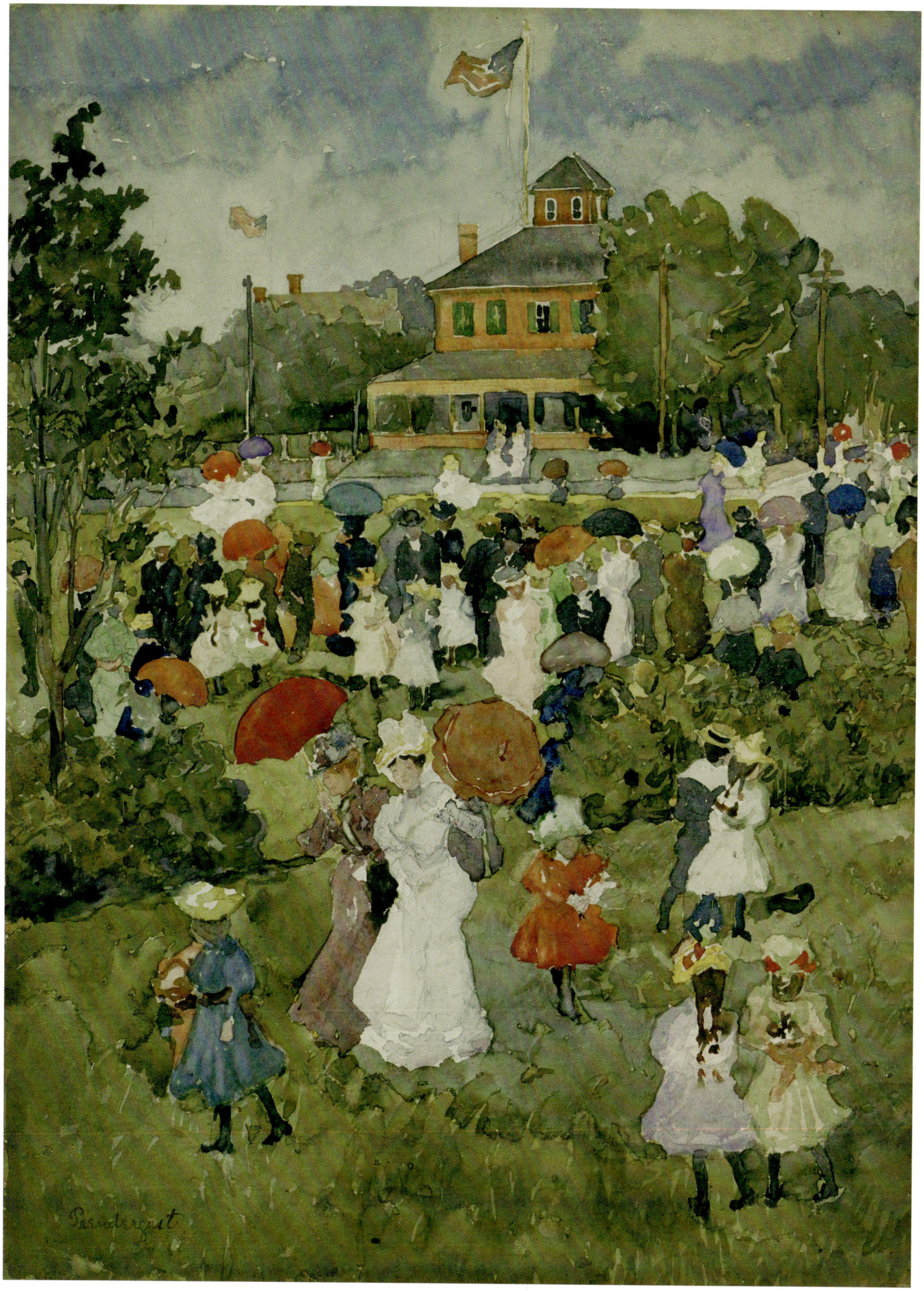

of John Singer Sargent's. American paintings elsewhere at the fair were declared "distinctively American" and proof of a true American school. It was observed in exhibitions in New York, one of which paired the Americans Twachtman and Weir with the Frenchmen Monet and Besnard, that "the brilliant sunshiny and open-air effects . . . seem to have a more powerful influence on American students than on Frenchmen."[32]

Impressionism retained its appeal to American progressive artists and collectors throughout the 1890s as Boston artists like Maurice Brazil Prendergast edged his audience closer to post-Impressionism within a recognizable American context. Prendergast mixed popular resort imagery with fashionably dressed revelers in such well-known American sites as Franklin Park in Boston (Fig. 4) and Central Park in New York City, as well as the newly created beach hotels along the New England coast. His individualism was unmistakable; but when the stylishness of his scenes became perhaps a bit too French, he made sure an American flag claimed his Impressionist paintings for the American national school. Childe Hassam also turned to recognizably American subjects to the extent that by 1910 the critic Harriet Monroe declared him "so American" that he fulfilled the publisher Henri Rochefort's prophecy that "the Americans would refine and adapt this principle [Impressionism] and make it fruitful."[33]

While American Impressionists such as Hassam and other members of "The Ten" continued to establish themselves as "an institution"[34] well into the twentieth century, by 1900 Impressionism had lost its identity as avant-garde. Younger Americans began investigating post-Impressionist styles, including Cézanne, Matisse, and their own urban realism and symbolism that would be shown in the 1908 exhibition of "The Eight." The term *Post-Impressionism* came into widespread use after 1910 thanks to Roger Fry's adoption of it for his exhibitions of modernist art at the Grafton Galleries in London. However, Impressionism was not lost in these surveys of contemporary art; rather, it took its place as a forerunner of modernism, and Impressionist artists such as Monet and Renoir were newly appreciated for their abstract qualities. In New York's own such exhibition, the International Exhibition of Modern Art, also called the Armory Show (1913), both French and American Impressionists were prominently on view. Although there were some disturbing omissions of important American Impressionists (such as Chase and Sargent),[35] others, such as Cassatt, Robinson, Weir, Twachtman, Butler, and Hassam, were included and thus cemented their importance in the national narrative of modern art.

If the Giverny group contemporary with the Armory Show—Frederick Frieseke, Richard E. Miller, and Lawton Parker as well as many other Americans—continued to paint in the original Impressionist style, they need only look at the respect accorded Impressionism in that exhibition to justify their choice. Furthermore, the

FIGURE 4. Maurice Brazil Prendergast (American, born in Canada, 1858–1924), *Franklin Park, Boston*, 1895–97, watercolor over black chalk on ivory wove watercolor paper, 17 ½ × 13 ⅛ in. (44.5 × 33.3 cm), Terra Foundation for American Art, Daniel J. Terra Collection, 1999.111

prices put on the Impressionist paintings in the Armory Show were the highest in the exhibition, with Renoir and Monet over $10,000 and the Americans asking $5,000 to $6,000. In contrast, Matisse and Picasso both had works for less than $2,000 and Duchamp's *Nude Descending a Staircase* was marked at just over $300.[36]

Aside from the monetary importance of Impressionism in the United States, the style, both the French and American versions of it, had been adopted by Americans as a source of national pride—an ongoing reminder of American open-mindedness and embrace of the new. By 1913 that moral high ground was even ceded by the French. When Francis Picabia came to New York from Paris that year to promote his cubist style, he harked back to the American adoption of Impressionism and appealed to them to embrace once more the "New Movement in Art" with their characteristic "love of liberty."[37] In the end, because of this national identity, the story of Impressionism was claimed by Americans and continues to have a special role in the national art history, whether produced by French or American artists. Whose Impressionism is it? An interesting question . . .

Notes

1. For Monet's presence in Paris in the 1860s, see Paul Hayes Tucker, *Claude Monet: Life and Art* (New Haven: Yale University Press, 1995), chapter 3.

2. Cassatt's American artistic partner in Paris, Eliza Haldeman, writing to her parents, May 8, 1868, in *Cassatt and Her Circle: Selected Letters,* ed. Nancy Mowll Mathews (New York: Abbeville Press, 1984), 54.

3. The art press commented on the extraordinary number of Monets sold to American collectors starting in the 1880s. Wynford Dewhurst documents American owners in *Impressionist Painting: Its Genesis and Development* (London: George Newnes, 1904), 37, 47–48.

4. American writers saw the Impressionists carrying on the ideals of the 1830 July Revolution, which promised "freedom and individuality of vision." See "The Fine Arts," *Chicago Daily Tribune,* September 14, 1890, 38.

5. Paul Hayes Tucker, *Monet in the '90s: The Series Paintings* (New Haven: Yale University Press, 1989), especially chapters 3 and 5.

6. Ibid., 138–41.

7. Ibid., 141 n. 46.

8. "History of French Art," *Chicago Daily Tribune,* December 8, 1888, 12.

9. "Art Exhibit Grand," *Chicago Daily Tribune,* April 30, 1893, 41.

10. For an analysis of the American market for Impressionism, see Laura Meixner, "'Gambling with Bread': Monet, Speculation, and the Marketplace," *Modernism/Modernity* 17, no. 1 (2010): 171–99.

11. Mary Cassatt to Camille Pissarro, November 27, 1889, in Mathews, *Cassatt and Her Circle,* 213: "M. Eugene Manet told me that an American had wished to buy the picture & it was to prevent its leaving France that the subscription was opened. I wish it had gone to America—."

12. See Frances Weitzenhoffer, *The Havemeyers: Impressionism Comes to America* (New York: Harry N. Abrams, 1986); and Alice Cooney Frelinghuysen, Gary Tinterow, Susan Alyson Stein,

Gretchen Wold, and Julia Meech, *Splendid Legacy: The Havemeyer Collection* (New York: Metropolitan Museum of Art, 1993). Havemeyer also owned works by Cassatt, Weir, and Chase.

13. Cassatt to Weir, March 10, 1878, in Mathews, *Cassatt and Her Circle*, 137.

14. "Art in Paris," *New York Times,* April 27, 1879, 2.

15. For example, in a June 1891 letter to Camille Pissarro, Cassatt asks whether he would take pupils and how much would he charge. Mathews, *Cassatt and Her Circle*, 220–21.

16. "It is perhaps hoped that a land ready to accept novelties on their own merits, a people less encumbered than the Europeans with traditions in art, may receive [Impressionism] with more sympathy than it has obtained abroad." "Neo-Impressionists," *New York Times,* February 15, 1891, 4.

17. "Pictures at the Union League," *New York Times,* February 13, 1891, 4.

18. See Michael Leja's discussion of Helen Abbott Michael (Celen Sabbrin) and her focus on science in Monet's work in *Looking Askance* (Berkeley: University of California Press, 2004), chapter 3.

19. Tucker, *Monet in the '90s,* 54.

20. Ibid.

21. See Nancy Mowll Mathews, *Moving Pictures: American Art and Early Film, 1880–1910* (Manchester, Vt.: Hudson Hills Press, 2005), especially chapter 2.

22. Will Low, *A Chronicle of Friendships, 1873–1900* (New York: Scribner, 1908), 448–49.

23. Theodore Robinson, "Claude Monet," *Century,* September 1892, 699: "It is a plausible theory that our forefathers saw fewer tones and colors than we . . . that the modern eye is being educated to distinguish a complexity of shades and varieties of color before unknown."

24. Kathleen Pyne, "Americans in Giverny: The Meaning of a Place," in *Impressionist Giverny: A Colony of Artists, 1885–1915*, ed. Katherine M. Bourguignon (Chicago: University of Chicago Press, 2007), 49.

25. See note 22.

26. A critic stops at Monet's painting: "Here is his own garden and queer home, made of two houses of different sizes bumped together at the top of a flight of stone steps." "Some Dazzling Pictures: Two French and Two American Painters of Sunlight," *New York Times,* May 4, 1893, 9.

27. Cora Roche Howland, "A Trip to Europe in an Arm Chair," *Chicago Daily Tribune,* May 24, 1906, 8.

28. Clara T. MacChesney, "Frieseke Tells Some of the Secrets of His Art," *New York Times,* June 7, 1914, SM7. "I had to be content with viewing [Monet's garden] from over the fence. Since strangers had abused the privileges formerly given."

29. Robinson, "Claude Monet," 699–700.

30. Low, *Chronicle of Friendships*, 450.

31. "Catalogue of Paintings and Sketches by Theodore Robinson on Exhibition at the Gallery of William Macbeth," typescript, February 2–16, 1895, Frick Art Reference Library.

32. "The Week in the Fine Arts," *New York Times,* May 7, 1893, 16.

33. Harriet Monroe, "Long Ago Prophecy of a French Critic Is Fulfilled in Hassam's Works," *Chicago Daily Tribune,* January 23, 1910, H4.

34. "The American Impressionist is an institution," says the critic for the *New York Times,* February 18, 1912, SM15.

35. See Susan Larkin, "'So Many Thrills, So Much Excitement': Elmer MacRae's Role in the Armory Show," in *The Armory Show at 100,* ed. Marilyn Satin Kushner and Kimberly Orcutt (New York: New-York Historical Society, 2013), 77.

36. Ibid., appendix A, "The Complete 1913 Armory Show Checklist," includes prices.

37. "Picabia, Art Rebel, Here to Teach New Movement," *New York Times,* February 16, 1913, 49.

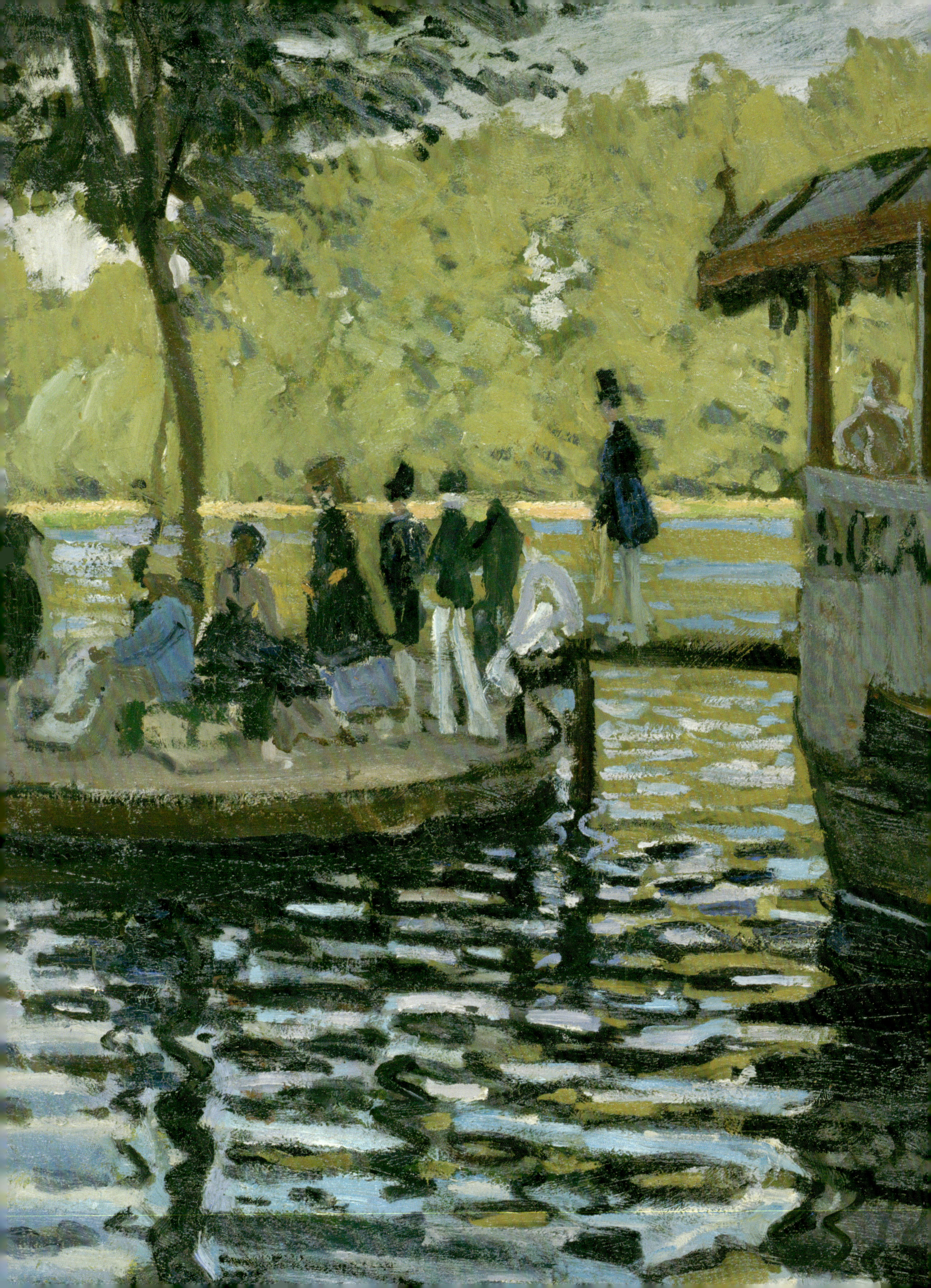

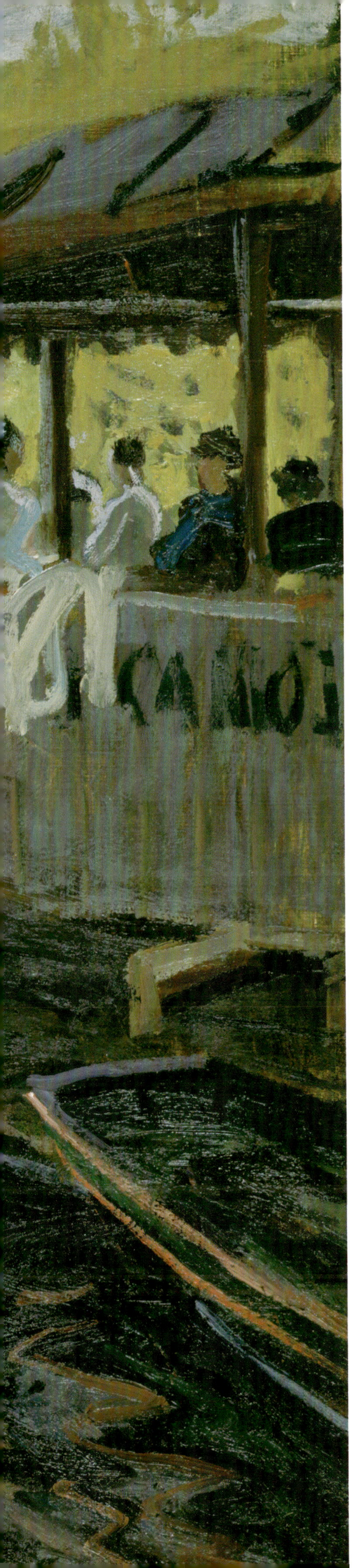

Framing Impressionisms

Mirrors of Dissonance and Realism in Literature and the Visual Arts

GAYLE ZACHMANN

There began to appear, sometimes perchance on the walls of the Salon, but far more frequently and certainly on those of the galleries of the rejected, curious and singular paintings.
—Stéphane Mallarmé

They've all gone crazy.
—Charles Francis Browne

In the latter decades of the nineteenth century, France experienced momentous changes in visual and print cultures as unprecedented modernization and scientific and technological innovation were swiftly absorbed into practices *and depictions* of modern life—on canvas, in literary production, cultural politics, and the press. The new, art-acquiring, leisure- and status-seeking public did not only see the "new art" in galleries, exhibitions, or Salons; they also read about it. Very similarly, although a few decades later, American Impressionism made its appearance, witnessing rich intersections between the visual arts in France and the United States, as well as literary and journalistic ones.

As transforming political and market economies refashioned social relations and even optical experience on both sides of the Atlantic, Impressionism would bear testimony, mirroring new visions and views of society, art, and cultural industry. Initial

Claude Monet (French, 1840–1926), *La Grenouillère* (detail, fig. 1), 1869

reactions to Impressionism were negative. And yet, in France and the United States of the late nineteenth and early twentieth centuries, the once scandalous poetry of everyday life in painting would take a place of honor, often justified by the very arguments on which the new painting had originally been spurned, those of mimesis, or the faithful representation of nature. On the one hand, Impressionists were criticized for too little of it; their "shocking" images did not conform to academic conceptions of realistic representation. However, they were also attacked for mirroring far too much; forgoing idealized historical events and heroic figures, their journalistic canvases reflected fruit picking, dance halls, sprawling contemporary land- and urban-scapes, everyday faces, barmaids, boating parties, train stations, park walks, and picnics.

First called *intransigeants* in France for their rejection of convention, unfinished surfaces, strangely cropped scenes of modern and mundane life, and their destabilizing renderings of instantaneity, light, and reflection, the Impressionists would soon be associated with the scientific, aesthetic, and sociopolitical discourses deployed to justify them.[1] And framing Impressionism was by no means a uniquely visual endeavor. Sung by literary proponents as a revolutionary art of both dissidence and democracy, Impressionist disruptions of tradition were rapidly linked to (praiseworthy) literary and societal ones. In France, writers would scramble to re-brush art, literary, and national master narratives, displaying the Third Republic's "new art"—*in literature and in painting*—as a more immediately accessible—and therefore more legitimate "real," one grounded in individual observation, visual memory, and effect, as well as the social and political histories underwriting the individual, artistic agency, and national image.[2]

Narratives associated with American and French Impressionism often include "the encounter." American painters arrive in France, and born of that meeting of the minds and eyes—a collision of visual cultures—American Impressionism will emerge. Interaction, however, was far more complex, traversing art, literature, and philosophical writings throughout the nineteenth century, and much prior.[3] Still, within art criticism, the label "American Impressionism" has received much attention, and even suspicion. Is it American? Or is it really French? Issues of origins and imitation aside, the dialogic relationships between these two movements remain rich.

For those familiar with American Impressionism, the name Hamlin Garland most likely rings a bell, perhaps less for his novelistic production or calls to a locally colored, decentered American art than for John Rewald's oft-cited declaration that Garland's 1894 *Crumbling Idols: Twelve Essays on Art Dealing Chiefly with Literature, Painting, and the Drama* was "probably the first all-out defense of the movement to be written in English."[4] Although possibly the first apology for American Impressionism, the first case for Impressionism in English is much more likely that of modern poet-critic par excellence, Stéphane Mallarmé (1842–1898), whose essay "The Impressionists and Edouard Manet" was published in English in *Art Monthly Review* in September 1876, soon after the second Impressionist group exhibition in Paris.[5] Rather than merely describe the work of the Impressionists as painting—so to speak—a verbal picture, Mallarmé sought first and foremost to situate the new art form historically, aesthetically, and ideologically. As did Garland's 1894 *Crumbling Idols*, the 1876 piece linked Impressionism to modern, scientifically bolstered visions and new relations to space and time in both literature and the visual arts. What might their discussions tell us about their parallel concerns and common ideological contexts and assumptions?[6]

As would Garland's treatise, Mallarmé's "The Impressionists and Edouard Manet" invokes the literature-painting analogy to justify the "new art." He legitimates the "sudden light" of Impressionist dissidence with recourse to historical precedents, modern life, and parallel trends in the verbal arts. Calling up French writers Charles Baudelaire and Émile Zola[7] as an "enlightened few" who "voluntarily abandoned conventionalism" (446), Mallarmé states that in painting, Edouard Manet, the French artist and precursor to Impressionism, "followed a similarly divergent course, seeking the truth, and loving it when found, because being true it was so strange, especially when compared with the old and worn-out ideals of it" (450).

Mallarmé finds great affinity between Manet and several contemporaries, including Monet, Sisley, and Pissarro. He underscores their "push together towards new and unexpected horizons, and fresh-formed truths" (461). Addressing Monet's pictorial innovations (Fig. 1), he writes: "Claude Monet loves water, and it is his especial

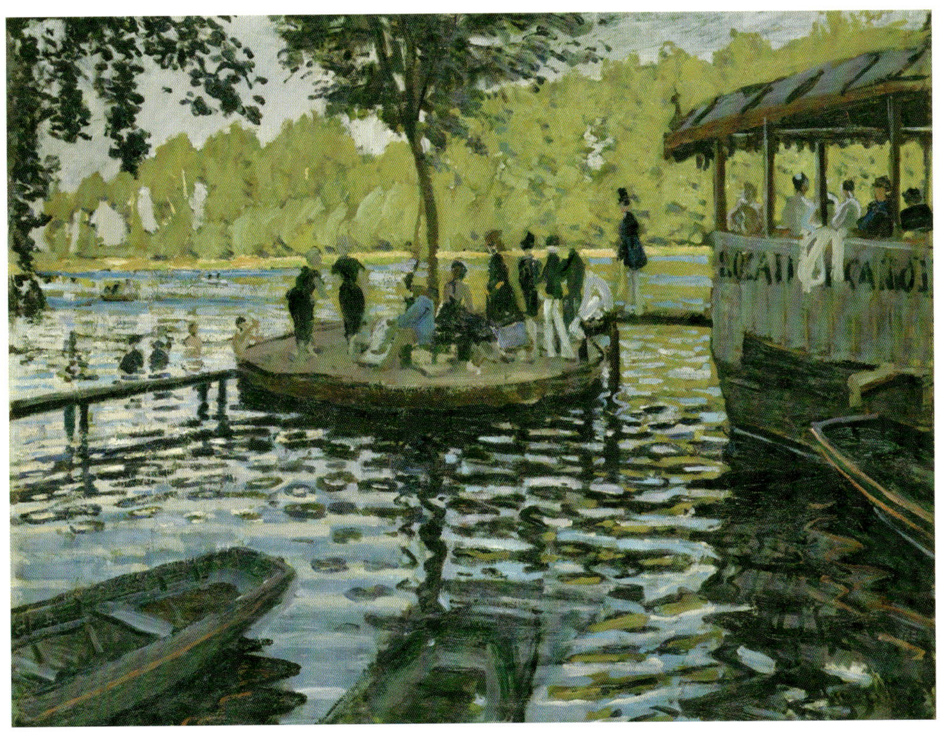

FIGURE 1. This was one of seventeen landscapes by Monet included in the second Impressionist group exhibition in 1876. Claude Monet (French, 1840–1926), *La Grenouillère*, 1869, oil on canvas, 29 ⅜ × 39 ¼ in. (74.6 × 99.7 cm), The Metropolitan Museum of Art, H. O. Havemeyer Collection, Bequest of Mrs. H. O. Havemeyer, 1929, 29.100.112; Image copyright © The Metropolitan Museum of Art. Image source: Art Resource, NY

gift to portray its mobility and transparency, be it sea or river, grey and monotonous, or coloured by the sky. I have never seen a boat poised more lightly on the water than in his pictures or a veil more mobile and light than his moving atmosphere. It is in truth a marvel" (462).

For Mallarmé, Impressionism in literature and the visual arts is born of the ability of the "true artist" to seize what is "captivating" in modern, "ambient" life, a modern understanding of "new laws of space and light" (451), and never a matter of slavish imitation. Explaining that the public has been fooled by "an artificially classic science," that they are "dupes of a civilized education," he pronounces Impressionism's effects "a new delight at the recovery of a long obliterated truth" (457–58), its dissonant scenes "an extraordinary and quasi-original newness of vision" that "make[s]

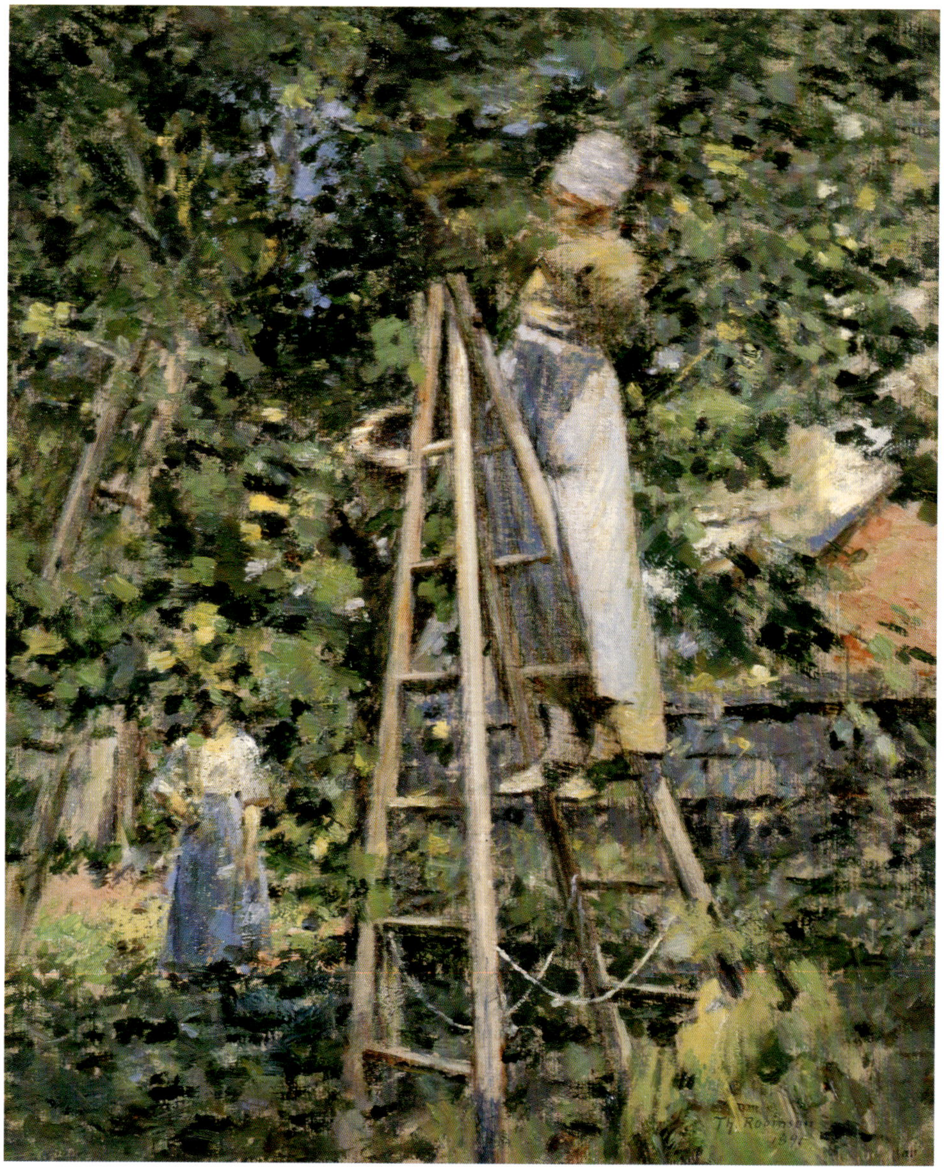

FIGURE 2, PLATE 7. Theodore Robinson (American, 1852–1896), *Gathering Plums*, 1891, oil on canvas, 22 × 18 in. (57.2 × 55.9 cm), Georgia Museum of Art, University of Georgia, Eva Underhill Holbrook Memorial Collection of American Art, Gift of Alfred H. Holbrook, 1945.76

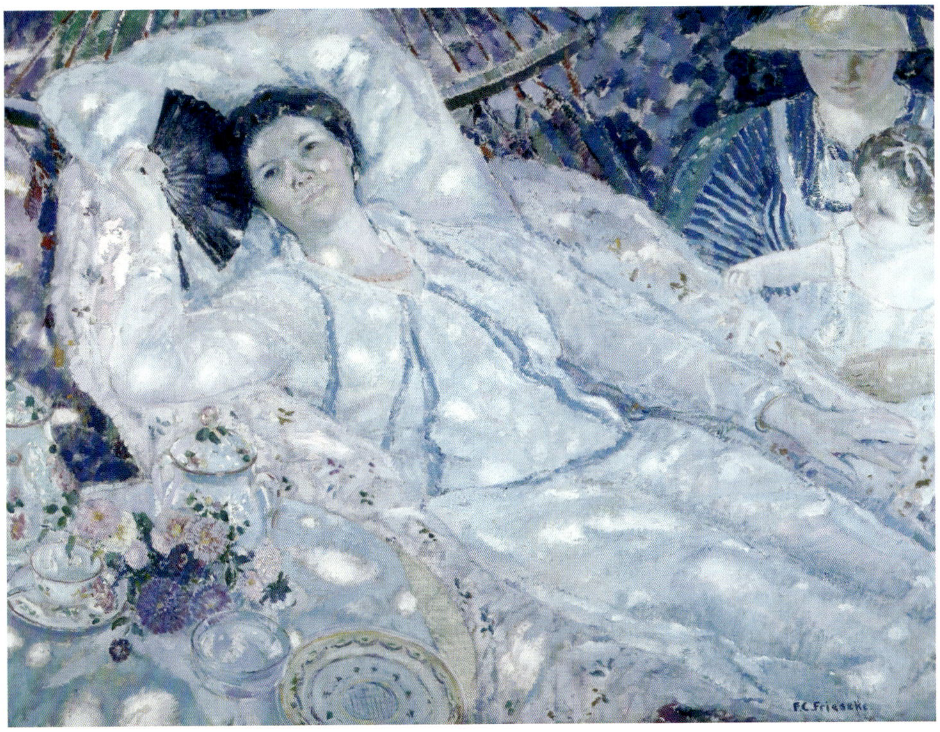

FIGURE 3, PLATE 13. Frederick Carl Frieseke (American, 1874–1939), *The Hammock*, by 1915, oil on canvas, 38 ⅝ × 51 ⅝ in. (98.1 × 131.1 cm), Telfair Museums, Savannah, Georgia, Museum purchase, 1917.3

us understand when looking on the most accustomed objects the delight we should experience could we but see them for the first time" (466).

Clarifying the aims and practices of the new art for "the mighty numbers of an universal suffrage" (468)—newcomers to a new artistic market—Mallarmé affirms that the Impressionists are "visionaries" in a "confused and hesitating age" (466). He declares Impressionism "the principal and real movement of contemporary painting" (466–67), appealing to social and revolutionary analogies, and proudly reclaiming the inclusive heritage of the French Revolution for the emerging art's everyday visions: "The participation of a hitherto ignored people in the political life of France is a social fact that will honour the whole of the close of the nineteenth century. A parallel is found in artistic matters. . . . To day the multitude demands to see with its own eyes" (467–68).

Nearly twenty years later, the poet, novelist, essayist, and short fiction writer Hamlin Garland, in *Crumbling Idols,* would decry the blind imitation of masters in praise of individual freedom, justifying the mirroring of everyday activities as might be seen in Theodore Robinson's *Gathering Plums*, 1891 (Fig. 2, Pl. 7), or the surprising use of light, color, cropping, and theme reflected in Frederick Carl Frieseke's visually assonant *The Hammock*, by 1915 (Fig. 3, Pl. 13). Proposing Impressionism as most apt to portray new visions of America, Garland relates the movement in painting to literary practices and theories as well as to social and political ones, concurring with Hutcheson Macaulay Posnett that "the true makers of national literature are the actions and thoughts of the nation itself" (3).

Like Mallarmé, Garland invoked democratic movements to validate impressionistic views, and he too linked aesthetic revolution to historical ones—justifying artistic independence and new realisms as legacies of the American Revolution. He insisted that, like Impressionism in painting, the new literature reject models of those "blinded" by instruction and "deal truthfully and at close grapple with the facts of his immediate present" (51). And as had Mallarmé, Garland justified Impressionism's claims to referentiality, marketing its incongruous mimesis as well as its potential as both document and democratic provocation: the new artist "sees life in terms of what it might be, as well as in terms of what it is; but he writes of what is, and, at his best suggests what is to be" (52).[8]

Both Mallarmé and Garland deploy Impressionism as form and pretext for cultural journalism and social criticism. Both harken back to revolutions to similar ends, and both would engage the public with texts whose sociopolitical and ideological calls to artistic independence link national identity and the figure of the artist as cultural reporter and social agent. Impressionism came to the fore as France's cultural nationalism affirmed the enfranchisement of new sectors and phenomena of the nascent Republic. As Wolfgang Schivelbusch notes in *The Culture of Defeat*, post-1870s France would recast defeat and civil war as a blessing and as impetus for a new kind of nation, reframing narratives of the republican individual and social inclusion in life and in art as cultural state glory in the name of humanity.[9] That being said, the foregrounding of scenes from daily life does not only exalt; seeing as if for the first time precludes neither opportunities nor invitations to social criticism—quite the contrary.

Less overtly critical of society than its French counterpart, American Impressionism is considered euphemistic rather than acerbic.[10] And yet Garland's vision of Impressionism seems no less challenging of dominant discourses. Here, too, the interest in open air and modern life meets a scientific and justificatory gaze bolstered by a political one. And while Garland appeals to the mythology of the American Revolution, he also acknowledges a more recent watershed that "divided the old from the new"—the 1861–65 American Civil War, conjuring the place of trauma in post–civil war societies' reconsiderations of national values in life and in art (84). Indeed, the dual revolutions serve at once to justify and to enshroud these radical movements, memorializing them within well-established and comfortable national narratives. The real origins and futures of Impressionism's shocking new way of seeing the world are for Mallarmé and Garland, indeed, much more contemporary upheavals. Both writer-critics call for national regeneration, new visual arts, and new literatures that would record, mirror, and ultimately, provoke.

Notes

1. In addition to "impressionists," the painters associated with *plein air* painting, high pitch, and surprisingly cropped tableaux of modern life were called "realists, "Japonistes," and "veritists." See William H. Gerdts, *American Impressionism* (New York: Abbeville Press, 2001); Robert L. Herbert, *Impressionism: Art, Leisure, and Parisian Society* (New Haven: Yale University Press, 1988); Linda Nochlin, *Realism* (London: Penguin, 1990); Philip G. Nord, *Impressionism and Politics: Art and Democracy in the Nineteenth Century* (London: Routledge, 2000); John Rewald, *The History of Impressionism,* rev. ed. (New York: Museum of Modern Art, 1961); and *American Impressionism and Realism: The Painting of Modern Life, 1885–1915,* curated by H. Barbara Weinberg, Doreen Bolger, and David Park Curry (New York: Metropolitan Museum of Art, 1994).

2. If journalism was to be the orator and *sine qua non* of the Republic, the informed republican citizen, and by extension the art-acquiring public, Impressionism—visual and verbal—was to be its reporter, documentation, and art.

3. Hamlin Garland, for example, opens his *Crumbling Idols* with reference not to a French painter but to the French historian and philosopher Hippolyte Taine. Garland, *Crumbling Idols* (Chicago: Stone and Kimball, 1894), 1 (hereafter cited parenthetically in the text).

4. John Rewald, *The History of Impressionism,* rev. ed. (New York: Museum of Modern Art, 1961), 610.

5. Stéphane Mallarmé, "The Impressionists and Edouard Manet," *Art Monthly Review*, September 30, 1876, 117–22, reprinted in Stéphane Mallarmé, *Oeuvres complètes*, vol. 2, ed. Bertrand Marchal (Paris: Gallimard, 2003), 444–70 (hereafter cited parenthetically in the text). For an extended discussion of the essay and the metaphor of photography, see Gayle Zachmann, *Frameworks for Mallarmé: The "Photo" and the "Graphic" of an Interdisciplinary Aesthetic* (New York: State University of New York Press, 2008), particularly chapters 4 and 5.

6. Although the ambit of my remarks targets ideological commonalities that underwrite how literary figures frame discussions of Impressionism, intertextual relationships between the two arts may occur at multiple levels, including shared subject matter and formalistic coincidences, with analogical appropriations in literature of characteristics traditionally associated with the visual arts such as the cropping and the pausing of time one sees in Mallarmé's syntactic play with punctuation and blanks, or the representation and justification of unverisimilar shadow colors evoked by Spencer or Garland.

7. Baudelaire, scandalous poet of the *Fleurs du mal,* the modern city, the *flâneur,* and "the heroism of modern life," would also take on the role of writer-critic. See his *Salon de 1846* and *Salon de 1859* in particular. Zola, known for his theorization of the experimental novel, is associated with naturalistic theories and depictions of the impacts of heredity, race, and milieu on lives not previously deemed worthy of representation. Both Baudelaire and Zola were additionally early supporters of Manet and of avant-garde writers and painters. See T. J. Clark, *The Painting of Modern Life: Paris in the Art of Manet and His Followers* (New York: Knopf, 1985); and Harrison C. White and Cynthia A. White, *Canvases and Careers: Institutional Change in the French Painting World* (Chicago: University of Chicago Press, 1992).

8. Garland assimilated Impressionist practices and visions to what he will interchangeably call "realist" and "veritist" ones in literature.

9. Wolfgang Schivelbusch, *The Culture of Defeat: On National Trauma, Mourning, and Recovery,* trans. Jefferson Chase (New York: Picador, 2001).

10. Noted by Gerdts in *American Impressionism*, among others.

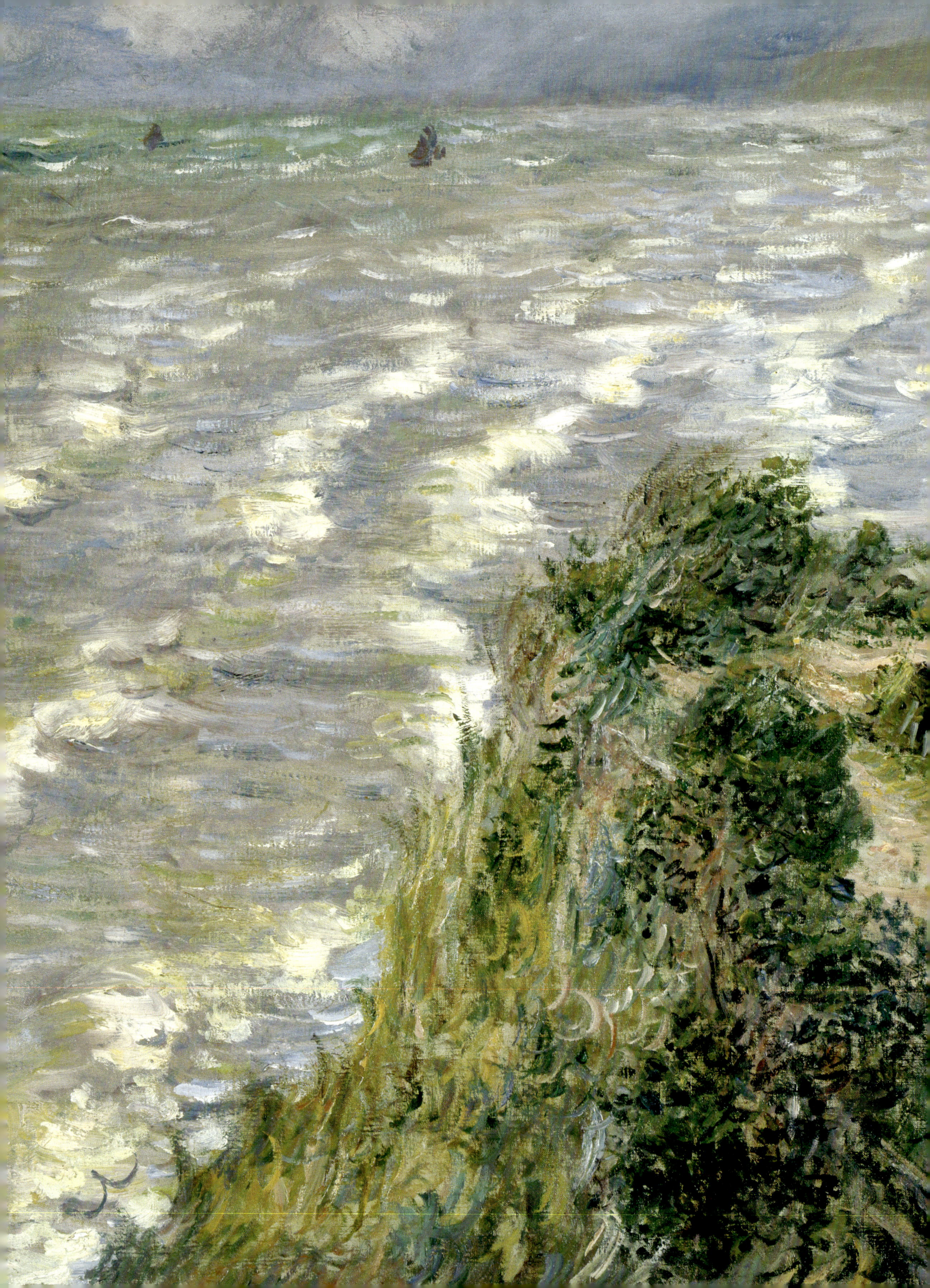

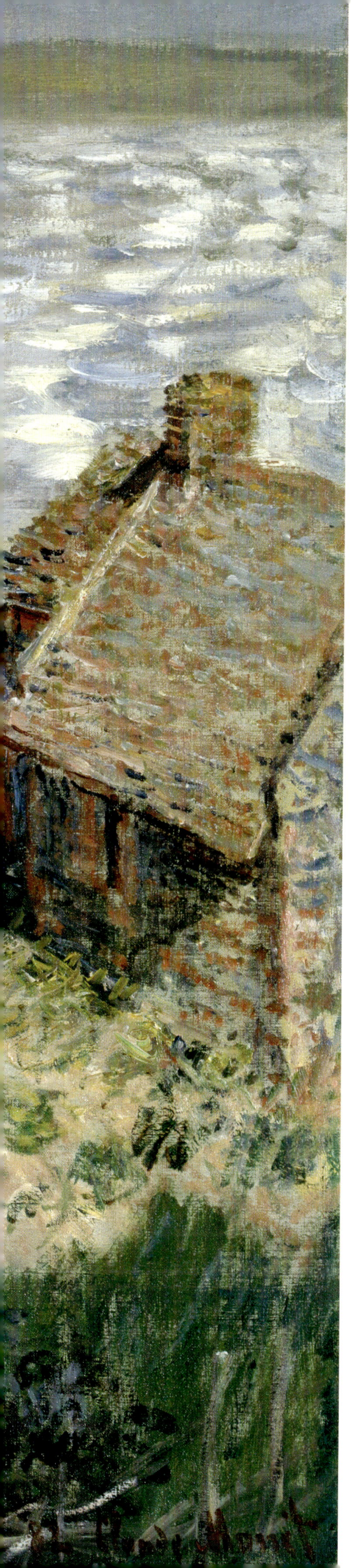

Seeing Nature, Poetically

Proust and Impressionism

CAROL J. MURPHY

In Marcel Proust's iconic modernist novel, *In Search of Lost Time,*[1] the narrator, seeking truth through art, asks what it means to "see poetically" in a description of a seascape by the text's fictional painter, Elstir. Elstir, whose name is a partial anagram of the last name of the American expatriate artist James Abbott McNeill Whistler (Fig. 1, Pl. 66),[2] is a composite figure of several painters of the late nineteenth century, including Claude Monet, whose work *Impression, Sunrise,* 1873, provided the name for the Impressionist movement.[3] Proust's meticulous description, in its conflation of poetic truth with artistic vision, captures not only what the artist sees—a seascape in Normandy (Fig. 2, Pl. 22)—but also, and especially, the act of seeing as a subjective process of encoding perceptions and impressions. The narrator remarks that what appears to the eye of the painter and is translated spontaneously onto the canvas is a representation of nature as felt experience, before the overlay of thought.[4] This visual "impression," a dynamic field of sensations, colors, and reflections of light, is rendered technically through rapid brushstrokes in "a web of pigment."[5] For Proust, Elstir's efforts "to reproduce things not as he knew them to be but according to the optical illusions of which our first sight of them is composed, had led him precisely to bring out certain of these laws of perspective, which were thus all the more striking, since art had been the first to disclose them."[6] These new

Claude Monet (French, 1840–1926), *Marée montante à Pourville (Rising Tide at Pourville)* (detail, fig. 2, pl. 22), 1882

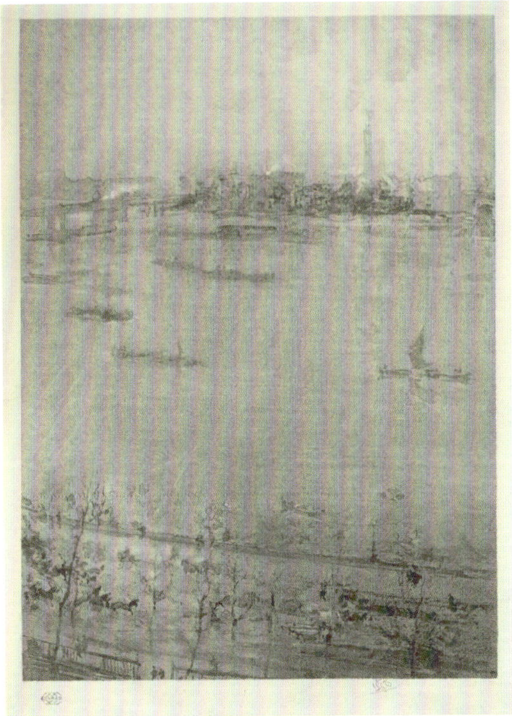

FIGURE 1, PLATE 66.
James Abbott McNeill Whistler (American, 1834–1903), *The Thames*, 1896, lithotint with scraping on paper, image: 10 7/16 × 7 3/8 in. (26.5 × 18.7 cm), sheet: 11 13/16 × 8 7/16 in. (30 × 21.4 cm), The Baltimore Museum of Art: The Conrad Collection, BMA 1932.17.19; Photography by Mitro Hood

"laws of perspective" described by Proust invite his reader, and by extension viewers of Impressionist paintings, to see and sense reality differently. Proust's passage about new ways of seeing nature, published more than forty years after the inception of the movement, offers insights into our understanding of American Impressionist paintings and their unique approaches to rendering the physical world.

Although Proust's narrator may have gone too far in attributing the discovery of new perspectives to the Impressionists, these artists, nonetheless, inherited and engaged with a visual culture that had started to change radically at the beginning of the nineteenth century.[7] Philosophical, scientific, and aesthetic theories of perception and sensation, together with numerous optical inventions, unsettled the once-stable relationship between viewer and viewed, privileging instead subjective and sensate vision as temporally and corporeally experienced. Traditional perspectival representations of the real, based on the model of the camera obscura, a device that reproduced an objective view of the world fixed in time and space,[8] had dominated the theory of vision since the Renaissance. The shift from geometric optics to new scientific theories that embraced a modern, embodied, and thus subjective observer of the real, transformed the nature of the viewer's relationship to the viewed from that of passive spectator to active producer. Such a dramatic change in concepts of the visual is chronicled by art theorist Jonathan Crary in his groundbreaking study *Techniques of the Observer: On Vision and Modernity in the Nineteenth Century.* Crary signals the importance of the work of the German writer and scientist Johann Wolfgang von Goethe, whose pioneering *Theory of Colours*, published in 1810, demonstrated that subjective visual phenomena such as retinal afterimages constituted an optical "truth" and not an "illusion"; our perception of colors is a product of the eye of the observer, not a simple reproduction of an already existing reality.[9] Goethe's ideas were shared and developed by others, including the philosopher Arthur Schopenhauer, whose aesthetic theories were linked to these new physiological discoveries. Like Friedrich Nietzsche, the German philosopher who compared seeing and sensibility to a "flood of impressions" from disparate stimuli, Schopenhauer highlighted the constructed nature of reality where the human subject was both "the site and producer of sensation."[10] Many other such revelations in physiology, psychology, chemistry, and physics (for example, the function of light waves in perception) revolutionized existing theories of sight and ultimately modified discourses on what it meant to be human. In addition, the discovery of optical devices, such as the stereoscope, the kaleidoscope, and the phenakistoscope, culminating in the invention of photography and prototypes for a cinematic recording of images in the later nineteenth century and into the twentieth, "delineated perception as a continuous process, a flux of temporally dispersed contents."[11] Other technological changes wrought by industrialized modern societies, such as train travel, and later on the automobile and the airplane, disrupted visual codes by affording, on the one hand, mobility and freedom from fixed temporal and spatial perspectives, but on the other hand, producing perceptual disjunction and defamiliarization. As Crary notes about the consequences of these inventions: "The disruption between internal sensation and external sign is irrevocably blurred."[12]

How did these new ways of seeing affect Impressionist paintings, and what did it mean, as Proust's narrator suggests, to see nature "poetically"? The insistence on subjectivity, flux, sensate perception, feeling, and mood engendered by the new visual culture is both subject and technique of French Impressionist landscape paintings. Blurry landscapes, flickers of reflected light, patches of color, shadows, tonal harmonies, and wavy, blended horizons that fuse or confuse sea or land with sky are some of the elements of their canvases that seek to render immediate and sensate reproductions of nature seen from the point of view of the artist as "freshly encountered and continually changing."[13] The art historian and critic Meyer Schapiro describes the Impressionists' poetic view of nature as "the contemplation of color, light, movement, texture, and the experience of their qualities as feeling-charged; they fuse to constitute a mood, a state of mind, a symbol of a complex essence of man and nature."[14] He also suggests, however, that this view of nature can be interpreted

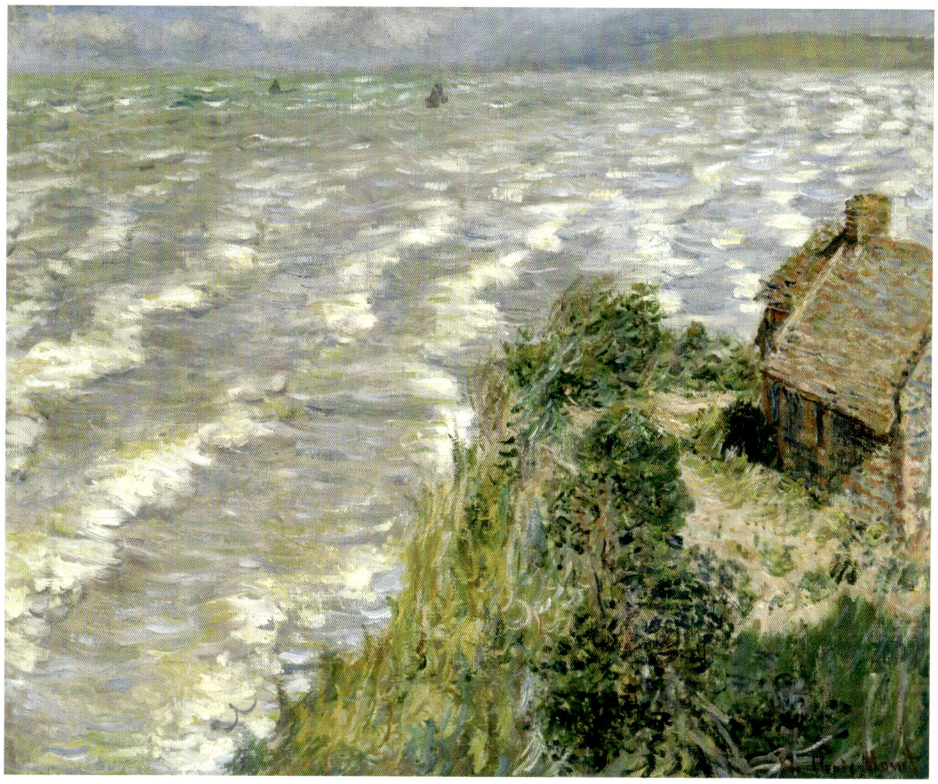

FIGURE 2, PLATE 22.
Claude Monet (French, 1840–1926), *Marée montante à Pourville (Rising Tide at Pourville)*, 1882, oil on canvas, 26 × 32 in. (66 × 81.3 cm), Brooklyn Museum, Gift of Mrs. Horace O. Havemeyer, 41.1260

as a kind of "frank and fresh realism" in that the Impressionists sought to capture appearances of nature rooted "in the direct observation of things."[15] If nature was poetic for the Impressionists, who chose to record the environment as experienced through the activity of sketching in the open air, featuring sites whose appearances changed dramatically according to time of day and the effects of light, seasons, and mood, it was also a practice tied in with new cultural mores of the industrialized nineteenth century and the rise of the leisure classes. No longer ruled by Mother Nature in its moralistic or mythological sense, the representation of the outdoors asserted the freedom of the individual, the value of the senses and their pleasures against a traditional philosophical or religious view of the environment.[16] Art historian Robert Herbert reminds us that during the time of the Impressionists nature was enjoyed as a personal experience and as such was tied in with the importance of tourism, which encouraged displacement for the painters who produced memorable works of art for their future collectors.[17] In the United States, French Impressionist landscapes were popular when introduced to the art-loving public in the 1880s, but in adopting the subject of landscapes the American Impressionists tended to express their ambivalence about progress and change in the natural world by overlaying these phenomena with a noticeable patina of nostalgia, unlike the French Impressionists, who veered away from the picturesque and the sentimental.[18]

As we view the landscapes, seascapes, and garden vistas of American Impressionism, we are reminded of this guiding principle of Impressionism: to capture the changing nature of the real in its subjectively observed and temporally determined refractions of light and color. This overall impression, a unity of the canvas, is what Proust's narrator, speaking of Elstir's seascapes, calls a "multiform and powerful unity."[19] We, as spectators, are invited to experience the pleasures of seeing nature poetically. Viewed from up close, the large and irregular masses of color produced by divided brushstrokes evoke fragments of flowers, skies, sunsets, shadows, rivers, and seas. As we back away, these are transformed into the powerful unity of a felt experience. In this activity of contemplative viewing, we, too, are engaged visually in producing the scene before us as "seen."

Notes

1. Marcel Proust, *Remembrance of Things Past,* vol. 1, *Swann's Way and Within a Budding Grove,* trans. C. K. Scott Moncrieff and Terence Kilmartin (New York: Vintage Books, 1982). Subsequent English translations have adopted the more accurate translation *In Search of Lost Time.* Proust's epic novel, whose seven volumes were published between 1913 and 1927, chronicles the social, historical, scientific,

and psychological transformations of French society from the Belle Epoque to the post–World War I era in a new aesthetic discourse. Over the course of the novel, the narrator's gradual revelation of his own vocation as an artist is inspired by two other fictional artists in addition to Elstir: Vinteuil, a musician, and Bergotte, a writer.

2. Monet met Whistler (1834–1903) in 1862 at the studio of Charles Gleyre. See George T. M. Shackelford and Fronia E. Wissman, *Monet, Renoir, and the Impressionist Landscape* (Ottawa: National Gallery of Canada; Boston: Museum of Fine Arts, 2000), 12. Although Whistler is not considered an Impressionist artist per se, his "Nocturnes" and "Harmonies" series revealed innovative use of color, tonal harmonies, and evocative scenes. See Richard J. Boyle, *American Impressionism* (New York: Little, Brown, 1974), 61–72. The name "Elstir" also references the French painter Paul César Helleu (1859–1927), who was befriended by the American artists John Singer Sargent and Whistler and knew Proust personally. See *American Impressionism and Realism: The Painting of Modern Life, 1885–1915*, curated by H. Barbara Weinberg, Doreen Bolger, and David Park Curry (New York: Metropolitan Museum of Art, 1994), 51–52.

3. *Impression, soleil levant* was shown in the first Independent Impressionist Exhibit in 1874, before the name of the group was coined. The name "Impressionist" is attributed to the art critic Louis Leroy, who referenced Monet's title in a scathing review of the show in the newspaper *Le Charivari* in 1874.

4. Meyer Schapiro, *Impressionism: Reflections and Perceptions* (New York: George Braziller, 1997), 25. Proust's passage reads: "The effort made by Elstir to strip himself, when face to face with reality, of every intellectual notion, was all the more admirable in that this man who made himself deliberately ignorant before sitting down to paint, forgot everything that he knew in his honesty of purpose (for what one knows does not belong to oneself), had in fact an exceptionally cultivated mind" (*Remembrance*, 1:898–99).

5. Schapiro, *Impressionism*, 31.

6. Proust, *Remembrance*, 1:897.

7. Schapiro, *Impressionism*, 206–29. Schapiro reminds us that although the Impressionists did not consult scientific treatises, and that their canvases were often studied by scientists themselves, the Impressionists' connections to the new studies of perception and perspective led them to favor "variable, unstable forms under the dominance of light and atmosphere" (211). The subjectivity of the artist's viewpoint was central to their enterprise.

8. The camera obscura is a darkened chamber where light enters through a small opening that projects images of real objects onto a facing surface and not a plate or film. The optical principle known since Aristotle's time was given its name by Johannes Kepler in 1604.

9. Goethe writes: "Let the observer look steadfastly on a small coloured object and let it be taken away after a time while his eyes remain unmoved; the spectrum of another colour will then be visible on the white plane . . . it arises from an image which now *belongs to the eye*." Quoted in Jonathan Crary, *Techniques of the Observer: On Vision and Modernity in the Nineteenth Century* (Cambridge: MIT Press, 1990), 68–69. Emphasis in the original.

10. Ibid., 23, 75.

11. Ibid., 100.

12. Ibid., 24.

13. Schapiro, *Impressionism*, 15.

14. Ibid., 275.

15. Ibid., 69.

16. Ibid., 88.

17. Robert L. Herbert, *Impressionism: Art, Leisure, and Parisian Society* (New Haven: Yale University Press, 1988), especially chapter 6.

18. Weinberg, Bolger, and Curry, *American Impressionism and Realism*, 54.

19. Proust, *Remembrance*, 1:894.

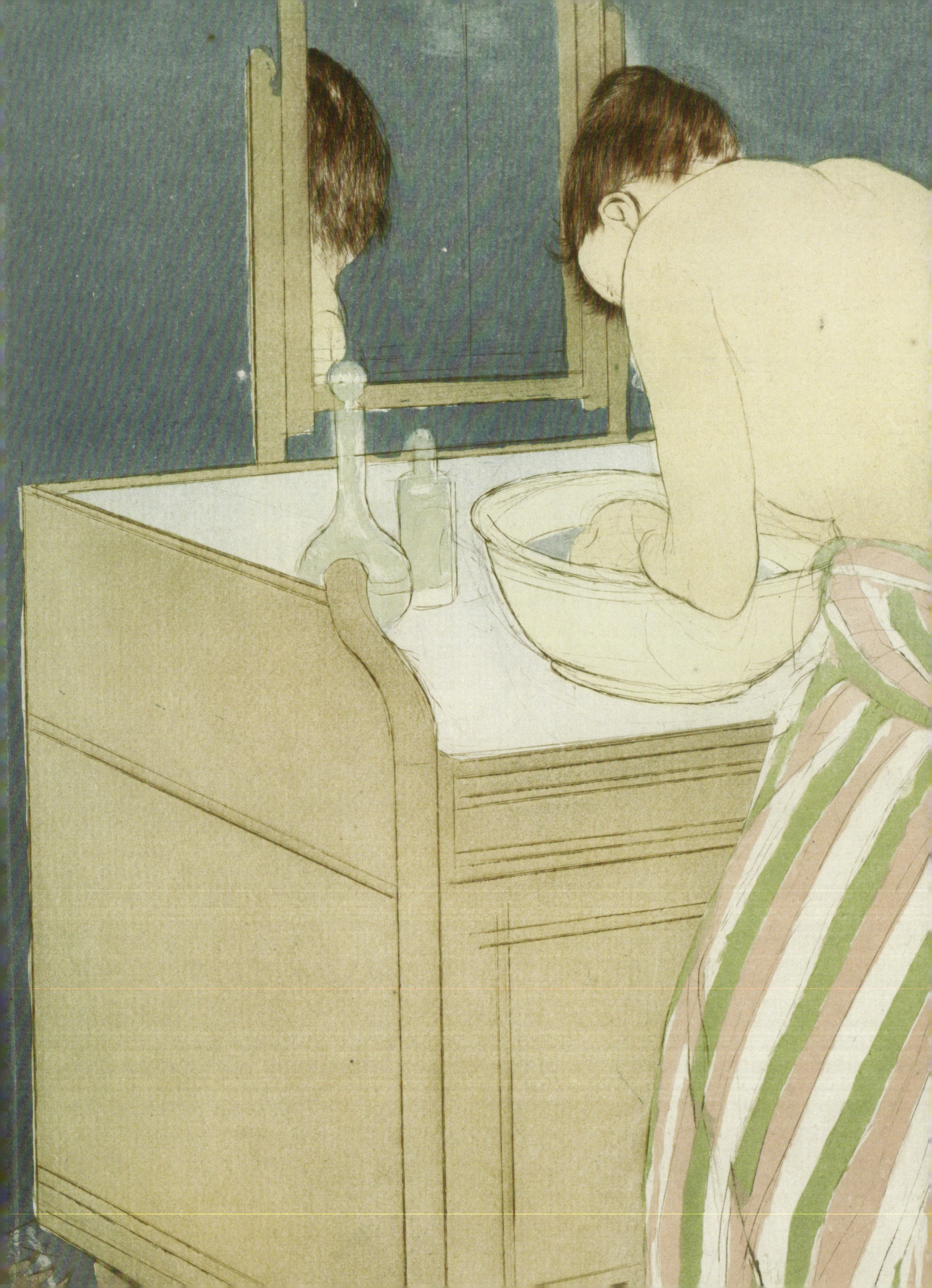

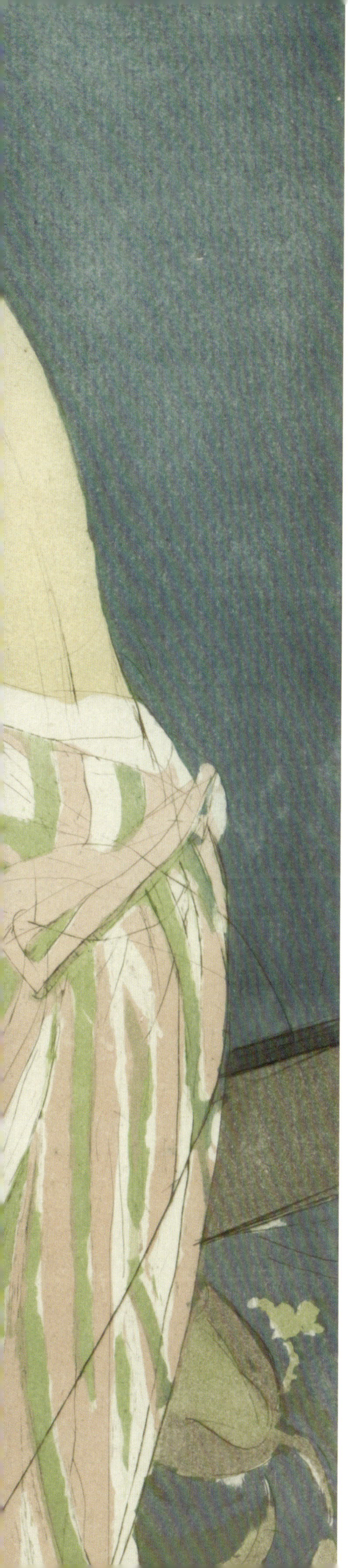

Imprinting Impressionism

The Graphic Work of Mary Cassatt, Frank Benson, and Childe Hassam

COURTNEY A. MCNEIL

IN PAINTING, the style, technique, and objectives of Claude Monet can be seen to have influenced the work of the American Impressionists in a myriad of ways. Yet, unlike many of these Americans (and most of his French peers), Monet confined his forays into printmaking to creating drawings for reproduction in the print media or to allowing other artists to create reproductions of his paintings through etching, lithography, or wood engraving, and is not known to have engaged in any printmaking with his own hands. By contrast, many well-known American Impressionist painters were tremendously inspired by the Etching Revival movement of the mid-nineteenth century and embraced the challenge of mastering various technically demanding printmaking media, having already achieved recognition and success with their painting, in order to find a new outlet for their artistic expression. Their interest flourished despite the fact that several of the key characteristics of Impressionism, such as its bright color palette and its portrayal of glimmering sunlight, do not seem particularly well suited to the confines of an etching plate. Practical concerns, such as the affordability of prints and the visibility they provided for an artist's paintings, also played a role in the fervor with which American Impressionist painters applied themselves to printmaking. This essay will consider the printmaking output and objectives of three American Impressionists—Mary Cassatt, Frank Benson, and Childe Hassam—in contrast to Monet's engagement (or lack thereof) with various printmaking media.

Mary Cassatt (American, 1844–1926), *Woman Bathing* (detail, pl. 61), 1891

Printmaking enjoyed a long and storied history in Europe as a fine art form dating back to the fifteenth century. By the early nineteenth century, though, the "fine art print" was on the decline, and for the most part, prints were used to reproduce works of art in other media, such as paintings or drawings. The tide began to shift once again with the dawn of the Etching Revival in the middle of the nineteenth century—first in France, then spreading to Britain and the United States. In France, printmakers of the Barbizon school, such as Jean-Baptiste-Camille Corot, Jean-François Millet, and Charles-François Daubigny, began producing highly finished plates depicting realistic, non-idealized scenes from nature, as opposed to the mythologically inspired landscapes that were more conventional at that time. The beautiful and often haunting prints of Charles Meryon combined realism with elements of fantasy and generated even more interest in printmaking, both in France and abroad.

Inspired by the potential for innovative artistic expression offered by printmaking, many French Impressionists would create prints, with major contributions to the field being made by Camille Pissarro, Félix Bracquemond, Edgar Degas, and Jean-François Raffaëlli, and with some worthwhile efforts by other major painters who would only dabble in printmaking, such as Alfred Sisley, Paul Cezanne, Pierre-Auguste Renoir, Berthe Morisot, and Gustave Caillebotte.[1] Monet was the only major French Impressionist who never engaged in any type of printmaking with his own hands. Prints after Monet's paintings and drawings do exist, but they were created through printing methods that did not require the hands-on participation of the artist. These methods included gillotage (Fig. 1) (a relatively new process, often used for commercial applications, in which Monet used a special type of coated paper to create drawings after his paintings that could then be reproduced line by line), reproductive etchings and wood engravings (in which a professional etcher or wood engraver translated a painting by Monet onto an etching plate or wood engraving block), and a collaborative limited edition lithographic portfolio designed and printed by lithographer William Thornley (for which Monet selected the works to be reproduced and is believed to have had input into the final product).[2]

If, unlike nearly all of his Impressionist peers, Monet was not interested in exploring the potential for innovative artistic expression offered by printmaking, why did he engage in (or allow others to engage in) the reproduction of his drawings and paintings as summarized above? As described by James A. Ganz, Monet's primary motivations appear to stem from a desire to have more control over how his work was reproduced as well as to promote his exhibitions and better market his oil paintings.[3] Although Monet was likely not paid for the drawings he created for publication in newspapers and journals, he recognized the value of such collaborations with the press in order to promote and ensure the success of his exhibitions. Lamenting

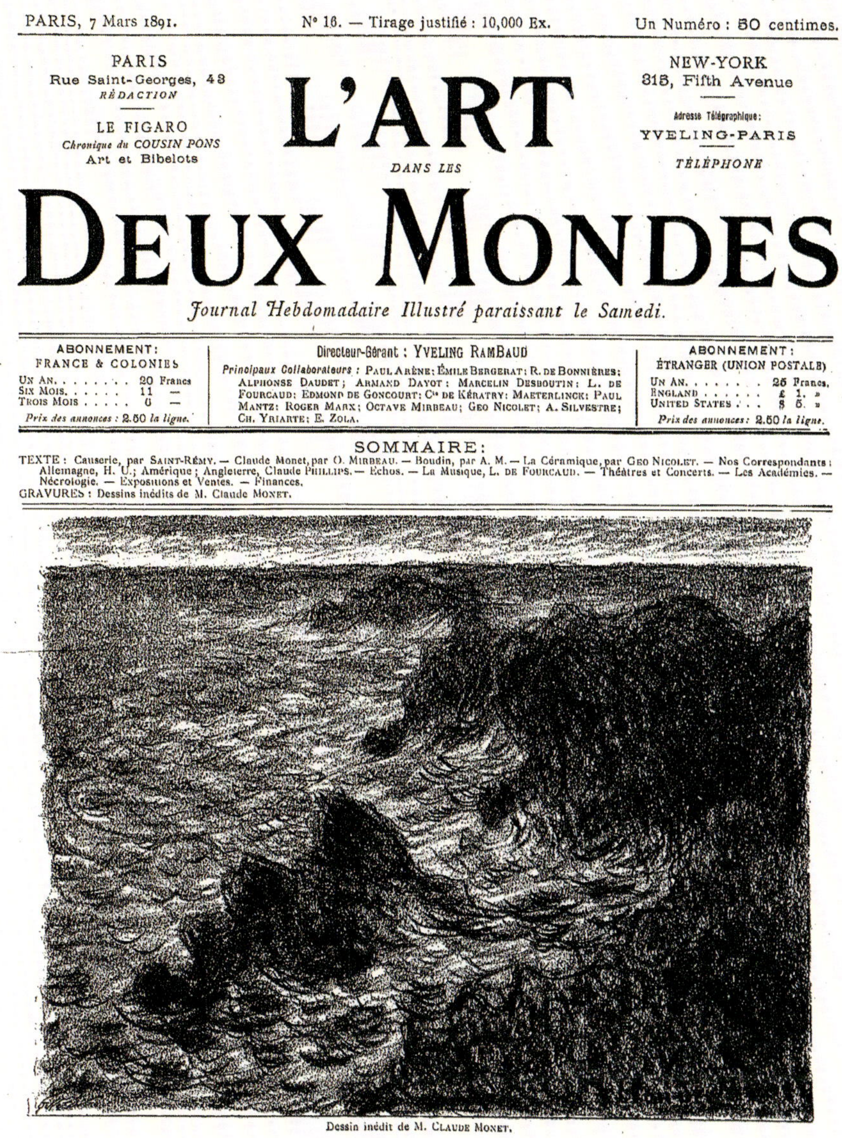

PARIS, 7 Mars 1891. N° 16. — Tirage justifié : 10,000 Ex. Un Numéro : 50 centimes.

PARIS
Rue Saint-Georges, 43
RÉDACTION

LE FIGARO
Chronique du COUSIN PONS
Art et Bibelots

L'ART
DANS LES
DEUX MONDES

NEW-YORK
815, Fifth Avenue

Adresse Télégraphique:
YVELING-PARIS
TÉLÉPHONE

Journal Hebdomadaire Illustré paraissant le Samedi.

ABONNEMENT:
FRANCE & COLONIES
Un An. . . . . 20 Francs
Six Mois. . . . . . 11 —
Trois Mois . . . . . 6 —
Prix des annonces : 2.50 la ligne.

Directeur-Gérant : YVELING RAMBAUD
Principaux Collaborateurs : PAUL ARÈNE; ÉMILE BERGERAT; R. DE BONNIÈRES; ALPHONSE DAUDET; ARMAND DAYOT; MARCELIN DESBOUTIN; L. DE FOURCAUD; EDMOND DE GONCOURT; Cte DE KÉRATRY; MAETERLINCK; PAUL MANTZ; ROGER MARX; OCTAVE MIRBEAU; GEO NICOLET; A. SILVESTRE; CH. YRIARTE; E. ZOLA.

ABONNEMENT:
ÉTRANGER (UNION POSTALE)
Un An. . . . . 25 Francs.
England . . . . . . £ 1. »
United States . . . $ 5. »
Prix des annonces : 2.50 la ligne.

SOMMAIRE:
TEXTE : Causerie, par SAINT-RÉMY. — Claude Monet, par O. MIRBEAU. — Boudin, par A. M. — La Céramique, par GEO NICOLET. — Nos Correspondants : Allemagne, H. U.; Amérique ; Angleterre, Claude PHILLIPS. — Echos. — La Musique, L. DE FOURCAUD. — Théâtres et Concerts. — Les Académies. — Nécrologie. — Expositions et Ventes. — Finances.
GRAVURES : Dessins inédits de M. Claude MONET.

Dessin inédit de M. CLAUDE MONET.

FIGURE 1. After Claude Monet (French, 1840–1926), *The Côte Sauvage*, 1891, gillotage in *L'Art dans les deux mondes*, March 7, 1891, Sterling and Francine Clark Art Institute, Williamstown, Massachusetts

a poorly attended exhibition at Durand-Ruel Gallery in 1883, he complained to the gallery proprietor: "And we'd be blind not to see the truth staring us in the face, not to recognize that the exhibition was ill-prepared and poorly advertised. It is necessary at all costs to secure in advance the cooperation of the press, since even intelligent art-lovers are more or less responsive to the noise made by the newspapers."[4]

In addition to inspiring the Impressionists (aside from Monet), the French etching revival was extremely influential on the father of the Etching Revival in England, Francis Seymour Haden, an acclaimed surgeon, a collector and student of Old Master prints, and an accomplished etcher in his own right. Although Haden's work is much less known today than that of his younger and much more famous brother-in-law, James Abbott McNeill Whistler, Haden played a vital role in legitimizing etching as a fine art form (Fig. 2). His fervent writings on the merits of the print were widely read, and he helped establish the Society of Painter-Etchers in 1880. Haden is also credited with first introducing Whistler to etching and for encouraging him to study and utilize the medium, and it is difficult to overstate the impact that Whistler's prints, with their spare lines and atmospheric printing, would have on an entire generation of printmakers. In addition to urging Whistler to first take up the etching needle, Haden also shared his passion for creating and studying etchings with an American audience during an extensive lecture tour in 1882–1883.[5]

During his lecture tour, Haden encountered enthusiastic practitioners of etching in art communities from the East Coast to the Midwest. The New York Etching Club had been founded in 1877, and in the 1880s similar organizations would be founded in Boston, Philadelphia, Cincinnati, and Brooklyn.[6] The first generation of participants in the American Etching Revival included Stephen Parrish, Charles A. Platt, Henry Farrer, R. Swain Gifford, Mary Nimmo Moran (Fig. 3), and others. Working almost exclusively with landscapes as their subjects, they were interested in capturing realistic and luminous views of their surroundings. These artists were printmakers first and foremost, not painters who also dabbled in printmaking. But as printmaking became more popular in the United States (due to the work of this first generation of artists and to greater exposure to prints by Whistler and his contemporaries) and an American school of printmaking became more established, greater numbers of artists were inspired to take up the etching needle, including many of the leading American Impressionist painters.

Mary Cassatt is known to have produced around 250 prints, beginning in 1879 (the same year she first exhibited with the French Impressionists) and continuing through about 1910.[7] Her prints typically consisted of drypoint, aquatint, and soft-ground etching, or some combination thereof. As described by Nancy Mowll Mathews, Cassatt had no interest in printmaking during the early years of her artistic career, considering it (alongside drawing) to be a lesser branch of art.[8] Cassatt's early opinions about printmaking were informed by her time as a student during the first half of the 1860s at the Pennsylvania Academy of the Fine Arts, where the curriculum was heavily influenced by printmaker John Sartain. Best known for mezzotints reproducing paintings by other artists, Sartain espoused a curriculum that focused heavily on the mastery of drawing techniques before allowing students to move on to painting. Cassatt was impatient with this type of repetition and would not develop a sincere interest in printmaking until she was exposed to the innovative ways in which her French Impressionist colleagues (Degas in particular) were utilizing printmaking to create dazzlingly inventive works of art. Cassatt approached her

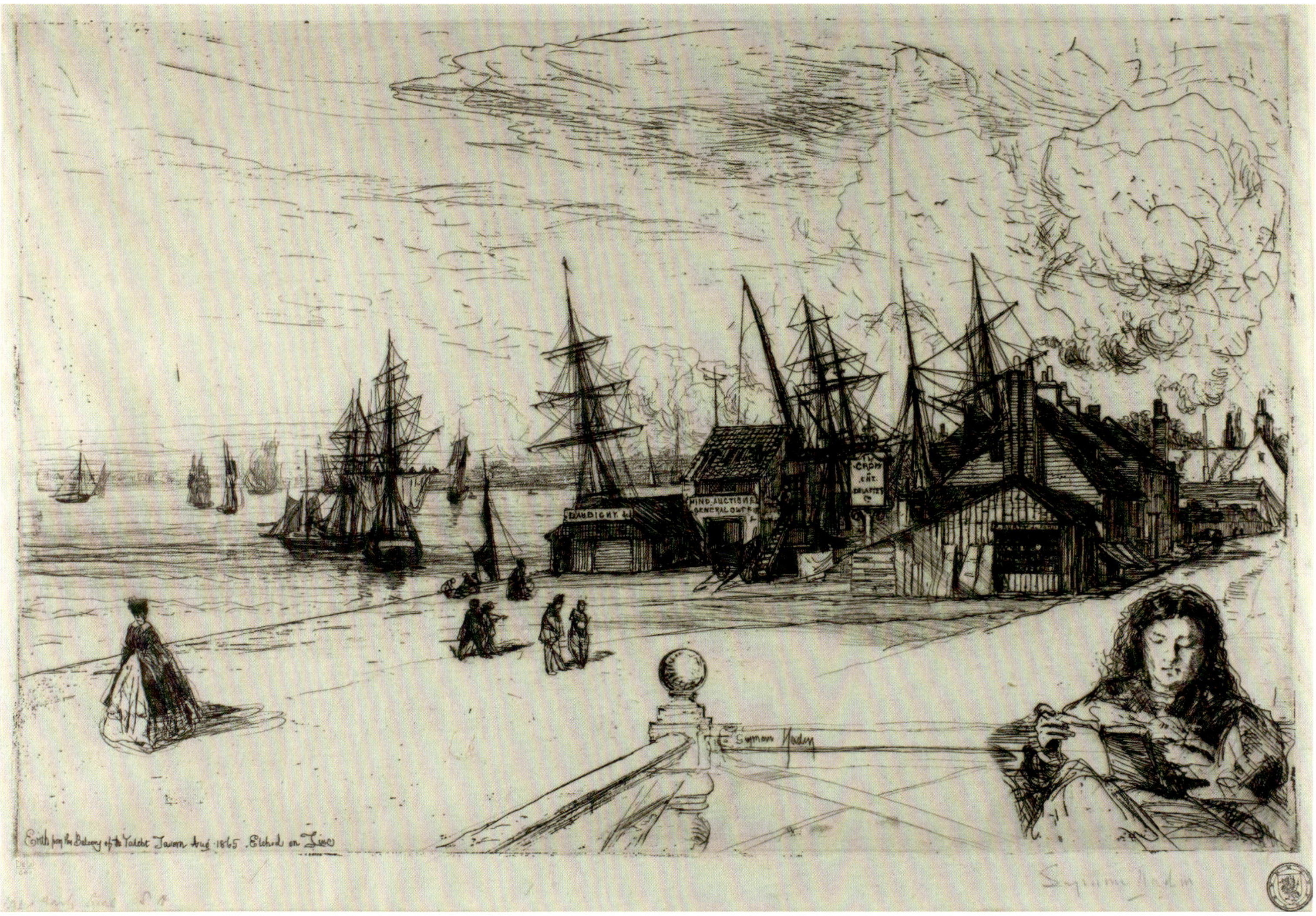

FIGURE 2. Francis Seymour Haden (English, 1818–1910), *Yacht Tavern, Erith*, 1865, etching from a zinc plate on ivory China paper, image/plate: 9 ⅜ × 14 27⁄32 in. (23.8 × 37.7 cm), sheet: 10 15⁄64 × 15 9⁄32 in. (26 × 38.8 cm), The Art Institute of Chicago, Wallace L. DeWolf Collection, 1910.501

prints like a painter; as described by Mathews, "she was willing to draw, paint, dust, heat, bite, and scrape the plate to force from it the extended range of expression she knew was possible from her work in other media."[9] Cassatt's typical subject matter for her prints, intimate domestic scenes featuring women and children (Pl. 55, Pl. 58 and Pl. 60), closely paralleled the subjects of her paintings, and her stylistic approach was heavily influenced by the widespread popularity of Japanese prints at that time. These facts did not go unnoticed by contemporary critics. Christian Brinton noted of her color prints in 1906 (Pl. 61): "Her subjects are much the same as in oils or pastel, but the simplicity of her contour and the clarity of her two or more flat tones give these chance episodes of domestic existence a charm as rare as it is engaging. Though they inevitably suggest Japanese color prints, the plates in no degree lack that deliberate personal impress which distinguishes Miss Cassatt's handling of any medium."[10]

Frank Benson dabbled in etching while he was a student at the School of the Museum of Fine Arts in Boston from 1880 to 1883, but he largely abandoned printmaking until much later in his career. When Benson picked up his etching needle again he was a well-established artist in his fifties, and he embraced the medium with gusto. He would go on to become one of the most prolific printmakers among the American Impressionists, creating more than 350 prints (mainly etchings and drypoints, with just a handful of known lithographs) between 1914 and 1942 and earning a reputation as "dean of American etchers."[11] Unlike Cassatt and Hassam, the subject matter for Benson's etchings did not parallel the subjects of his oil paintings: while his best-known paintings typically portray children and women in bright, sun-dappled landscapes, his prints mainly depict sporting subjects and are populated by ducks, other waterfowl, and the occasional hunter (Pl. 79). His exploration of this subject area is so extensive that he is largely credited with inventing and popularizing the genre of the sporting print. While ducks in flight could easily become prosaic in another artist's hands, Benson's talent for composition and uncanny ability to translate sunlight and atmosphere into the black-and-white format of etching yielded a remarkable body of work. In a glowing review of Benson's first exhibition of etchings, in 1915, critic Royal Cortissoz declared: "His wild fowl are bathed in light. The waters on which they move positively take on color through the skill with which he illuminates them."[12] Praise for his etching technique continued as Benson's career in printmaking progressed. Writing nearly twenty years later, in 1934, Childe Reece stated: "Benson is not only selective, he is the delineator of light and air. His birds are enveloped in atmosphere, they never float in a vacuum or against an impalpable sky."[13]

Another American Impressionist painter who was also a prolific printmaker was Childe Hassam, who produced 380 known etchings and drypoints as well as 45 known lithographs.[14] Like Benson, Hassam dabbled in printmaking early in his career (during the 1880s), then turned away from the medium for several decades. Also like Benson, he made his public debut as an etcher with an exhibition of prints in late 1915.[15] Hassam returned to printmaking sometime in the early 1910s and began focusing seriously on it during the summer of 1915. Elizabeth E. Barker makes a compelling argument that Hassam's return to etching was informed and encouraged by his close friend and fellow founder of "The Ten," J. Alden Weir.[16] Weir was no longer actively making prints at that time; he had engaged in printmaking for a relatively brief interlude (from the late 1880s through early 1890s), but the years he spent making prints had an indelible impact on him. Hassam took Weir's encouragement to heart, and his aptitude for the medium was remarkable. As soon as he had mastered the basic techniques of etching during that productive summer of

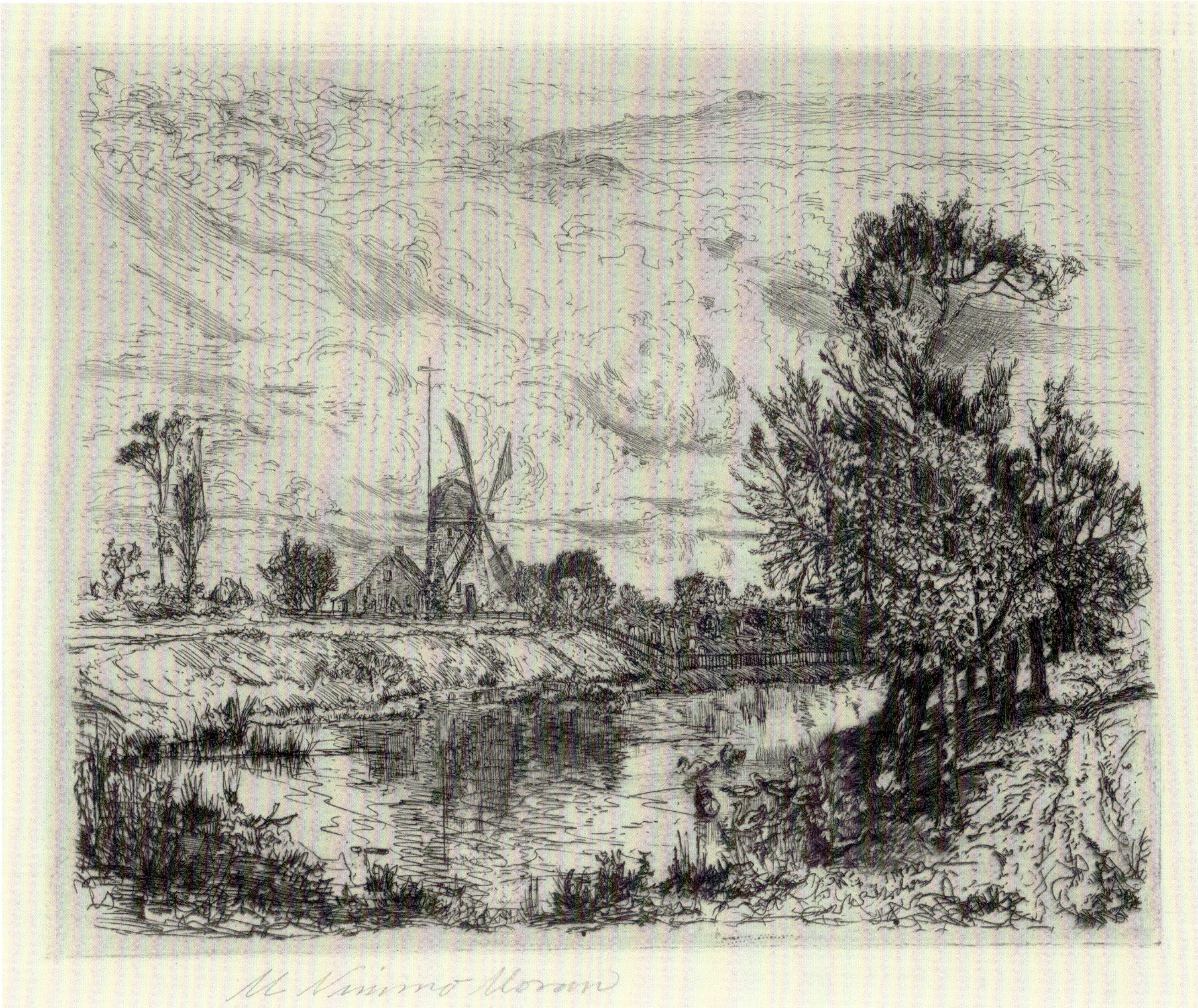

FIGURE 3. Mary Nimmo Moran (American, born in Scotland, 1842–1899), *The Goose Pond, Easthampton, Long Island*, 1881, etching, platemark: 7 1/16 × 8 7/8 in. (18 × 22.5 cm), Museum of Fine Arts, Boston, Gift of Sylvester Rosa Koehler, K1499; Photograph © 2015 Museum of Fine Arts, Boston

1915, he began producing extraordinary plates that seemed to be the result of years of practice rather than a few weeks. Hassam's subjects—the landscape, the figure in the landscape, contemporary urban views, and domestic interiors—closely parallel the subjects of the oil paintings that had already brought him great fame as an artist. Examples include *Easthampton* (Pl. 77), *The Willow Pool* (Pl. 75), and *Washington's Birthday (Fifth Avenue & 23rd Street)* (Pl. 72).

Hassam's style of printmaking differed from that of many of his contemporaries in one significant way: his plates were typically full of marks from edge to edge. Just as a painting would be covered in brushstrokes over the entire surface of the canvas, the designs of Hassam's etchings typically contained great detail in all areas—not only the primary subject of the print, but also the foreground and the background. The prints of Whistler (Pl. 67) or other artists associated with the Etching Revival typically featured a spare, linear style and often gave as much importance to blank areas of the composition as they gave to the ostensible subject of the works. Compare the level of finish of any of Hassam's prints to Weir's *By Candlelight* (Pl. 62), Cassatt's *The Mirror* (Pl. 54), or Benson's [*Second Island Outlet*] (Pl. 78). Hassam's prints could hardly be described as "unfinished," a criticism often leveled against progressive printmakers at the time. Cortissoz praised this unique aspect of Hassam's prints in a review of his etching debut in 1915. After describing the artist's first foray into printmaking as "uneven," he elaborates: "Those that are good are so good as to be positively exciting. In fact, no etcher has appeared in recent years with so fresh a quality, with so original a style. It is not a linear style in the Whistlerian sense. You do not savor Mr. Hassam's line as a thing beautiful in itself. But you love it for its adequacy in the expression of what he has to convey."[17] What Hassam conveyed in his etchings, according to Cortissoz, was a "wonderfully delicate fabric of line and light and shade,"[18] a description that could easily be applied to the dappled sunlight and pervasive crosshatching of *Easthampton* (Pl. 77) or *The Willow Pool* (Pl. 75).

After considering the printmaking output of Cassatt, Benson, and Hassam, one important similarity emerges: all three artists began their serious engagement with printmaking only after achieving considerable success in oil painting. This fact raises the question of why these painters, at the height of their fame, would turn to a new, technically challenging medium with which they had almost no experience. The possible answers are many. As discussed above, it can be surmised that Monet's engagement with printmaking (albeit very limited) stemmed from his desire to control how his work was represented in the media and to better promote his paintings. Some of these practical, publicity-driven concerns can be attributed to the Americans as well. Prints exist in multiples, and historically they have commanded prices significantly lower than those of oil paintings. These combined factors allow prints to be disseminated much more broadly than paintings could ever be. As Mary Cassatt declared, "nothing, I believe, will inspire a taste for art more than the possibility of having it in the home. I should like to feel that amateurs in America could have an example of my work, a print or an etching, for a few dollars. That is what they do in France. It is not left to the rich alone to buy art; the people—even the poor—have taste and buy according to their means. And here they can always find something they can afford."[19] This point is echoed in an article describing the goals of the newly formed Painter-Gravers of America in 1917 (of which Childe Hassam was founding chairman), in which a writer for the *New York Times* stated: "The print is more in keeping with the democratic tendencies of today. It can be bought within the means of a greater number, and fifty or more collectors may enjoy their separate impressions of one print."[20] Yet even if prints were successful in raising general awareness of contemporary American art among the public and in broadening the spectrum of collectors who could afford to hang art in their own homes, it would take the sale of many prints to equal the sale of a single painting by one of these highly sought-after artists. While Cassatt's and Benson's prints are known to have met with commercial success, Hassam's (despite being widely touted by insiders in the print world) would never prove to be a commercially viable endeavor. In what is likely a thinly veiled shot at his colleague Benson, Hassam once remarked, "Not doing ducks and dogs my prints are rarely very successful."[21]

If prints were not the panacea that would remedy these artists' financial concerns, why did they engage in printmaking with such sustained energy? As an American school of printmaking became more established during the final decades of the nineteenth century and the first decades of the twentieth, the medium's popularity was so pervasive that it was simply difficult, if not impossible, for professional artists to ignore it. As one critic analyzing the prevalence of printmaking stated in 1915: "One benefit in a fashion is that everybody follows it. There is no chance for talent to lie fallow or remain obscure. Everybody is tested. Nobody escapes."[22] Perhaps even more importantly, printmaking provided a means of original artistic expression, as well as a true challenge to artists who, it could be argued, had long ago mastered the use of paint and brush. It required artists to master the handling of new and unfamiliar artistic tools, to understand the sensitive workings of a printing press (whether they did this work themselves or outsourced their printing to a professional), and to consider the varied visual effects that could be achieved through the use of antique papers, the reworking of a plate through multiple states, or the way in which excess ink was wiped from a plate. This challenge, and the opportunity it provided for a new mode of artistic expression, captivated Cassatt, Benson, and Hassam and resulted in unique bodies of printed work that are a testament to the artistic possibilities of printmaking.

Notes

1. A detailed study of the prints of the French Impressionists is beyond the scope of this essay, but a thorough and well-researched examination of the subject can be found in Michel Melot's *The Impressionist Print* (New Haven: Yale University Press, 1996).

2. An insightful and thorough study of Monet's drawings for reproduction can be found in James A. Ganz's "Drawing for the Mass Media," and a detailed history and analysis of the Thornley lithographic portfolio can be found in Ganz's "Monet in Print," both in James A. Ganz and Richard Kendell, *The Unknown Monet: Pastels and Drawings* (Williamstown, Mass.: Sterling and Francine Clark Art Institute, 2007), 183–213 and 215–39.

3. See Ganz, "Drawing for the Mass Media."

4. Claude Monet to Paul Durand-Ruel, March 7, 1883, quoted in ibid., 195.

5. The purpose of Haden's trip was "advancing the art of painter-etching, of which he is acknowledged to be a master." "Dr. Seymour Haden's Visit: What He Has Done in This Country—His Success and Gratification," *New York Tribune,* January 14, 1883, 10. During his visit he lectured in New York, Boston, Philadelphia, Baltimore, Cincinnati, Chicago, Milwaukee, and Detroit. Haden stated that a reception in his honor at the Pennsylvania Academy for the Fine Arts attracted fifteen hundred guests.

6. Cincinnati Etchers Club was founded in 1879; Philadelphia Society of Etchers and Boston Etching Club in 1880; Brooklyn Scratchers Club in 1881. For more information on the circumstances surrounding the formation of these groups, see James Watrous, "Entering the Mainstream of Printmaking," in *A Century of American Printmaking, 1880–1980* (Madison: University of Wisconsin Press, 1984), 3–27.

7. The most comprehensive reference for Cassatt's graphic work is Adelyn D. Breeskin, *The Graphic Work of Mary Cassatt: A Catalogue Raisonné*, 2nd ed. (Washington, D.C.: Smithsonian Institution Press, 1979).

8. Nancy Mowll Mathews, "The Color Prints in the Context of Mary Cassatt's Art," in *Mary Cassatt: The Color Prints* (Williamstown, Mass.: Williams College Museum of Art, 1989), 19–20.

9. Ibid., 27.

10. Christian Brinton, "Concerning Miss Cassatt and Certain Etchings," *International Studio* 27 (February 1906): vi.

11. For a catalogue raisonné of Benson's prints, see Adam E. M. Paff and Arthur William Heintzelman, *Etchings and Drypoints by Frank W. Benson: An Illustrated and Descriptive Catalogue* (Boston: Houghton Mifflin, 1917–59). Benson is referred to as "dean of American etchers" by Childe Reece in "Frank W. Benson," *Prints* 4, no. 4 (1934): 1–11.

12. Royal Cortissoz, "Painter-Etching and Its Only Perfect Path in Art: Signs of Its Possible Development at the Hands of Americans—Mr. F. W. Benson's Brilliant Studies of Wild Ducks," *New York Tribune,* December 5, 1915, 3.

13. Reece, "Frank W. Benson," 8.

14. For a catalogue raisonné of Hassam's drypoints and etchings, see Royal Cortissoz and Leonard Clayton, *Catalogue of the Etchings and Dry-points of Childe Hassam* (San Francisco: Alan Wofsy Fine Arts, 1989); for a catalogue raisonné of the lithographs, see Fuller Griffith, *The Lithographs of Childe Hassam*, U.S. National Museum, *Bulletin* 232 (Washington, D.C.: Smithsonian Institution, 1962). For an insightful overview of Hassam's engagement with printmaking, see Elizabeth E. Barker, "'A truly learned weaving of light and dark': Hassam's Prints," in *Childe Hassam: American Impressionist*, curated by H. Barbara Weinberg (New York: Metropolitan Museum of Art, 2004).

15. To fans of etching, these two 1915 exhibitions (Hassam at Keppel and Company and Benson at Kennedy Gallery)

marked a turning point for American printmaking. Royal Cortissoz remarked at the time: "Only last week we had occasion to record what is practically Mr. Childe Hassam's debut as an etcher, and to rejoice in his adoption of the needle. Now comes, at the Kennedy Gallery, an exhibition of prints by Mr. Frank W. Benson, one of the Boston members of the Ten American Painters. He, too, has begun to etch in very recent years, and he, too, makes us glad of his new efforts. Is there, then, some reason for believing that a revival of etching is presently to be witnessed in American art?" Cortissoz, "Painter-Etching," 3. Another critic playfully remarked at the time: "The undoubted success of both Mr. Benson and Mr. Hassam will no doubt swell the lists of the etchers enormously. It seems so easy! Nobody fails!" "What Is Happening in the World of Art," *New York Sun*, December 12, 1915, 8.

16. Barker, "'A truly learned weaving,'" 269, 281–82 n. 12.

17. Royal Cortissoz, "The Art of Childe Hassam Studied at Full Length," *New York Tribune,* November 28, 1915, 3.

18. Ibid.

19. Cassatt, conversation with Louisine W. Havemeyer, quoted in Louisine W. Havemeyer, *Sixteen to Sixty: Memoirs of a Collector* (New York: Ursus Press, 1993), 284.

20. "'Painter-Gravers' Aim to Cultivate American Taste for Graphic Art," *New York Times,* March 25, 1917.

21. Childe Hassam to Frederic Newlin Price, February 7, 1932, Ferargil Galleries Records, 1900–1963, Archives of American Art, Smithsonian Institution, reel N68–14, frame 115. Quoted in Barker, "'A truly learned weaving,'" 271.

22. "What Is Happening in the World of Art," 8.

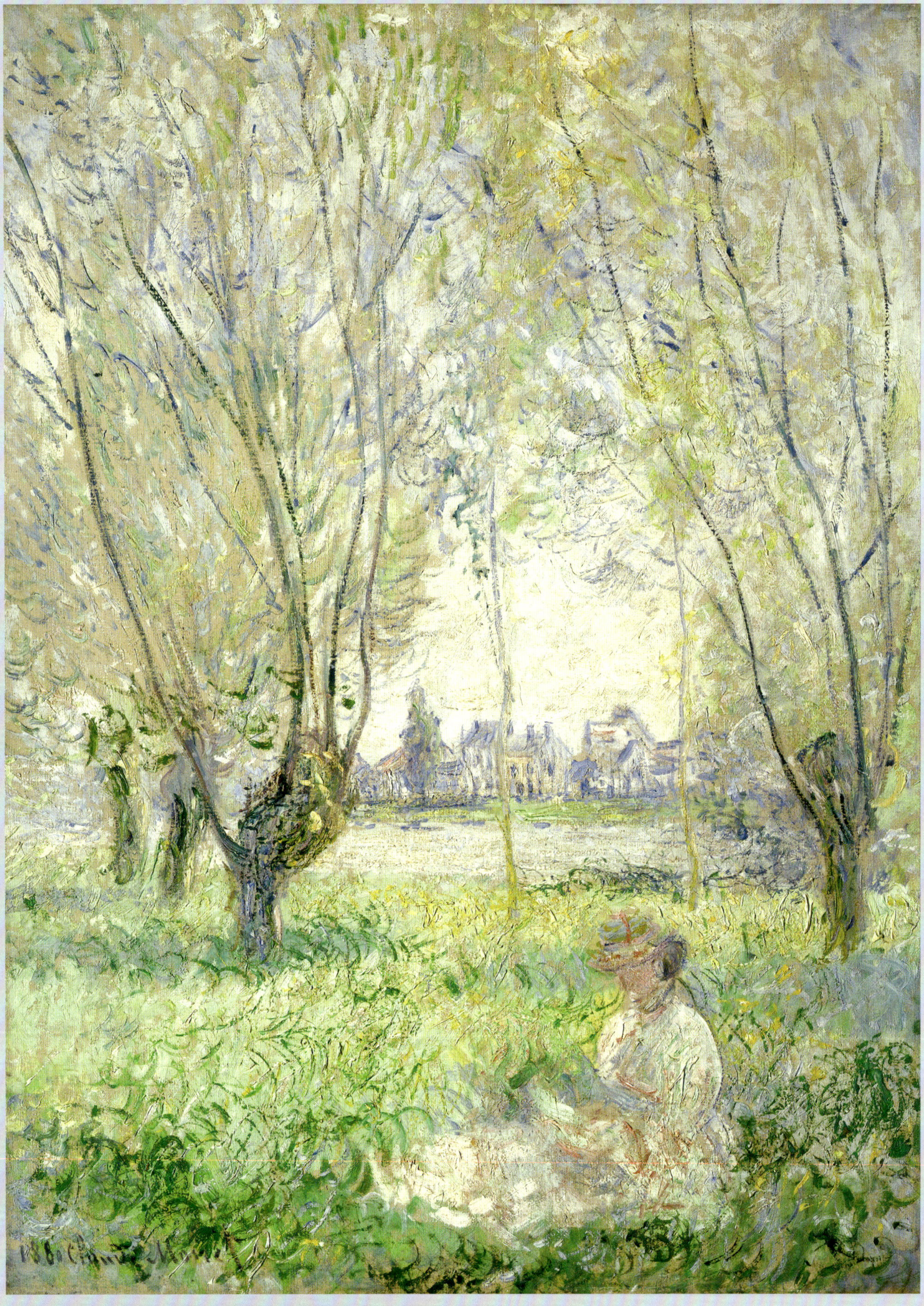

Women and the Nature of Impressionism

MELISSA LEE HYDE & ERIC J. SEGAL

CLAUDE MONET once told his friend, the American Impressionist painter Lilla Cabot Perry, that "he wished he had been born blind and then had suddenly gained his sight so that he could have begun to paint . . . without knowing what the objects were that he saw before him." He also instructed Perry: "When you go out to paint, try to forget what objects you have before you. . . . Merely think, here is a little square of blue, here an oblong of pink, here a streak of yellow, and paint it just as it looks to you, the exact color and shape, until it gives your own naïve impression of the scene before you."[1]

Monet's comments to Perry are one of the clearest surviving statements about Impressionist principles. They conceive of painting as essentially about painting itself, so that what matters in a painting is technique and treatment of light—actual subject matter does not matter. Understood in this way, Impressionist subjects, painterly technique, and treatment have nothing to do with historical context, identity, class, gender, or nationalism. The paintings are, rather, the product of a naive or innocent eye. When we look at a breezy, sun-drenched Impressionist painting of a field of oats (Pl. 3) or of people enjoying the leisure of a Sunday afternoon, it is easy to believe that what you see is what you get. However, the Impressionist ideal of an innocent eye has been contested, or at least problematized, by nearly every critic or scholar who has written about the "new painting," as it was first termed.

Much of this critical inquiry has focused on the role of women and on gender.[2] We take up this line of questioning here in order to think about a selection of images by French and American Impressionists who were part of the art colony at Giverny

FIGURE 1. Claude Monet (French, 1840–1926), *Woman Seated under Willows*, 1880, oil on canvas, 31 15/16 × 23 5/8 in. (81.1 × 60 cm), Courtesy National Gallery of Art, Washington, D.C., Chester Dale Collection, 1963.10.178

FIGURE 2. Claude Monet (French, 1840–1926), *In the Woods at Giverny: Blanche Hoschedé at Her Easel with Suzanne Hoschedé Reading*, 1887, oil on canvas, 36 × 38 ½ in. (91.4 × 97.8 cm), Los Angeles County Museum of Art, Mr. and Mrs. George Gard De Sylva Collection, M.46.3.4; Digital Image © 2015 Museum Associates / LACMA, Licensed by Art Resource, NY

that grew up around Monet in the 1880s and 1890s. If we assume there is more to these paintings than meets the eye, what can they tell us about cultural understandings of women, both in the depiction of women as painted subjects and as agents who render images of their own?

Monet, in his advice to Perry, would seem to be—in modern parlance—gender-blind. As recounted by Perry herself, he makes no reference to her sex, but assumes that she has access to painterly objectivity like his and possesses the artistic skills to put it into practice. Yet matters of gender have always been entirely visible to those who look for them. Already in the 1870s, French critics of Impressionism disparaged its "effeminate" emphasis on color rather than on firmly drawn figures.[3] Although there was nothing intrinsically feminine in Impressionist techniques, observers could make such claims with critical effect, an effect bolstered by pointing to notable women Impressionists like Berthe Morisot and Mary Cassatt (Pl. 42), who were seen to paint "naturally" feminine subjects in a feminine manner.[4] In the face of "persistent fears of Impressionist effeminacy," Monet's response in the 1890s was to bring a new "vigorous muscularity" to his painting, achieving what one critic termed a "victory over nature"—a nature that was implicitly understood as feminine.[5] From the first then, gender has been central to Impressionist practice and the debates about it, even if the term *gender* only came to be used as a category for critical analysis in the later twentieth century.[6]

Matters of gender are perhaps most literally visible in the figures of women depicted in Impressionist canvases where, far from being rendered solely as "squares of blue, oblongs of pink, and streaks of yellow," these are value-laden representations of women that embody—and sometimes complicate—normative social roles and conventional symbolic associations. Nowhere is this truer than in the Impressionist subject of the woman outdoors, a favorite of both French and American painters.[7] These paintings, which typically show women at leisure, sometimes with their children, sitting, strolling, languorously reclining, boating, picnicking, drinking tea, present only a partial and often idealized view of women and of middle-class life.[8] Whether in a garden or in a less-cultivated landscape setting, these representations evoke the persistent cultural myth of the intimate identification between women and nature.[9] But social ideals—including restrictive ones—are also represented here, with women regularly appearing as passive, pliant, even decorative figures of visual delectation; only rarely are they active agents or intellectual beings.[10]

In *Woman Seated under Willows*, 1880 (Fig. 1), Monet hews to his own advice, treating the figure as so many moments of color. Objective though his approach may be, he depicts woman and nature as interchangeable and equivalent. Indeed, a close look at the brushwork shows that—except for a black line defining the contour of the sitter's back—it is difficult to determine exactly where she ends and the luxurious vegetation begins.[11] Yet despite this objective (even objectifying) treatment, Monet's female sitters were typically women about whom he was anything but objective; the model in this case was most likely Alice Hoschedé, his future wife.[12] In some of his other images, such as *In the Woods at Giverny: Blanche Hoschedé at Her Easel with Suzanne Hoschedé Reading*, 1887 (Fig. 2), the women possess a presence and agency that resists any easy equivalence between woman and nature.[13] Here the models are his future stepdaughters, Blanche and Suzanne Hoschedé. Monet's representation of Blanche, herself in the act of representing a landscape *en plein air*, suggests a relationship between women and nature that is active and engaged, and as we will see,

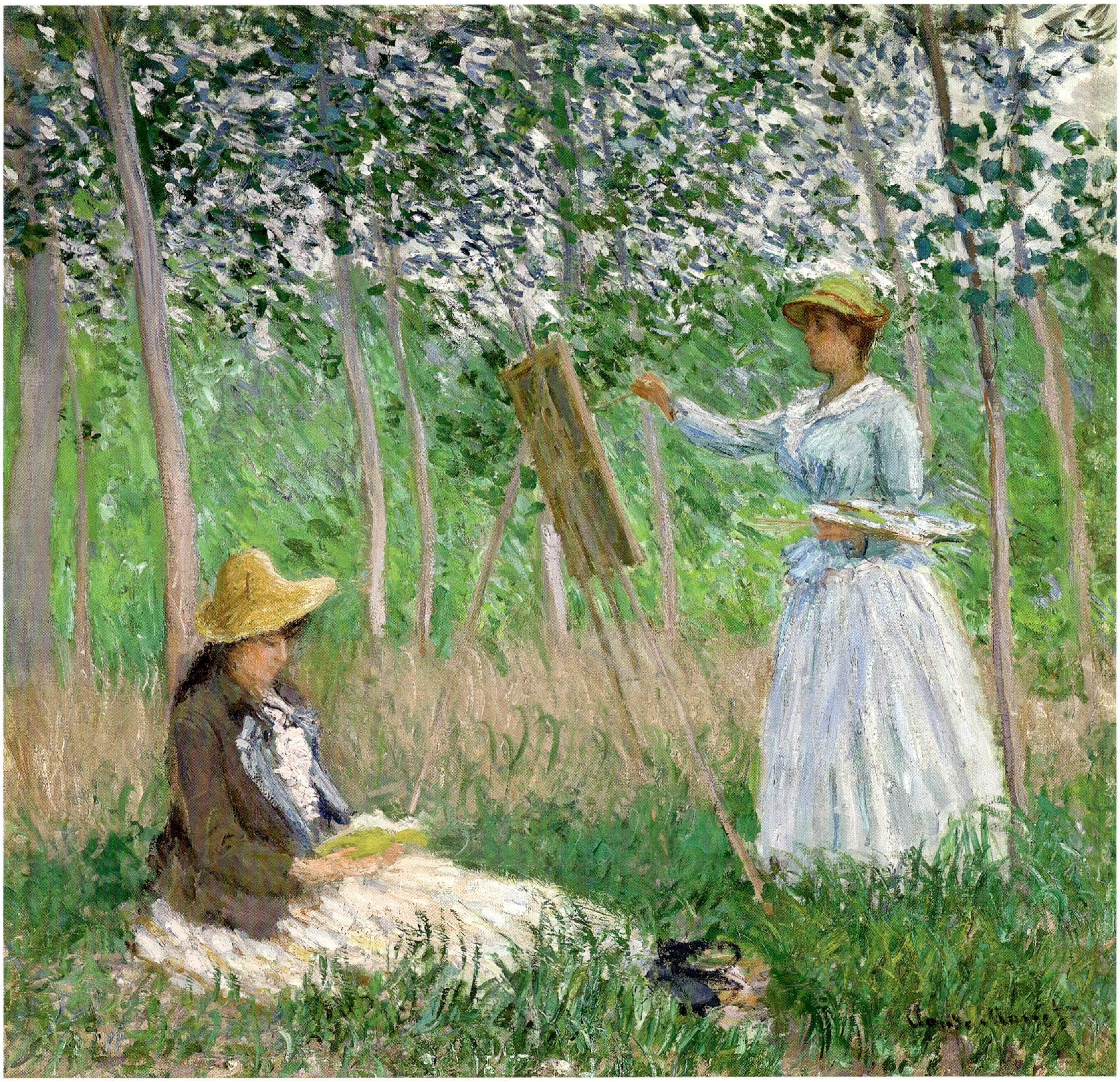

also quite uncommon in the history of art.[14] Suzanne would later marry Theodore Earl Butler (Pl. 10), who, like Lilla Cabot Perry, was part of a group of Americans gathering at Giverny after 1887, many inspired by Monet's example. Among them, the subject of woman and nature was commonly taken up by artists who employed Impressionist techniques, even as the themes they explored around this motif varied at times in unexpected ways.

One such artist is Frederick Carl Frieseke, best known for his pleasing paintings of women in garden settings, of which *Lilies*, by 1911 (Fig. 3, Pl. 11), is a prime example. Set in the garden of Le Hameau, a house that Frieseke and his wife rented at Giverny, next door to Monet, it shows one woman in a straw hat trimmed with flowers standing before an enormous bank of white lilies.[15] Her informal white tea gown makes her look rather like a lily herself. The woman seated before her—probably Frieseke's wife, Sadie—wears a floral-patterned pelisse that visually rhymes with the lush, blossoming garden around them. The title of the painting reinforces the conceptual equivalence between women and nature, and seems to refer to the women as much as to the flowers. So, on one level, the painting can be read as a conventional image of woman as a form of domestic floral decoration that harmonizes with the flowery gardens. But a closer consideration of the image reveals incongruous features that strike a discordant note in a scene that is also about modern social intercourse.

This afternoon tea, served by the seated figure, takes place in a well-ordered but confined space marked by a well-tended lawn and flowerbeds, an edged walkway, and the riotous backdrop of lilies and plants screening a trellised house beyond. The lady of the house is placed squarely—even immovably—with her back to her guest, in a garden chair that creates a visual web of lines around her. As a decorative form she is thoroughly congruent with the colors of the garden, as well as the tea set before her, and becomes an extension of the agreeable domestic scene. By contrast, her guest appears awkwardly trapped on the too-narrow path between two capacious chairs—one of them faces us, empty, and markedly set apart from the tea table, the other occupied by her hostess. With her left hand placed on the back of the seated woman's chair to steady her balance and her right hand lifting her white peignoir out of harm's way from the many-colored pollens in the flowerbed, she appears unlikely to find her way forward or back. This sense of containment, the woman's slightly off-balance posture, and her gaze out at the artist/viewer, suggests—whether intentionally or not—the possibility of a certain tension or constraints in the experience of women in modern social life.[16] Importantly for our purposes, this standing figure, whose white dress most suggests an affinity with nature, is ill at ease in the very garden setting that *ought* to be "home" to both flowers and to women conceptually associated with nature. Frieseke has taken up the theme of women as nature, but he ends with an image that paradoxically denaturalizes that same theme.

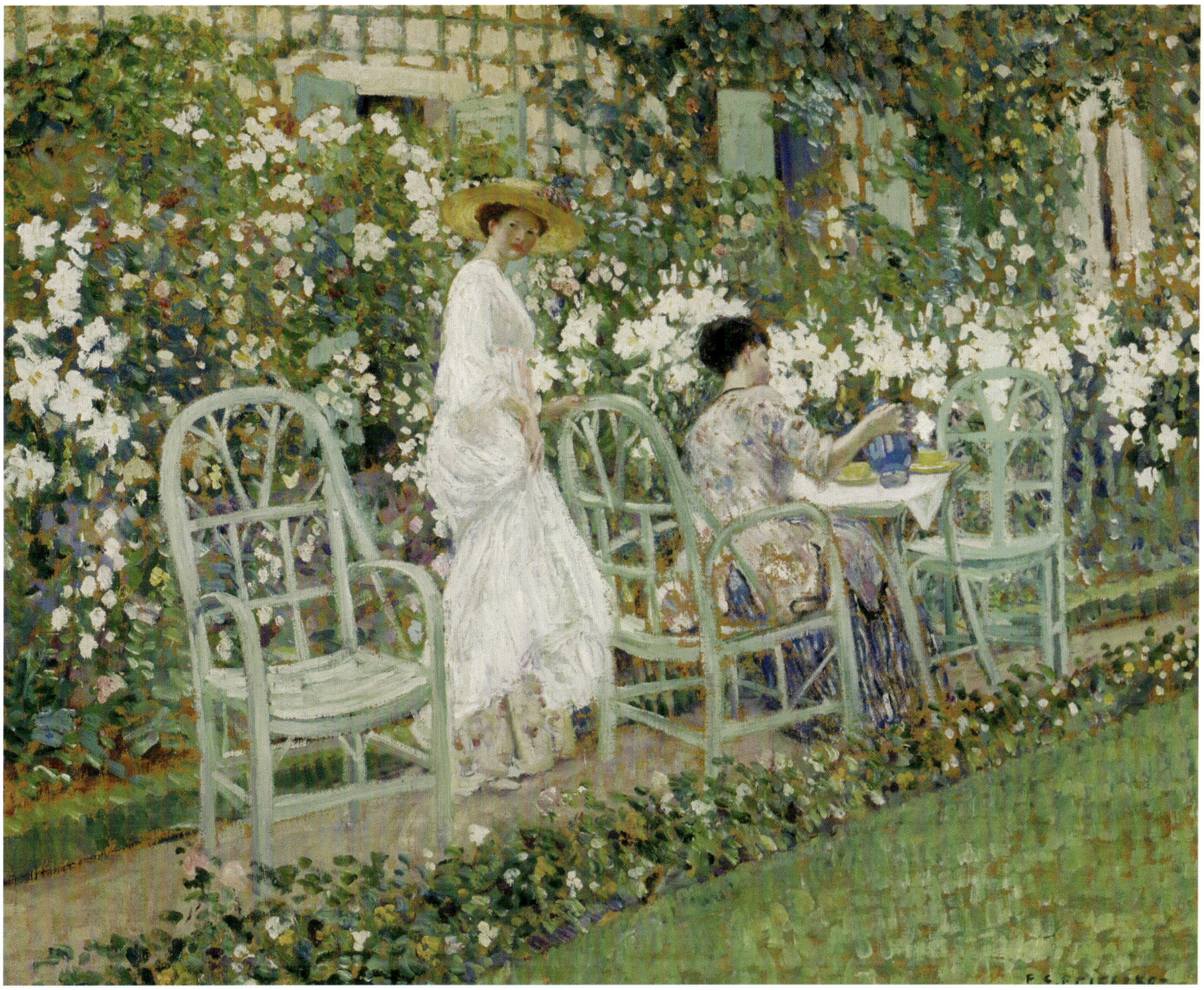

FIGURE 3, PLATE 11.
Frederick Carl Frieseke (American, 1874–1939), *Lilies*, by 1911, oil on canvas, 25 ¾ × 32 ⅛ in. (65.4 × 81.6 cm), Terra Foundation for American Art, Daniel J. Terra Collection, 1999.55

We might view this painting and the relationship it posits between women and nature in another, slightly different, light if we consider the fact that Sadie Frieseke was an avid gardener. In other words, *Lilies* depicts a garden that was itself the product of a woman's thought and effort, so that the equivalence proposed between women and nature here evokes a nature that the woman herself had a hand in shaping, for it is *her* garden.

Other paintings in the current exhibition take up the theme of women and nature so that we see this cultural conception filtered through a range of individual responses, which can differ even within the work of a single artist. For example, Frieseke's *The Garden Umbrella*, by 1910 (Pl. 12), has none of the tensions of his *Lilies,* for here the women are so completely integrated into the landscape through brushwork and color as to blur the distinction between them and their natural surroundings.

Helen Maria Turner's *Lilies, Lanterns, and Sunshine,* 1923 (Pl. 49), though thematically similar to Frieseke's *Lilies,* presents a pleasing view of two women on a sun-dappled garden terrace, whose proximity to each other and to the picture plane (and therefore to the artist herself) suggests a sense of self-containment and cozy domestic complicity between women who seem very much in their element, which here happens to be Turner's own garden.[17] Meanwhile, in Childe Hassam's ravishingly lovely *French Tea Garden* (also known as *The Terre-Cuite Tea Set*), 1910 (Pl. 35), Hassam too equates the lady with the flourishing plant life around her through his treatment of her gown and hat. At the same time, he delicately renders her face, arms, and hands in a way that distinguishes her from her surroundings, suggests interiority and individual presence, and thereby complicates the suggestion that she is merely a delicate flower. She is wearing a wedding ring, and has a thimble on her finger, as she does needlework at a tea table set for two—the painter himself being her implied companion. The painting thus explores the harmony—if not equivalence—of woman's domestic craft and the painter's creative art.[18]

We now want to turn to other instances in which traditional relationships between woman and nature are complicated by the intervention of woman herself. How do things change when the landscape painter is a woman? As noted earlier, Monet's depiction of a woman painting *en plein air* was uncommon, especially in France, though he painted Blanche Hoschedé painting outdoors several times. In fact, Hoschedé was, like Perry, Monet's sometime apprentice, and she quite frequently accompanied him on his painting excursions.[19] He must not have been troubled by the disheveling effects of painting outdoors, as Berthe Morisot's husband, Eugène Manet, had been. In a letter of 1875 to her sister, Morisot reported that she had had to abandon her efforts to paint in the open air during a holiday excursion in England, after a frightful wind blew her hat off and her hair got in her eyes. She wrote: "Eugène was in a bad humour as he always is when my hair is in disorder."[20] Three hours after setting out, they were back in their holiday cottage. This incident hints at some of the proprieties that made it difficult for women to practice landscape painting at all. Though Morisot managed to do quite a bit of it anyway, the very conditions necessary for producing an Impressionist landscape were anything but gender-blind. Concern for the niceties of appearance would have been beyond imagining in the case of a Monet. In fact, his battling of the elements for hours on end is very much a part of the heroism of his victories over nature. Significantly, too, Morisot's anecdote reminds us that she was accompanied by her husband. Unlike male artists, women lacked the "freedom to go about alone," as the painter Marie Bashkirtseff once lamented.[21]

Perhaps by the late nineteenth century cultural attitudes had changed or were different enough in the United States that the obstacles faced by women like Turner and Perry were less daunting when they took up painting landscapes.[22] Like most Impressionists, Turner did a great many figures *en plein air*, but she also painted "pure" landscapes. These tend to depict the garden of her own house at Cragsmoor.[23] Perry's *paysages*, such as *A Stream Beneath Poplars,* circa 1890–1900 (Pl. 1), venture beyond her own domestic sphere, though sometimes they only appear to do so, as in the case of *Landscape in Normandy,* 1890 (Pl. 2). A letter from her husband, Thomas Perry, to a family friend reveals that she painted *Landscape in Normandy* one fine August day from the window of his room in their Giverny house. Thus *Landscape in Normandy* might be said to represent a woman's point of view, not in the essentialist way one finds in nineteenth-century criticism, but in the sense that Perry's act of painting from the confines of her husband's room can be understood as an instance in which a woman literally painted from a position that would not have been adopted by most male *plein air* painters.[24] Her physical position comports with the social positioning of women in the domestic sphere, while the composition of the painting itself suggests the contrary, namely, that what we see is a view of the out-of-doors painted out-of-doors.[25] This is what most of Perry's landscapes actually were: *plein air* landscapes in the usual sense, and in this she was unusual as a woman artist.

In fact, Perry was an exceptional figure on a number of counts. She began her painting career late, at the age of thirty-nine, at which time she had been married for ten years and had three small children. All of this was exceedingly rare for a woman artist, since most women who chose the challenging life of a professional artist elected to remain single. Rarer still, she also became the breadwinner in the family.[26] Portraits were her primary source of income, and she frequently painted everyday scenes of women and children (including her own), "feminine" subjects that were preferred by other women associated with Impressionism, whether by choice or by necessity.[27] It is clear, though, that Perry's genre of choice was landscape. She returned to it almost exclusively during the Roaring Twenties, when she was in her eighties. By that time she was at last free to do as she pleased, as she explained in a letter to her friend Bernard Berenson: "Thank Heaven I can in my old age give up the bondage of painting portraits. . . . I am devoting my small remaining strength to what Monet begged me to do and said was my forte: Pleine Air [*sic*] and Paysages."[28]

In closing, then, we wish to emphasize that landscapes by Perry and by other women of her time are quite uncommon in the history of art. By virtue of their very existence, such paintings are remarkable and, like those of their male counterparts, inflected with a whole set of cultural meanings that circulate around women (and men), nature, and landscape painting, confirming that there is much more to these pictures than first meets the eye.

Notes

1. Lilla Cabot Perry, "Reminiscences of Claude Monet from 1889 to 1909," *American Magazine of Art,* March 1927, 119–25, reprinted in Meredith Martindale, Pamela Moffat, and Nancy Mowll Mathews, *Lilla Cabot Perry: An American Impressionist* (Washington, D.C.: National Museum of Women in Art, 1990), 116.

2. Of the vast literature on this subject, some of the most important examples include Tamar Garb, *Women Impressionists* (New York: Rizzoli, 1986); Griselda Pollock, "Modernity and the Spaces of Femininity," in *Vision and Difference: Femininity, Feminism and the Histories of Art* (London: Routledge, 1988), 50–90; Anne Higonnet, *Berthe Morisot* (Berkeley: University of California Press, 1995); Norma Broude, *Impressionism: A Feminist Reading* (New York: Rizzoli, 1991); Ruth E. Iskin, *Modern Women and Parisian Consumer Culture in Impressionist Painting* (Cambridge: Cambridge University Press, 2007); and Nancy Mowll Mathews, *Mary Cassatt* (New York: Abrams in association with the National Museum of American Art, Smithsonian Institution, 1987).

3. Anthea Callen, "Technique and Gender: Landscape, Ideology and the Art of Monet in the 1890s," in *Gendering Landscape Art,* ed. Steven Adams and Anna Gruetzner Robins (Manchester: Manchester University Press, 2000), 42.

4. Tamar Garb, "Berthe Morisot and the Feminizing of Impressionism," in *Perspectives on Morisot*, ed. T. J. Edelstein (New York: Hudson Hills Press, 1990), 57–66.

5. Callen notes that Monet turns from painting figures in landscapes to painting his subjects in series, such as the famous Rouen cathedral series, and the *Grainstacks*. Callen says the "vigorous muscularity of Monet's facture . . . serves to distance him from the effeminacy associated with the painterly touch of a Renoir or a Morisot" ("Technique and Gender," 41).

6. See Joan W. Scott, "Gender: A Useful Category of Historical Analysis," *American Historical Review* 91, no. 5 (1986): 1053–75.

7. See John House, "Women Out of Doors," in *Women in Impressionism: From Mythical Feminine to Modern Woman,* ed. Sidsel Maria Søndergaard (Milan: Skira, 2006), 157–223. Men, of course, are represented in many Impressionist scenes of leisure, and their depiction is no less subject to analysis in terms of gender. However, depictions of women, singly or in small groups, were particularly favored by many Impressionists.

8. For discussion see, in this volume, Louise M. Newman, "The 'Woman Question' in American Impressionist Painting, 1880–1920."

9. Tamar Garb, "Renoir and the Natural Woman," in *The Expanding Discourse: Feminism and Art History,* ed. Norma Broude and Mary D. Garrard (New York: Icon Editions, 1992), 295–311.

10. Garb has observed that unlike their male counterparts, "women Impressionists presented images of women resonant with dignity and self-containment" (*Women Impressionists*, 26).

11. Indeed, Monet had declared his intention to paint figures "like a landscape." Quoted in *The Annenberg Collection: Masterpieces of Impressionism and Post-Impressionism,* ed. Susan Alyson Stein and Asher Ethan Miller (New York: Metropolitan Museum of Art, 2009), 79.

12. Mary Mathews Gedo, *Monet and His Muse: Camille Monet in the Artist's Life* (Chicago: University of Chicago Press, 2010), 215.

13. For discussion of this issue see Stein and Miller, *The Annenberg Collection,* 79–80.

14. Concerning the iconography, we have been able to identify only a handful of paintings from this era of women shown working *en plein air*, none of them French: Alfred James Munnings, *Laura Knight Painting* (undated); John Singer Sargent, *Jane Emmet and Wilfred de Glehn at the Fountain, Villa Torlonia, Frascati* (undated); John Sloan, *Helen Taylor Sketching* (1916); Joaquín Sorolla, *Maria*

Painting in El Pardo (1907); Alfred Stevens, *Painting at the Beach* (1880); and David Woodlock, *A Landscape Painter* (undated). One notable French image of women painting landscapes is to be found in a fashion plate from *Le Moniteur de la mode*, 1886, which shows two stylish Parisian coquettes in a landscape, one seated before a tiny easel, the other holding her painterly accoutrements like fashion accessories. Here landscape painting is presented as a fashionable amateur practice that provides a pretext for appearing in the latest fashions for the outdoors. See Marie Simon, *Mode et peinture: Le Second Empire et l'impressionnisme* (Paris: Hazan, 1995), 66.

15. This is the same house that the Perrys rented for nine summers. Museo Thyssen-Bornemisza, *Colección Carmen Thyssen-Bornemisza*, ed. Javier Arnaldo, vol. 2 (Madrid: Museo Thyssen-Bornemisza, 2004), 222.

16. For a different reading of this painting see discussion on the website for the Terra Foundation of Art, http://www.terraamericanart.org.

17. Pollock argues in "Modernity and the Spaces of Femininity" that proximity and compositional compression are features of the work of other female Impressionists. See also note 10.

18. Gari Melchers's *Unpretentious Garden*, 1903–1909 (Pl. 46), Theodore Robinson's *Gathering Plums*, 1891 (Pl. 7), and Robert Vonnoh's *Jardin de paysanne (Peasant Garden)*, 1890 (Pl. 6)—treat class and labor in the context of gardens, orchards, and peasant houses in interesting ways that space will not allow us to explore here.

19. She had a long and successful career as a landscape painter. Sophie Fourny-Dargère, *Blanche Hoschedé Monet, 1865–1947: Une Artiste de Giverny*, exh. catalogue, April 2–June 6, 1991 (Vernon, France: Musée municipal, 1991). See also Philippe Piguet, *Blanche Hoschedé-Monet, un destin impressionniste* (Rouen: Editions Points de vues, 2010).

20. Quoted in Higonnet, *Berthe Morisot*, 130.

21. Marie Bashkirtseff, *The Journal of Marie Bashkirtseff* (London: Virago Press, 1985), 347. We are aware of only two late-nineteenth-century examples of women landscape painters depicted by women, namely, by a Norwegian, Kitty Kielland, and by a Dane, Caroline Mundt; in the other images of women painting landscapes, listed in note 14, the women are in essence accompanied by the men painting them, even when shown alone.

22. In 1871, *Godey's Lady's Book* published an article titled "Painting as a Profession for Women," which looked favorably on the possibility but also asserted that "the working conditions of a landscape artist or illustrator—painting or drawing outdoors, sometimes living in a tent—were 'obviously impossible for a woman,' especially an unmarried woman." Quoted in Sue Rainey, *Creating Picturesque America* (Nashville: Vanderbilt University Press, 1994), 105.

23. Jane Ward Faquin, *Helen M. Turner: The Woman's Point of View* (Memphis: Dixon Gallery and Gardens, 2010). A photograph showing Turner painting in her own garden can be found in Carol Lowrey, *A Legacy of Art: Paintings and Sculptures by Artist Life Members of the National Arts Club* (New York: Hudson Hill, 2007), 183.

24. Perry comments that she only once saw Monet paint indoors. Martindale, Moffat, and Mathews, *Lilla Cabot Perry*, 117.

25. Not only is Perry assuming a view at her husband's window, but Thomas Perry also noted that she depicted a field that Monet often painted. In effect, the position she takes within the home for this particular canvas has her seeing from her husband's vantage point what Monet saw. Ibid., 28.

26. As pointed out in ibid., 105–8.

27. Women only painted certain Impressionist subjects—not nudes or prostitutes. See Pollock, "Modernity and the Spaces of Femininity."

28. Quoted in Martindale, Moffat, and Mathews, *Lilla Cabot Perry*, 96.

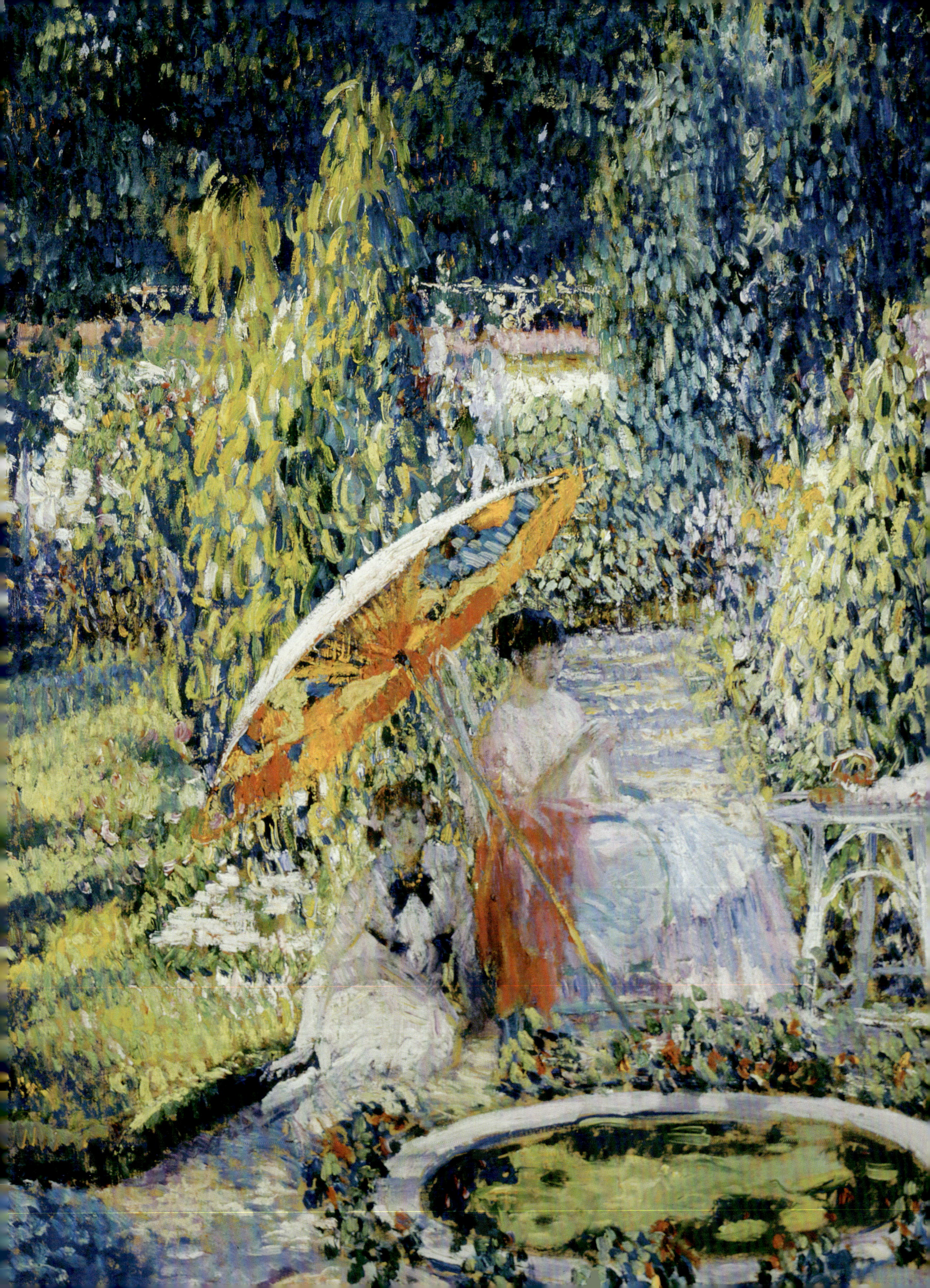

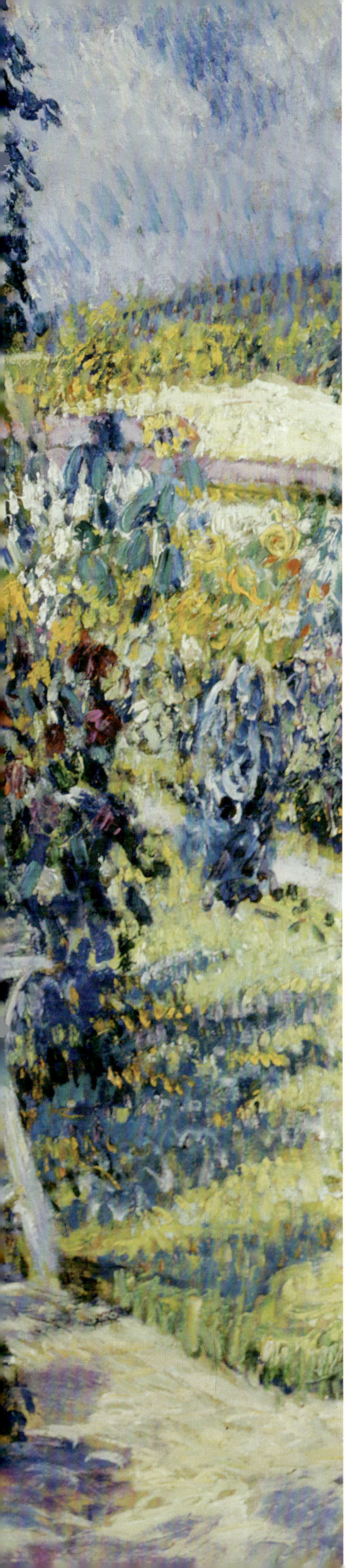

The "Woman Question" in American Impressionist Painting, 1880–1920

LOUISE M. NEWMAN

American Impressionism is generally understood as offering a conservative perspective in terms of its subject matter—an obscuring of the increasing political conflict, social turmoil, and economic disparities that characterized American society during the Gilded Age—yet modern (for its time) in its technique and methods of representation. As one art historian has written, "in contrast to the swiftly changing social and political landscape, American Impressionism presented images of stillness, solitude and optimism."[1] Today, the consensus among art historians, as well as the viewing public, seems to be that these are lovely paintings, in part because of their subject matter but also because of style and technique: softened lines, brilliant color, diffused light.[2]

Yet in the late nineteenth century, American art critics were sometimes enthralled, sometimes repulsed by the new techniques, and art connoisseurs who valued symbolic compositions did not always find the subject matter suitable. Thinking about the skepticism of nineteenth-century viewers might prompt us to reflect on why today we find them so lovely. Is it simply that we no longer find the techniques off-putting, accustomed as we are to the Abstract Expressionism that was to follow? Or are we attracted to the idealism informing these works, seeing in them evidence of a world we wistfully believe once existed? Or perhaps we are drawn to these paintings because they seem highly symbolic to us—as we can discern in

Frederick Carl Frieseke (American, 1874–1939), *The Garden Umbrella* (detail, pl. 12), by 1910

them references to European masters, along with new elements and styles from non-Western sources. Finally, do we respond so favorably because we find in them some transcendent meaning?

Many of the works featured in this exhibition use women as subjects in ways that moved beyond traditional portraiture or classic nudes. In this respect, American Impressionists followed the example of their French counterparts. The picturesque scenes of bourgeois leisure activities by Renoir, Degas, and Monet are familiar to most of us. During the 1870s and 1880s, for example, Monet painted several series of figural subjects in which his extended family served as models for pictures that were more about explorations of light, color, and painterly bravura than strict portraiture (Fig. 1).[3]

FIGURE 1. Claude Monet (French, 1840–1926), *Woman with a Parasol—Madame Monet and Her Son*, 1875, oil on canvas, 39 ⅜ × 31 ⅞ in. (100 × 81 cm), Courtesy National Gallery of Art, Washington, D.C., Collection of Mr. and Mrs. Paul Mellon, 1983.1.29

Despite great variations in style and composition, the representations of women and domesticity represented in this exhibition demonstrate remarkable consistency. Whether situated indoors or *en plein air*, whether painted in somber or bright colors, whether "realistically" or "impressionistically" rendered, the female subjects are often depicted in contented repose—strolling, picnicking, reading, drinking tea, playing music, eating breakfast, embracing children, doing their toilettes. Often the female figures are deeply absorbed in their solitude or happily engaged in daily rituals. As the art historian Debra Mancoff has observed of Mary Cassatt's paintings, "instead of being confining, the settings"—modestly furnished bedrooms, sun-filled parlors, walled gardens—"are always pleasant, and more importantly, private; they define a realm where a woman can spend her time alone, content with her own company and fulfilled in the richness of her experience" (Fig. 2).[4]

Is it possible, then, to approach American Impressionist painting as a kind of documentary record, offering glimpses into elite women's lives, or at least into the cultural values that upheld "woman's sphere" as an ideal? Victorians understood the home as a realm that women controlled and where they were supposed to be happiest,[5] yet the cultural historian Kristin Hoganson, describing how middle- and upper-class American women decorated their homes with foreign objects, argues that these "cosmopolitan interiors can be read as protests against the constraints of women's domesticity," and in particular as "protests against the narrowness of *American* domesticity."[6] The cover illustration for Hoganson's book is *Morning News,* an Impressionist painting by Helen M. Turner, and so the question arises what meanings American female consumers imparted to Impressionist paintings created by American, as opposed to French, artists and to female, as opposed to male, artists.

Moreover, given that most American men spent much less time at home, as their work and leisure activities increasingly took place in the "public sphere," we might also wonder whether Victorian men and women responded to these paintings

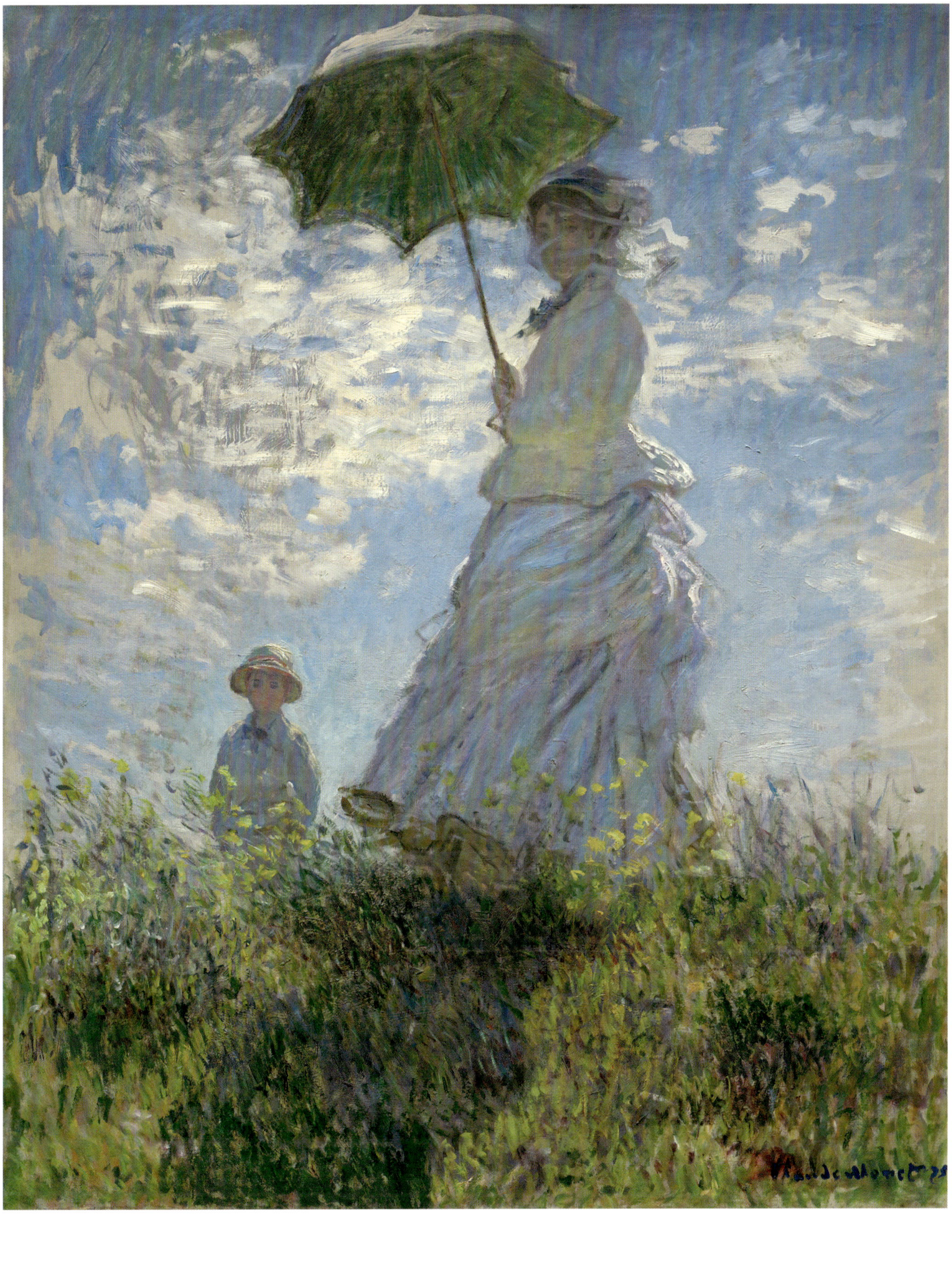

FIGURE 2. Mary Cassatt (American, 1844–1926), *The Child's Bath*, 1893, oil on canvas, 39 ½ × 26 in. (100.3 × 66.1 cm), The Art Institute of Chicago, Robert A. Waller Fund, 1910.2

differently, given how different their lives were. It's a hard question to answer, not least because historians have been able to gather more information concerning men's reactions to Impressionism than women's.[7] For example, a French male critic is known to have marveled at how Cassatt "succeeded in expressing . . . the joyful peace, the tranquil friendliness of the domestic interior,"[8] but would Mary Ead, an American woman, have had the same response, given the profound isolation and boredom she experienced as a young faculty wife at a small college in California in the 1890s? Ead, who was well educated and had taught before she married, describes how she has come to feel about reading and having tea: "Unrestrained reading produces stupefaction and revolt. At times when one longs to be abroad in the thick of things, books do not altogether suffice the spirit." Commenting on the different ways that she and her husband feel about sharing a cup of tea at the end of the day, Ead writes, "And on days when no social visit or visitor throws a bright ray of fellowship into the home, the lone wife feels that she has nothing to say over the teacups to beguile the tired man, who, for his part, has been among inspiring people all day and feels the contrast of a dull home, she fears."[9]

It is impossible to know how many Victorian women shared Ead's ambivalence about domesticity, but we do know that extensive discussions about the "woman question" were published in U.S. print media, beginning in the 1870s and extending into the next century, as more and more women voiced dissatisfaction with the confinement of woman's sphere and sought access to activities and opportunities outside the home that had traditionally been denied them. For example, articles by and about Frances Elizabeth Bellenden Clarke (1854–1943), a British suffragist and feminist author who was well known for her "New Woman" novels, appeared in American periodicals with some regularity during this period. In 1894, Clarke, publishing under her familiar pseudonym, Sarah Grand, wrote, "In the club and periodical, at the dinner-table and on the [lecture] platform," "what girls were, are, will be, and should be is the constant question. . . . [A]lthough women generally are becoming conscious that some great change is taking place in their position, they are as yet unaware of the nature of it."[10]

The woman question first emerged in the United States as a cultural concern in the decades following the Civil War as more and more white, middle-class women attended college. In 1870 there were just 11,000 women enrolled in institutions of higher learning. By 1900 this number had grown to 85,000, 36.8 percent of all students enrolled (but just 2.8 percent of all women age 18–21). By 1920 the numbers had more than tripled: 283,000 women, 47.3 percent of all college students (7.6 percent of women age 18–21).[11] Although the numbers may now seem inconsequential, to contemporaries this dramatic rise was hugely significant, reflecting the social

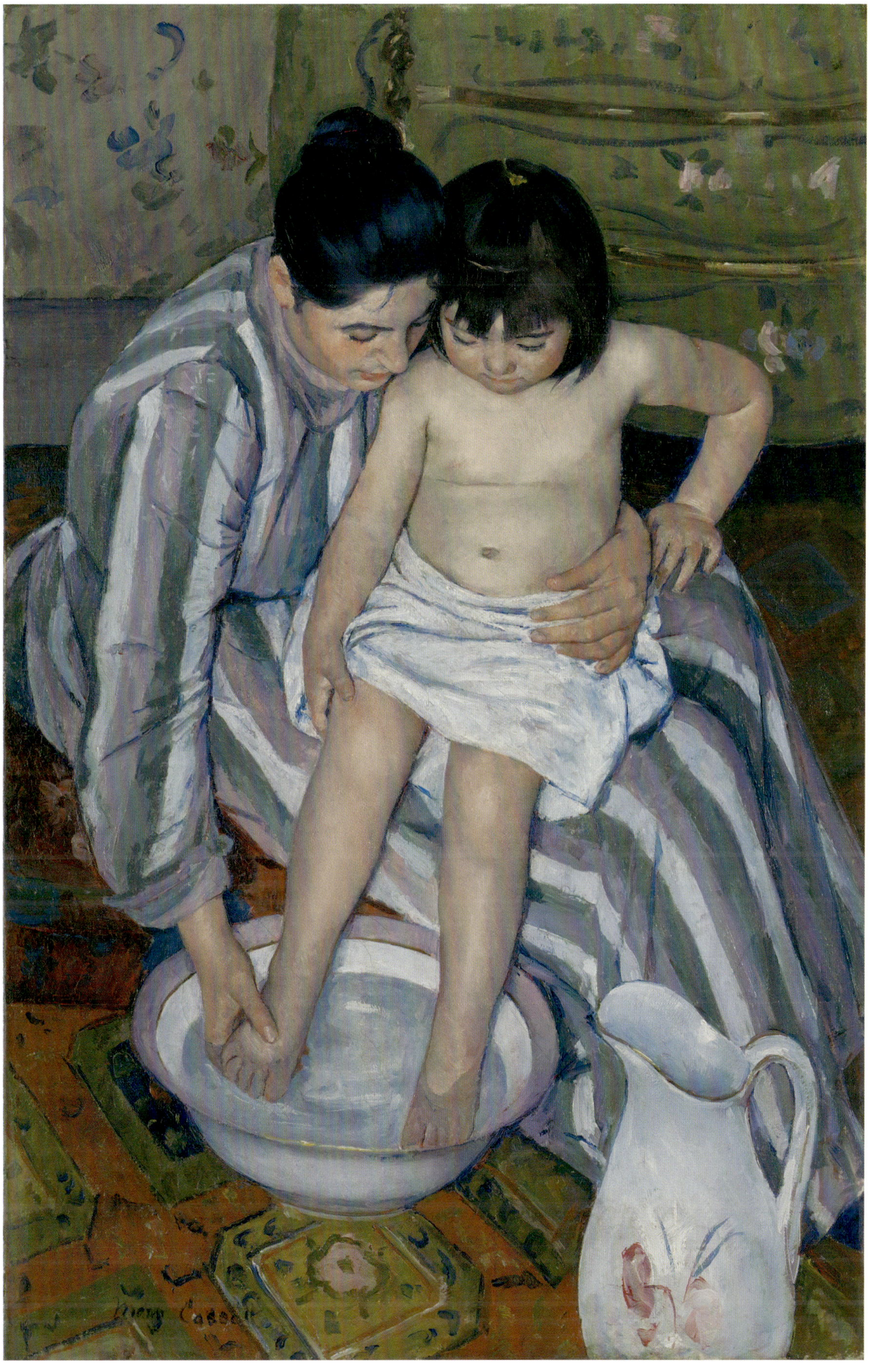

changes affecting American women's lives at the time and fueling middle-class women's increasing involvement in social and political reform, such as the temperance, labor, and suffrage movements.

In the face of such widespread changes, elites had to rethink the purpose of education for the "modern woman"—a term that the journalist Elizabeth Bisland (1861–1929) used in the 1890s to describe an emerging class of women who were delaying marriage for several years, or avoiding it altogether, to pursue other interests. The modern woman's desire for an "independent" life was severely criticized by social commentators, politicians, ministers, and educators. Such women were castigated for being selfish and refusing to fulfill their social obligation to have children and thereby "advance the race."[12] Although historians now understand that the birthrates of all groups of women were declining in this period—a phenomenon attributed in part to the increasing urbanization of society—to most contemporaries it seemed that birthrates were only falling among the upper classes, fueling concern that "civilization" would decline as the "lower classes" out-reproduced their purported social superiors.[13]

In this highly charged atmosphere, most white middle- and upper-class women felt they had to make a choice: either marry and have a family, or retain the freedom and independence to devote themselves to a lifelong pursuit.[14] To pursue an avocation like art—especially if one was determined to earn one's living from it—was a bold and courageous act for women to take in the second half of the nineteenth century. Mary Cassatt (1844–1926) is often cited as an example of such a woman, and her scornful branding of women whom she considered amateurs (and who were generally married) should be understood in this context.[15] Cassatt's decision to make art her life's work occurred in the 1870s, but two generations later the same dynamics still held. As Cleveland schoolteacher Bertha Monroe Rickoff observed in 1893: "How long before the spirited American society girl will have some higher ambition placed before her than social success. . . . [Even] in art studies and literary society she may find occupations, which, while being more soul-satisfying than fancy work, lack the stamp of purpose, because essentially amateur." Or as the British painter and suffragist Mary Sargant Florence (1857–1954) lamented in 1916: "No one knows better than I the limitations of my own work. . . . but it is because the energy, time, imagination, and physical strength that men use freely for their art has in my case had to go in ceaseless struggling . . . not for money only but for the 'right' to work."[16]

As a documentary record, then, these paintings offer only a partial picture. We may glimpse some of the rituals and routines of elite women's lives—the intimate activities (the combing of hair and bathing of children) and the social activities that engaged women of the upper classes (visiting for tea, holding musicales at home, promenading in the park, going to the theater)—but much about these women's lives is omitted. The belief that women's lives were centered in the home is true but not the whole truth. Most women's lives extended beyond the domestic sphere: some worked for wages, some inspected factories, some served on municipal governing boards, some planned public events. Many were active in church and charitable endeavors, labor organizing, and social reform movements. Perhaps most relevant here, some women organized art exhibitions and helped to introduce American Impressionist paintings to new audiences.[17] None of this subject matter finds its way into American Impressionist painting, which for the most part remained focused on the domestic lives of elite women, but even here there are significant omissions. We seldom see how much effort is involved in household management and childrearing; there are relatively few representations of the working-class women who made the lives of these privileged women possible—the maid who brings the tea, the nanny who puts the children down for a nap, the cook who prepares the dinner meal—in short, the many servants, tutors, and nannies who populated these households but are just outside the frame.

But what we do see—and contemporaries discerned this as well—is the deep respect, even reverence, accorded to women's lives. However idealized these women may be, these figures are not shrouded in mystery or sexually objectified. They are not one-dimensional icons of mothers, virgins, or whores. These women are individualized and have thoughts of their own. The sensuality, intelligence, energy, and engagement captured on canvas may be, in the end, what we find most lovely.

Notes

1. David R. Brigham, *American Impressionism: Paintings of Promise* (San Francisco: Pomegranate, 1997), 10.

2. Ibid.

3. For a discussion of Monet's figural series, see Paul Hayes Tucker, *Monet in the '90s: The Series Paintings* (New Haven: Yale University Press, 1989), 22–26.

4. Debra N. Mancoff, *Mary Cassatt: Reflections of Women's Lives* (New York: Stewart, Tabori and Chang, 1998), 41.

5. Many examples could be cited here, but Elizabeth Bisland's is interesting for being articulated by a woman who understood women's yearnings for independence but nonetheless felt that women were fools for relinquishing the realm that would provide them the most security and happiness. See Elizabeth Bisland, "The Modern Woman and Marriage," *North American Review* 160, no. 463 (June 1895): 753–55.

6. Kristin Hoganson, *Consumers' Imperium: The Global Production of American Domesticity, 1865–1920* (Chapel Hill: University of North Carolina Press, 2007), 34, emphasis in original.

7. This is not surprising, since most professional art critics at this time were men. Male critics commenting on paintings by

female artists often discerned something especially feminine in their work. In addition to Joris-Karl Huysmans's comment on Cassatt (see note 8 below), see Duncan Phillips's comments about Helen Turner (1858–1958) in his memoir, *A Collection in the Making* (New York: E. Weyhe, 1926), 56–57, as well as an anonymous critic's observations about Helen Turner published in *The Spur* (New York, March 1921), both quoted in Jane Ward Faquin, *Helen M. Turner: The Woman's Point of View* (Memphis: Dixon Gallery and Gardens, 2010), 12. Although nineteenth-century art critics often felt that women artists brought a special sensitivity to their subjects, I am unable to discern such gender differences when comparing the works of Frederick Frieseke, William Merritt Chase, and Childe Hassam with those of Mary Cassatt, Lilla Cabot Perry, and Helen Turner.

8. Upon viewing the 1881 Impressionist exhibition in Paris, Joris-Karl Huysmans, a contemporary of Cassatt's, described a special sensibility in Cassatt's work, "a flutter of feminine nerves" and a "note of tenderness," which he believed differentiated her work from that of her male French colleagues. He attributed this quality to both her nationality and her gender: "This indeed is the most characteristic quality of her talent, that Mlle. Cassatt, who, I believe, is an American, paints French women, but manages somehow to introduce into her Parisian interiors an 'at home' feeling. She has succeeded in expressing, as none of our own painters have managed to do, the joyful peace, the tranquil friendliness of the domestic interior." Quoted in Mancoff, *Mary Cassatt,* 56.

9. Nonetheless, even Ead upheld domesticity as an important ideal: "By nature and training I believe in the sweet old fashioned ideals of home, in its peace and rest as a retreat from the world." Her solution to women's restlessness and dissatisfaction was for women to find a larger interest that they could pursue before they had children and then resume after their children were grown. Mary Ead, *Sewanee Review* 23, no. 4 (1915): 412, 416.

10. Sarah Grand, "The Modern Girl," *North American Review* 158, no. 141 (June 1894): 707. For a listing of Sarah Grand's "New Woman" novels, see the World Catalog (http://worldcat.org/identities/lccn-n83-227407/) and search Library of Congress listings (http://catalog.loc.gov). Biographical information is available at http://en.wikipedia.org/wiki/Sarah_Grand and http://www.litencyc.com/php/speople.php?rec=true&UID=1836.

11. These statistics originally appeared in Mabel Newcomer's *A Century of Higher Education for American Women* (New York: Harper and Row, 1959), 46, and are assembled into a table in Louise Michele Newman, ed., *Men's Ideas/Women's Realities* (New York: Pergamon Press, 1985), 62.

12. Bisland believed that a woman's "instinct" for childrearing meant that women would be happiest and best off married, and like many of her generation, she felt that women did not have sufficient energy to devote to both homemaking and career: "Using all her energies for her own needs, she can not give vigor to her children. If she employ for her own ends her store of life she robs the child." Bisland, "The Modern Woman and Marriage," 735.

13. These concerns reflected white elites' racial fears about the sharing of political power, social mixing, and miscegenation. For an overview of contemporaries' concerns about the meaning of declining birthrates, see Newman, *Men's Ideas/Women's Realities,* 105–55.

14. Mary Ead, *Sewanee Review* 23, no. 4 (1915): 409–17, describes the five to ten years after college that ambitious young women spent pursuing careers before they married, commenting that "independent women are coming more and more to regard marriage as a matter of definitely giving up a 'career'" (414). Ead did not understand that American women had been expressing such ambivalence for more than twenty years.

15. According to Nancy Mowll Mathews, Cassatt's foremost biographer, "there is no doubt that Cassatt was profoundly feminist from an early age. She held women in as high esteem as she held men, if not higher in some ways. She believed in a woman's right to education and advancement in the world outside of the home. She was fully aware of and did not hesitate to raise her voice against the vast injustices suffered by women in modern life." Mathews, *Mary Cassatt: A Life* (New York: Villard Books, 1994), 307–8. See also Griselda Pollock, *Mary Cassatt: Painter of Modern Women* (New York: Thames and Hudson, 1998), 7.

16. Bertha Monroe Rickoff, "Women and the World," *North American Review* 157, no. 143 (October 1893): 451. Mrs. (Mary) Sargent Florence is quoted in *International Studio* 59 (July 1916): iii.

17. Mary Cassatt and Lilla Cabot Perry played a major role in educating the American public about Impressionist painting. For Perry's role, see Meredith Martindale, Pamela Moffat, and Nancy Mowll Mathews, *Lilla Cabot Perry: An American Impressionist* (Washington, D.C.: National Museum of Women in the Arts, 1990); and Wilhelmina Cole Holladay, *A Museum of Their Own: National Museum of Women in the Arts* (New York: Abbeville Press, 2008). For Cassatt's role, see Mathews, *Mary Cassatt;* and H. Barbara Weinberg, "Mary Stevenson Cassatt (1844–1926)," Heilbrunn Timeline of Art History, http://www.metmuseum.org/toah/hd/cast/hd_cast.htm.

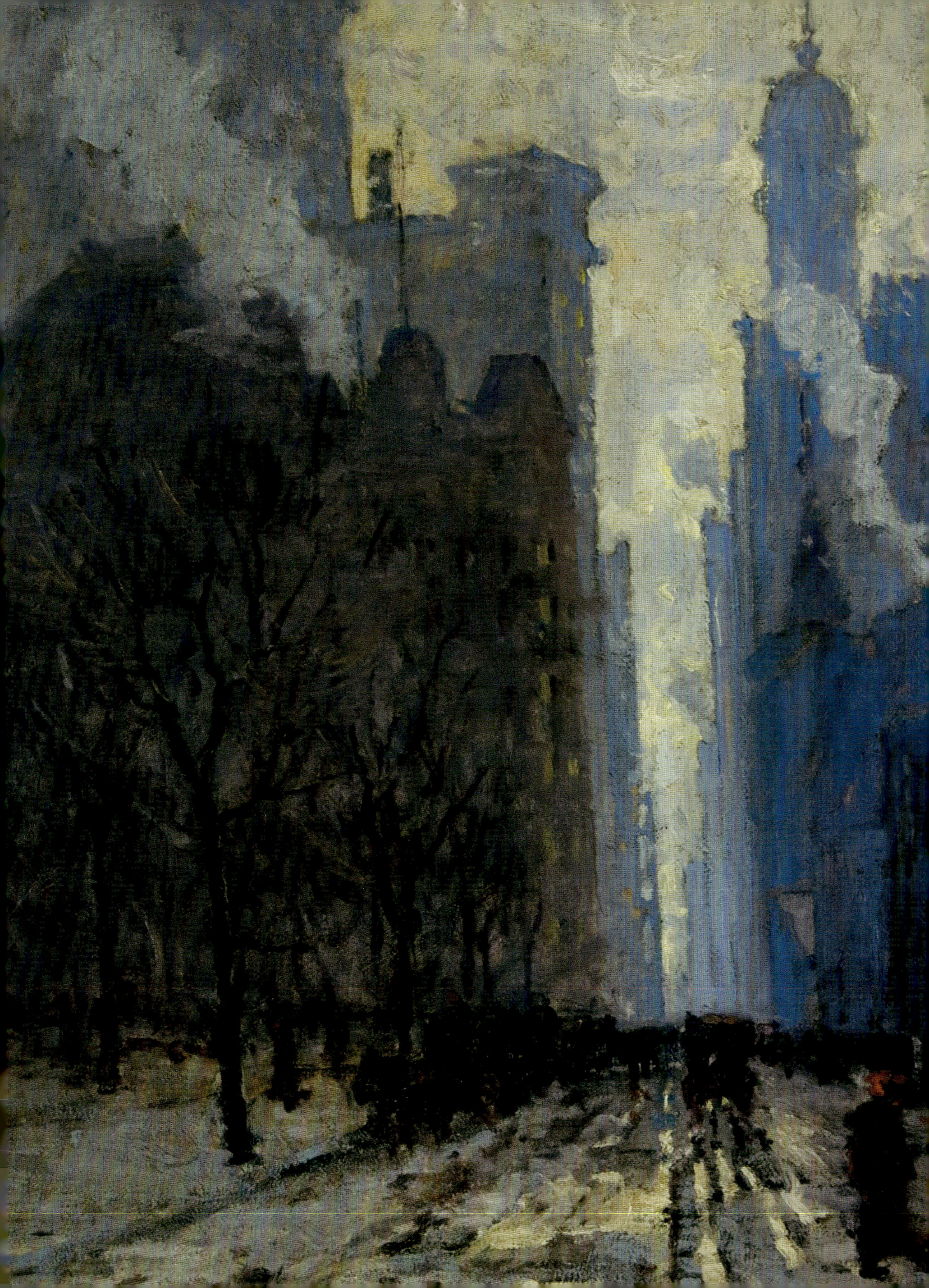

Constructing Landscapes

Impressionism, Urban Parks, and the City Beautiful Movement

SEAN PATRICK ADAMS

When the photographer and "muck-raking" reformer Jacob Riis described the "vast human pig-sty" of New York City's Mulberry Bend in his book *How the Other Half Lives*, he had a larger point to make. For Riis and many other reformers, the landscape of the industrial American city sowed disease, crime, and disorder. Urban spaces seemed crowded and disorganized collections of shops, manufactories, and hastily constructed living spaces; the swelling ranks of industrial workers drawn from home and abroad only added to the chaos and confusion that Riis sought to document in 1890. "In the scores of back alleys, of stable lanes and hidden byways, of which the rent collector alone can keep track, they share such shelter as the ramshackle structures afford with every kind of abomination rifled from the dumps and ash barrels of the city," he wrote. "Here, too, shunning the light, skulks the unclean beast of dishonest idleness."[1] Riis's inclusion of photographs like *The Mulberry Bend Area in New York's Little Italy* (Fig. 1), in which the dirty streets surrounded by listing, ramshackle buildings betray the crude utilitarian nature of American cities, hammered home the point to readers. *How the Other Half Lives* is probably the most famous indictment of urban living conditions in late-nineteenth-century America, and in it Riis raised questions that dominated reform circles for two decades: What could be done about the living and working conditions in American cities? Was urban space destined to be dirty, cramped, and unhealthy? What was the social impact of these dire conditions? Could Americans ever reconcile this dystopian industrial present with their traditional preference for wide-open rural spaces?

Jonas Lie (American, born in Norway, 1880–1940), *Dusk on Lower Broadway* (detail, pl. 41), c. 1910

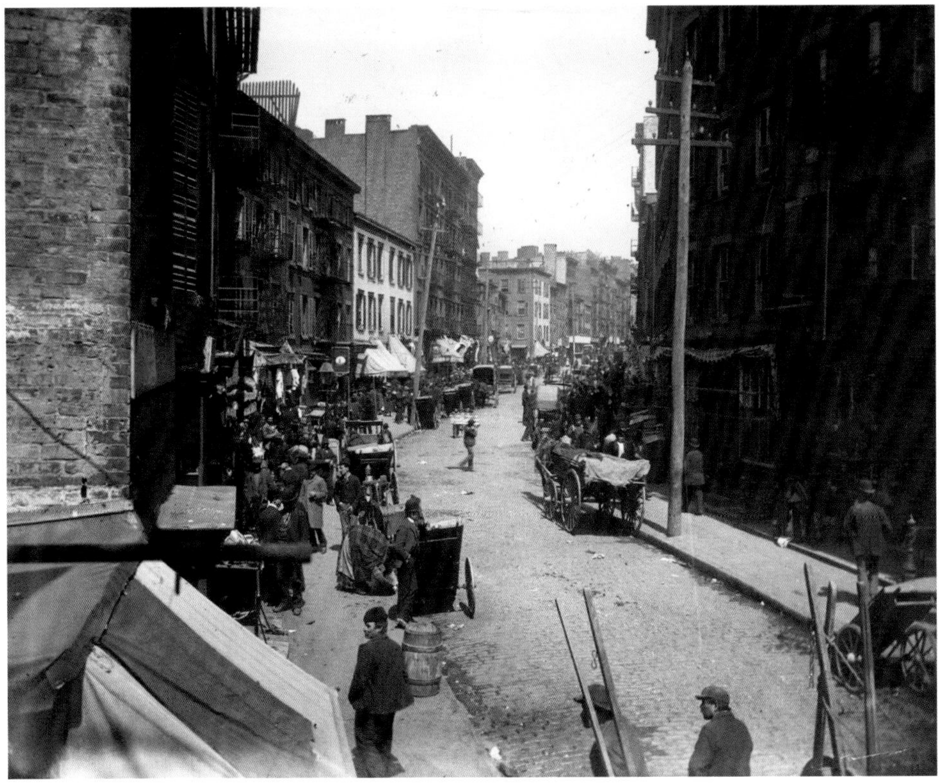

FIGURE 1. Jacob Riis (American, 1849–1914), *The Mulberry Bend Area in New York's Little Italy*, from *How the Other Half Lives; Studies Among the Tenements of New York* (New York: Charles Scribner's Sons, 1890). Jacob Riis/Hulton Archive/Getty Images

By 1903, a journalist from Rochester, New York, believed that he had the definitive answer to these questions. In that year, Charles Mulford Robinson wrote *Modern Civic Art; or, The City Made Beautiful*, in which he outlined an "urban evolution" that was becoming apparent in reformist circles. "The love of nature, the lately aroused consciousness of what may be called sentiment for landscape, brings vegetation into the busy city to soften and brighten," he argued, "and then the spirit of practical philanthropy—so evident to-day—locates playgrounds, builds schools, and insists that modern civic art shall pervade all quarters of the town, remodeling alleys as well as avenues."[2] Robinson's argument that improving the American city's physical surroundings would have a positive moral effect upon the population is an articulation of an amorphous set of programs across the nation's large cities and small towns that historians refer to as the City Beautiful movement. Although it lacked a distinct center or leader, this movement inspired a slew of lectures, programs, and institutions dedicated to the improvement of the urban landscape.

Robinson gave articulation to a phenomenon that was already occurring simultaneously throughout hundreds of towns and small cities across the United States, even as larger cities like Boston or New York served as the most prominent examples. Six years before Robinson wrote *Modern Civic Art*, for example, the blighted Mulberry Bend that Riis described in *How the Other Half Lives* had become Mulberry Bend Park—a green space with tree-lined lanes that curved gracefully to offer New Yorkers a respite from the daily grind of the industrial economy. In this same spirit,

City Beautiful advocates cleaned streets, planted shrubs, removed trash, redesigned urban spaces, and dedicated themselves generally to the notion that industrialization had created a crisis in American cities that needed a solution. Although they could never quite coalesce around a central core of principles or policies, by 1905 more than twenty-four hundred organizations were dedicated to these ideas.[3]

More a loosely organized set of principles than a tightly focused program, the City Beautiful movement drew from several sources. If the movement had a founder, it was likely Frederick Law Olmsted, the famous architect and designer of New York City's Central Park. This project, begun in 1857 and finally completed in 1873, aimed to provide New Yorkers with access to rural landscapes while enjoying the amenities of modern life. Paved walkways, scenic bridges, benches, and structures such as the Gothic Belvedere Castle were as essential to Central Park as the trees or rocky outcrops. By blending the elements of city and country life, Olmsted was, in many ways, the first urban planner to advocate "greening" the American city by remaking its infrastructure with parks and open spaces.[4] Another indirect influence on the City Beautiful movement came from Chicago's World's Columbian Exposition in 1893. The architect Daniel Hudson Burnham conceived of a uniquely American version of neoclassical structures, in which exhibits and buildings reflected a sense of order and rationality. At the center of this built landscape stood the White City, a cluster of white stuccoed structures and broad boulevards. Burnham's vision played to rave reviews, as the White City suggested that foresight and planning could make urban spaces areas of sublime beauty even as they served a function.[5] Finally, an often unheralded influence came in the form of small women's clubs across the nation. These ad hoc volunteer societies applied nineteenth-century notions of domesticity to reduce urban blight. Since women were in charge of maintaining the home as a tidy, comforting shelter against the tumultuous male sphere of work and politics—this was an ideal rarely achieved but often lauded in prescriptive journals and books—middle- and upper-class women suggested that this domestic sphere could be extended outward into the streets and slums. But unlike Olmsted's or Burnham's grand plans, women's clubs often had more modest, but perhaps more realistic, goals. In Westport, Connecticut, for example, the Women's Town Improvement Association raised enough money to build two thousand feet of sidewalk. Despite this clear influence from the work of ambitious and talented women, professional men drawn from the ranks of architects, journalists, and city planners dominated the City Beautiful movement. The 1900 formation of the National League of Improvement Associations—one of the many national organizations affiliated with the movement—gave force to the notion that expertly assembled large-scale plans should form the backbone of City Beautiful projects.[6]

Adherents of the City Beautiful movement shared several philosophical

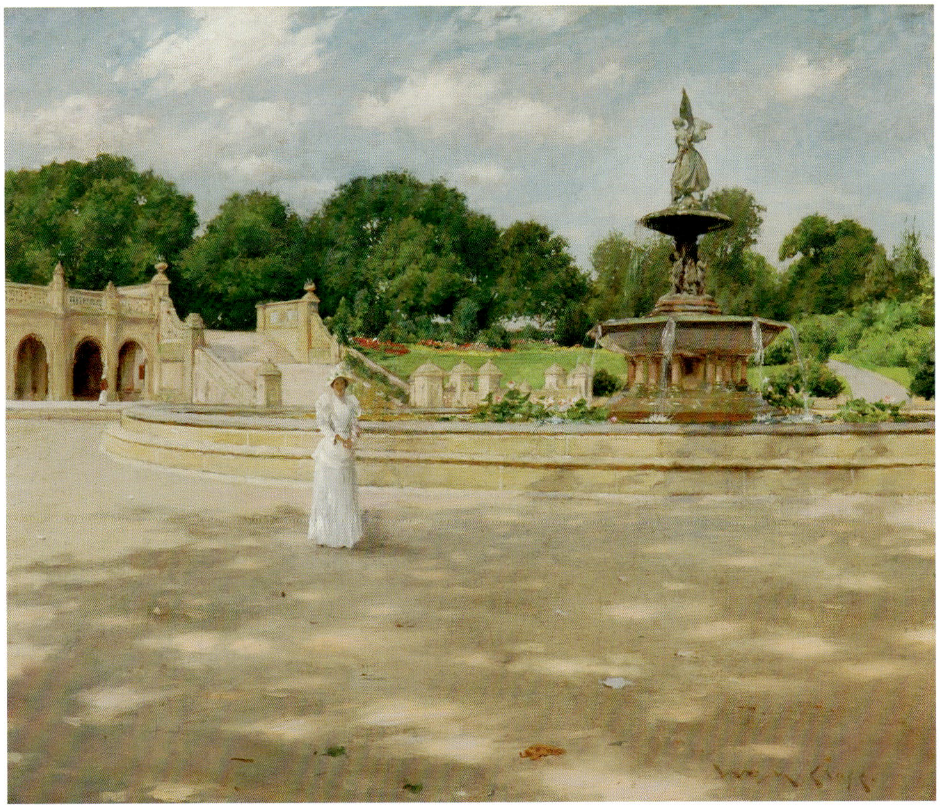

FIGURE 2. William Merritt Chase (American, 1849–1916), *An Early Stroll in the Park*, 1890, oil on canvas, 20 ⅜ × 24 ½ in. (51.8 × 62.2 cm), Montgomery Museum of Fine Arts, Montgomery, Alabama, The Blount Collection, 1989.2.4

assumptions. Like the women's clubs of the late nineteenth century, City Beautiful advocates were most successful at local, ad hoc projects. The invigorating properties of public art, for example, formed one tenet. The streets of American cities, they argued, were cluttered with trash, brash advertisements, and the undisguised by-products of commercial and manufacturing activity. Municipal art in the form of arches, statuary, and murals could alleviate this blight by replacing functional elements of urban life with ones designed to inspire the imagination. The National Sculpture Society's triumphal—yet temporary—arch in New York's Madison Square (1899–1900), for example, used the return of Admiral George Dewey as a way to demonstrate the transformative powers of public art.[7] Massive reworkings of existing urban landscapes represented another wing of the City Beautiful movement. In St. Louis, the Civic League—two-thousand-members strong by 1902—coordinated the construction of public bathrooms, condemned unsightly billboards, and envisioned a network of broad boulevards aimed at transforming public space. John Olmsted—Frederick's nephew—presented an extensive park, boulevard, and playground network for the emerging industrial city of Seattle, Washington.[8]

In the end, the City Beautiful movement did not offer a retreat or retrenchment to an idealized rural America; its proponents wanted to soften the blow of industrialism even as they recognized its permanence in the urban landscape. This reconciliation is reflected in the work of several American Impressionists. Jonas Lie, for example, an American artist born in Norway, painted both rural and urban scenes. In *Dusk on*

Lower Broadway, circa 1910 (Pl. 41), and *Path of Gold*, circa 1915 (Pl. 39), he portrays the kind of urban space that City Beautiful proponents would find comforting: the clean lines of buildings and bridges convey order and energy, outweighing the smoke plumes necessary for industrial life. Lie's work applied the Impressionist methods of using color and light to depictions of the built landscapes of urban America.[9] Other American Impressionists sought to convey the particular beauty of parks in their work. The European-trained American artist William Merritt Chase, for example, painted scenes of New York City's parks that attempted to portray the ways in which they incorporated natural beauty into urban life. Chase's vision in paintings like *An Early Stroll in the Park*, 1890 (Fig. 2), depicting Central Park's Bethesda Terrace and Fountain, emphasized urban parks' imposition of order on nature; these parks were not meant to be pristine or untouched slices of nature, but improved ones. This faith in improvement was one of the hallmarks of the City Beautiful movement, and the work of many American Impressionists reflected that theme perfectly. Rather than portray Jacob Riis's harsh urban climate with a gritty realism, a theme that a younger generation of realist painters known as the Ashcan school was pursuing at this time, many American Impressionists instead chose to reflect Charles Mulford Robinson's optimistic vision of urban spaces through creative uses of color and light. And although not explicitly tied to the City Beautiful movement, the American Impressionists certainly offer a way to appreciate its sentiments today.[10]

Notes

1. Jacob Riis, *How the Other Half Lives: Studies Among the Tenements of New York* (New York: Scribner, 1890), 55–56.

2. Charles Mulford Robinson, *Modern Civic Art; or, The City Made Beautiful* (New York: Putnam, 1903), 14.

3. Paul Boyer, *Urban Masses and Moral Order in America, 1820–1860* (Cambridge: Harvard University Press, 1978), 262–65; William H. Wilson, *The City Beautiful Movement* (Baltimore: Johns Hopkins University Press, 1989), 78–86.

4. Theodore S. Eisenman, "Frederick Law Olmsted, Green Infrastructure, and the Evolving City," *Journal of Planning History* 12 (November 2013): 287–311.

5. The influence of the World's Columbian Exhibition on the City Beautiful movement has been overstated by previous generations of historians, but the Chicago project did share many of the aesthetic and social principles of the City Beautiful movement. Jon Peterson, "The City Beautiful Movement: Forgotten Origins and Lost Meanings," *Journal of Urban History* 2 (1976): 415–34; Wilson, *The City Beautiful Movement*, 53–74.

6. Bonj Szczygiel, "'City Beautiful' Revisited: An Analysis of Nineteenth-Century Civic Improvement Efforts," *Journal of Urban History* 29 (2003): 107–32.

7. Peterson, "The City Beautiful Movement," 419.

8. Wilson, *The City Beautiful Movement*, 147–67.

9. William H. Gerdts and Carol Lowrey, *Jonas Lie (1880–1940)* (New York: Spanierman Gallery, 2005), 23–26.

10. *American Impressionism and Realism: The Painting of Modern Life, 1885–1915,* curated by H. Barbara Weinberg, Doreen Bolder, and David Park Curry (New York: Metropolitan Museum of Art, 1994), 138–52.

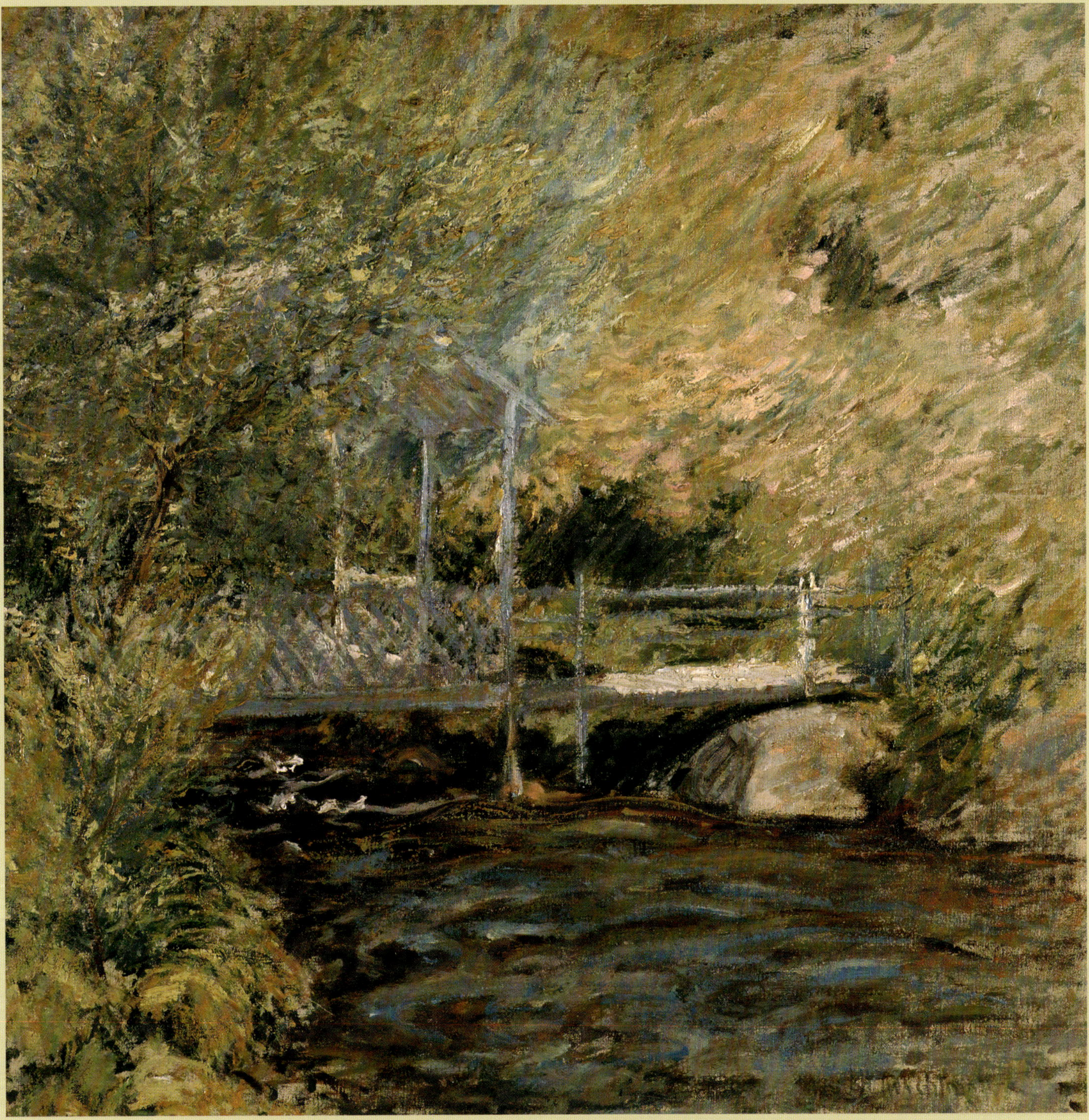

A Taste for What "Moves" Us

The Audiences of American Impressionism

SOPHIA KRZYS ACORD

LIKE ANY NEW ARTISTIC STYLE, Impressionism has traveled a winding road to arrive at the widespread popularity that it enjoys today in the United States. Indeed, Impressionism met with some definite skepticism by the American public at its initial reception. As one visitor remarked at an 1892 Boston exhibition, "Why, that isn't painting . . . that's paint."[1] Our tastes in art and in culture more generally reveal much about our opportunities and aspirations as individuals and as a society. As a result, to understand the rise of American Impressionism from a handful of distributed artist colonies to an artistic movement we need to consider the social makeup of turn-of-the-century America (who patronized art and why) as well as the changing system by which art was disseminated and exhibited (how art was made accessible). Of course, another important aspect of this story is our love for art and the ways in which American impressionism has come to appeal to our eyes, minds, and hearts.

This American story may begin in 1865 with the end of the Civil War, which brought greater wealth and mobility to many in the northern states and a renewed interest in all things foreign.[2] In particular, the nation's elite classes privileged European art for the cosmopolitan status it conveyed. American collectors admired the art of Monet above all others, and even sought out work by French Impressionists not well liked in France. Although American artists such as Mary Cassatt introduced American patrons to French Impressionism and were largely responsible for its success in the United States, these same collectors were largely uninterested in

FIGURE 1, PLATE 20. John Henry Twachtman (American, 1853–1902), *The Little White Bridge*, c. 1896, oil on canvas, 24 ⅝ × 24 ⅝ in. (62.6 × 62.6 cm), Georgia Museum of Art, University of Georgia, Eva Underhill Holbrook Memorial Collection of American Art, Gift of Alfred H. Holbrook, 1945.90

American artists who were incorporating Impressionist techniques. For new members of American high society, European art was seen as superior to American art: it was "Art with a capital A."[3] In major cities like New York and Boston, these wealthy social groups became tastemakers for the arts by forming charitable corporations governed by civic-minded trustees hailing from leading families. And, in the second half of the nineteenth century, these corporations went to work creating and refining the nation's first modern art museums.

So Impressionist painting emerged at roughly the same time as America's founding museums, concert halls, and other fine art institutions. These institutions, such as Boston's Museum of Fine Arts or Hartford's Wadsworth Atheneum, played an important role in distinguishing the "fine arts" from curiosities such as bearded women, mermaids, and other forms of "popular" culture.[4] Indeed, the nature of museum art was shaped by a number of distinct choices, including eliminating reproductions and collecting only original works of art, hiring trained art historians as curators, and distinguishing between professional and amateur artists.[5] Although some of the nation's first museums did collect American art—the Hudson River school was especially popular—the sentiments of the social groups that supported the museums also informed the tendencies of what they exhibited. Museums' interest in collecting only "proven" artists meant that the old European masters were included, but living artists and unconventional styles were often disregarded.

The privileging of European art that had already been consecrated by critics, curators, and royals likely worked against the recognition of new American Impressionist art by these traditional patrons. It may not be coincidental, then, that nineteenth-century American artists were highly individualized and chose to work in smaller groups and colonies outside the mainstream art world.[6] Indeed, following Monet and the Salon de Refusés, which established itself independently from the French Salon, American Impressionist artists also abandoned the traditional, centralized artistic reward channel of the National Academy of Design in New York. Like those of their French brethren, the protests of American Impressionists were less ideological and more practical, citing bureaucratic attitudes, overly large membership, and old-fashioned exhibition practices.[7] And, as with Monet and his colleagues, operating outside these channels required American artists to become entrepreneurs and work directly with dealers to sell their paintings. The accompanying rise of art dealers, critics, and independent exhibitions in raising the visibility of American Impressionism went hand-in-hand with a new market for visual art: the middle class.

The new, upwardly mobile middle class looked at art with a different eye than their elite brethren did: not one of aspiring to the cosmopolitan, but rather one of articulating their own American identity. Indeed, rather than beginning and ending with

European art, the availability of multiple genres of art was an important element of constructing a more typical American taste.[8] As a result, American artists influenced by Impressionism chose to paint subjects that would be appealing to their new patrons: New England beaches, the countryside (Fig. 1), church scenes, and upper-class women in moments of domestic tranquillity (Fig. 2). It was decorative and uplifting, in both its colorful palette and storybook subject matter. In a time of increased immigration by "the great unwashed," the muted painterly lens focused on domestic comforts and middle-class values.[9] Americans purchased this art for many reasons, from social ambition and a love of "the finer things in life" to a dedication to supporting artistic professions and sharing art with less privileged communities.[10] The cultivation of an audience for American Impressionism among the middle classes

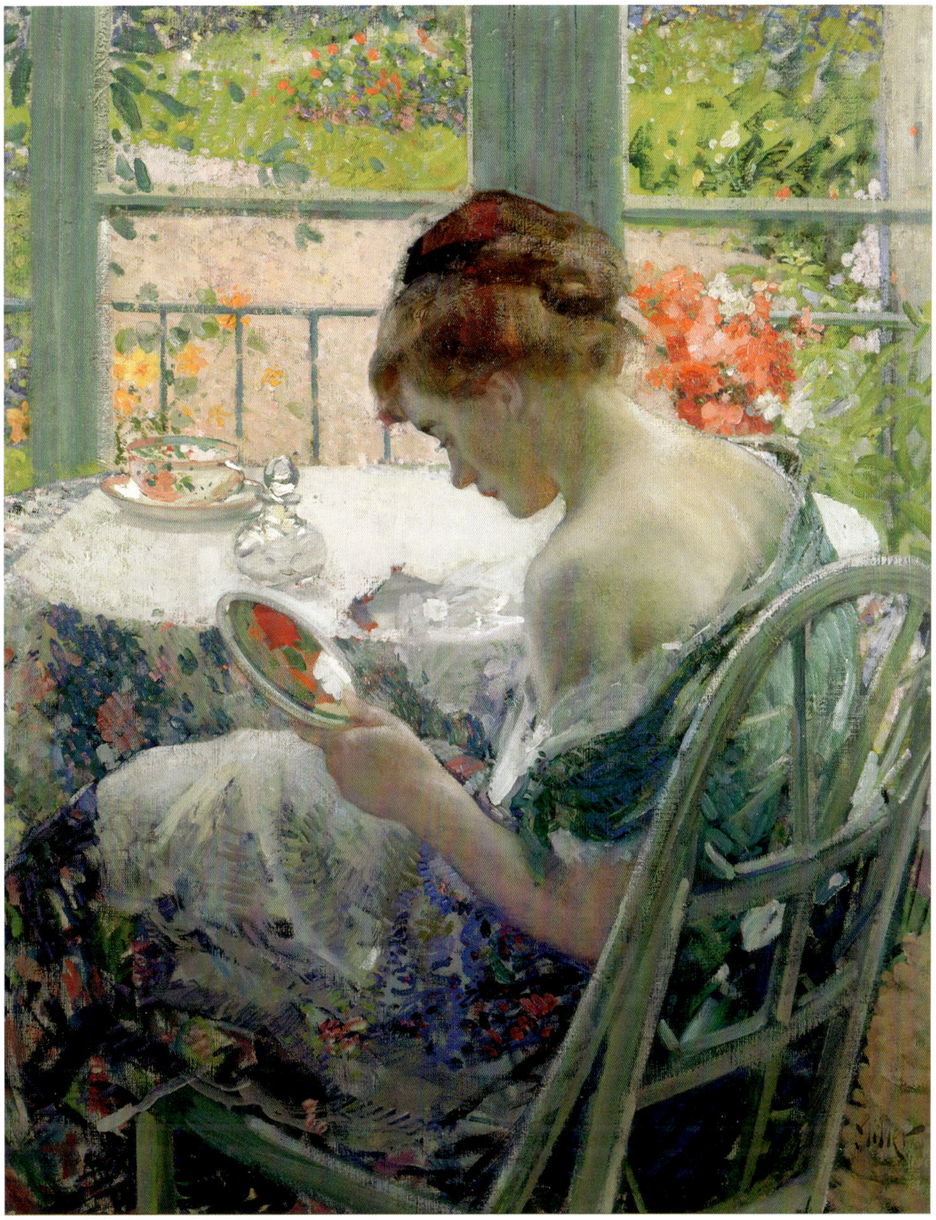

FIGURE 2, PLATE 51. Richard Emil Miller (American, 1875–1943), *La Toilette*, c. 1914, oil on canvas, 40 × 32 ½ in. (101.6 × 82.6 cm), The Columbus Museum, Georgia; Museum purchase made possible by Mrs. J. B. Knight, Jr., in memory of her husband

supported the reemergence of the wealthy American collector dedicated to building a nationalistic school of American art. Although American Impressionism was far from universally appreciated among more prominent patrons—some, like Charles Lang Freer and William T. Evans, enjoyed its "surface brilliance," while others, like Andrew Carnegie, found it overly sentimental and insufficiently democratic—their bequeaths to the Smithsonian and other American artistic institutions played an important role in setting the stage for a broader public appreciation of this work.

Interest in American Impressionism lay fallow from about 1930 until roughly 1960 as museums and collectors pursued more modern styles such as Cubism, Futurism and Abstract Expressionism. Following World War II, however, the art world in America exploded. More than 67 percent of museums exhibiting American art in the United States were founded after 1940. In New York City alone, the number of galleries handling American art multiplied from twenty to three hundred, the number of serious collectors (including corporations) of works by living artists increased from a dozen to thousands, and the number of exhibitions of living artists grew by more than 50 percent. At the same time, the 1965 creation of the National Endowment for the Arts expanded government support for the arts, and the rise of tourism, growing levels of education, and leisure time augmented visitors to art institutions.[11]

As part of this larger growth in cultural consumption, key art collectors played crucial roles in highlighting American Impressionism. In his second edition of *American Impressionism*, William Gerdts describes how "pioneer" collectors in the 1960s, such as Margaret and Ray Horowitz and Rita and Dan Fraad, prompted commercial establishments to seek out American Impressionism.[12] This rediscovery stimulated scholarly publications throughout the 1970s on American Impressionism, and was further amplified by two 1973 major museum exhibitions at the National Gallery of Art in Washington, D.C., and the Metropolitan Museum of Art in New York City, the latter dedicated to the Horowitz Collection. We continue to experience and add to the ripples of this renewed interest today.

But why did these contemporary collectors fall in love with American Impressionist works? As described by art collectors Nancy and Ira Koger in their foreword to the 1985 catalogue from an exhibition of works from their collection at Florida's Rollins College, "We like them because they are easy to live with, easy to understand. We like them because they represent a fairly close memory, a time we either experienced or heard about from our parents and grandparents. . . . Maybe we inherited our respect for the genteel tradition, or maybe it represents an ideal view of what we wished our childhoods had been, or maybe it is just a dream of what we wish life today would bring."[13] Perhaps our tastes are shaped by what we love as much as what we aspire to be.

The most interesting story about American Impressionism may be how it found its audiences and how its popularity endures into the present. Although French Impressionist painters like Monet greatly influenced American artists in their painterly techniques, American audiences also transformed the radical French Impressionist way of seeing the world into a means of projecting intimate scenes of American morality and family values. Indeed, the history of Impressionism reveals how public and private forces worked together to safeguard and promote American art, making it available to wider audiences throughout the country. And most importantly, every exhibition contributes to the identity of American Impressionism as a movement while also helping us to understand more deeply its role in American heritage and character. This prompts us to consider our roles, and that of this exhibition on Monet and American Impressionism, in building the future legacy of American Impressionism.

Notes

1. Quoted in Russell Lynes, *The Tastemakers: The Shaping of American Popular Taste* (New York: Dover, 1949), 158.
2. Moussa Domit, *American Impressionist Painting* (Washington, D.C.: National Gallery of Art, 1973), 17–19.
3. Richard J. Boyle, *American Impressionism* (Boston: New York Graphic Society, 1974), 143.
4. Paul DiMaggio, "Cultural Entrepreneurship in Nineteenth-Century Boston: The Creation of an Organizational Base for High Culture in America," *Media, Culture and Society* 4, no. 1 (1982): 34–35.
5. Paul DiMaggio, "Cultural Entrepreneurship in Nineteenth-Century Boston, Part II: The Classification and Framing of American Art," *Media, Culture and Society* 4, no. 4 (1982): 303–22.
6. Donelson F. Hoopes, *The American Impressionists* (New York: Watson-Guptill, 1972), 17–18.
7. Harrison C. White and Cynthia A. White, *Canvases and Careers: Institutional Change in the French Painting World* (New York: Wiley, 1965), 105–15; Boyle, *American Impressionism*, 149.
8. Vera L. Zolberg, *Constructing a Sociology of the Arts* (Cambridge: Cambridge University Press, 1990), 188–91.
9. Kathleen Pyne, *Art and the Higher Life: Painting and Evolutionary Thought in Late Nineteenth-Century America* (Austin: University of Texas Press, 1996), 222–31.
10. Lynes, *The Tastemakers,* 151–53.
11. Diana Crane, *The Transformation of the Avant-Garde: The New York Art World, 1940–1985* (Chicago: University of Chicago Press, 1987), 3–9.
12. William H. Gerdts, *American Impressionism*, 2nd ed. (New York: Abbeville Press, 2001), 3.
13. Donald D. Keyes, ed., *The Genteel Tradition: Impressionist and Realist American Art from the Ira and Nancy Koger Collection in Celebration of the Centennial of Rollins College* (Winter Park, Fla.: The George D. and Harriet W. Cornell Fine Arts Center, 1985), 8.

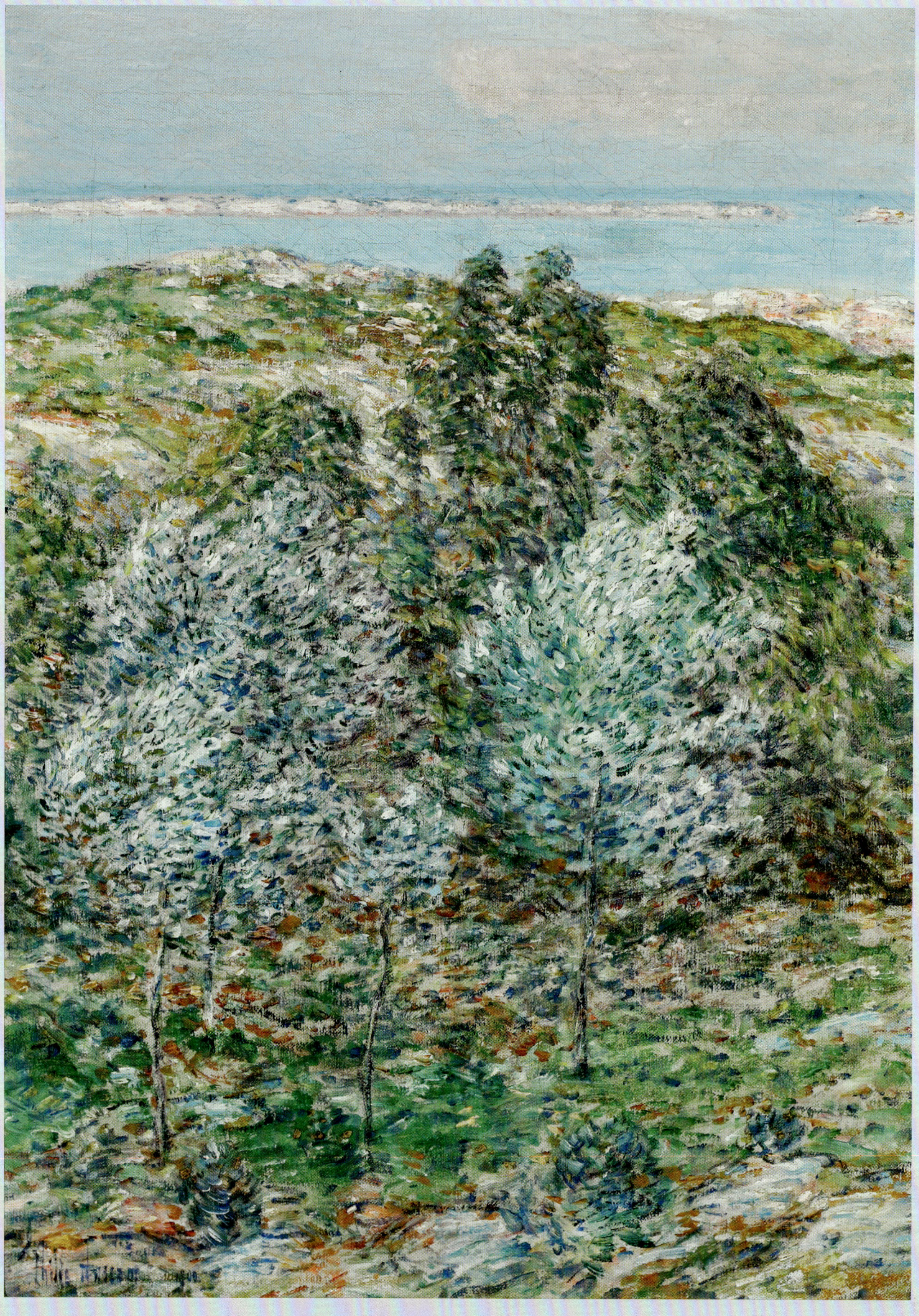

Winter Studio, 1901 (A Short Story)

STEPHANIE A. SMITH

I WALKED INTO the Holbein Studio Building at West Fifty-fifth as one girl, left it quite another. The couple who lived there had been friends of a friend of my mother's, a well-known poet who'd passed away years before the turn of the century. When I was five, and then again at six, Mother and I stayed with Celia Thaxter, on Appledore Island, before our family began to summer on the Vineyard. She and Mother were fond friends, even if, according to Father, she was "just a silly lady-writer." Poets, writers, and artists were, to his mind, frivolous, even if they'd achieved a measure of renown.

As Mother and I gained the second floor of the Holbein that winter's afternoon, I was annoyed. I didn't share my father's disdain for artists, but I didn't want to waste time with boring old people in an overheated studio. I was more interested in the new swan-bill corset, the "health-corset." Mother and I were still tight-lacing, which I thought terribly old-fashioned, even dangerous, and I'd been hoping she would buy us both ready-made swan-bills from Macy's. But Mama thought department stores vulgar, and put her foot down. We would not be caught traipsing into a place like *that*. Ever. Seems silly, but she has her ideas about what does, and does not, constitute being proper.

In response, I sulked. How was I to know that in a blink of an eye, women would ditch the corset, first in dribbles, these days in droves? At thirty-five, I'm a mother, not a fashion plate, but even so, I wouldn't be caught *dead* in a corset, *any* sort of corset. I'm modern, and proud of our progressive century.

Anyway, as I followed after Mother that day, I also dragged my feet, wondering how long we would have to tarry before we could go to tea. I was sure no artist would

Frederick Childe Hassam (American, 1859–1935), *Springtime Vision* (pl. 25), 1900 serve a proper tea. I pictured the husband as fat, a disheveled mess, with flecks of dry paint on a dirty shirt and the wife, blowsy, scattered. As I've said, I didn't entirely share my father's opinions, but I did share his social prejudices. Like many an upper-class girl in New York, I thought artists low, even if I enjoyed my own sketching lessons. Then again, I was encouraged to dabble, to gain a light cultural polish. Papa paid for a French governess, and a piano tutor, so I was well on my way to being a bauble for some soon-to-be-upstanding society bore to dangle on his arm.

I could not have known it then, but visiting that Holbein studio would alter my sense of possibility.

That man's vision changed everything.

It turns out that Celia Thaxter had told this painter he might offer me some guidance, as I grew up. She'd seen a few childhood sketches, and thought I had talent, but then she passed away, and time intervened. Mother, however, did not forget. She respected her friend's judgment, and she'd met Childe Hassam once at Appledore, long before he became famous. She thought to presume on this one chance meeting to persuade an artist of his stature to take an interest in me. It might prove, well, useful, in certain social circles.

We were ushered into the studio by Mr. Hassam himself, and he could not have been more different from what I'd imagined. Neatly dressed, stout but not fat, he was at first bluff and gregarious, but as the afternoon wore on, I realized he was also oddly reserved, even a bit secretive. Perhaps he had seen past my mother's trumped-up enthusiasm, into the social benefit she hoped to derive. His wife appeared a gentle soul, with a dash in her eye, and both of them seemed at ease, enjoying life in a way that my parents somehow did not. They seemed . . . I don't know, young, elastic, fresh.

I can't say now that I remember anything much of that brief visit, but Mr. Hassam's paintings, finished to unfinished, all of them, from the carefully framed oils—he framed them himself—down to a few watercolors just lying about, seemed to tighten the laces of my stays, cut off my wind. I went gasping around the studio as if I'd developed consumption, and in a way I had. I wanted to consume every last stroke of his hand. Suffice it to say I'd never seen anything the like. French Impressionism was just beginning to touch the American palette; for example, Claude Monet's prodigious talent was understood only by a handful, and anyway I lived bottled-up in old New York, where the "modern" was sniffed at, and art deemed a puzzle, unless you could prove it a sound investment.

He watched me, Childe Hassam, as I moved about, rapt. I was ever so taken with the one he'd titled *Isles of Shoals,* 1899. The quick-dash flecks of the sea-water's shimmering, simmering blues, the vivid, clear light he'd conjured and the sense of scale and space soaring out to the far horizon where the limpid blue of the sky kissed the choppy, glinting sea; the sculptural, tawny rock-cliffs I'd clambered across as a child,

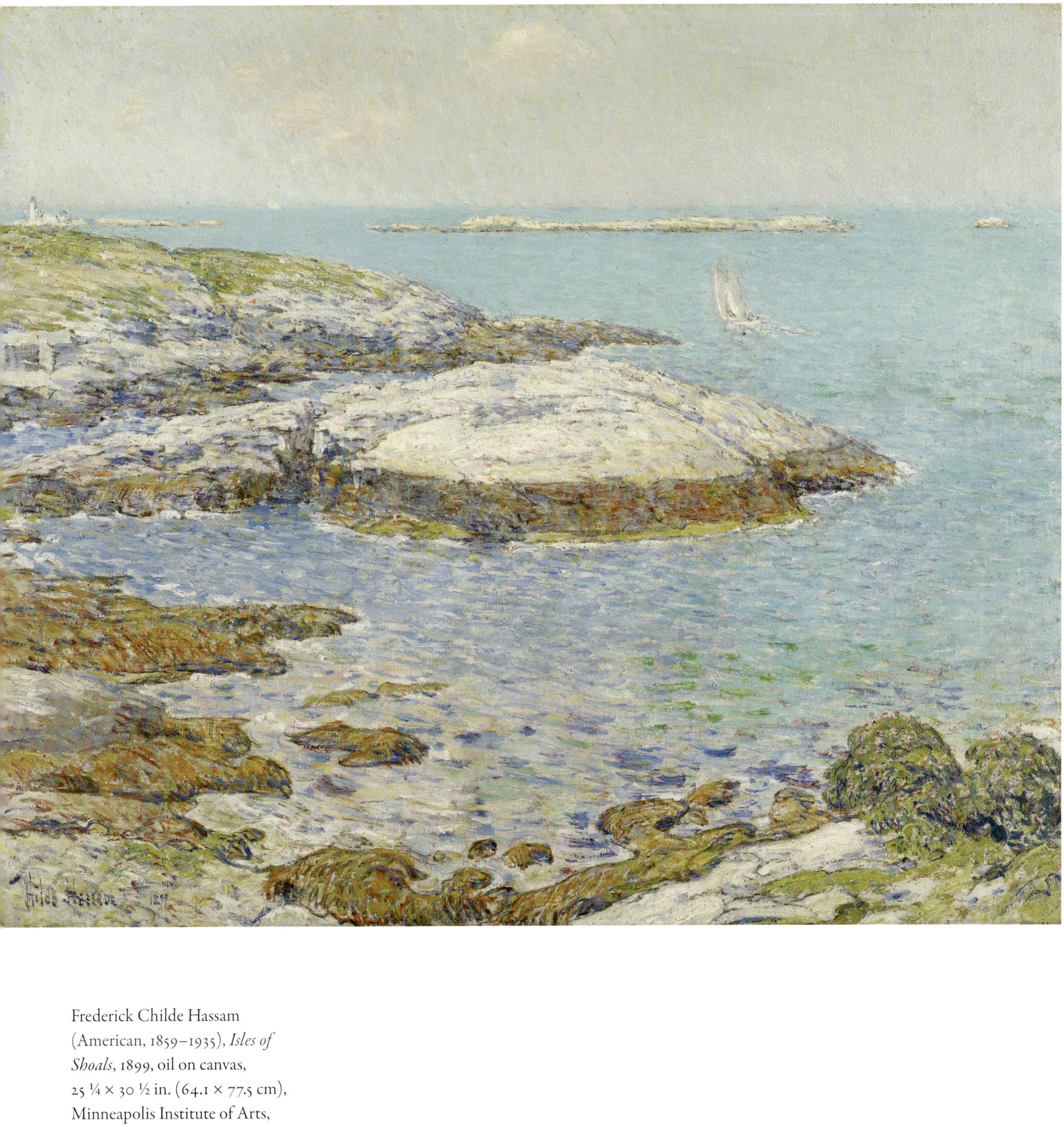

Frederick Childe Hassam (American, 1859–1935), *Isles of Shoals*, 1899, oil on canvas, 25 ¼ × 30 ½ in. (64.1 × 77.5 cm), Minneapolis Institute of Arts, Gift of the Martin B. Koon Memorial Collection, 14.115; Photo: Minneapolis Institute of Arts

all so stylized and yet so real, it brought me to Appledore as if we'd just stepped off the boat. I could smell sea-wrack, feel the brisk wind, taste the wine-heady colors of summer in the heart of winter.

"And did you find a favorite?" he asked me, as we readied to leave.

A favorite? How could I?

I'd already fallen in love with every line his hand had ever laid down. Shrugged halfway into my coat, I just stared at him, as if he had spoken in a tongue so foreign it didn't even register as language, which would have amused him since he enjoyed people mistaking him, the scion of a venerable, colonial New England family, for an exotic Arab, just because of his name.

"Muley," said his wife. "You're embarrassing the child."

"Am I?" he said, laughing. "That won't do. Forgive me, Miss Hendriks?"

Which of course only made me even more starved for air, though I managed to blurt out that everything had been "simply marvelous," which made me feel like a fool, especially when he laughed again.

We left, and that, it turns out, was that.

Well, almost. Mother had asked him to tutor me, and when he declined, tried to cajole him into accepting a portrait commission, but to no avail, he wasn't fond of portraits, didn't need commissions and besides, why have any monetary dealings with my parents? Proud of their Dutch heritage, both of them would've looked down their noses at him, socially, even as they would've bragged to their set of friends about having landed so rare a commission.

Then again, what might that have been like, to have been fifteen and taking *lessons* from the master of American Impressionism?

My imagination reels. I know I would have been petrified, perhaps overcome by his bearish, bullish masculinity. He was stubborn—his nickname was "Muley" in part due to that quality—and nearly thirty years my senior, but I imagine I would have swooned over his grandeur, his temper, his moods, and put it all down to genius.

Papa was delighted, of course, that Mother's designs had been baffled.

"What a shame," she murmured, shaking her head at breakfast, whilst Father smoked. "Irene obviously has talent. And besides, she is so lovely, isn't she? What a wasted opportunity. I mean for him."

But I, for one, was grateful to have escaped, and slowly, slowly turned the ardent awe Childe Hassam's work had inspired in me that afternoon into something else, a flexible, curious, inquiring self. I changed. The hard little social snob I was began to dissolve. I stopped my sketching lessons. I didn't paint, or draw, except in my mind's eye, where I would compose things quite unlike my girlish drawings. For years, Hassam's winter studio, in all its glorious exuberance, yet lingered, like the sweet afterburn of a hard liquor.

I did not marry any of the appropriate young men my father courted on my behalf; nor did I produce a bevy of grandchildren, as my mother so hoped. I wandered, and along the way I grew to know myself as a person, a whole person, no longer just a stuck-up plaything. And then, when I was finally an adult, I met Lee Hoving. He's not from wealth, or social class; he's a humble Vineyard farmboy, turned sculptor. We get by. My father's ire soon cooled, and Mother now dotes on Lee, so we have my inheritance, and the farm.

Not long after my son was born, I bought paint and brushes and canvas. That summer, with my fond husband's support, I worked, at a feverish pitch, my hand steered by the force of Hassam. I think my favorite to date is of my mother and son of a summer's eve, the swirl of white froth that is her dress, the low glare of a setting sun and the swift line of my boy's sweet, fat arm, reaching for stars unseen.

Although my husband has friends who know the Hassams fairly well, he and I have not met again, so I've never had the opportunity to tell him of his influence. I follow his career in the papers, my Mr. Childe "Muley Abdul" Hassam. I know that he gets annoyed when critics compare him, without flattery, to the great Monet, or call his *opus* too derivative of the French; I know he finds "modern" art tasteless. But the world changes, as it should; just this past February, the storied Holbein was suddenly torn down, sending the resident artists scrambling, and while I understand the loss, I can't find progress sad, can you? So if I could tell Childe Hassam anything at all, I would thank him for showing me another way of being. In his studio on that winter's day, a changeling hatched, a new creature altered by his eye for the exquisite light that illumines us all.

Plates

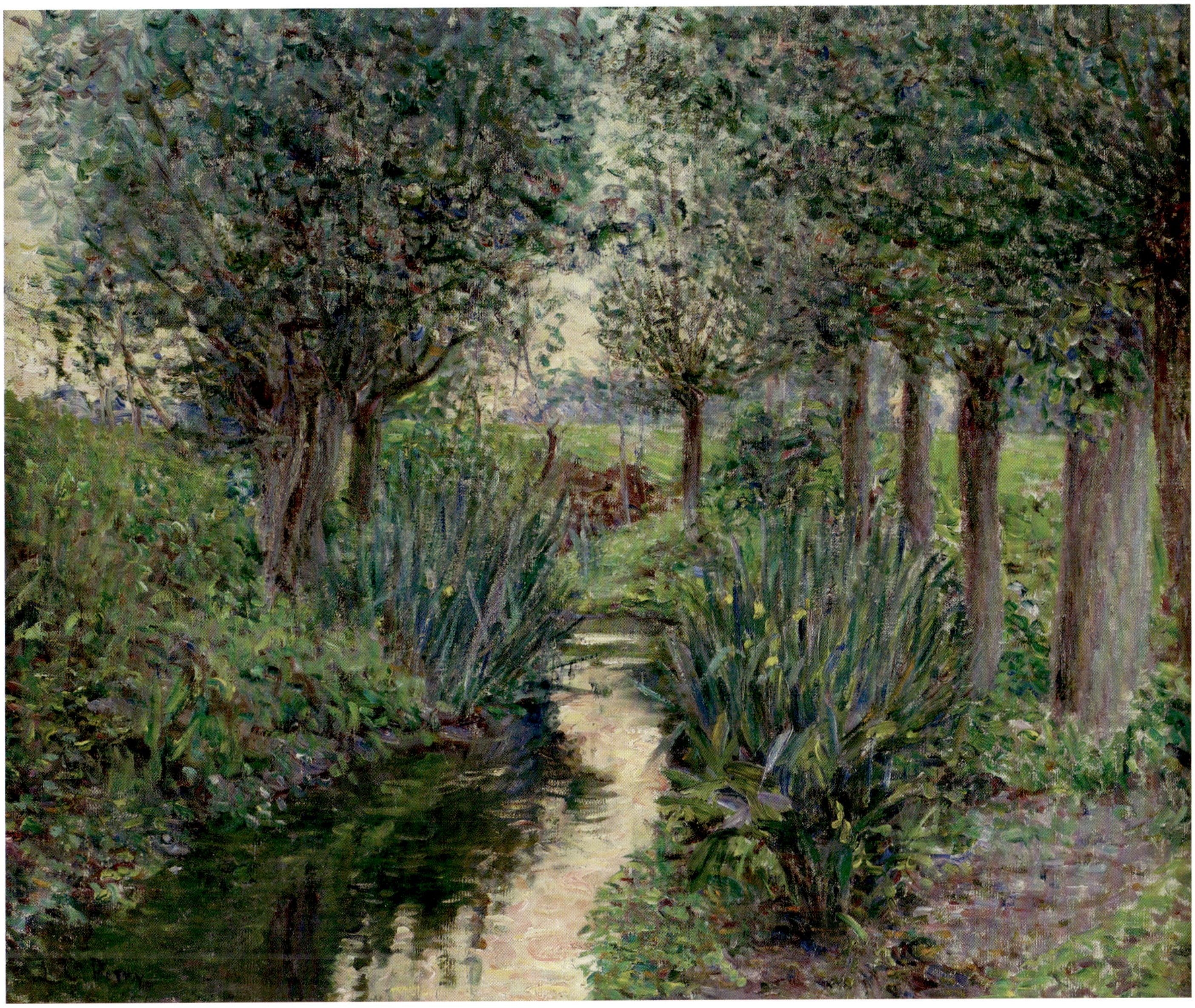

PLATE 1
Lilla Cabot Perry
(American, 1848–1933)
A Stream Beneath Poplars
c. 1890–1900
Oil on canvas
25 ¾ × 32 in. (65.4 × 81.3 cm)
Hunter Museum of American Art,
Chattanooga, Tennessee, Gift of Mr.
and Mrs. Stuart P. Feld
1973.21
Photo by James Madden, 204 Studios,
Chattanooga

PLATE 2
Lilla Cabot Perry
(American, 1848–1933)
Landscape in Normandy
1890
Oil on canvas
18 × 22 in. (45.7 × 55.9 cm)
Collection of the Newark Museum,
Bequest of Diana Bonnor Lewis, 1988
88.9

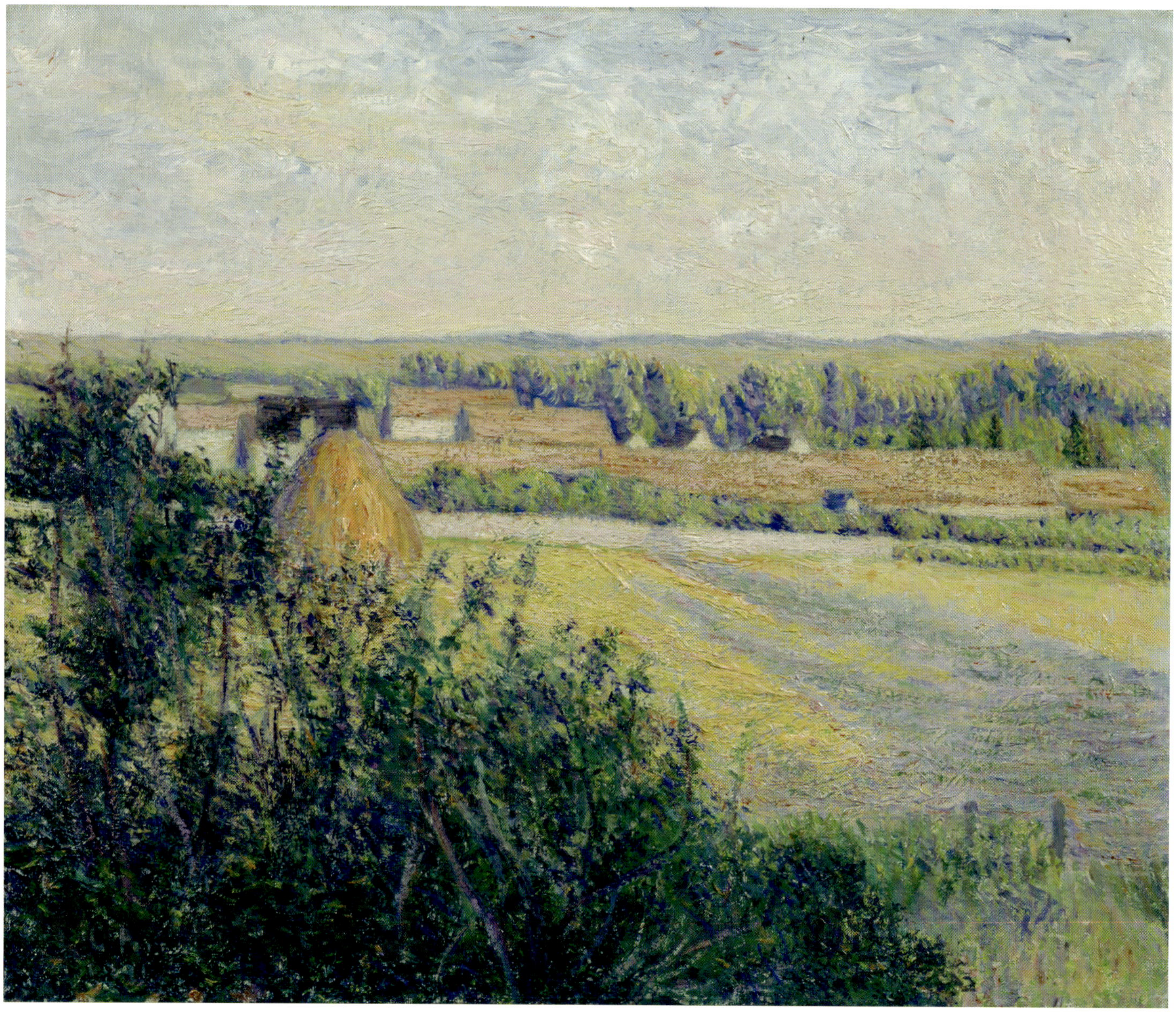

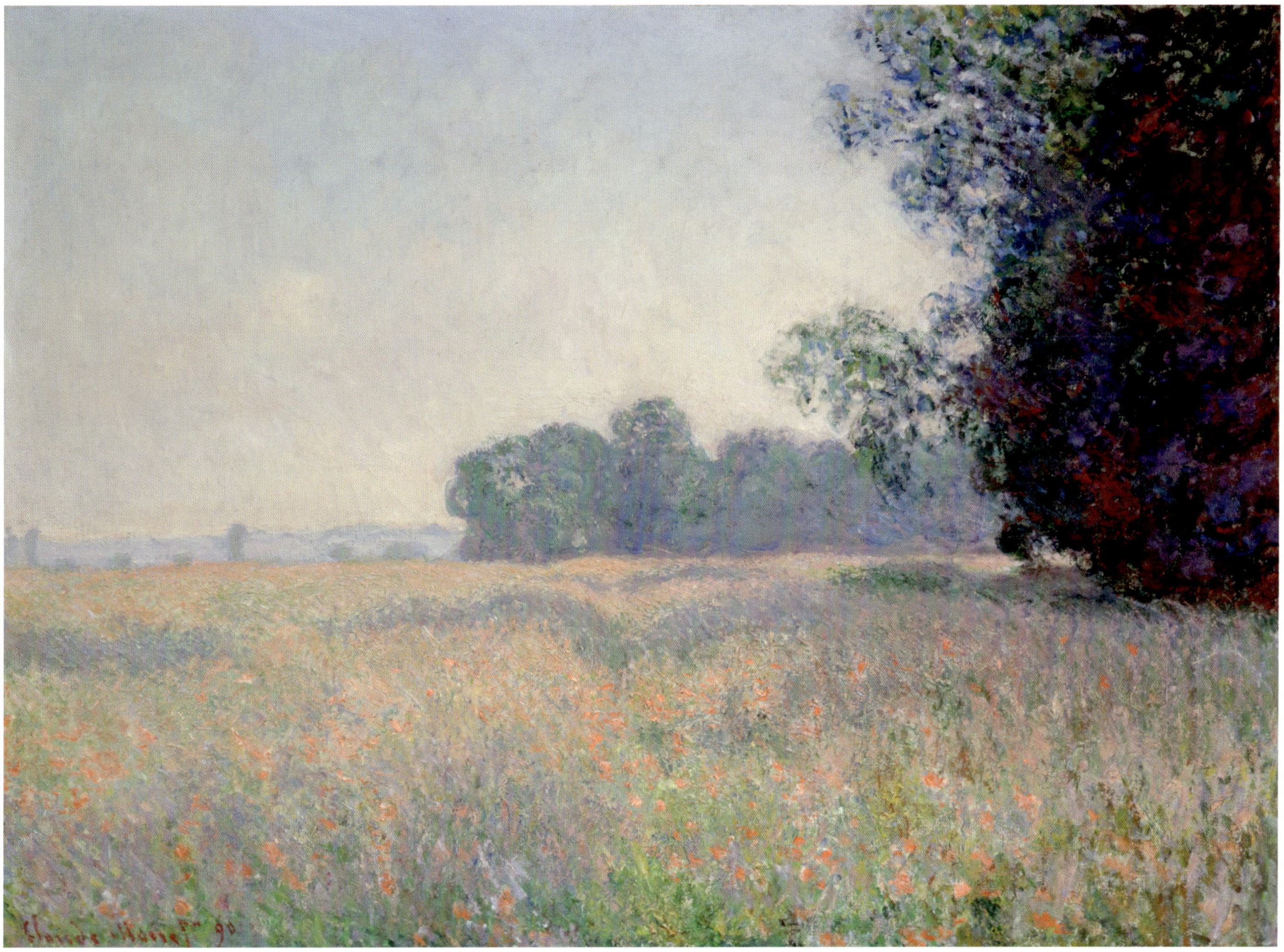

PLATE 3
Claude Monet
(French, 1840–1926)
Champ d'avoine (Oat Field)
1890
Oil on canvas
26 × 36 7/16 in. (66 × 92.6 cm)
Samuel P. Harn Museum of Art,
University of Florida, Gainesville,
Gift of Michael A. Singer
1999.6

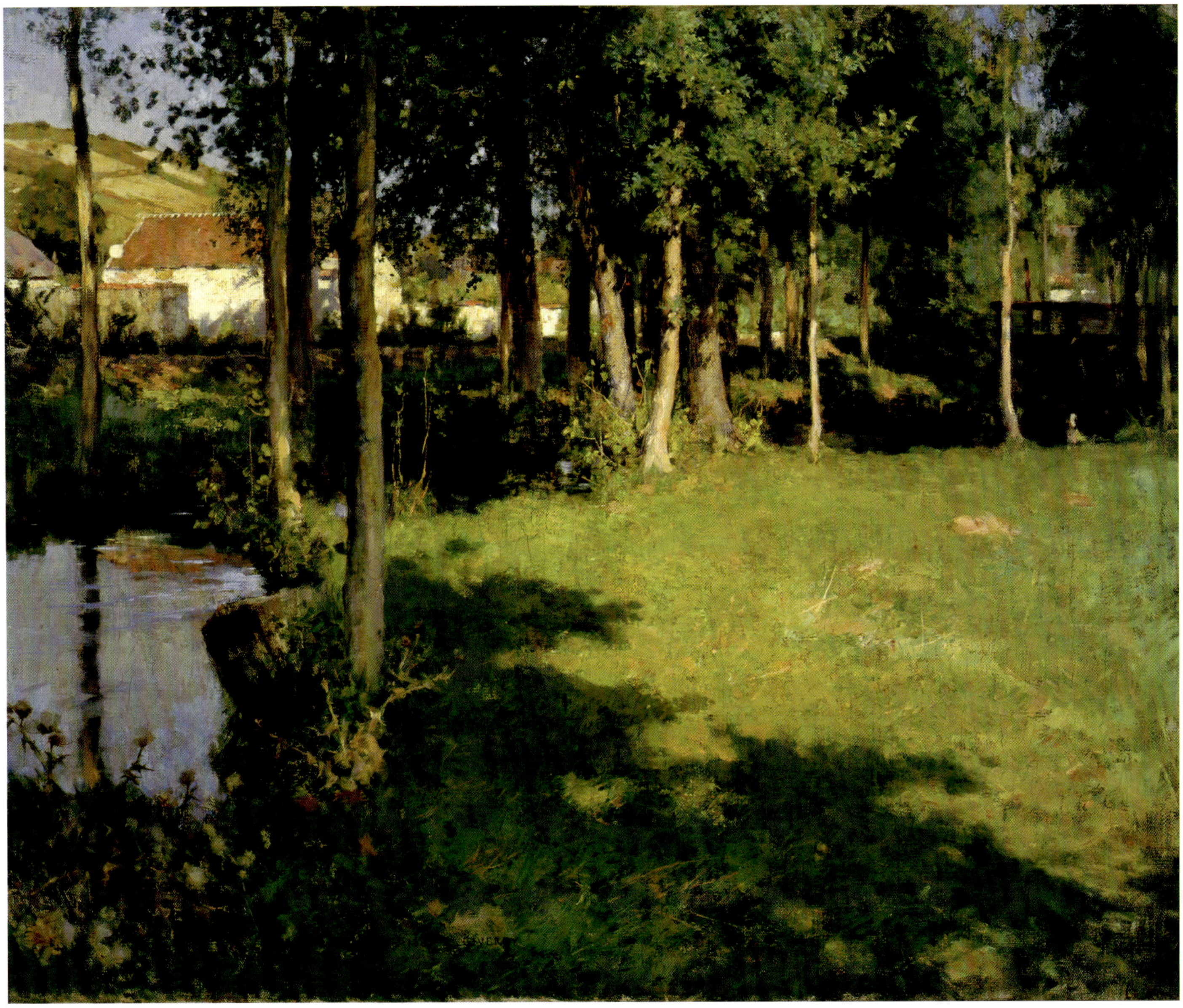

PLATE 4
Willard Leroy Metcalf
(American, 1858–1925)
Giverny
1887
Oil on canvas
26 × 32 ⅛ in. (66 × 81.6 cm)
Collection of The Art Museum at the University of Kentucky, Bequest of Addison M. Metcalf
1984.19.10

PLATE 5
Theodore Robinson
(American, 1852–1896)
Afternoon Shadows
1891
Oil on canvas
18 ⅛ × 22 in. (46 × 55.9 cm)
Samuel P. Harn Museum of Art,
University of Florida, Gainesville,
Museum purchase, funds provided by
Michael A. and Donna Singer
2007.7

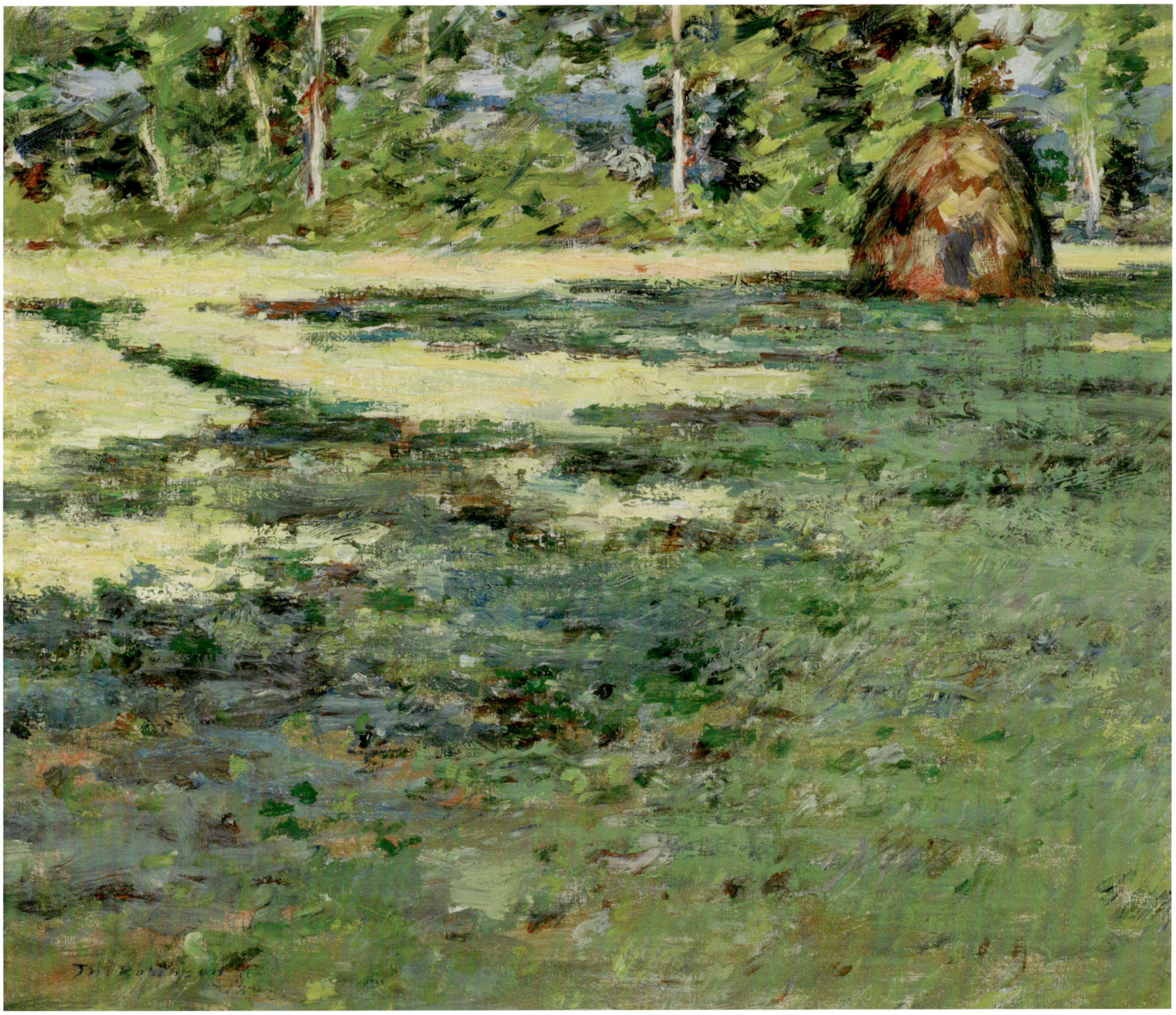

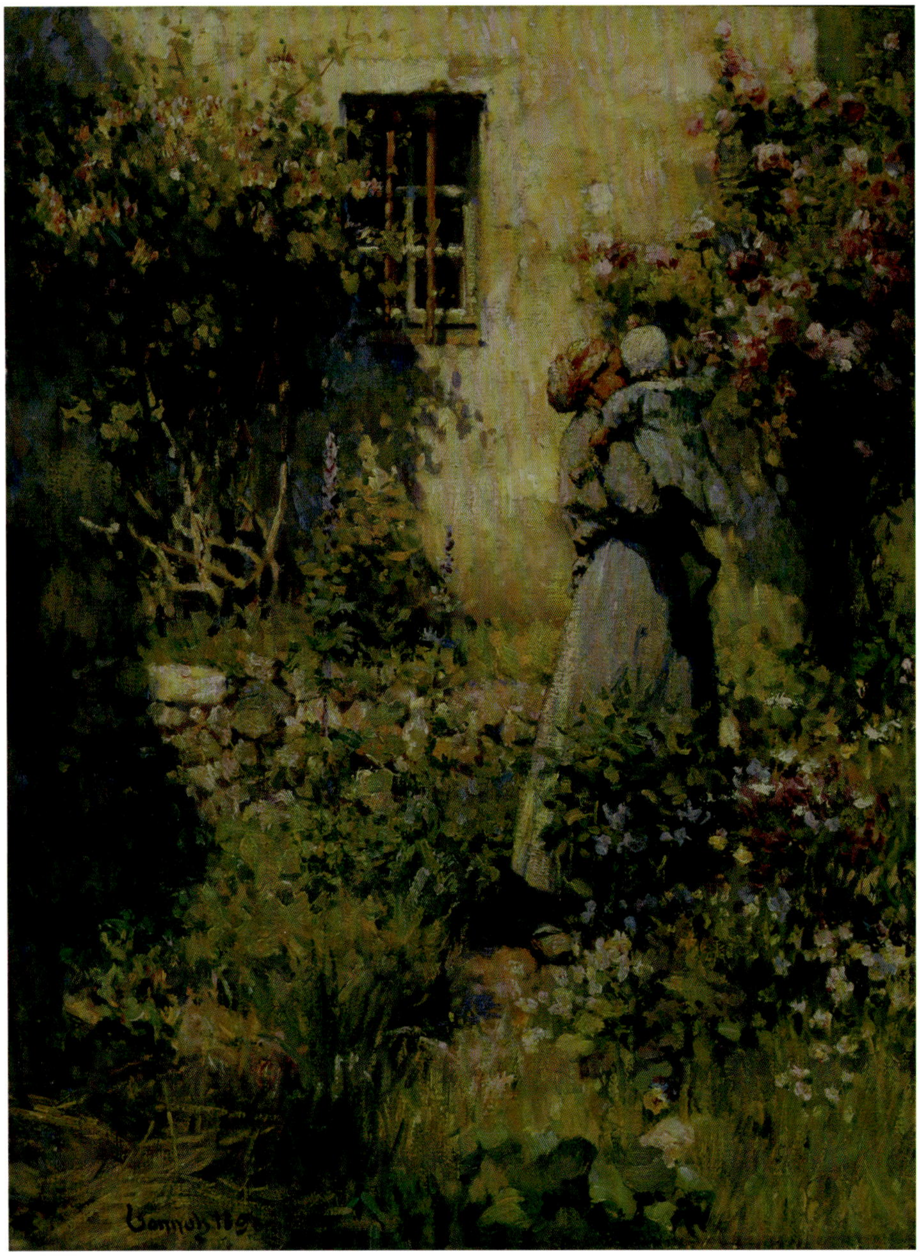

PLATE 6
Robert Vonnoh
(American, 1858–1933)
Jardin de paysanne (Peasant Garden)
1890
Oil on canvas board
25 ⅞ × 19 ¾ in. (65.7 × 50.2 cm)
Terra Foundation for American Art,
Daniel J. Terra Collection
1987.8

PLATE 7 (*facing page*)
Theodore Robinson
(American, 1852–1896)
Gathering Plums
1891
Oil on canvas
22 × 18 in. (57.2 × 55.9 cm)
Georgia Museum of Art, University of Georgia, Eva Underhill Holbrook Memorial Collection of American Art; Gift of Alfred H. Holbrook
1945.76

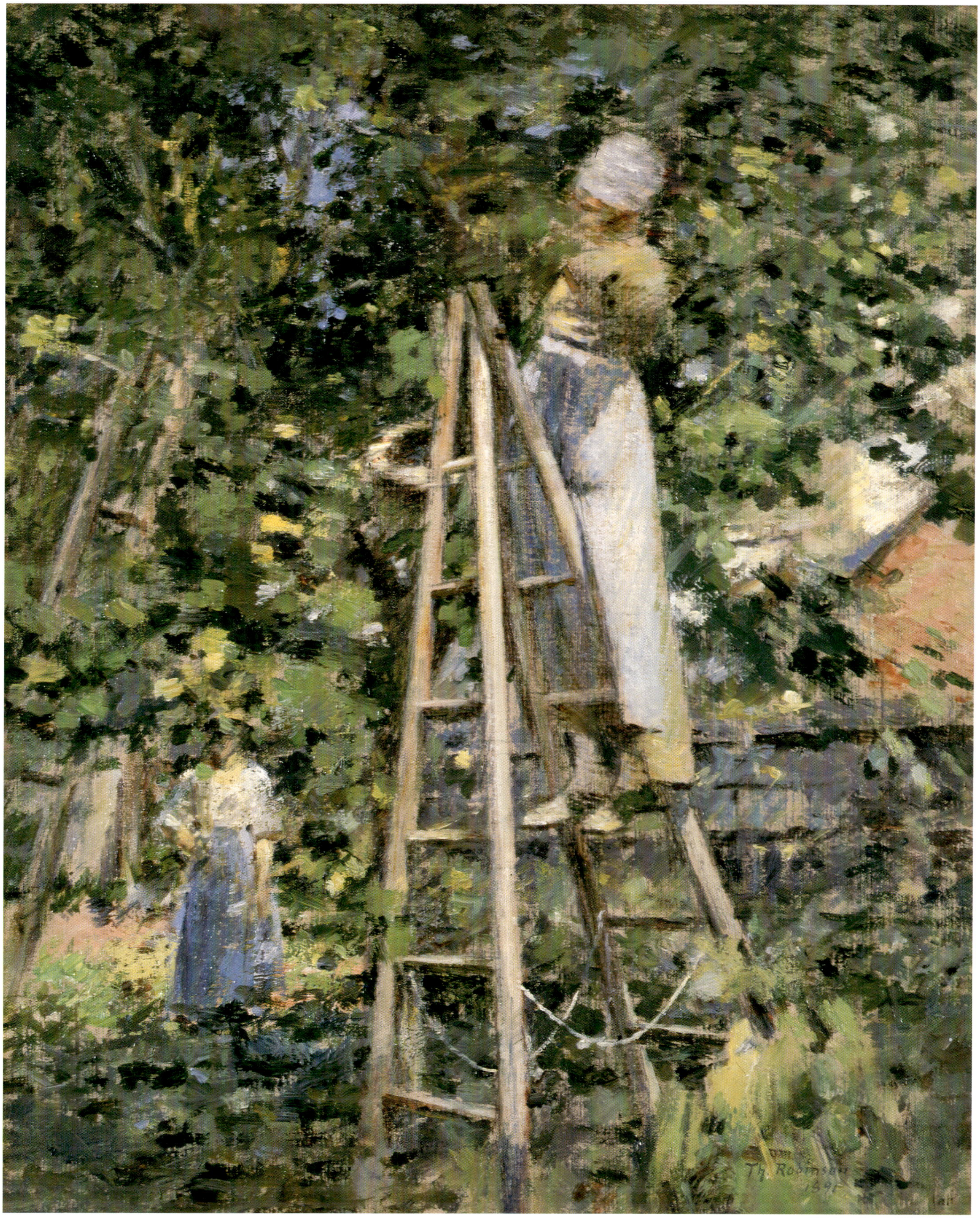

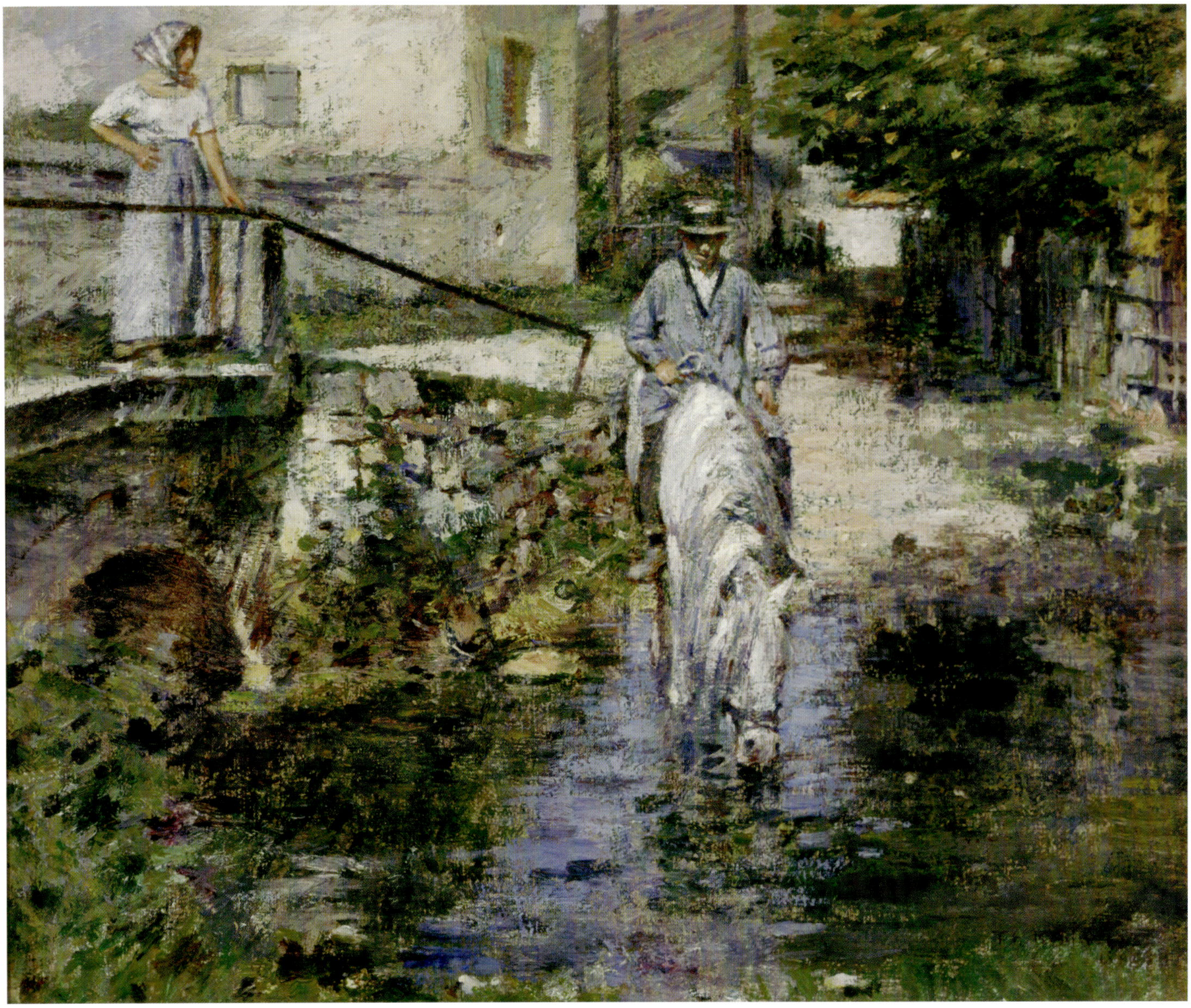

PLATE 8
Theodore Robinson
(American, 1852–1896)
Père Trognon and His Daughter at the Bridge
1891
Oil on canvas
18 ¼ × 22 ¹⁄₁₆ in. (46.4 × 56 cm)
Terra Foundation for American Art, Daniel J. Terra Collection
1988.29

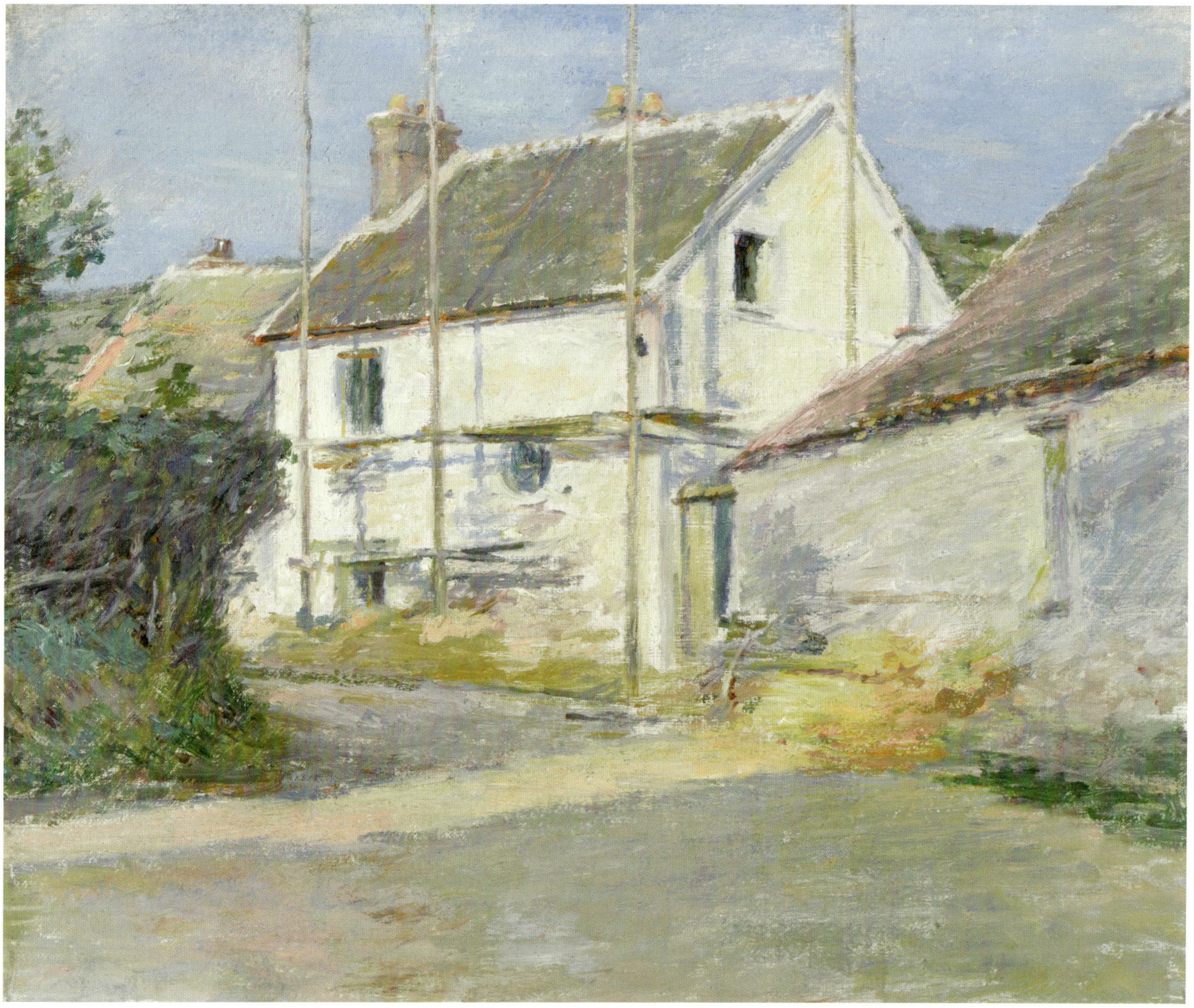

PLATE 9
Theodore Robinson
(American, 1852–1896)
House with Scaffolding, Giverny
1892
Oil on canvas
18 × 22 in. (45.7 × 55.9 cm)
North Carolina Museum of Art, Raleigh,
Gift of Mrs. Jacques Busbee
G.52.7.1

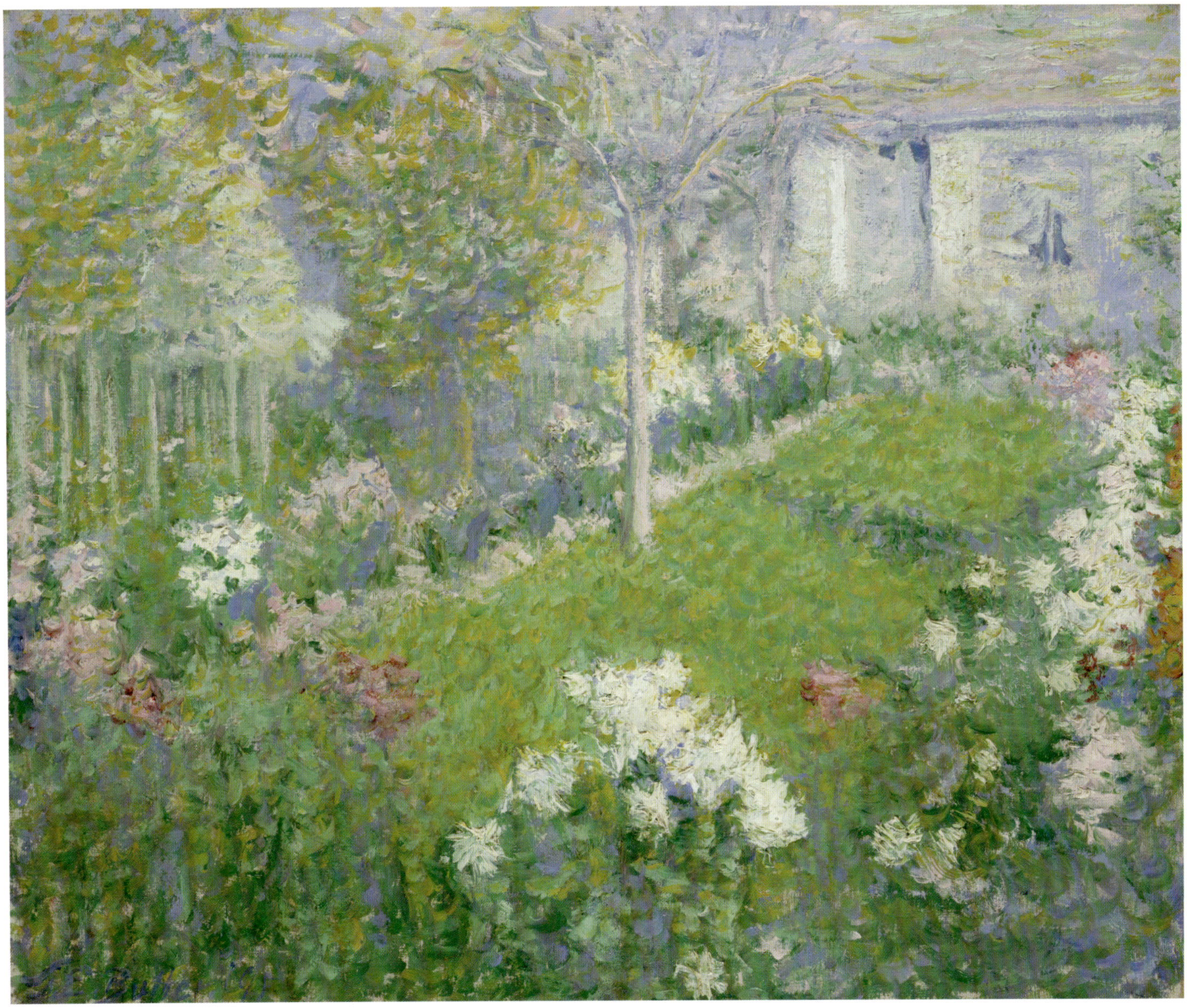

PLATE 10
Theodore Earl Butler
(American, 1861–1936)
Un Jardin, Maison Baptiste
1895
Oil on canvas
21 ⅛ × 25 ¾ in. (53.7 × 65.4 cm)
The Metropolitan Museum of Art, Gift of
Mr. and Mrs. Raymond J. Horowitz, 1976
1976.340.1

PLATE 11
Frederick Carl Frieseke
(American, 1874–1939)
Lilies
by 1911
Oil on canvas
25 ¾ × 32 ⅛ in. (65.4 × 81.6 cm)
Terra Foundation for American Art,
Daniel J. Terra Collection
1999.55

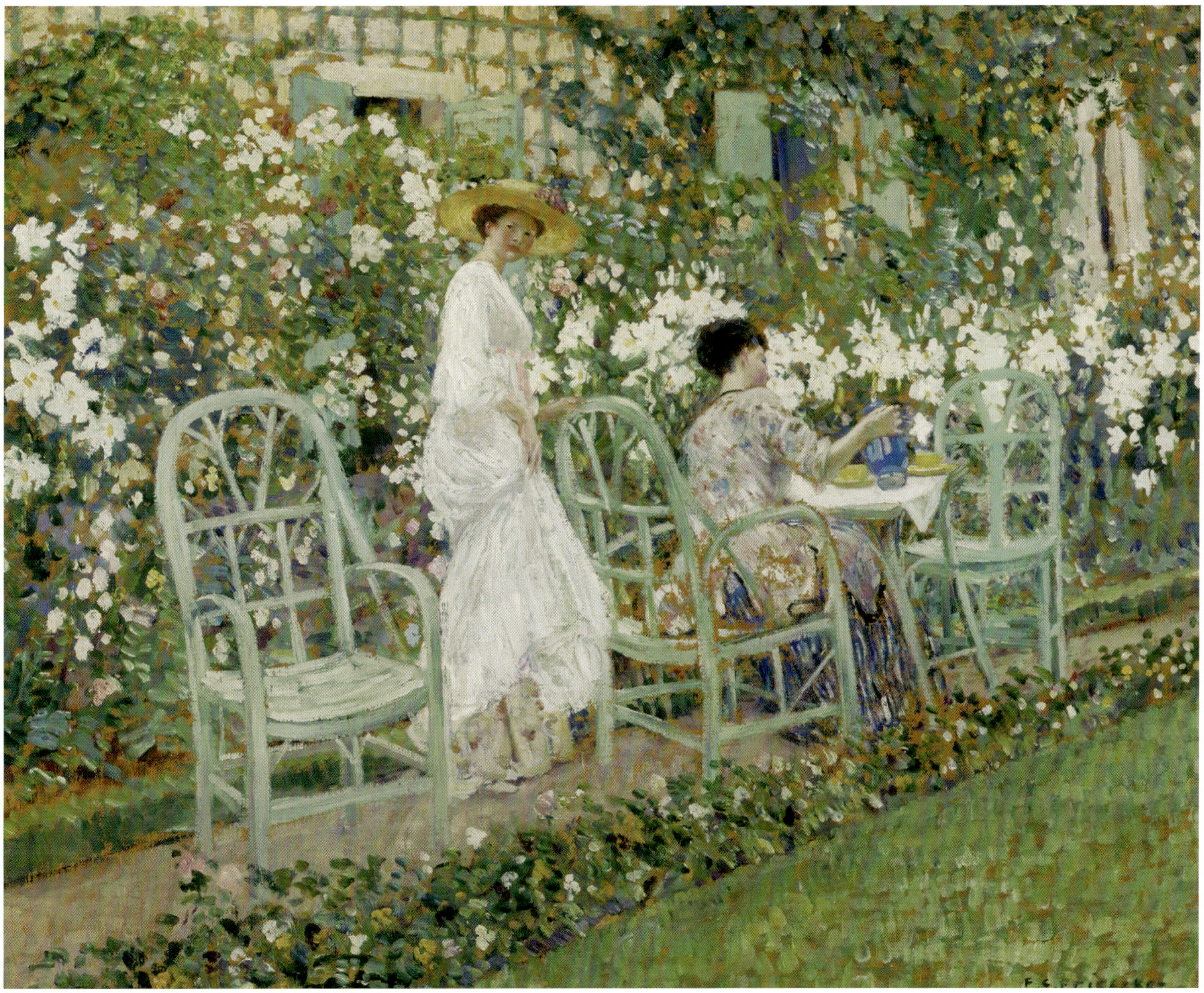

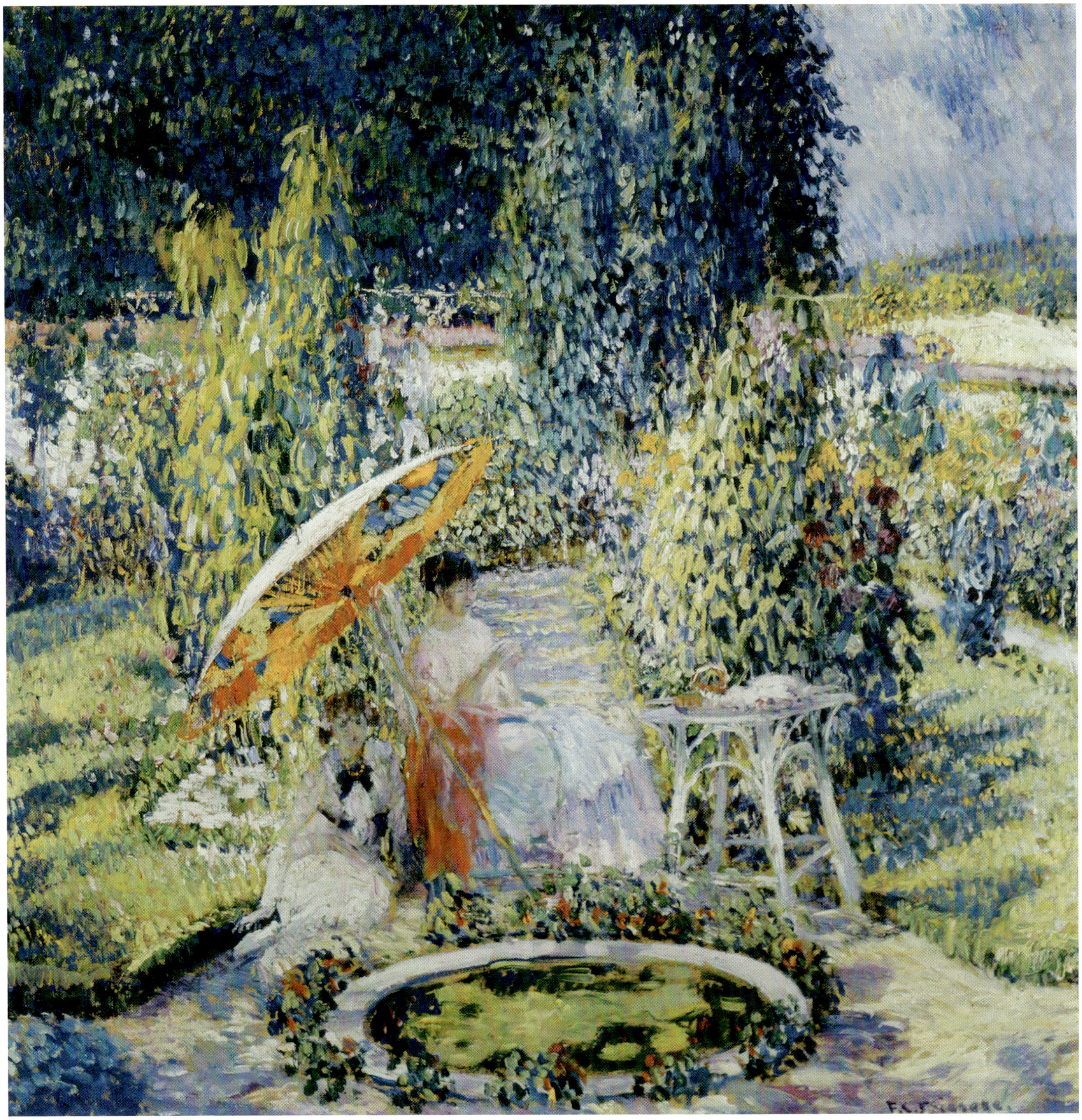

PLATE 12 (*facing page*)
Frederick Carl Frieseke
(American, 1874–1939)
The Garden Umbrella
by 1910
Oil on canvas
32 × 32 in. (81.3 × 81.3 cm)
Telfair Museums, Savannah, Georgia,
Bequest of Elizabeth Millar
(Mrs. Bernice Frost) Bullard
1942.7
Photo by Peter Harholdt

PLATE 13
Frederick Carl Frieseke
(American, 1874–1939)
The Hammock
by 1915
Oil on canvas
38 ⅝ × 51 ⅝ in. (98.1 × 131.1 cm)
Telfair Museums, Savannah, Georgia,
Museum purchase
1917.3
Photo by Peter Harholdt

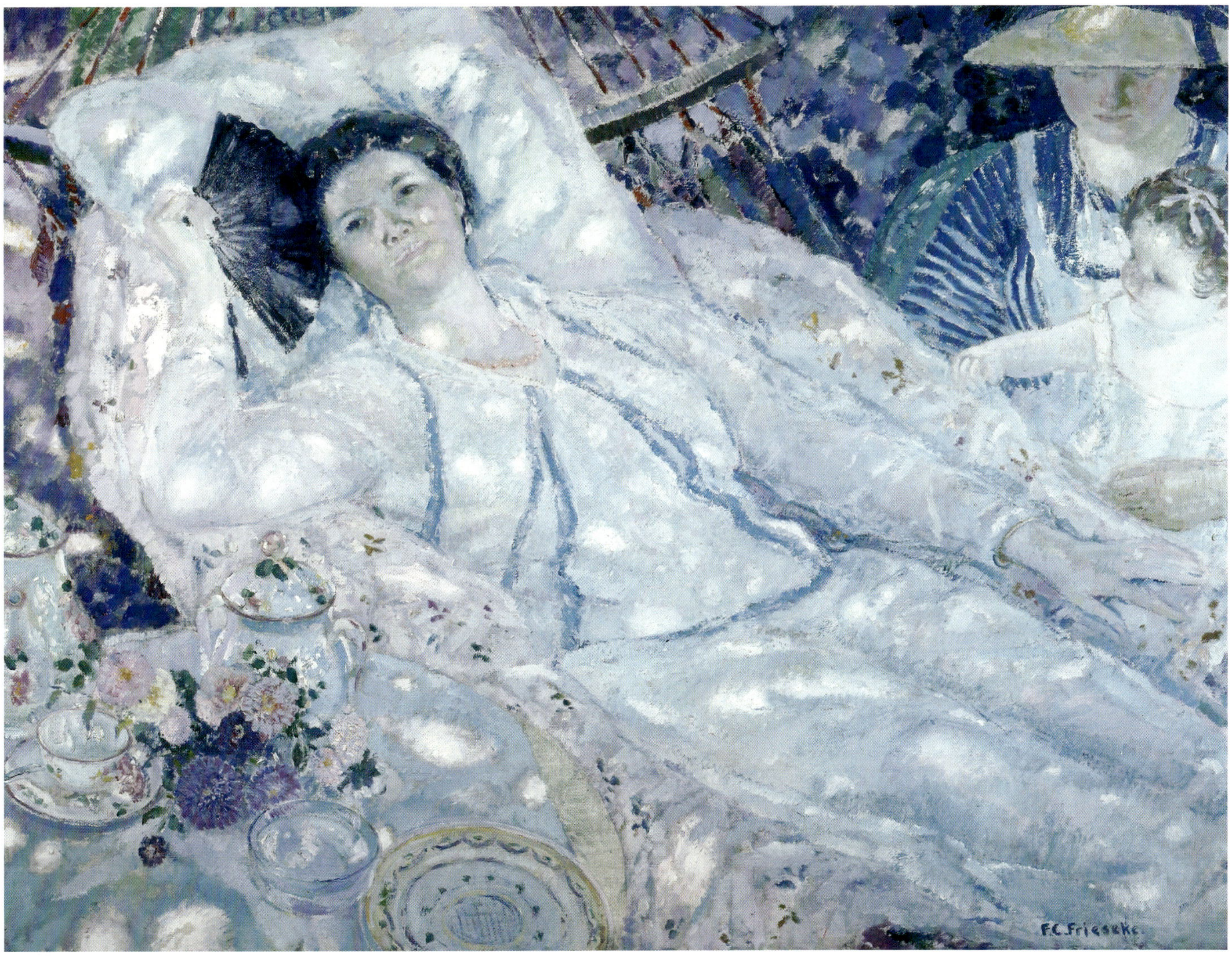

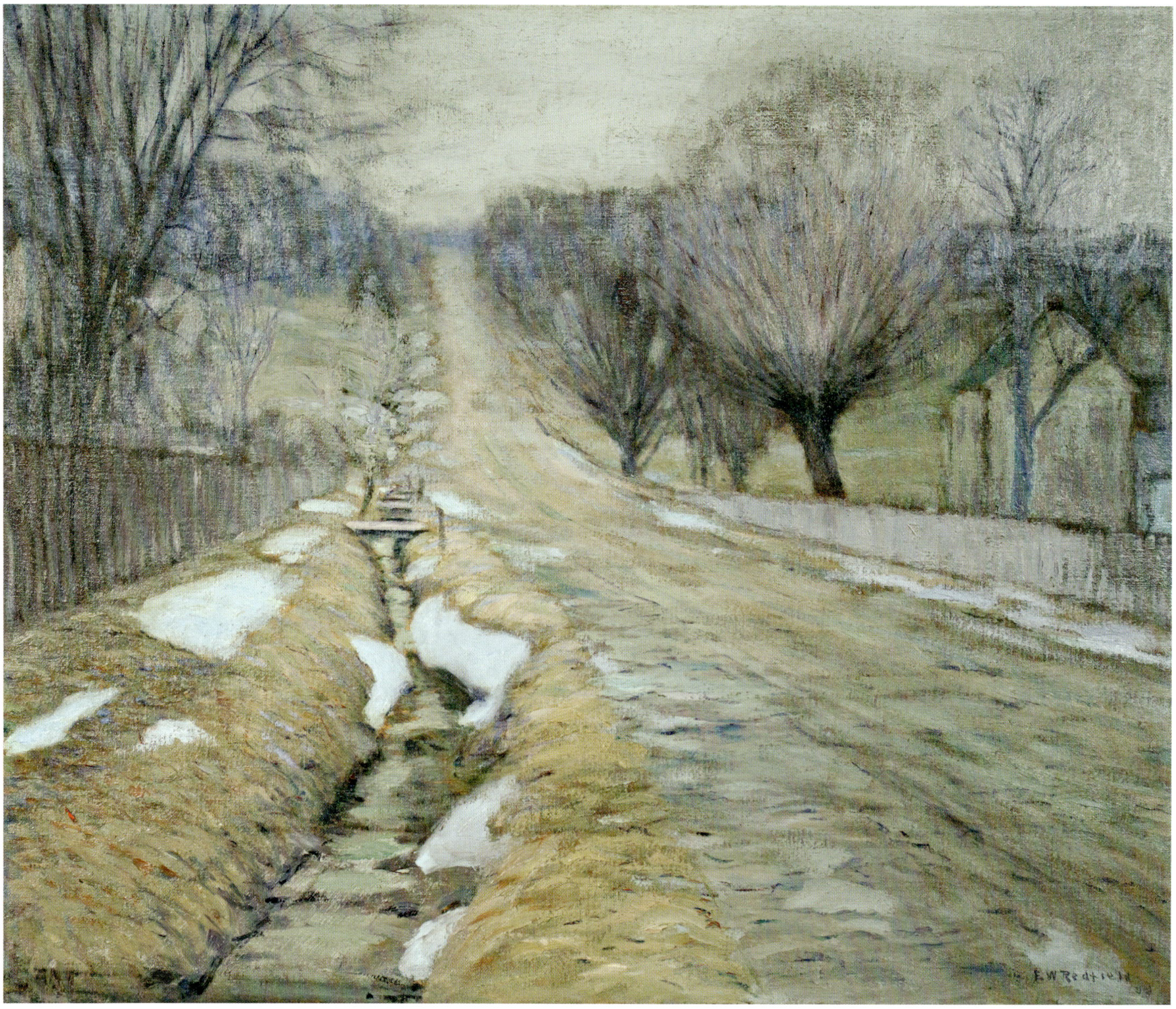

PLATE 14
Edward Redfield
(American, 1869–1965)
Bucks County Winter
1898
Oil on canvas
25 ¼ × 30 ¼ in. (64.2 × 76.9 cm)
Collection of The Art Museum at the University of Kentucky, Gift of Mrs. Mattie Schmidt Bowyer in memory of her husband Charles Henry Bowyer
1946.1.12

PLATE 15
Robert Vonnoh
(American, 1858–1933)
Winter Sun and Shadow
1890
Oil on canvas
18 × 24 in. (45.7 × 61 cm)
North Carolina Museum of Art, Raleigh,
Purchased with funds from the State of
North Carolina
72.1.5

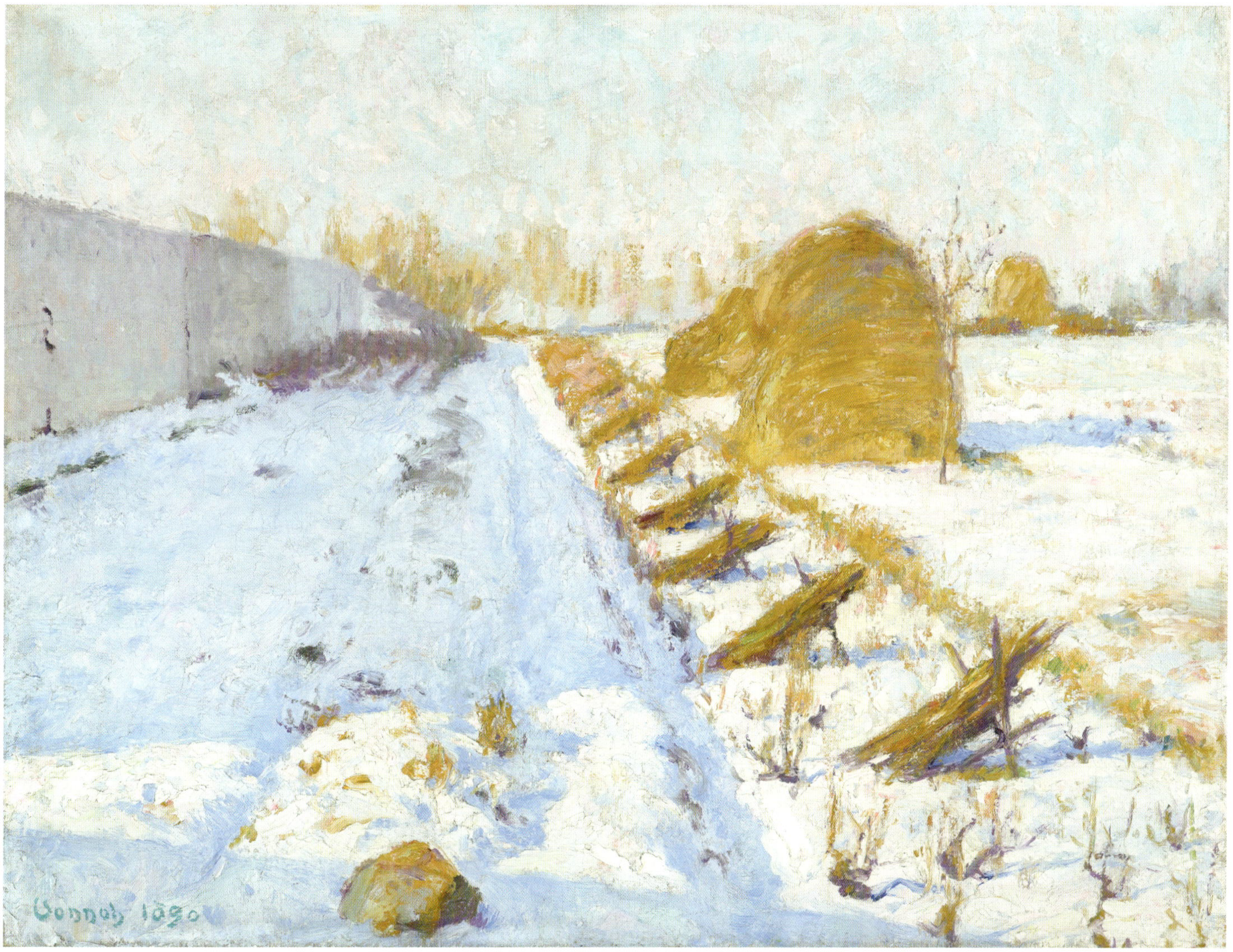

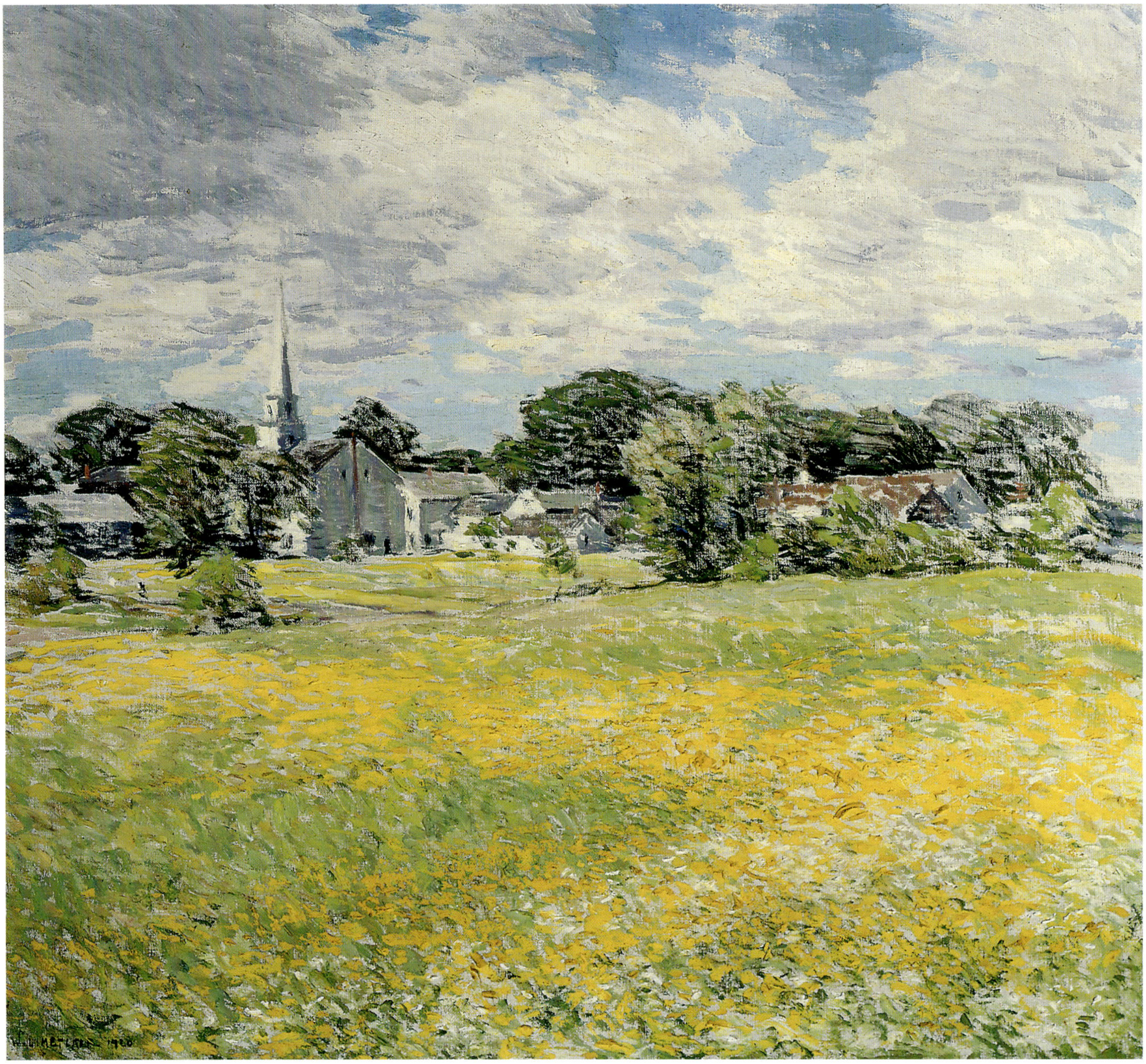

PLATE 16
Willard Leroy Metcalf
(American, 1858–1925)
Buttercup Time
1920
Oil on canvas
26 × 28 in. (66 × 71.1 cm)
Telfair Museums, Savannah, Georgia, Museum purchase 1926.1
Photo by Peter Harholdt

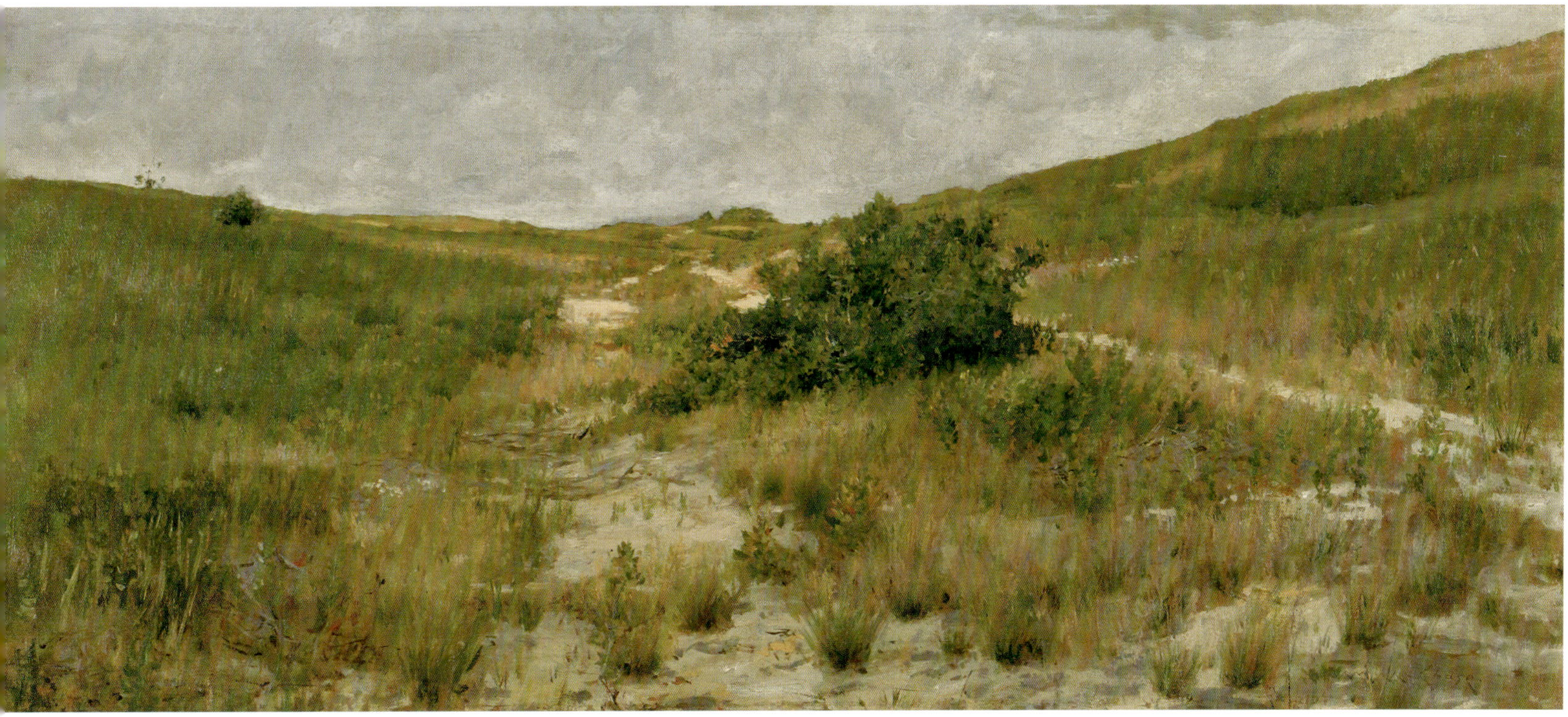

PLATE 17
William Merritt Chase
(American, 1849–1916)
Shinnecock Hills
c. 1892
Oil on canvas
20 × 46 ½ in. (50.8 × 118.1 cm)
Georgia Museum of Art, University of Georgia, Eva Underhill Holbrook Memorial Collection of American Art; Gift of Alfred H. Holbrook
1945.14

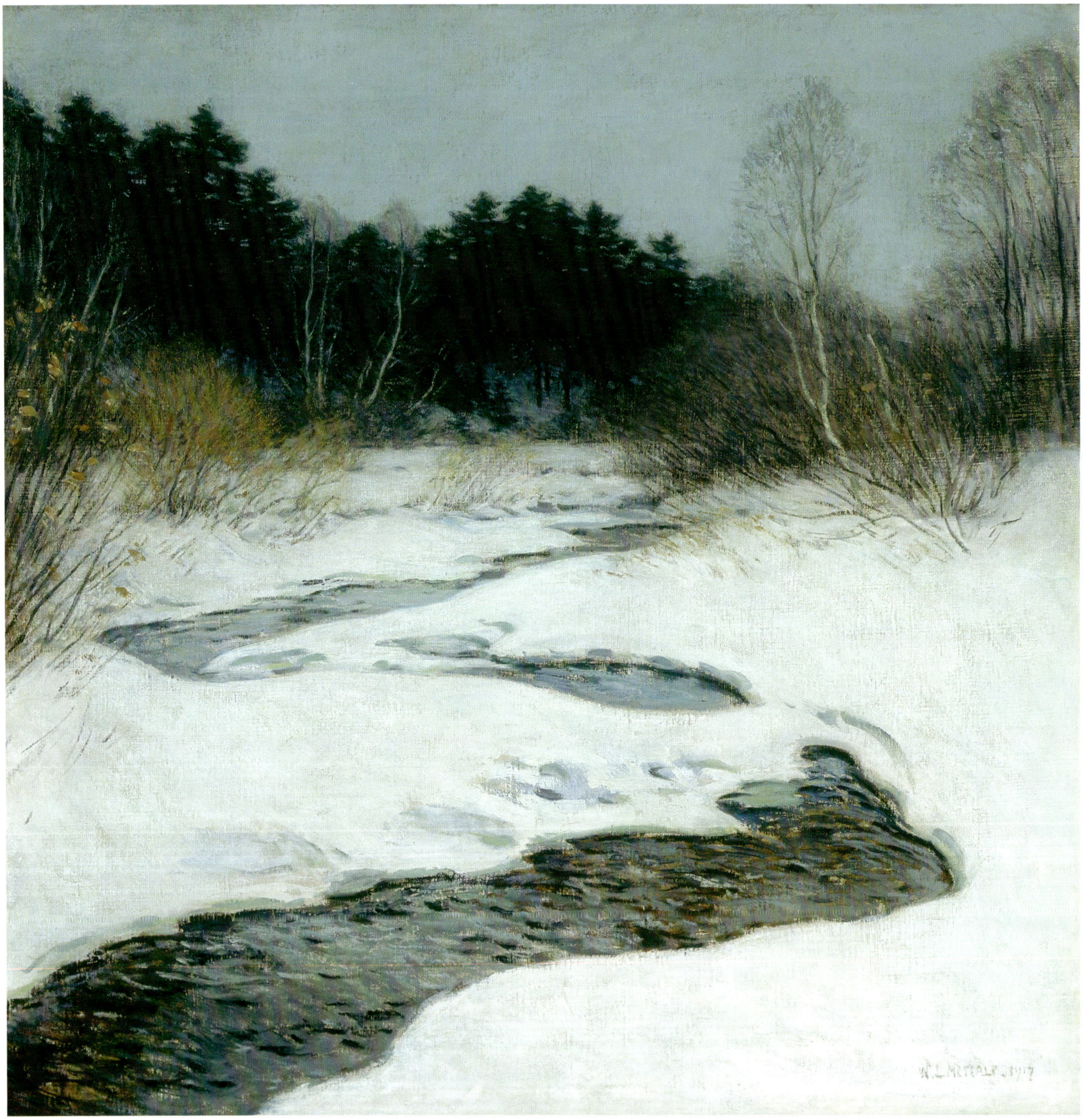

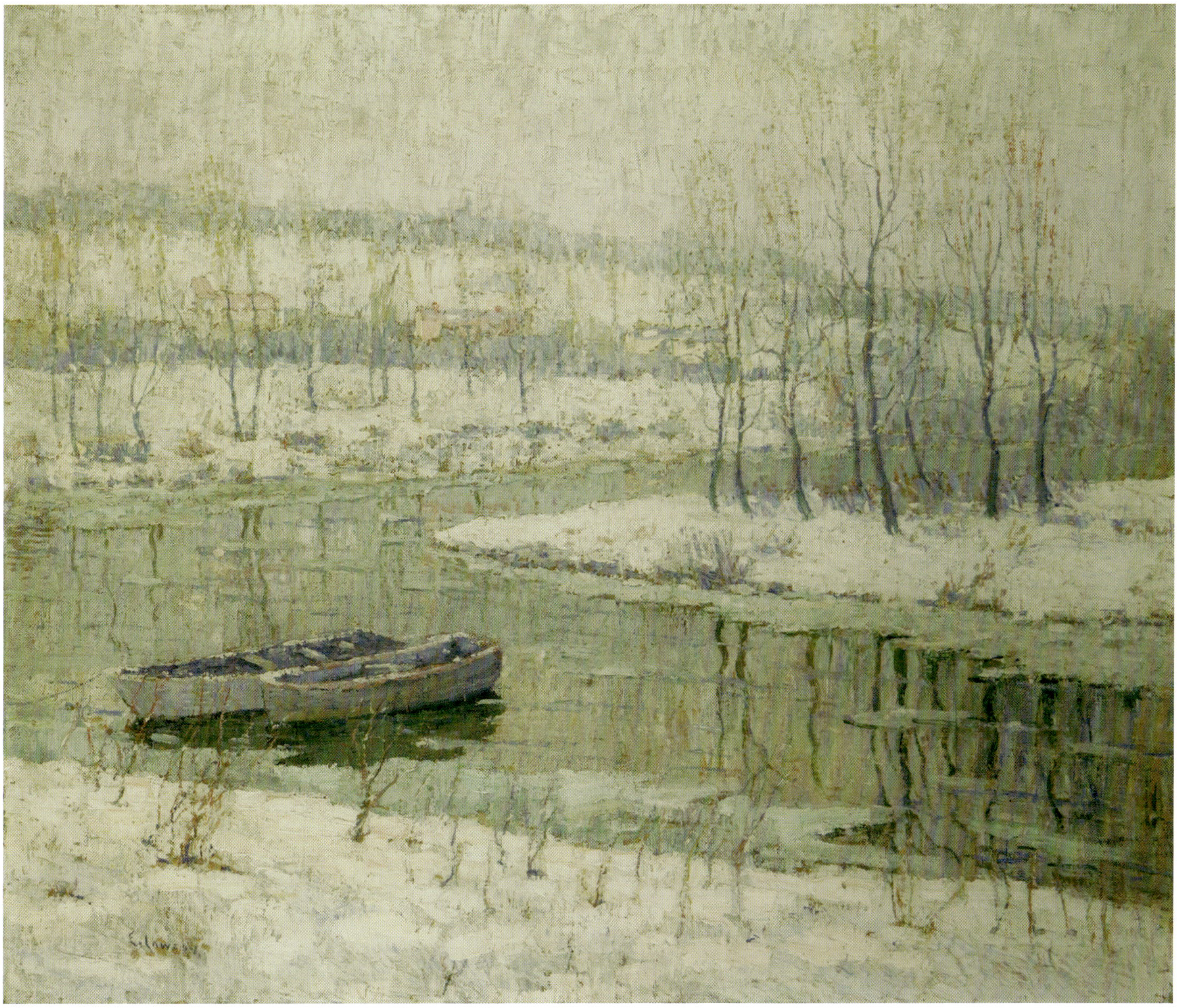

PLATE 18 (*facing page*)
Willard Leroy Metcalf
(American, 1858–1925)
The Thawing Brook
1917
Oil on canvas
36 ¼ × 36 in. (92.1 × 91.4 cm)
The Columbus Museum, Georgia, Gift of Jack Melchers Passailaigue, Sr., in memory of his late devoted wife, Mary Flournoy Passailaigue

PLATE 19
Ernest Lawson
(American, born in Canada, 1873–1939)
Spring Thaw
c. 1910
Oil on canvas
25 ¼ × 30 ⅛ in. (64.1 × 76.5 cm)
Terra Foundation for American Art, Daniel J. Terra Collection
1999.85

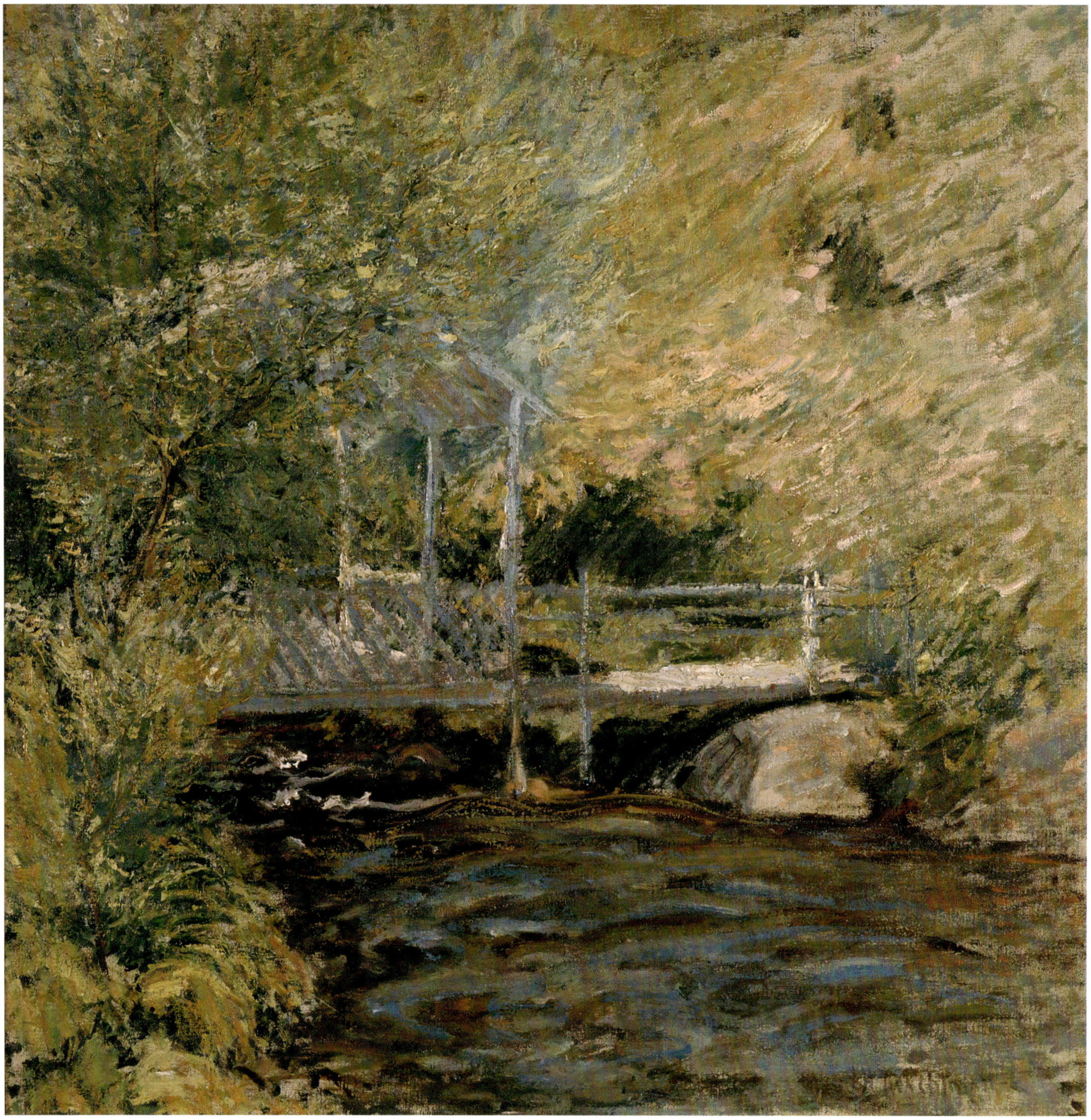

PLATE 20
John Henry Twachtman
(American, 1853–1902)
The Little White Bridge
c. 1896
Oil on canvas
24 5/8 × 24 5/8 in. (62.6 × 62.6 cm)
Georgia Museum of Art, University of Georgia, Eva Underhill Holbrook Memorial Collection of American Art; Gift of Alfred H. Holbrook
1945.90

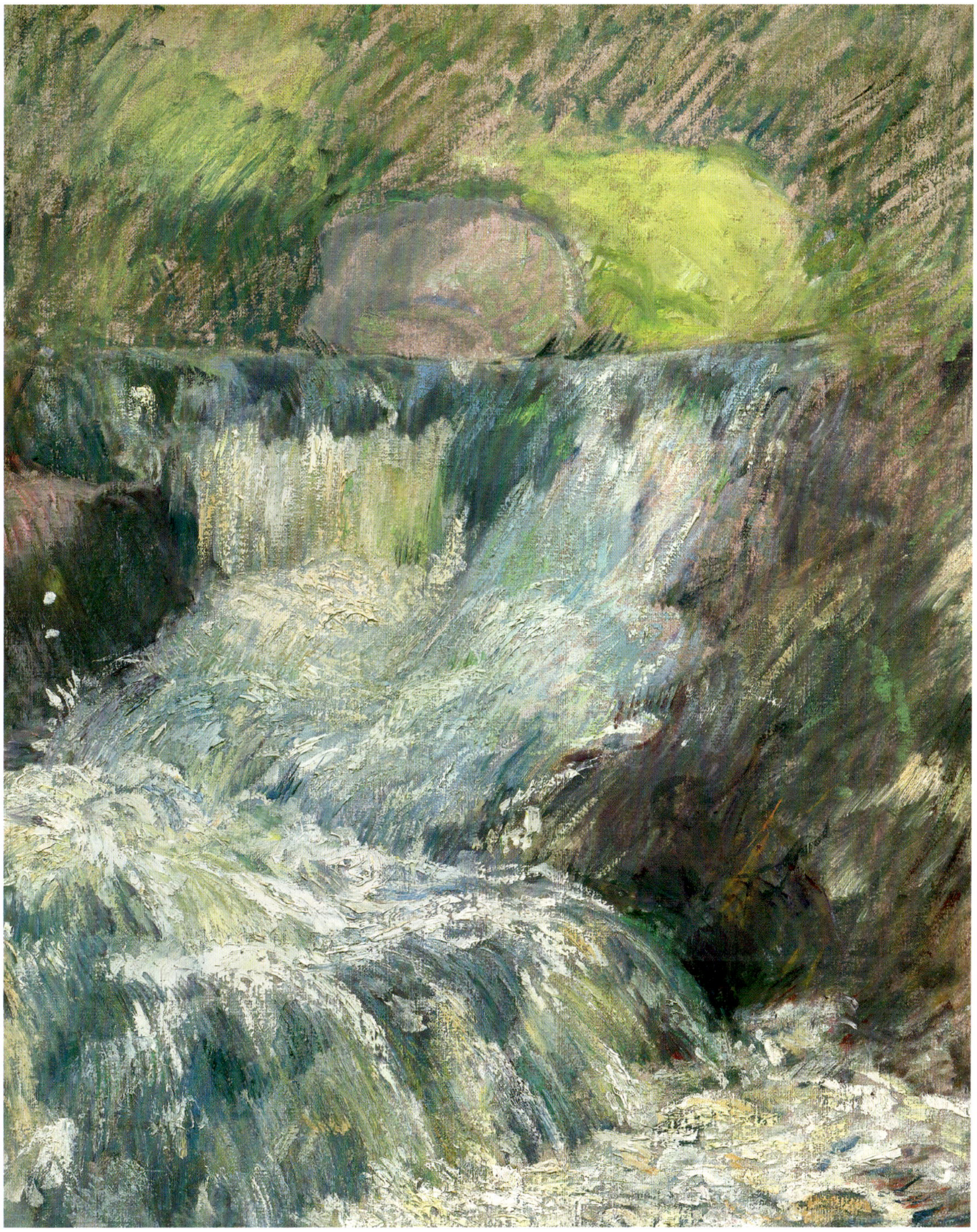

PLATE 21
John Henry Twachtman
(American, 1853–1902)
Horseneck Falls
c. 1900
Oil on canvas
30 × 25 in. (76.2 × 63.5 cm)
The Columbus Museum, Georgia,
Museum purchase made possible by
the Ella E. Kirven Charitable Lead
Trust for Acquisitions

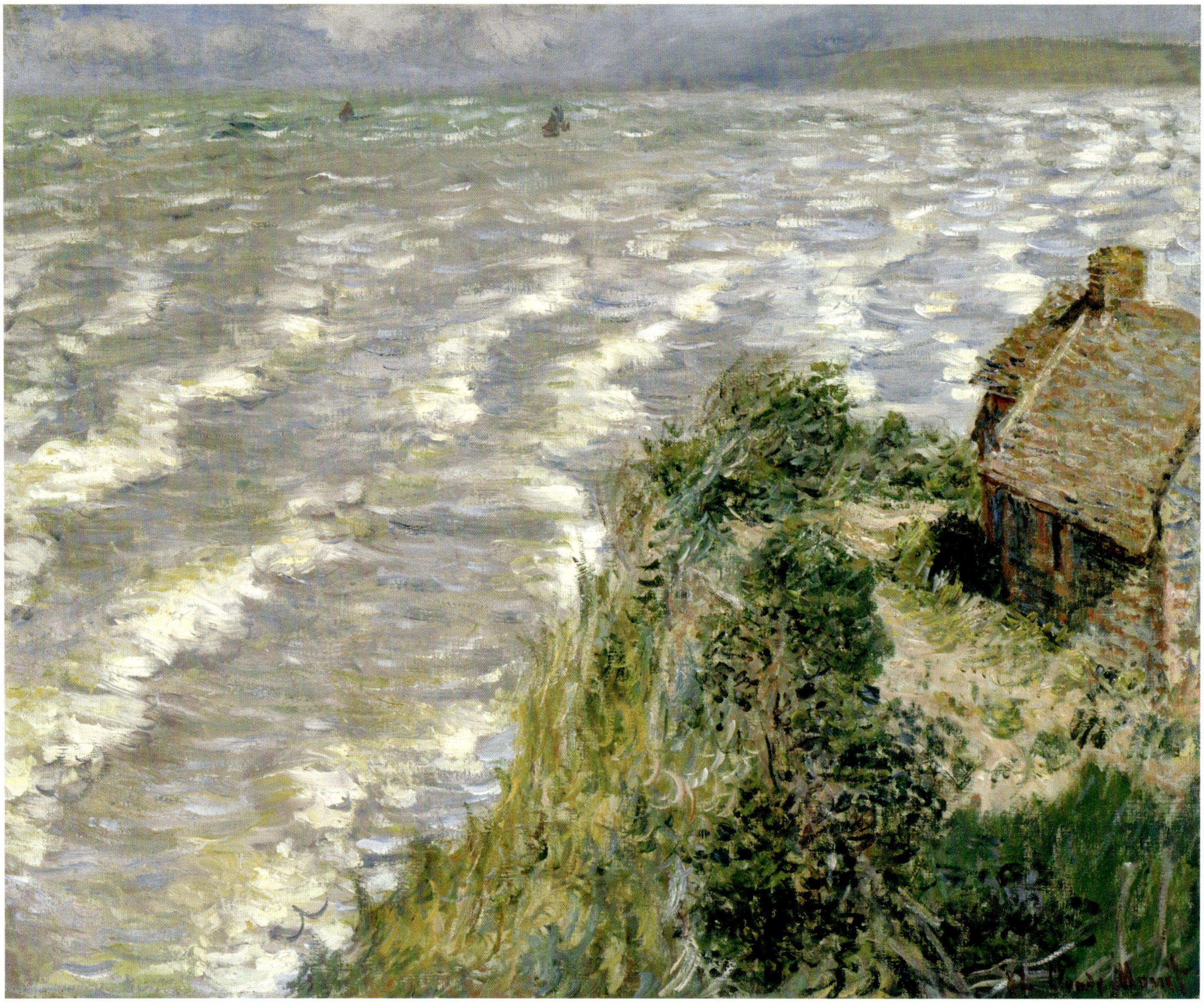

PLATE 22
Claude Monet
(French, 1840–1926)
Marée montante à Pourville
(Rising Tide at Pourville)
1882
Oil on canvas
26 × 32 in. (66 × 81.3 cm)
Brooklyn Museum, Gift of
Mrs. Horace O. Havemeyer
41.1260

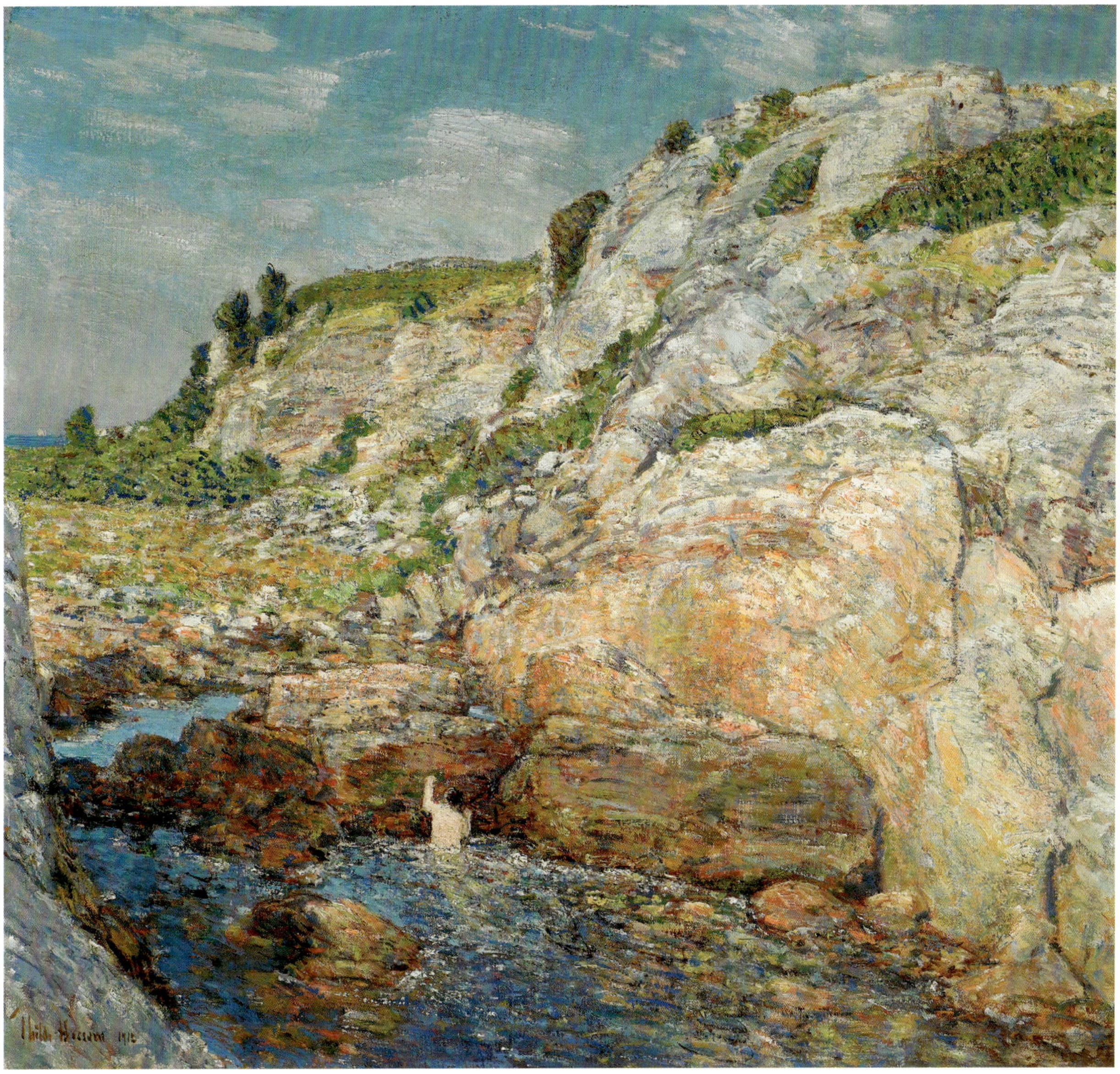

PLATE 23
Frederick Childe Hassam
(American, 1859–1935)
Northeast Gorge at Appledore
1912
Oil on canvas
24 ½ × 26 ½ in. (62.2 × 67.3 cm)
Samuel P. Harn Museum of Art, University of Florida, Gainesville, Museum purchase by exchange, gift of Louise H. Courtelis with additional funds provided by Michael A. Singer
2004.22

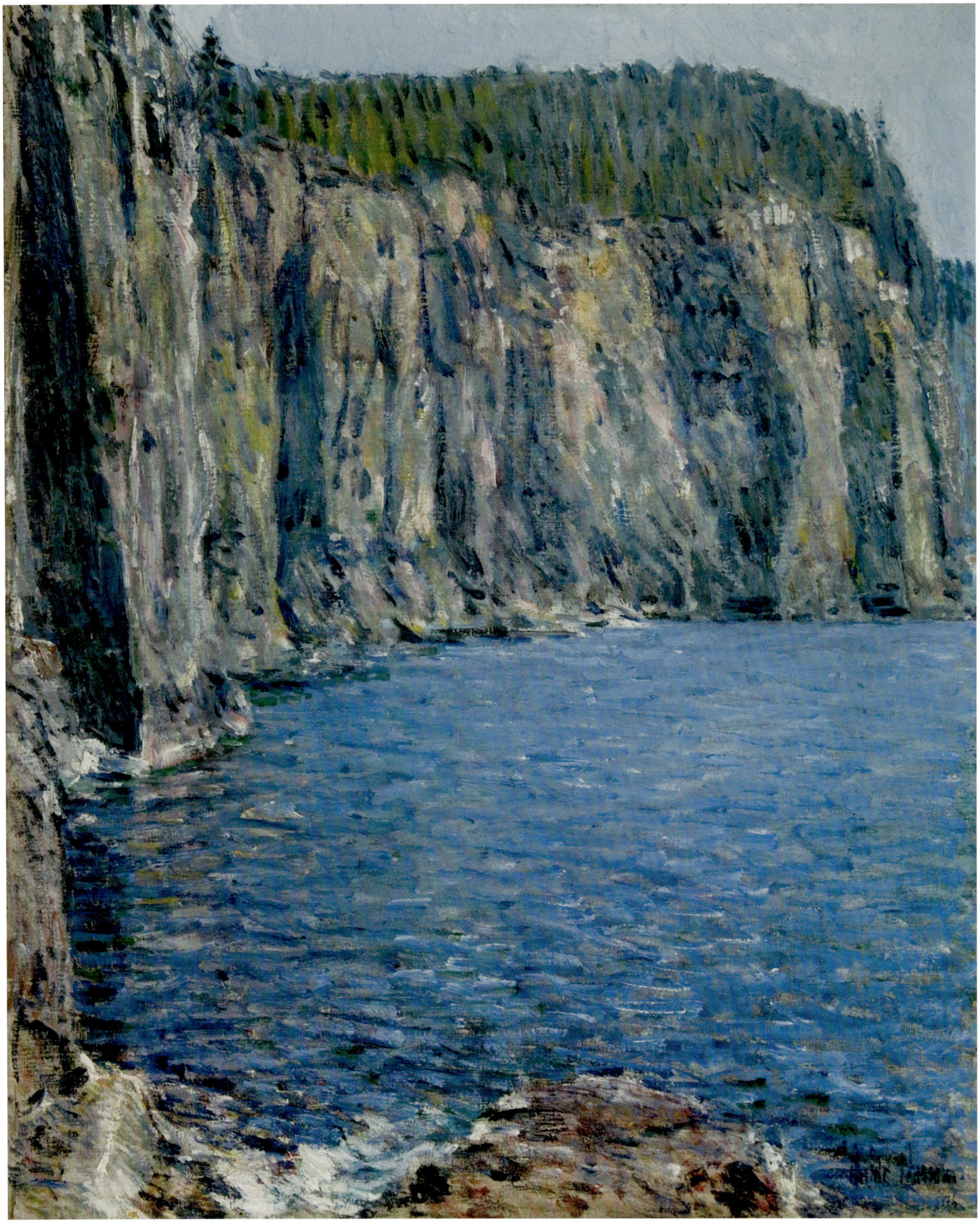

PLATE 24 (*facing page*)
Frederick Childe Hassam
(American, 1859–1935)
Ironbound
1896
Oil on canvas
30 × 25 in. (76.2 × 63.5 cm)
Cornell Fine Arts Museum, Rollins College, Gift of Laura and Sugurd Hersloff in memory of their father, Nils Hersloff
1957.003.P

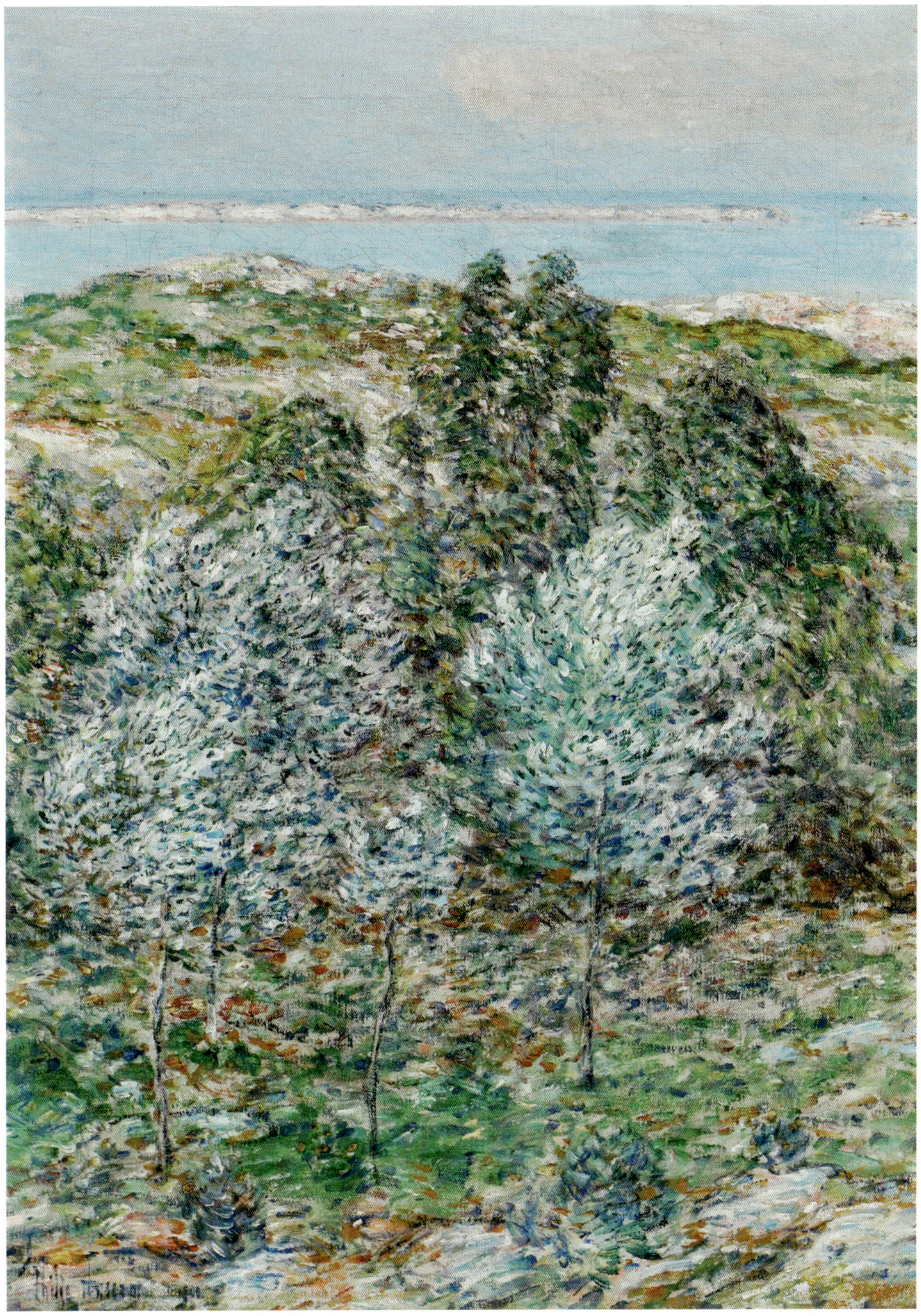

PLATE 25
Frederick Childe Hassam
(American, 1859–1935)
Springtime Vision
1900
Oil on canvas
21 ½ × 15 ½ in. (54.6 × 39.4 cm)
Samuel P. Harn Museum of Art, University of Florida, Gainesville, Bequest of Ruth P. Phillips
2005.23.1

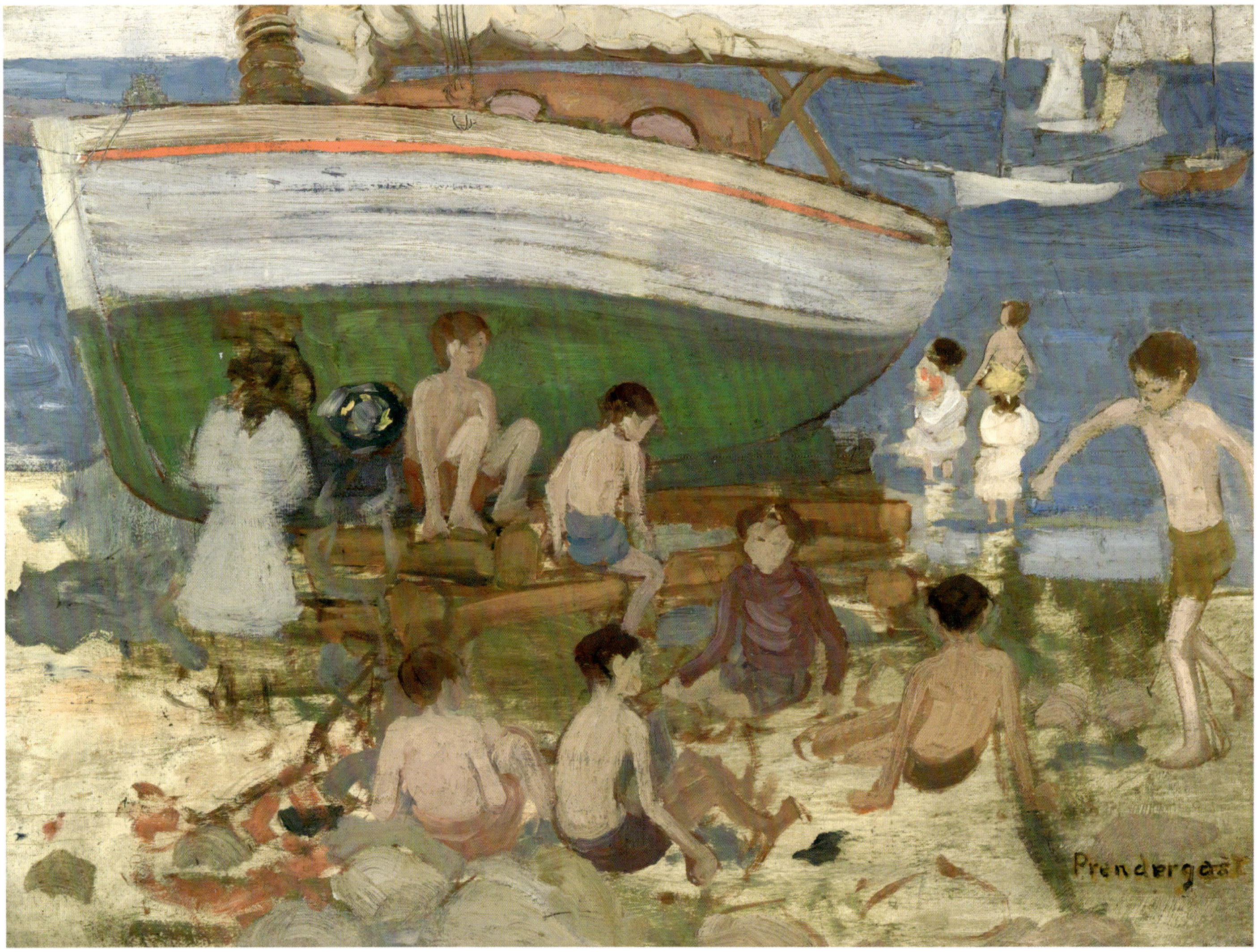

PLATE 26
Maurice Brazil Prendergast
(American, born in Canada, 1858–1924)
Low Tide
c. 1895–1897
Oil on panel
13 ½ × 18 in. (34.3 × 45.7 cm)
Williams College Museum of Art, Williamstown, MA, Gift of Mrs. Charles Prendergast
86.18.40

PLATE 27 (*facing page*)
Maurice Brazil Prendergast
(American, born in Canada, 1858–1924)
Surf, Nantasket
c. 1900–1905
Watercolor and pencil on paper
15 ⅜ × 11 ⅛ in. (39.1 × 28.3 cm)
Williams College Museum of Art, Williamstown, MA, Gift of Mrs. Charles Prendergast
86.18.60

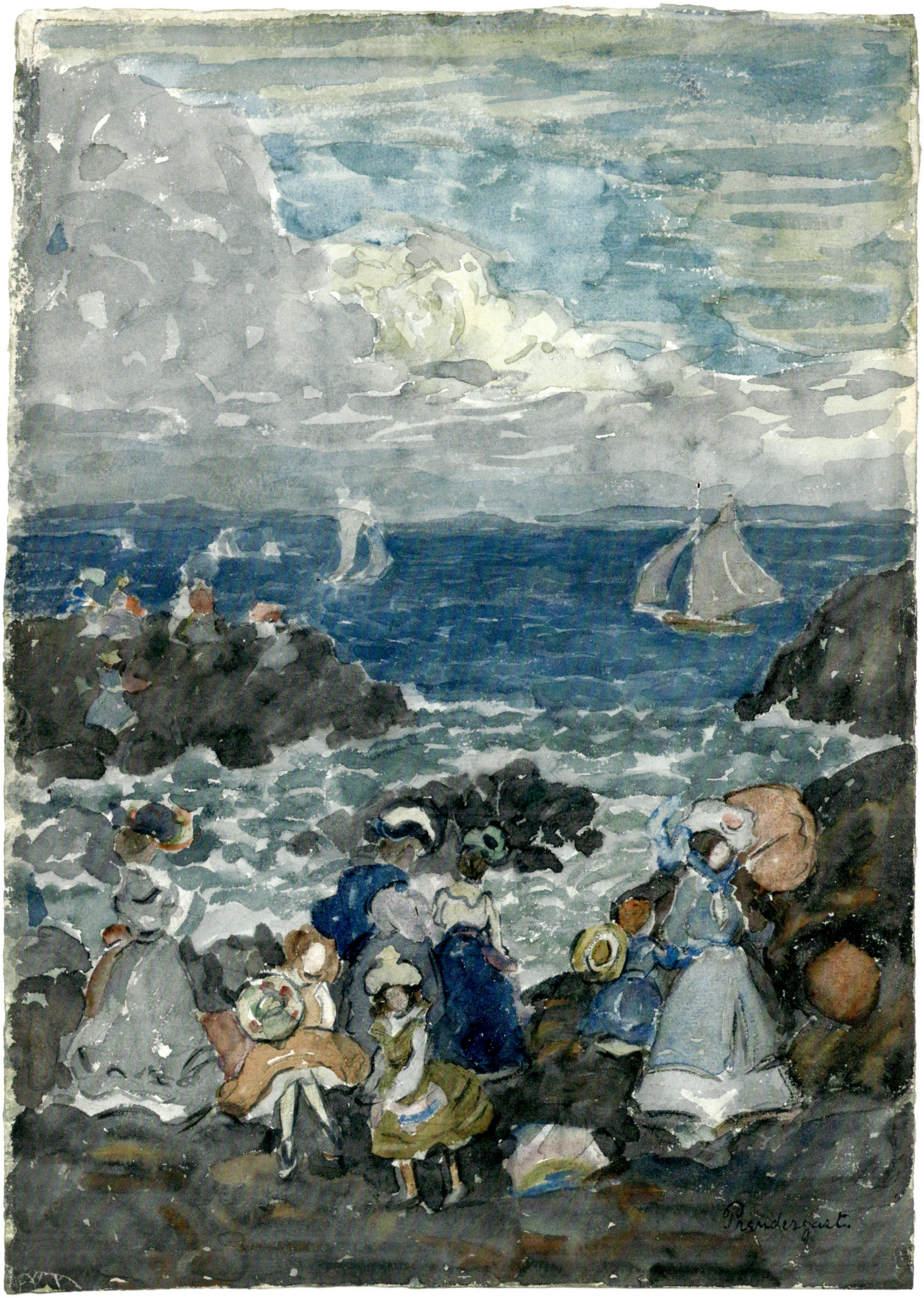
Prendergast.

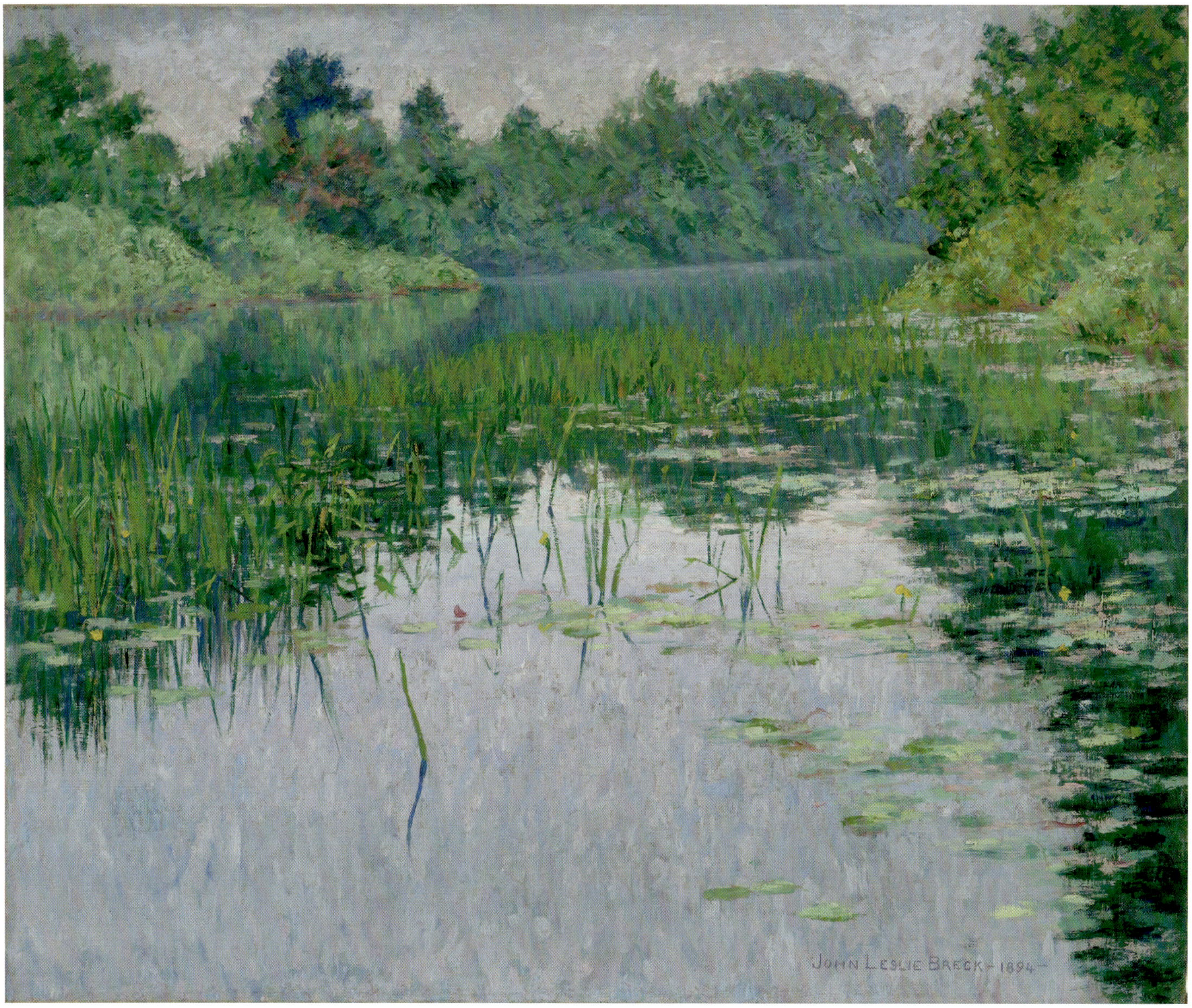

PLATE 28
John Leslie Breck
(American, born in China, 1860–1899)
Grey Day on the Charles
1894
Oil on canvas
18 × 22 in. (45.7 × 55.9 cm)
Virginia Museum of Fine Arts, Richmond
J. Harwood and Louise B. Cochrane Fund
for American Art
90.151
Photo: Katherine Wetzel

PLATE 29
Claude Monet
(French, 1840–1926)
Bridge at Argenteuil on a Gray Day
c. 1876
Oil on canvas
24 × 31 ⅝ in. (61 × 80.3 cm)
Courtesy National Gallery of Art, Washington, D.C., Ailsa Mellon Bruce Collection
1970.17.44

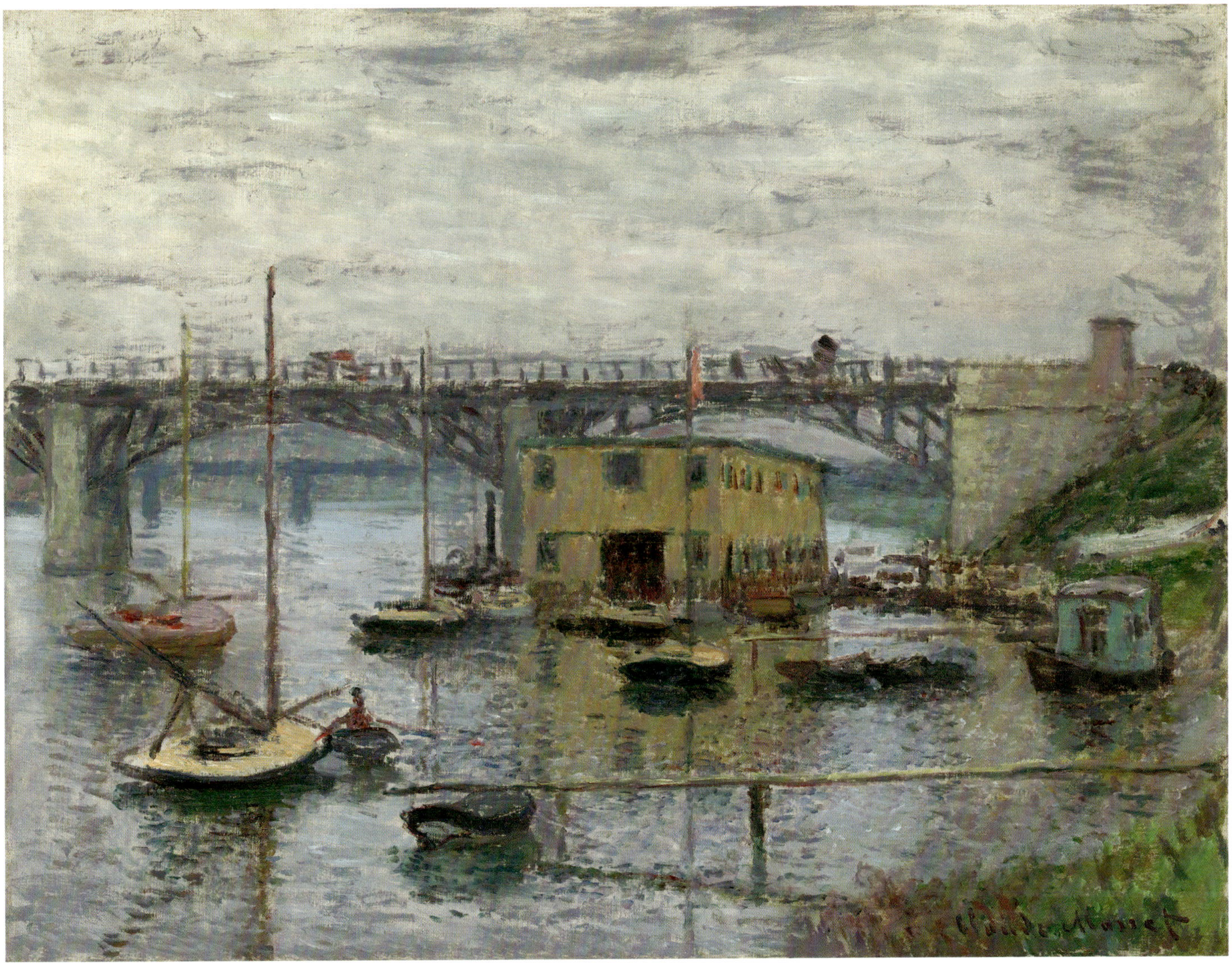

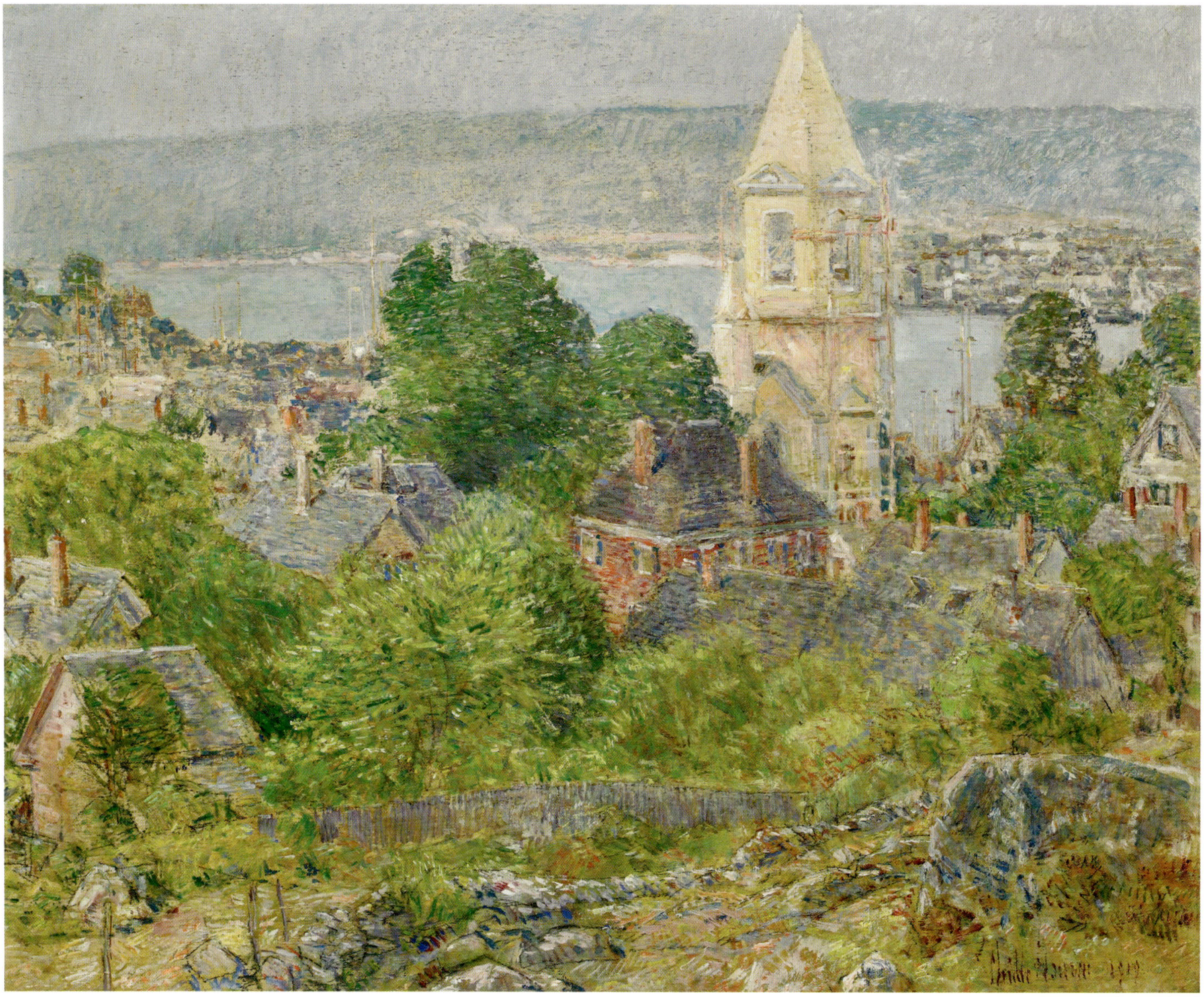

PLATE 30
Frederick Childe Hassam
(American, 1859–1935)
Gloucester
1919
Oil on panel
12 ⅝ × 16 in. (32.1 × 40.6 cm)
Samuel P. Harn Museum of Art,
University of Florida, Gainesville,
Gift from the Carol & Stephen Shey
Collection
2004.41

PLATE 31 (*facing page*)
Gari Melchers
(American, 1860–1932)
Bryant Park (Twilight)
c. 1906
Oil on canvas
34 ⅛ × 29 ½ in. (86.7 × 74.9 cm)
Gari Melchers Home and Studio,
University of Mary Washington

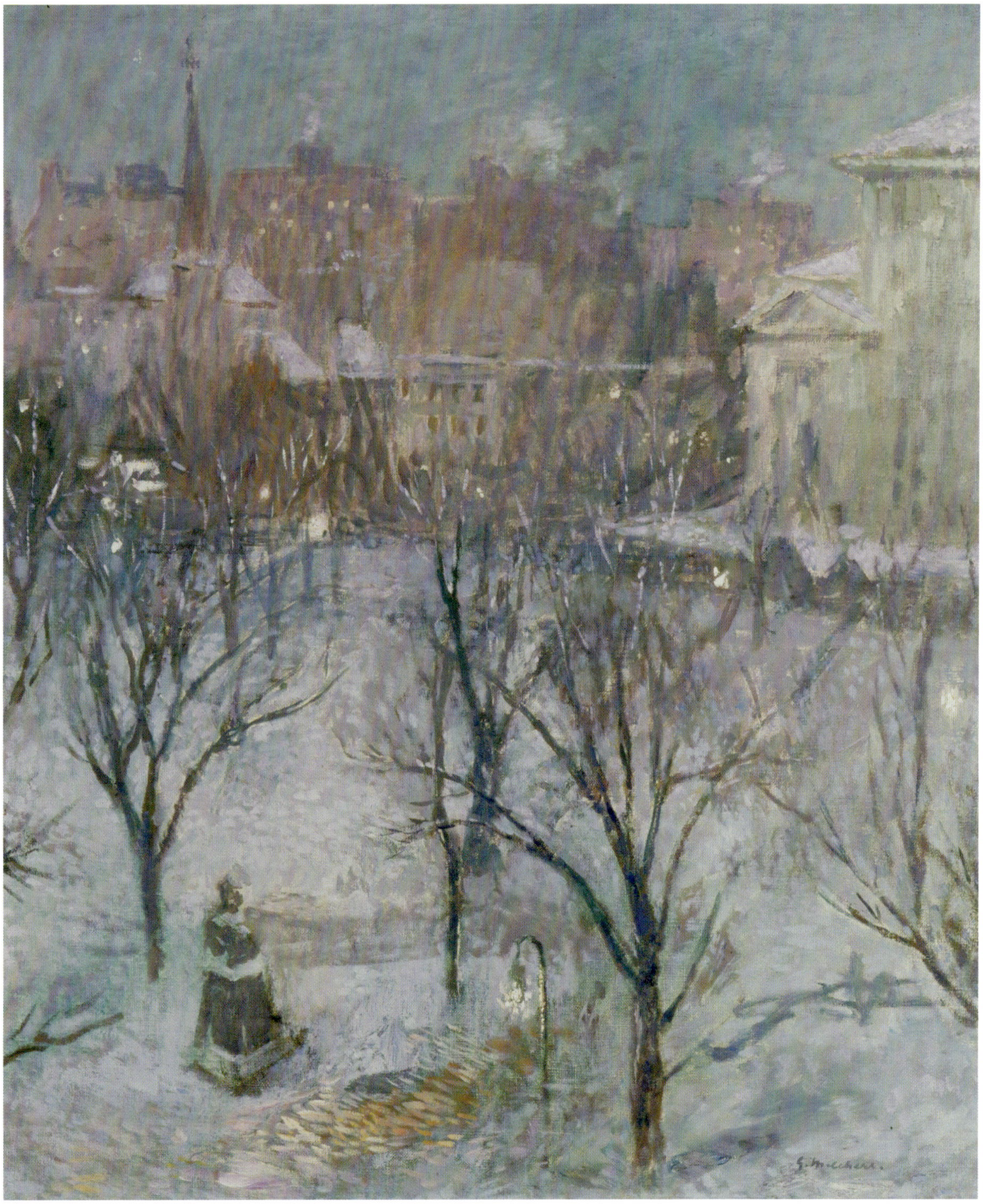

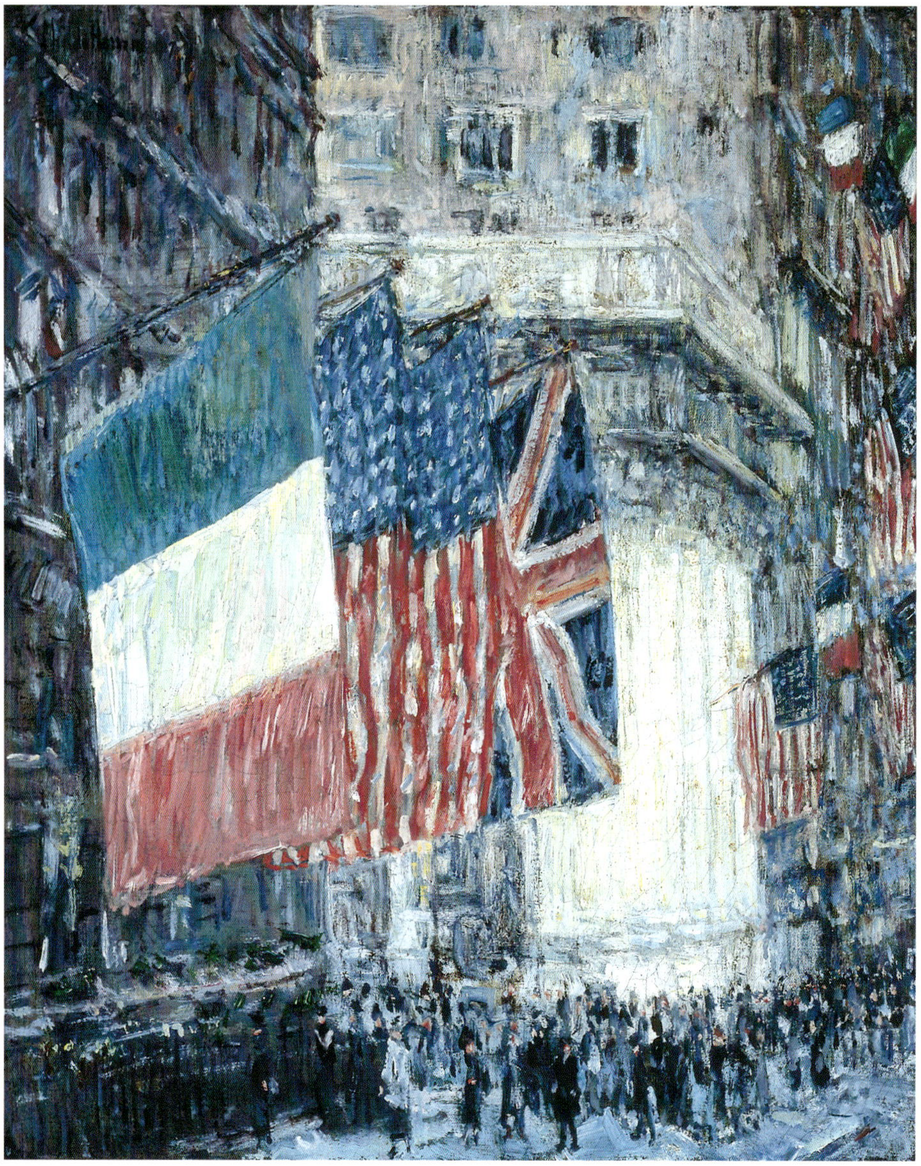

PLATE 32
Frederick Childe Hassam
(American, 1859–1935)
Avenue of the Allies
1917
Oil on canvas
18 ½ × 15 ⅛ in. (47 × 38.4 cm)
Telfair Museums, Savannah, Georgia,
Bequest of Elizabeth Millar
(Mrs. Bernice Frost) Bullard
1942.11
Photo by Peter Harholdt

PLATE 33
Guy C. Wiggins
(American, 1883–1962)
Columbus Circle, Winter
1911
Oil on canvas
33 ½ × 40 ¼ in. (85.1 × 102.1 cm)
Smithsonian American Art Museum,
Gift of William T. Evans
1911.4.2

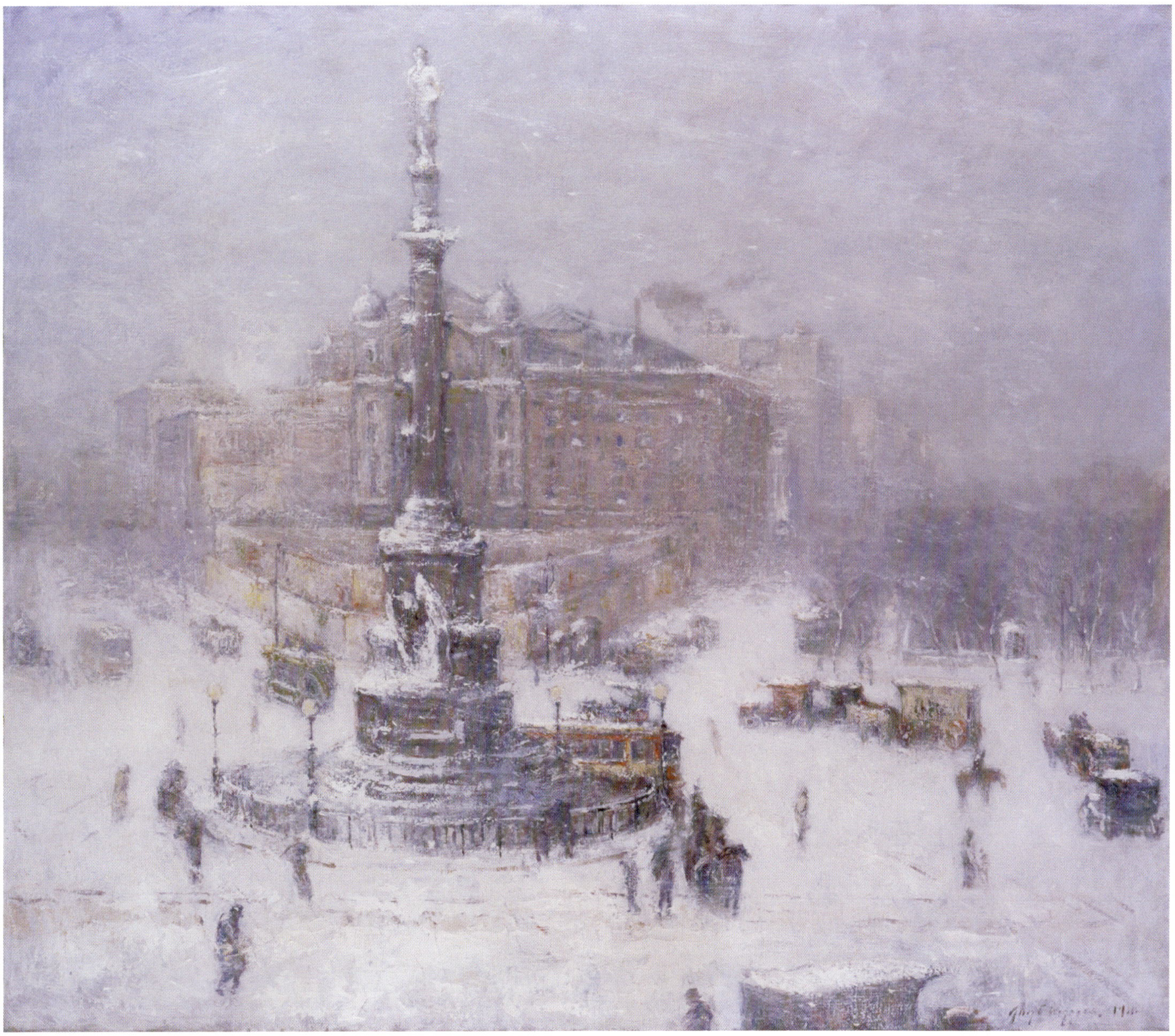

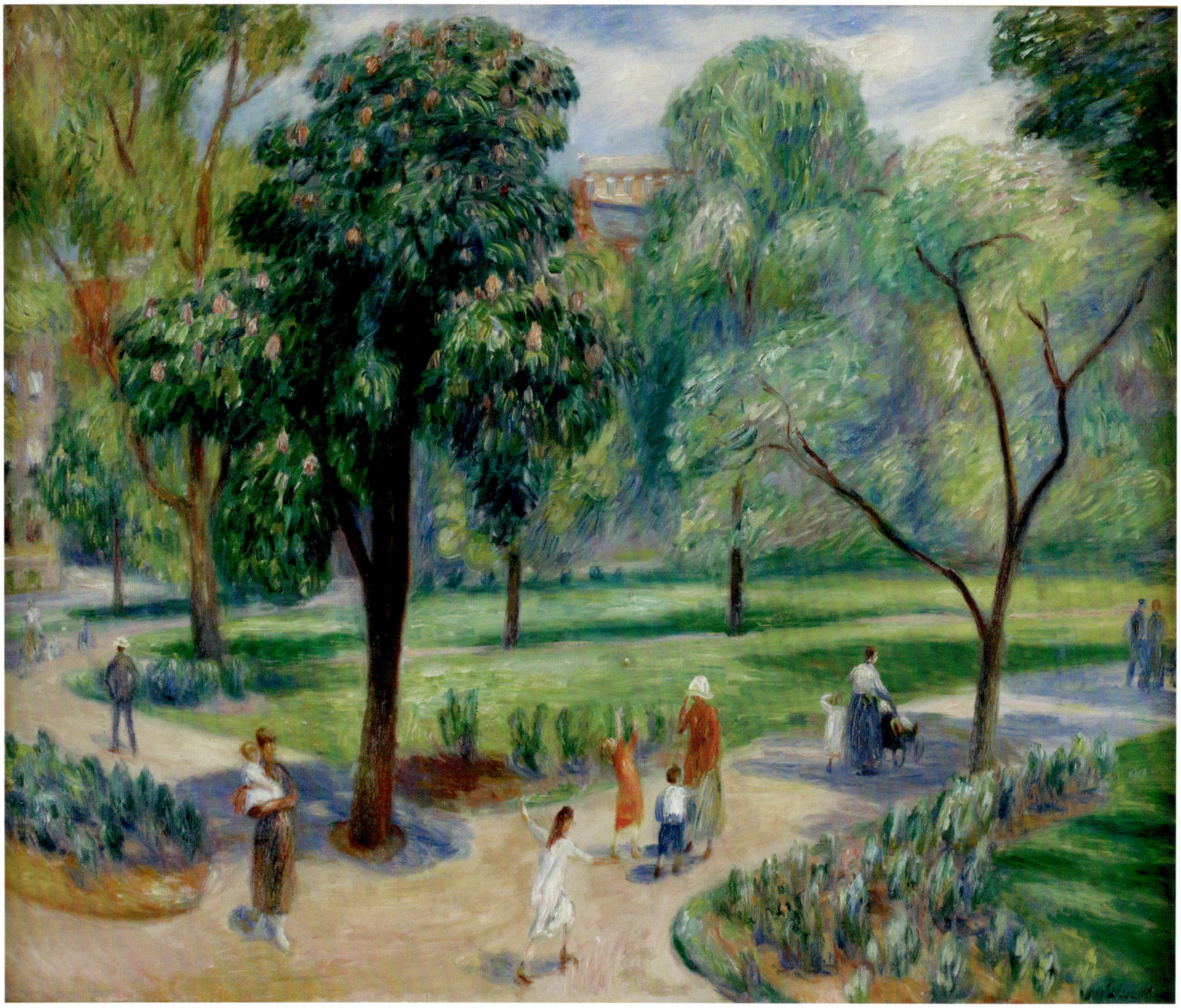

PLATE 34
William Glackens
(American, 1870–1938)
The Horse Chestnut Tree, Washington Square
c. 1915–1919
Oil on canvas
26 × 31 ¾ in. (66 × 80.6 cm)
Hunter Museum of American Art, Chattanooga, Tennessee, Museum purchase
1995.42
Photo by James Madden, 204 Studios, Chattanooga

PLATE 35
Frederick Childe Hassam
(American, 1859–1935)
French Tea Garden (also known as
The Terre-Cuite Tea Set)
1910
Oil on canvas
35 × 40 ¼ in. (88.9 × 102.2 cm)
Hunter Museum of American Art, Chattanooga,
Tennessee, Gift of the Benwood Foundation
1976.3.13
Photo by James Madden, 204 Studios,
Chattanooga

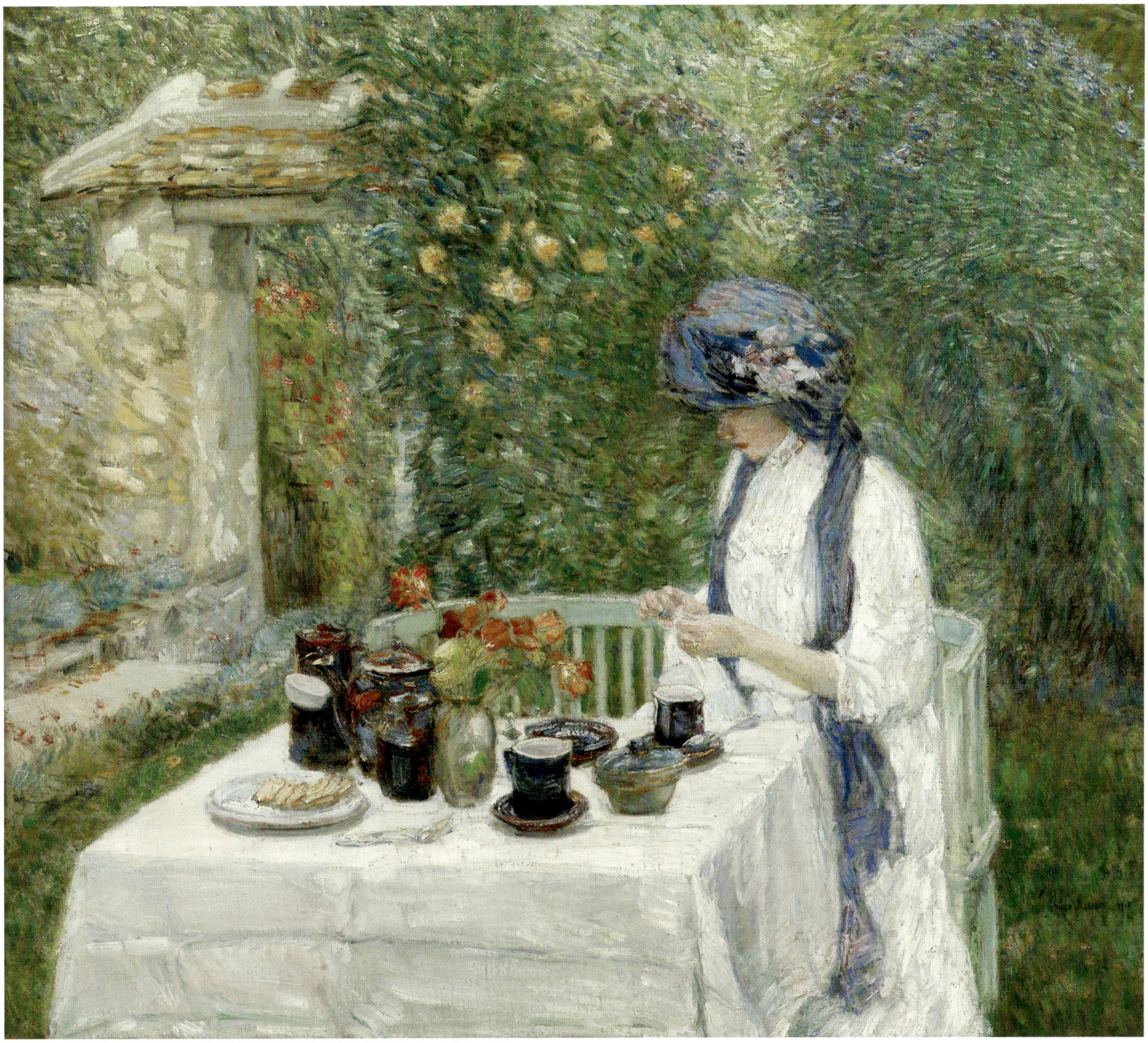

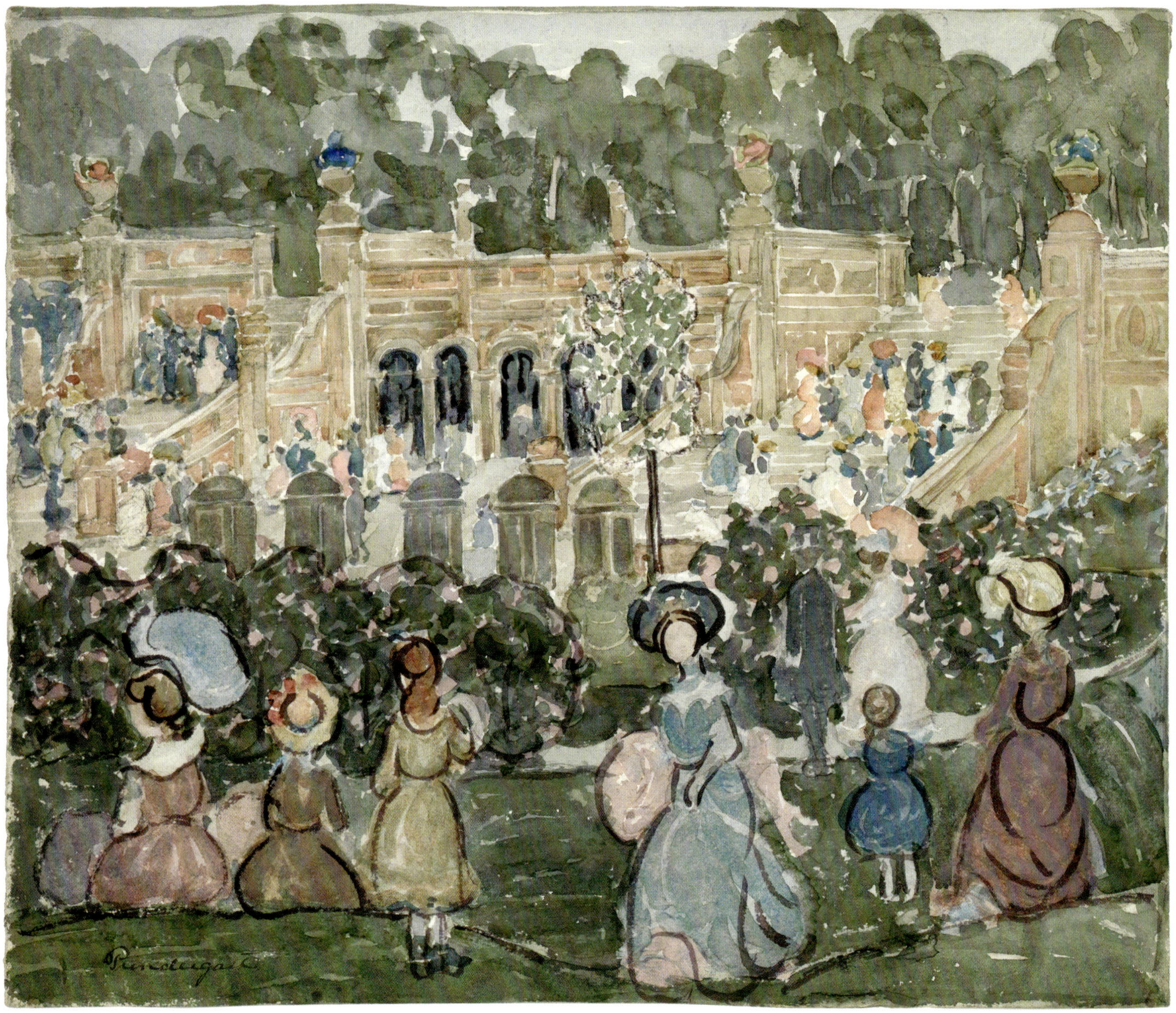

PLATE 36
Maurice Brazil Prendergast
(American, born in Canada, 1858–1924)
Central Park, New York
c. 1900–1903; reworked later
Watercolor, pencil, and gouache on paper
12 ¾ × 15 ½ in. (32.4 × 39.4 cm)
Williams College Museum of Art,
Williamstown, MA, Gift of Mrs. Charles
Prendergast
86.18.69

PLATE 37
Maurice Brazil Prendergast
(American, born in Canada, 1858–1924)
Salem Willows
1904
Oil on canvas
26 ¼ × 34 ¼ in. (66.7 × 87 cm)
Terra Foundation for American Art,
Daniel J. Terra Collection
1999.120

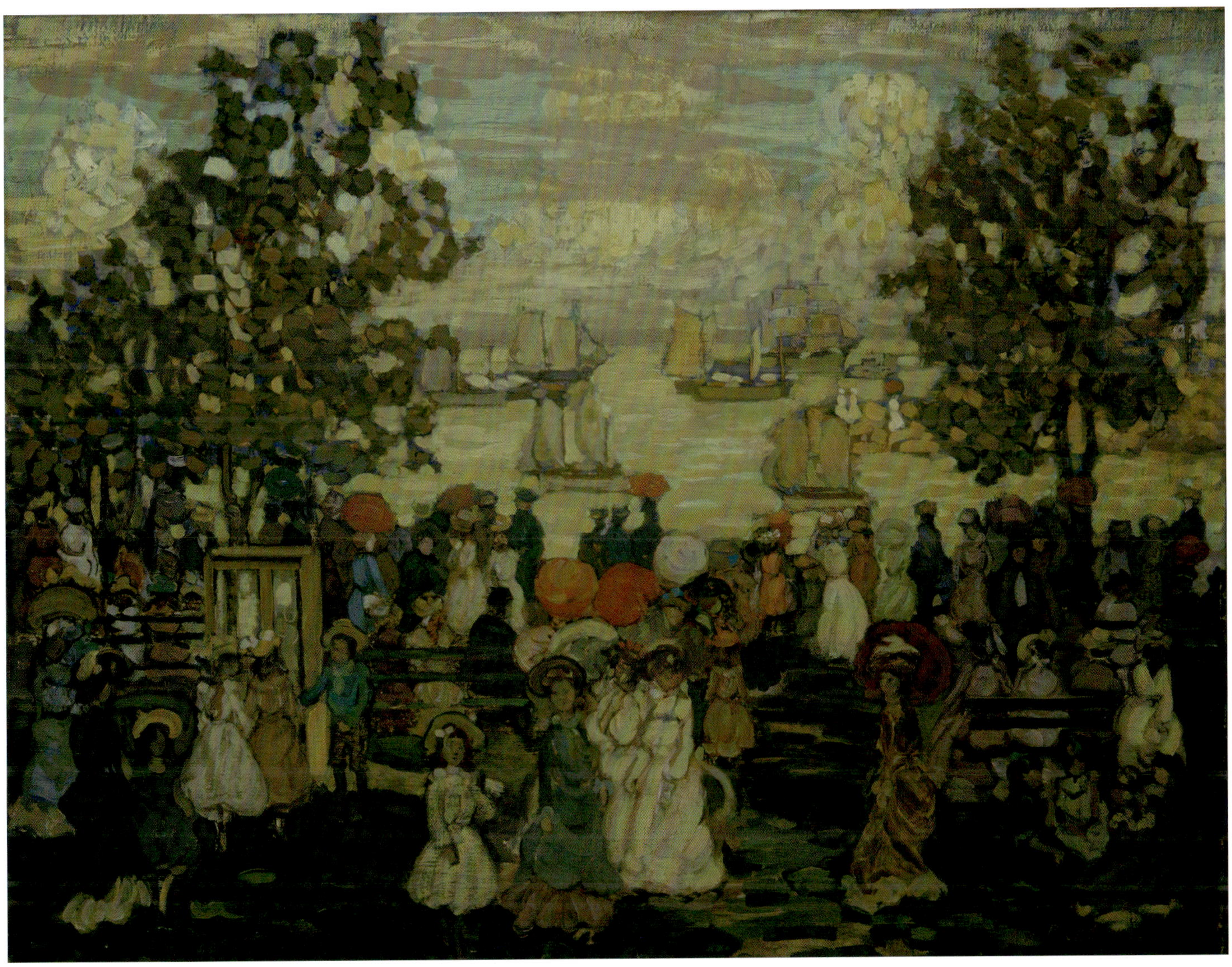

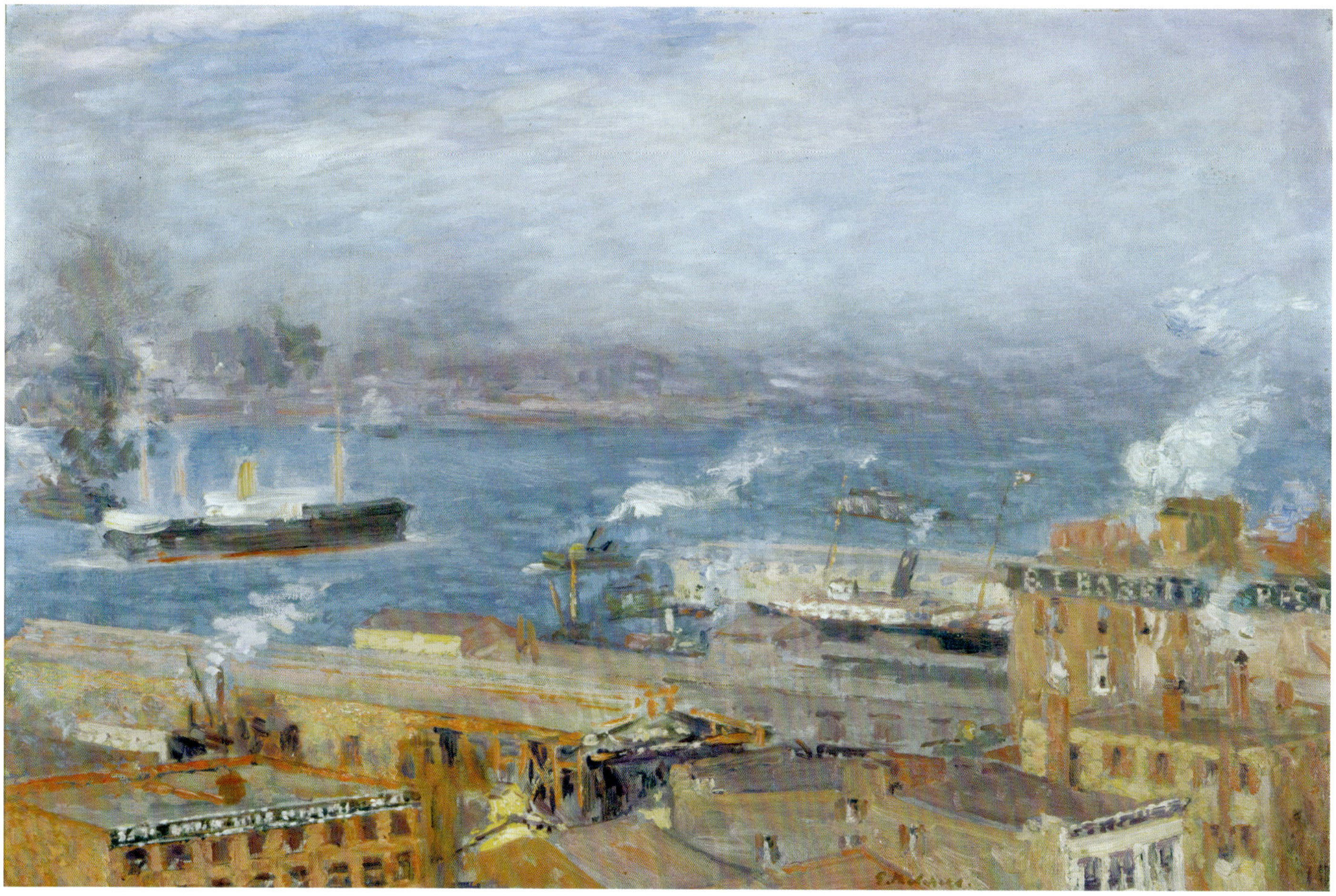

PLATE 38
Gari Melchers
(American, 1860–1932)
Hudson River
c. 1907
Oil on canvas
15 ½ × 23 ½ in. (39.4 × 59.7 cm)
Gari Melchers Home and Studio,
University of Mary Washington

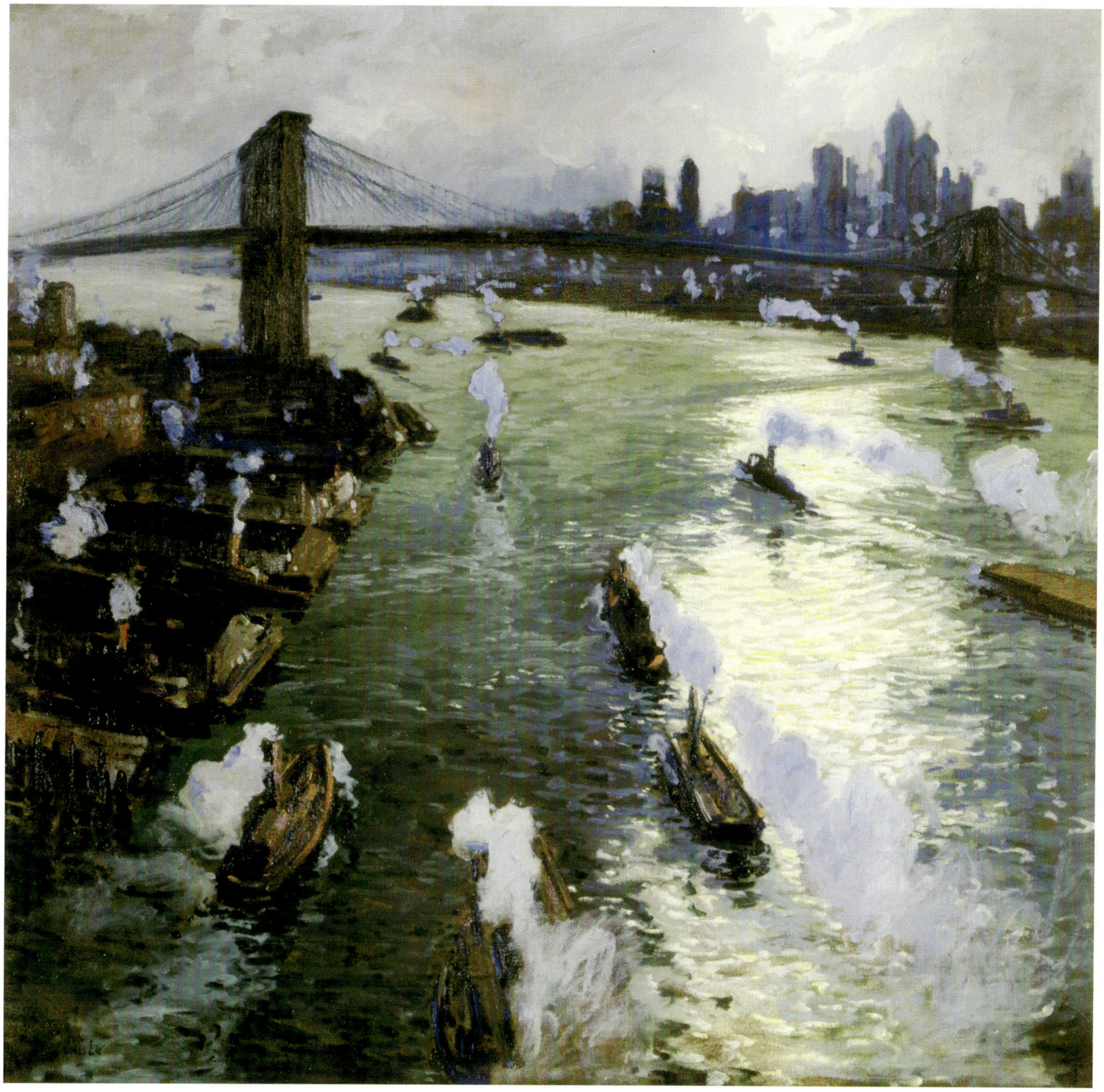

PLATE 39
Jonas Lie
(American, born in Norway, 1880–1940)
Path of Gold
c. 1915
Oil on canvas
34 × 36 in. (86.4 × 91.4 cm)
High Museum of Art, Atlanta, Georgia
J. J. Haverty Collection

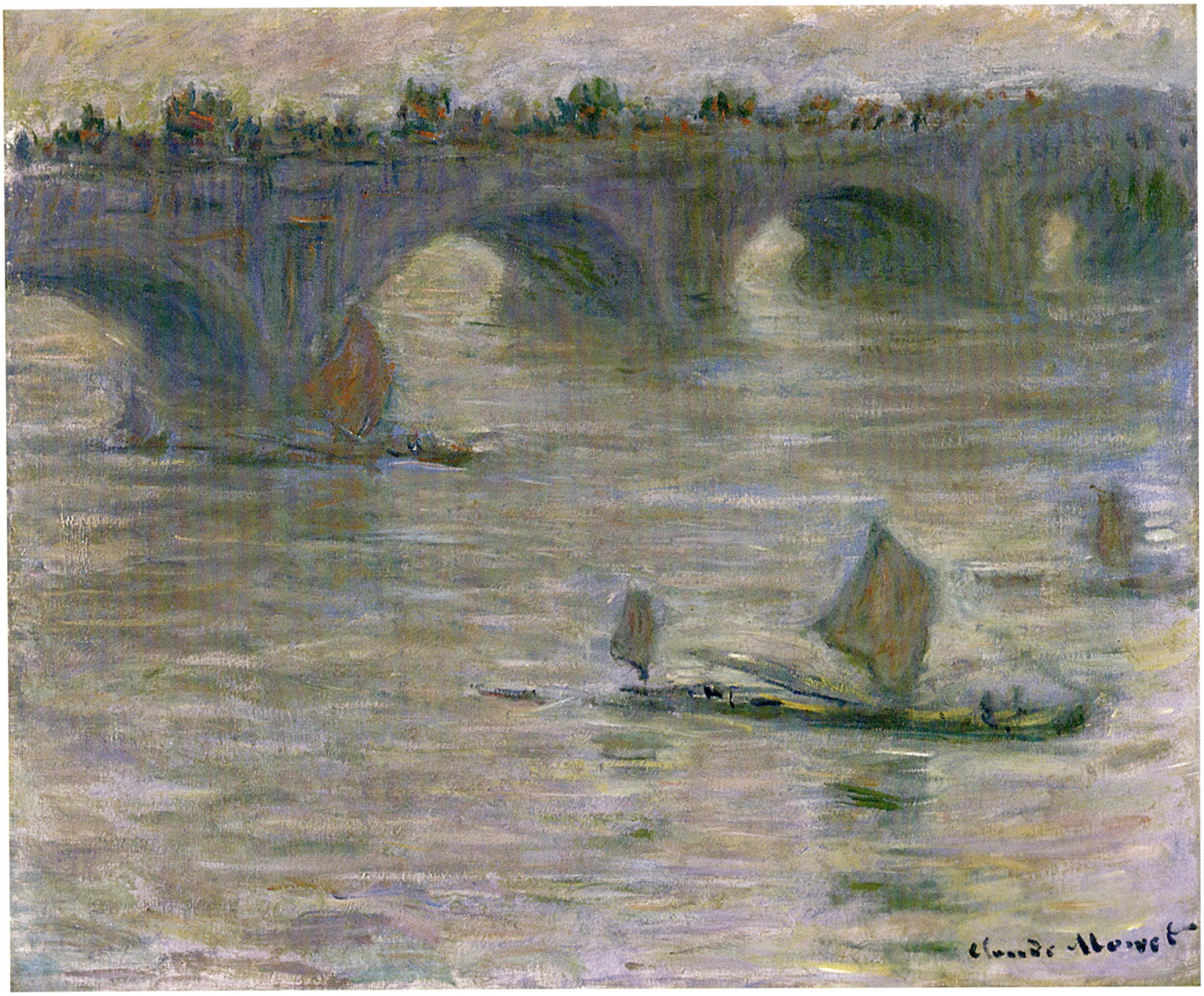

PLATE 40
Claude Monet
(French, 1840–1926)
Waterloo Bridge
1903
Oil on canvas
26 × 32 in. (66 × 81.3 cm)
Lowe Art Museum,
University of Miami, Florida
Gift of Ione T. Staley
60.057.000
USA/Bridgeman Images

PLATE 41 (*facing page*)
Jonas Lie
(American, born in Norway, 1880–1940)
Dusk on Lower Broadway
c. 1910
Oil on canvas
37 ½ × 31 ½ in. (95.3 × 80 cm)
Cornell Fine Arts Museum, Rollins College, Gift of the family in memory of Dr. James B. Thomas, rector of All Saints Episcopal Church, Winter Park, FL
1957.064.P

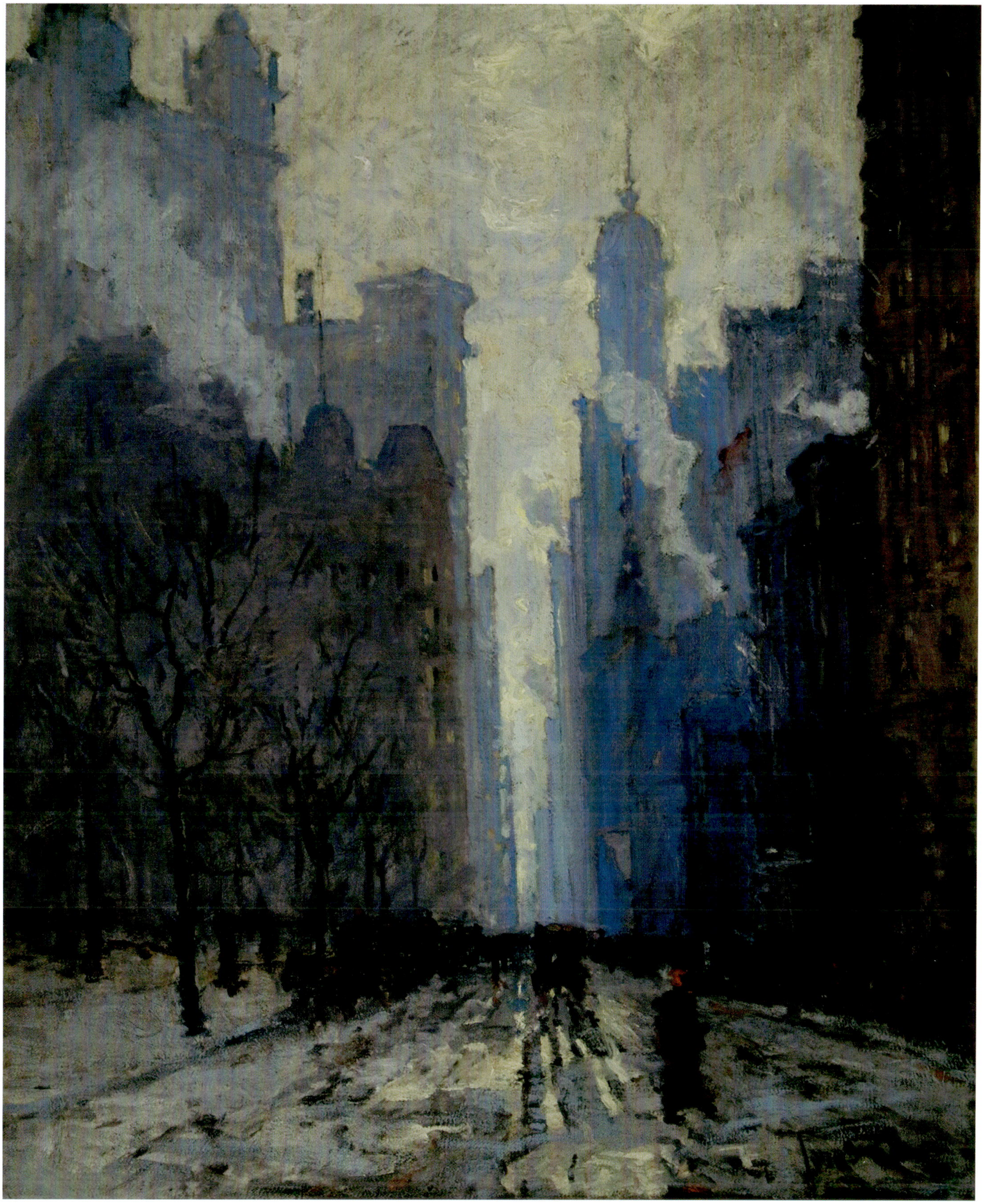

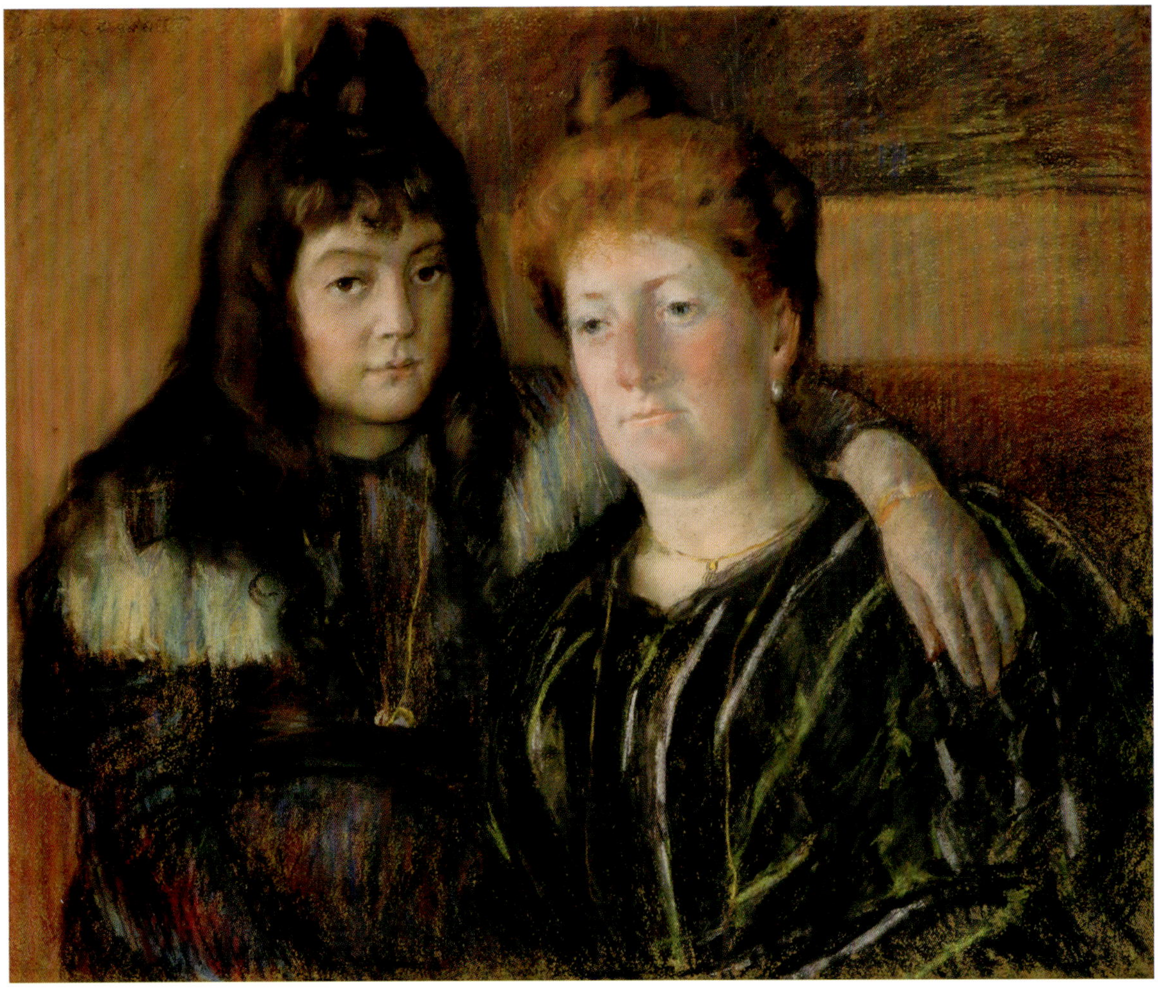

PLATE 42
Mary Cassatt
(American, 1844–1926)
Madame Gaillard and Her Daughter Marie-Thérèse
1897
Pastel on paper
22 ¾ × 28 in. (57.8 × 71.1 cm)
Courtesy of Reynolda House Museum of American Art, Winston-Salem, North Carolina, Gift of Barbara B. Millhouse
1975.2.1

PLATE 43 (*facing page*)
Joseph Rodefer De Camp
(American, 1858–1923)
The Red Kimono
c. 1919
Oil on canvas
53 ¾ × 46 ¼ in. (136.5 × 117.5 cm)
On loan from The Cummer Museum of Art & Gardens, Jacksonville, Florida, Museum Purchase
AP.1975.2.1

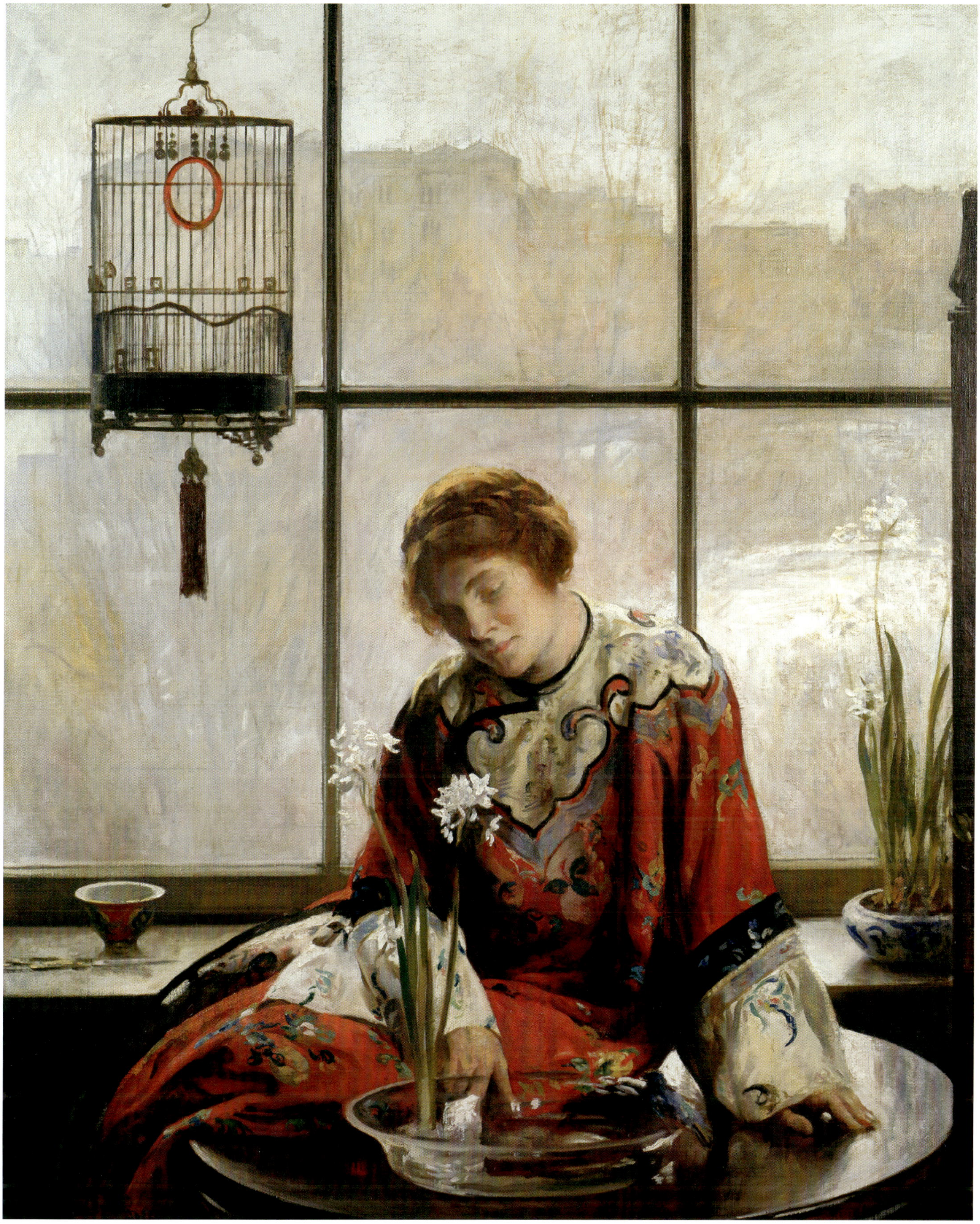

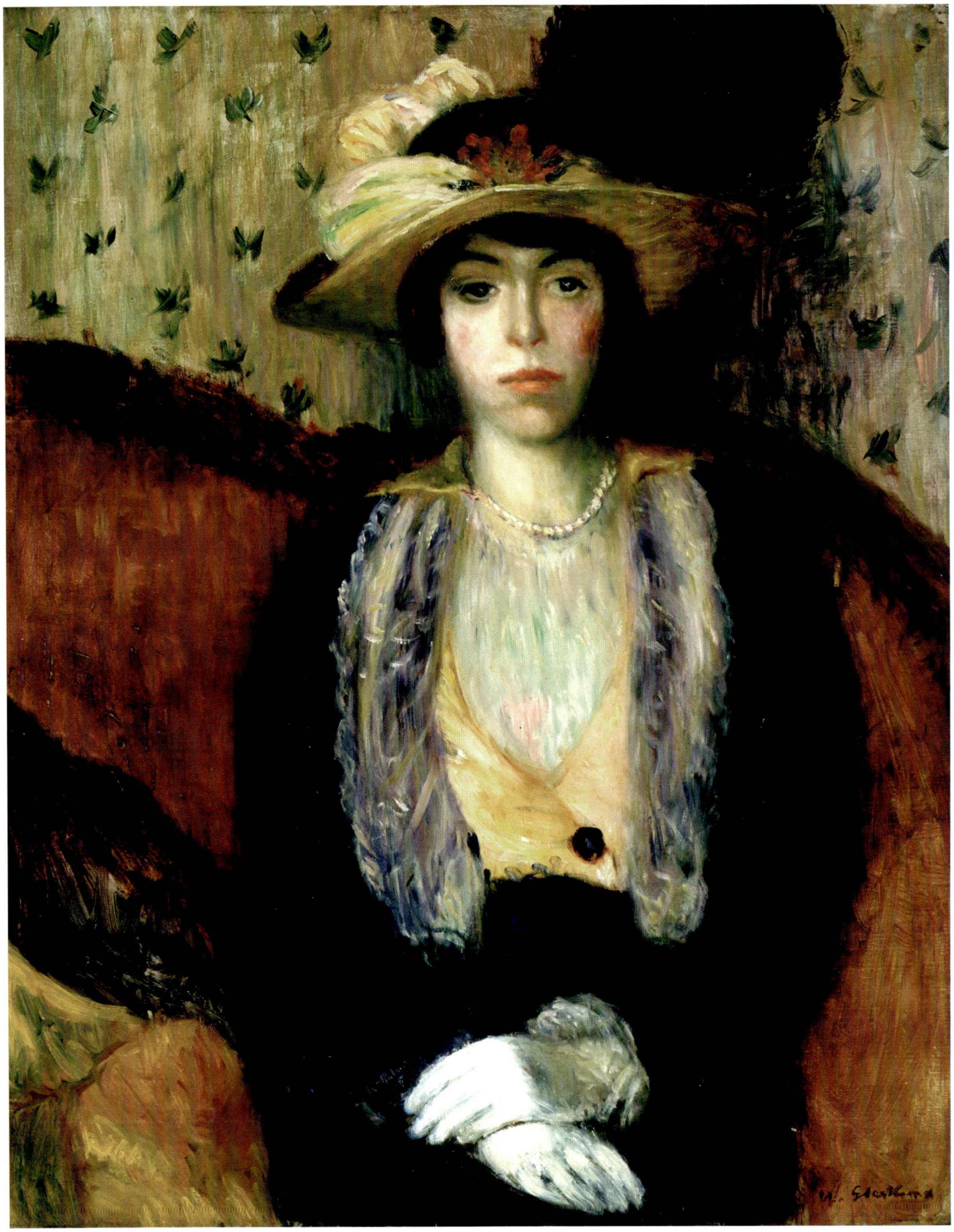

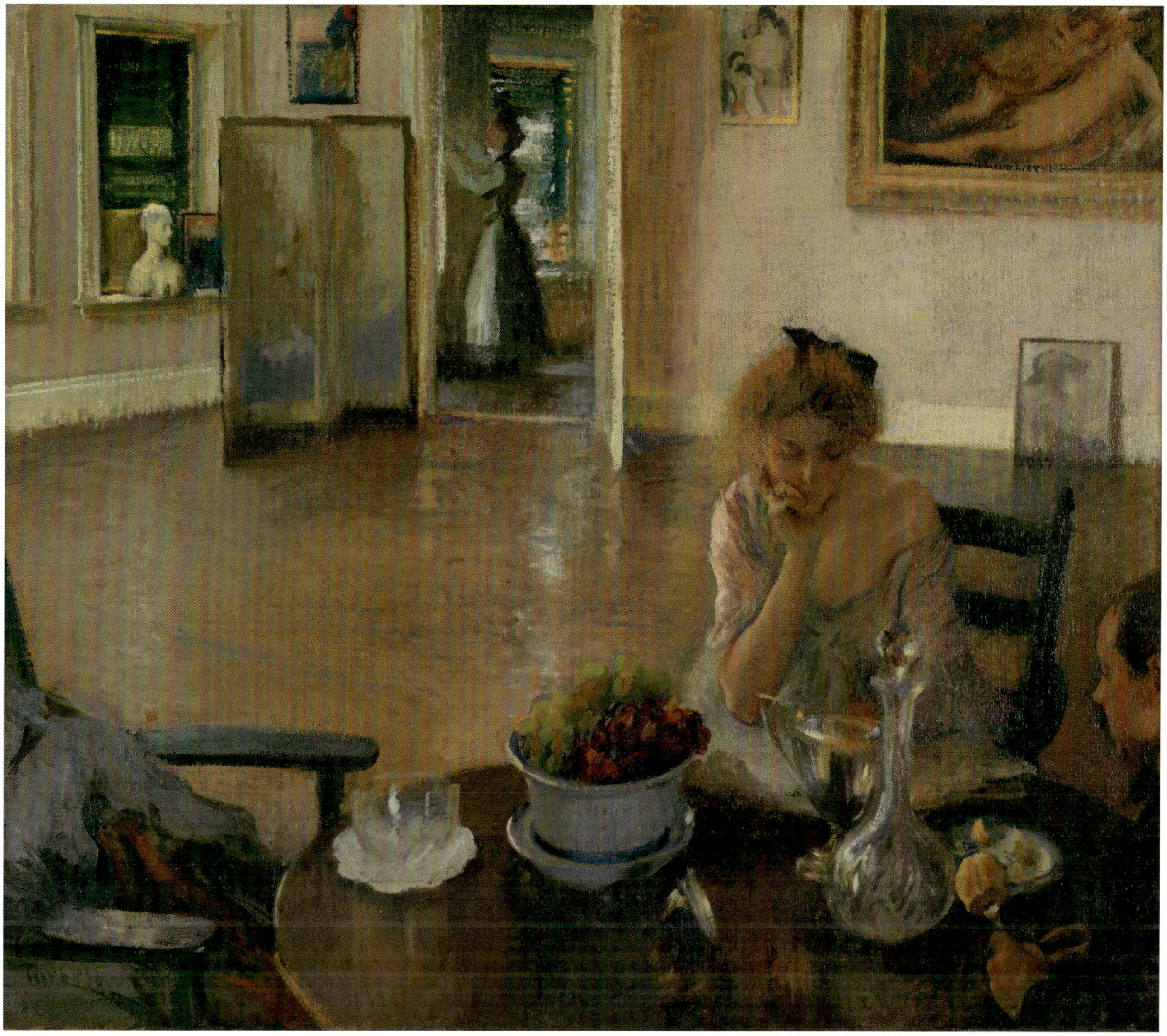

PLATE 44 (*facing page*)
William Glackens
(American, 1870–1938)
Miss Olga D.
1910
Oil on canvas
32 × 26 in. (81.3 × 66 cm)
Hunter Museum of American Art, Chattanooga, Tennessee, Gift of the Benwood Foundation
1976.3.11
Photo by J. Bradley Burns, Chattanooga

PLATE 45
Edmund C. Tarbell
(American, 1862–1938)
The Breakfast Room
c. 1903
Oil on canvas
25 × 30 in. (63.5 × 76.2 cm)
Courtesy of the Pennsylvania Academy of the Fine Arts, Philadelphia, Gift of Clement B. Newbold
1973.25.3

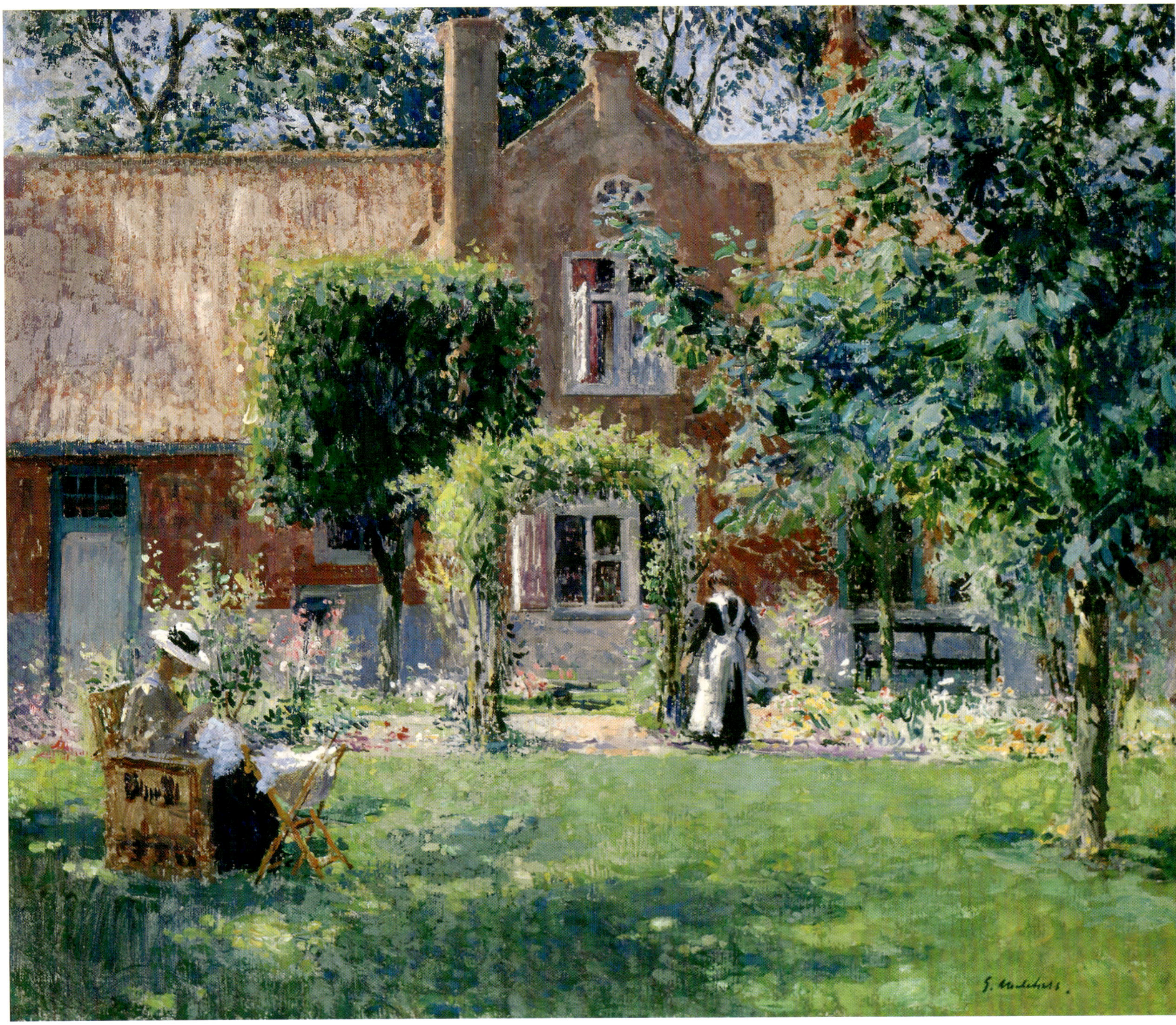

PLATE 46
Gari Melchers
(American, 1860–1932)
Unpretentious Garden
1903–1909
Oil on canvas
33 ¾ × 40 ¼ in. (85.7 × 102.2 cm)
Telfair Museums, Savannah, Georgia, Museum purchase, Button Gwinnett, Autograph Fund
1916.5
Photo by Peter Harholdt

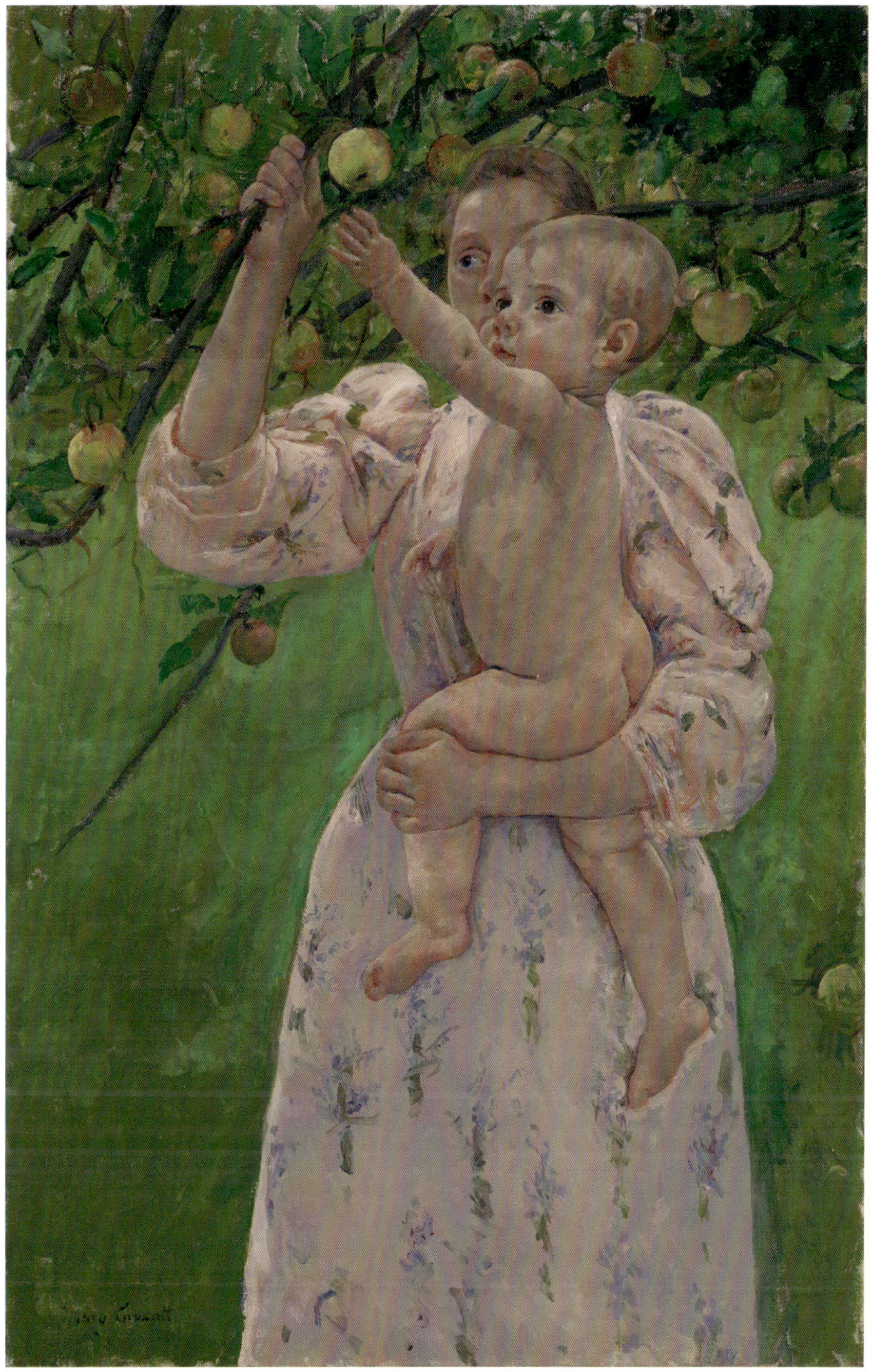

PLATE 47
Mary Cassatt
(American, 1844–1926)
Enfant cueillant un fruit
(Child Picking a Fruit)
1893
Oil on canvas
39 ½ × 25 ¾ in. (100.3 × 65.4 cm)
Virginia Museum of Fine Arts,
Richmond, Gift of Ivor and Anne Massey
75.18

Photo: Travis Fullerton

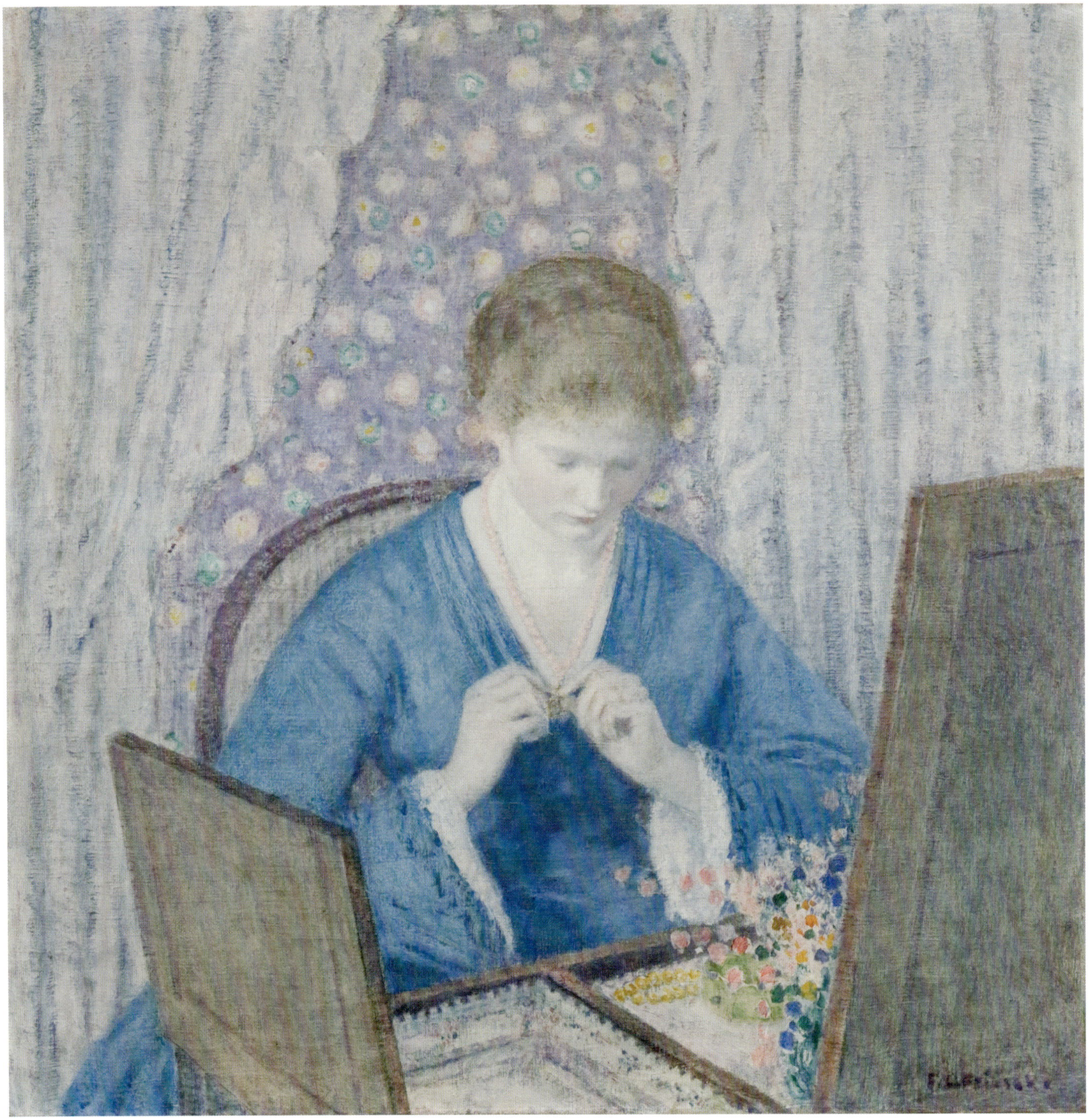

PLATE 48
Frederick Carl Frieseke
(American, 1874–1939)
Girl in Blue
by 1917–1919
Oil on canvas
32 × 32 in. (81.3 × 81.3 cm)
High Museum of Art, Atlanta, Georgia
Gift of Mrs. Joseph H. Boland
68.16

PLATE 49
Helen Maria Turner
(American, 1858–1958)
Lilies, Lanterns, and Sunshine
1923
Oil on canvas
36 ⅛ × 44 in. (91.8 × 111.8 cm)
Chrysler Museum of Art, Norfolk, VA,
Gift of W.B.S. Grandy
27.1.1

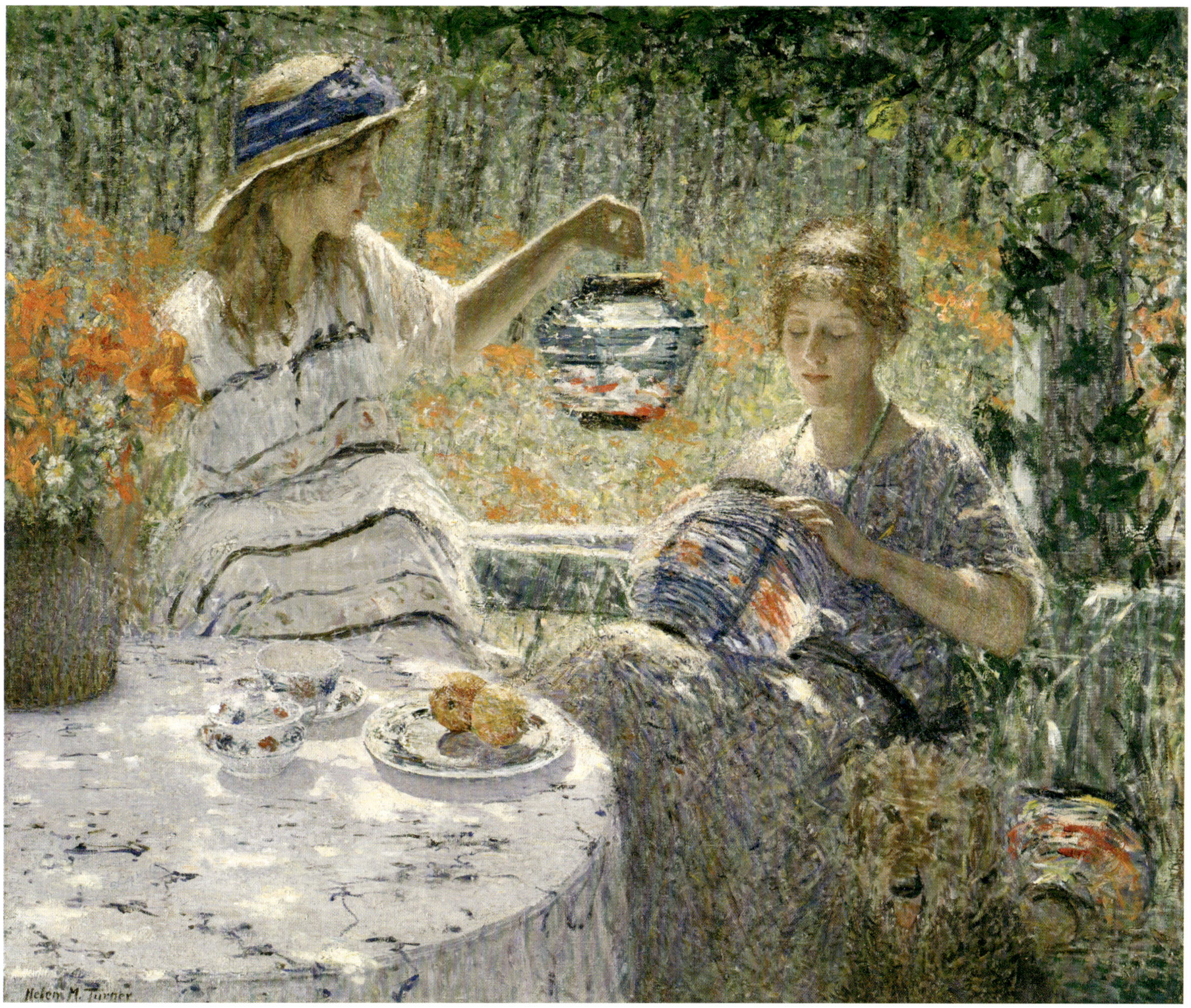

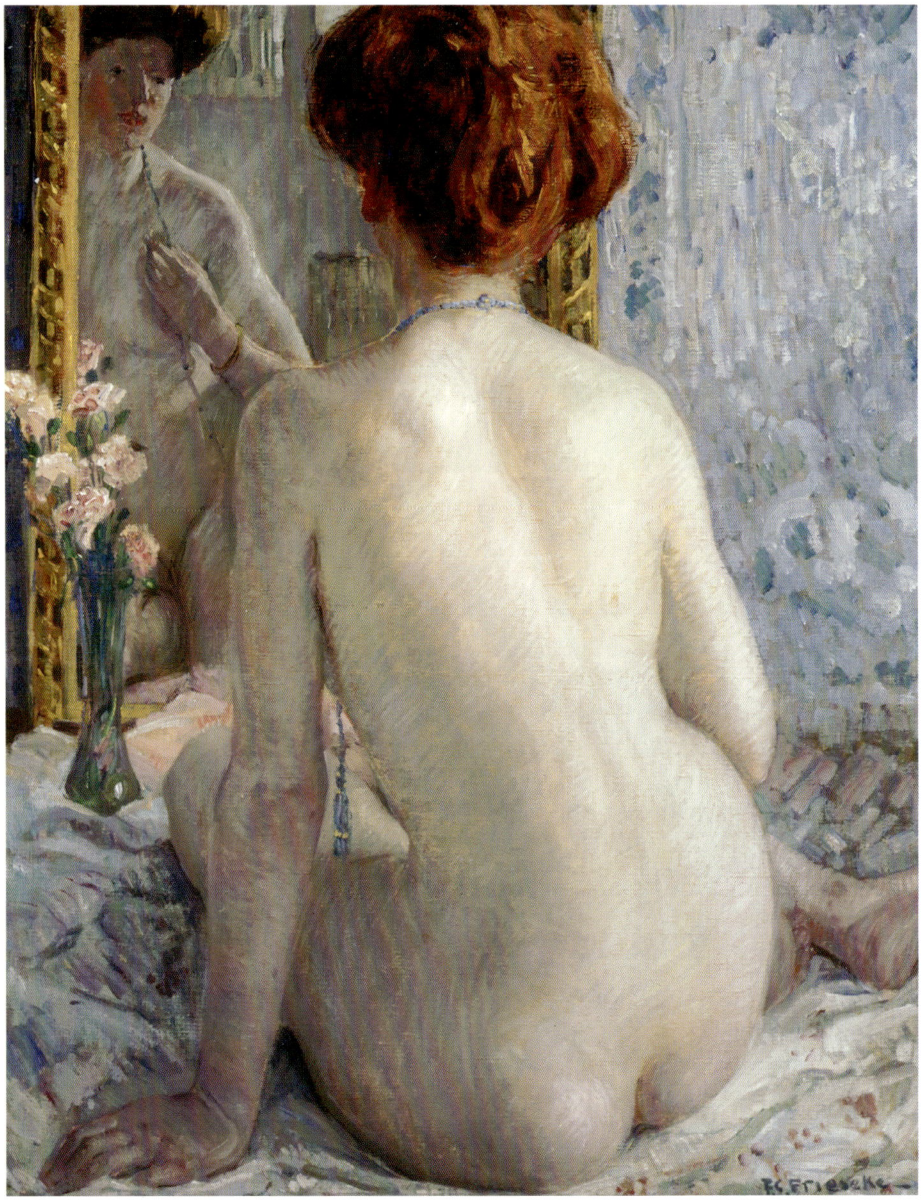

PLATE 50
Frederick Carl Frieseke
(American, 1874–1939)
Reflections (Marcelle)
by 1909
Oil on canvas
32 × 27 in. (81.3 × 68.6 cm)
Telfair Museums, Savannah, Georgia,
Museum purchase
1910.10
Photo by Peter Harholdt

PLATE 51 (*facing page*)
Richard Emil Miller
(American, 1875–1943)
La Toilette
c. 1914
Oil on canvas
40 × 32 ½ in. (101.6 × 82.6 cm)
The Columbus Museum, Georgia,
Museum purchase made possible by Mrs.
J. B. Knight, Jr., in memory of her husband

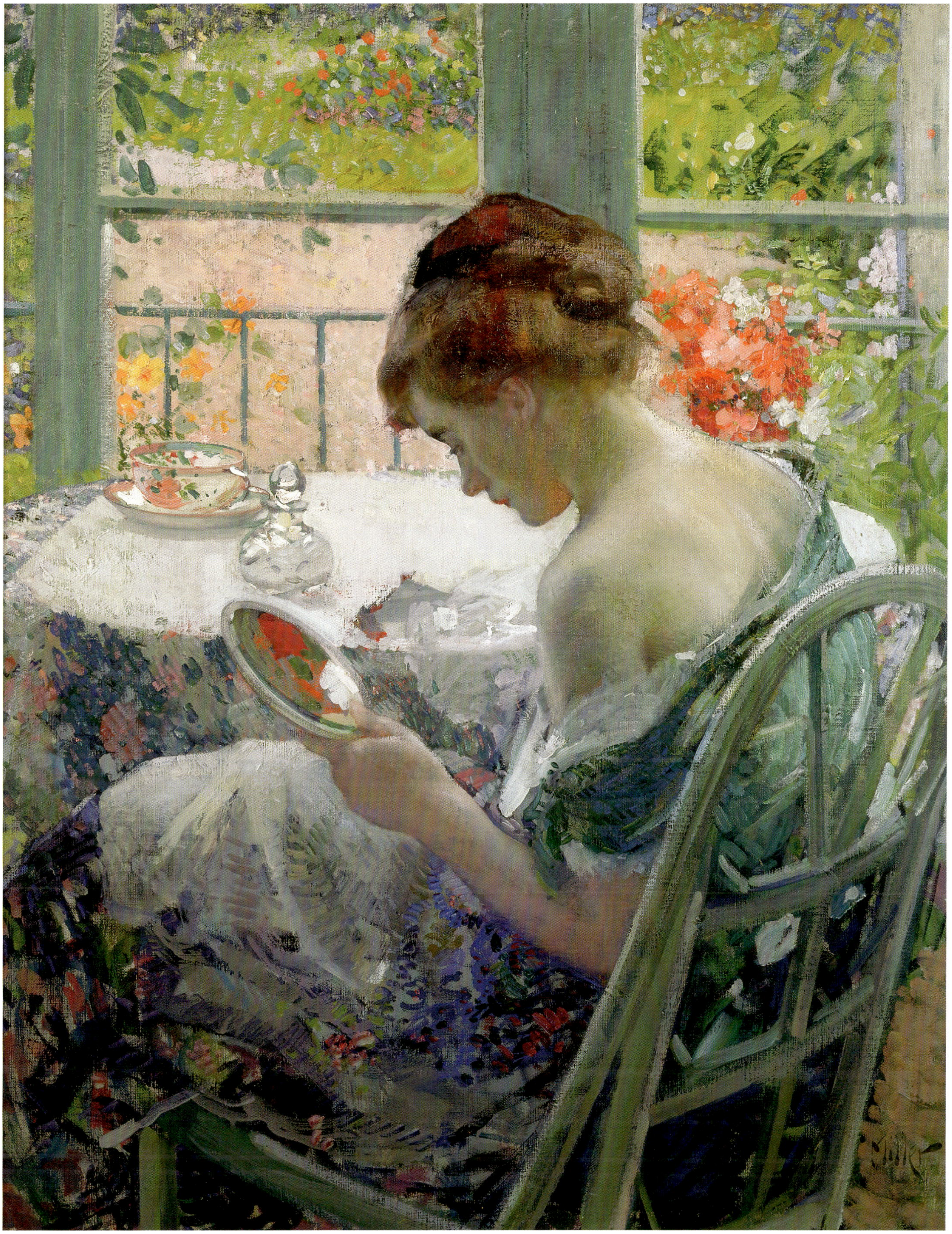

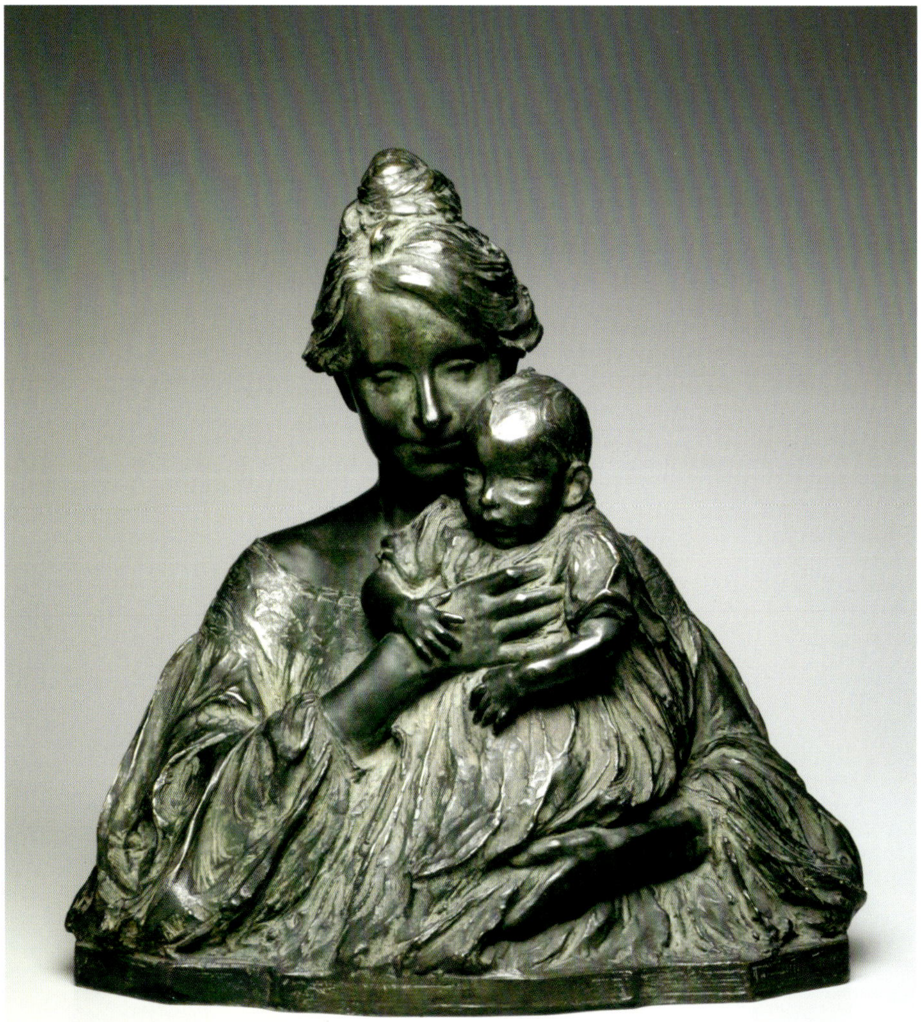

PLATE 52
Bessie Potter Vonnoh
(American, 1872–1955)
Modern Madonna
1904
Bronze
15 ⅛ × 15 × 8 ½ in. (38.4 × 38.1 × 21.6 cm)
Brooklyn Museum, Gift of the Artist
13.1062

PLATE 53 (*facing page*)
Bessie Potter Vonnoh
(American, 1872–1955)
Young Mother
1896
Bronze with green-and-brown patina;
lost-wax cast in 1913
14 × 13 × 15 ½ in. (35.6 × 33 × 39.4 cm)
Courtesy of the Pennsylvania Academy of the Fine Arts, Philadelphia. Gift of Mrs. Edward H. Coates in memory of Edward H. Coates
1923.9.8

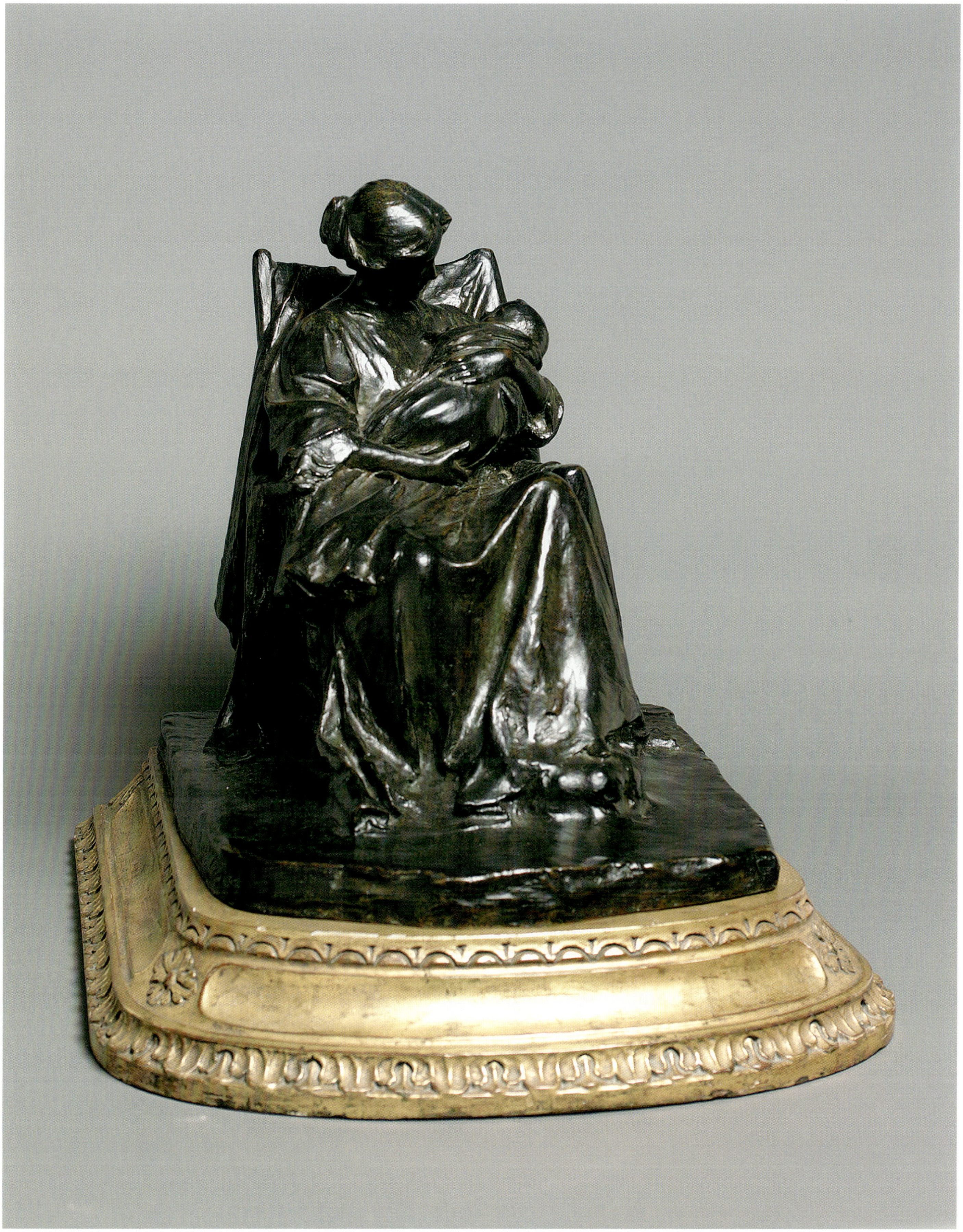

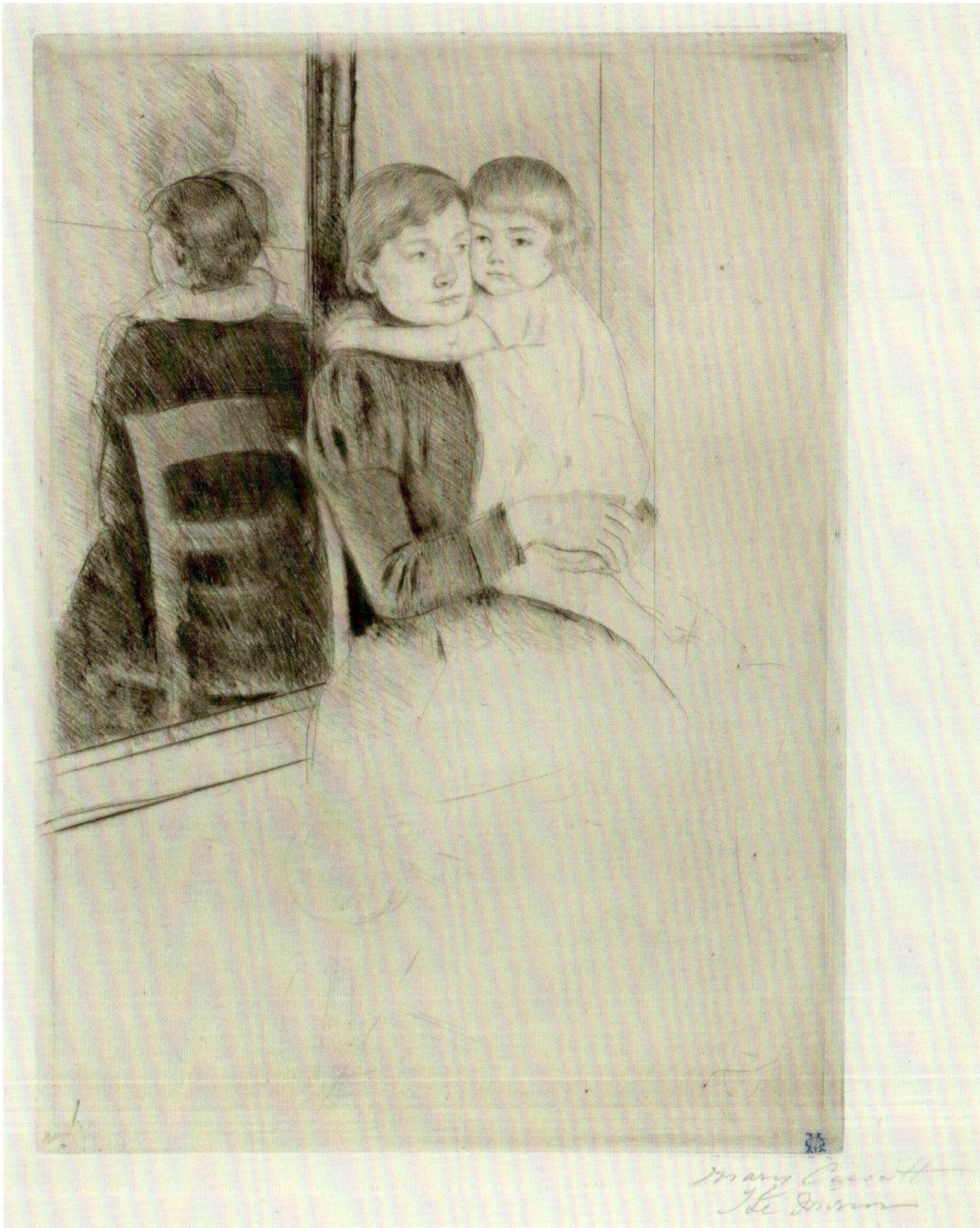

PLATE 54
Mary Cassatt
(American, 1844–1926)
The Mirror
1891
Drypoint on paper
Plate: 8 ⅞ × 6 9⁄16 in. (22.5 × 16.7 cm)
Sheet: 12 1⁄16 × 9 ⅜ in. (30.6 × 23.8 cm)
The Baltimore Museum of Art: The George A. Lucas Collection, purchased with funds from the State of Maryland, Laurence and Stella Bendann Fund, and contributions from individuals, foundations, and corporations throughout the Baltimore community
BMA 1996.48.508

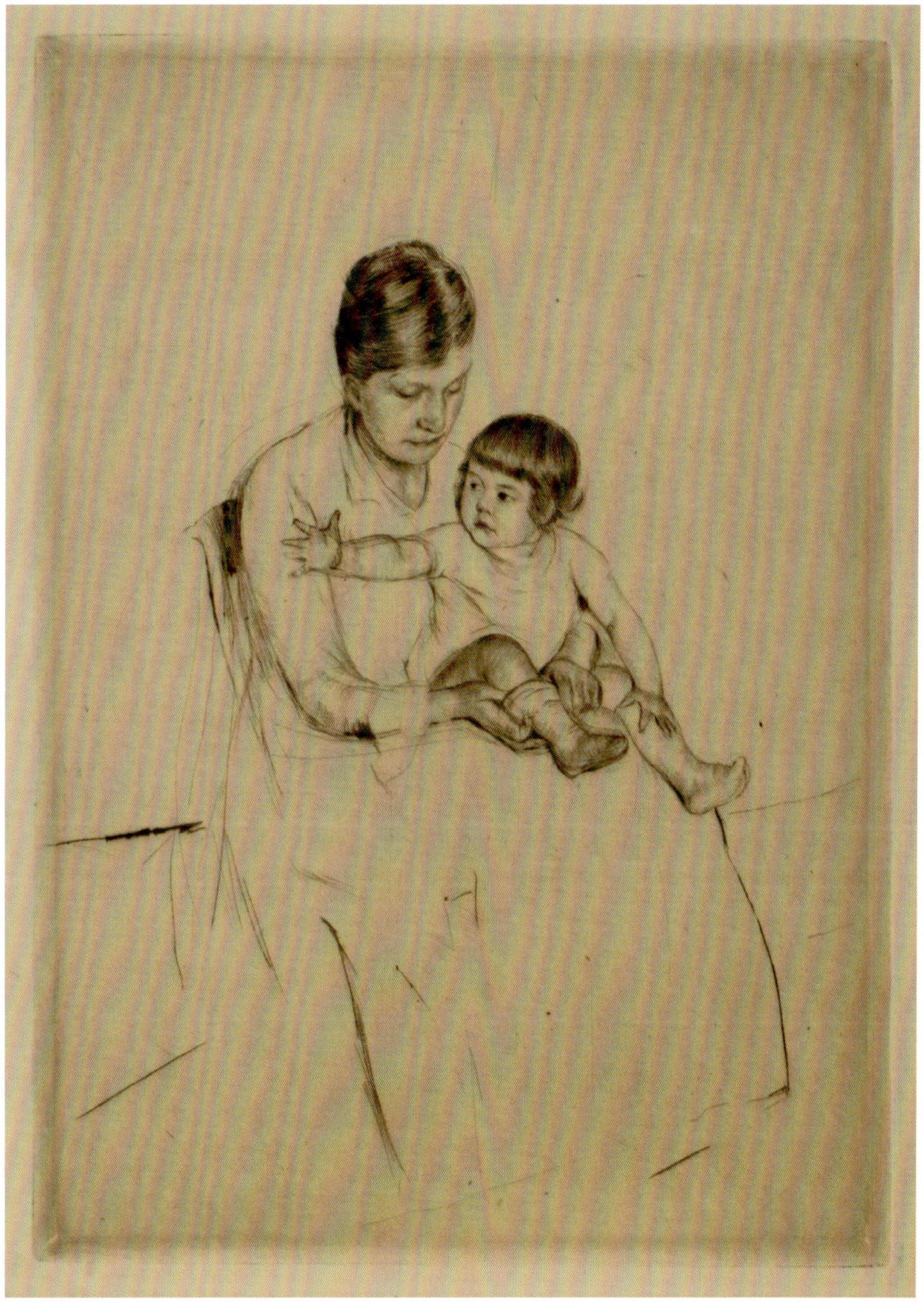

PLATE 55
Mary Cassatt
(American, 1844–1926)
The Stocking
c. 1890
Drypoint on paper
Plate: 10 1/16 × 7 5/16 in. (25.6 × 18.6 cm)
Sheet: 16 5/8 × 11 1/16 in. (42.2 × 28.1 cm)
Philadelphia Museum of Art,
Pennsylvania, Purchased with the
Joseph E. Temple Fund, 1949
1949-89-11

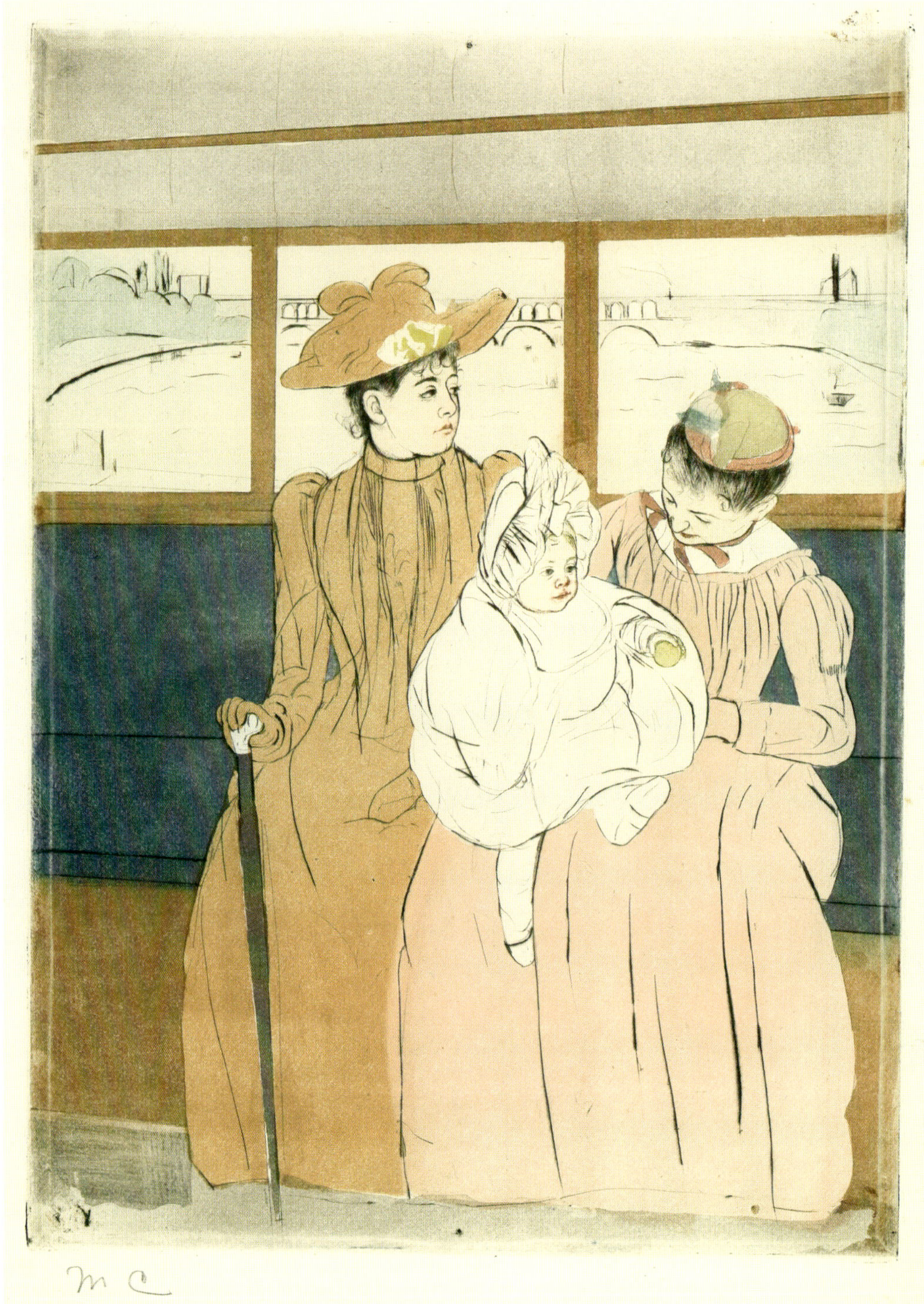

PLATE 56
Mary Cassatt
(American, 1844–1926)
In the Omnibus
1890–1891
Drypoint and aquatint, printed in colors on paper
14 ⅜ × 10 ⅝ in. (36.5 × 27 cm)
Courtesy of Adelson Galleries, Inc., New York

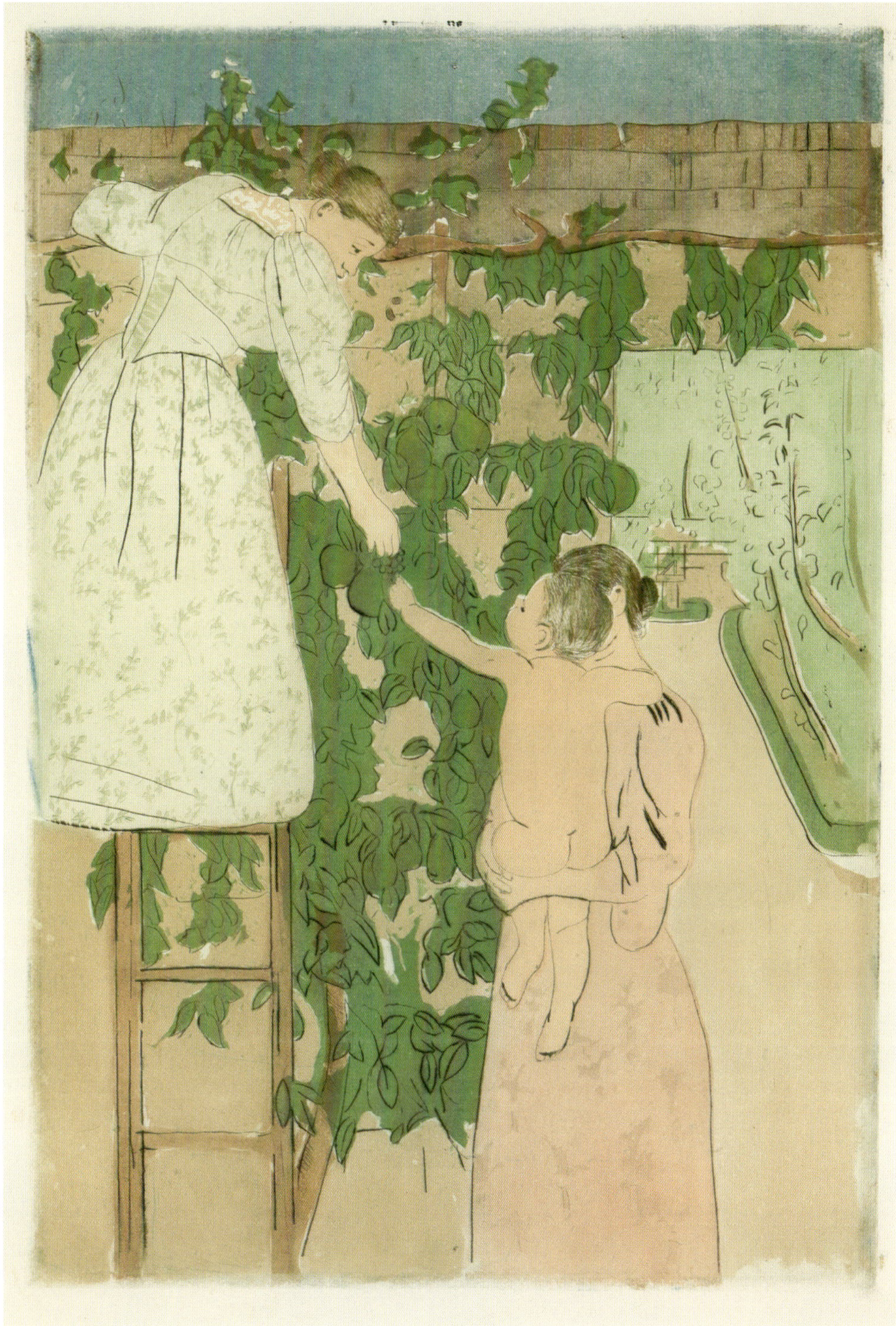

PLATE 57
Mary Cassatt
(American, 1844–1926)
Gathering Fruit
1893
Drypoint, soft-ground, and aquatint on paper
Plate: 16 ¾ × 11 ¾ in. (42.5 × 29.8 cm)
Sheet: 19 ⅝ × 15 ⅛ in. (49.8 × 38.4 cm)
Courtesy of Adelson Galleries, Inc., New York

PLATE 58
Mary Cassatt
(American, 1844–1926)
Tea
1890
Drypoint on paper
Image: 7 1/16 × 6 1/8 in. (17.9 × 15.6 cm)
Sheet: 13 1/4 × 9 7/8 in. (33.7 × 25.1 cm)
S. P. Avery Collection, Miriam and Ira D. Wallach Division of Art, Prints and Photographs, The New York Public Library, Astor, Lenox and Tilden Foundations

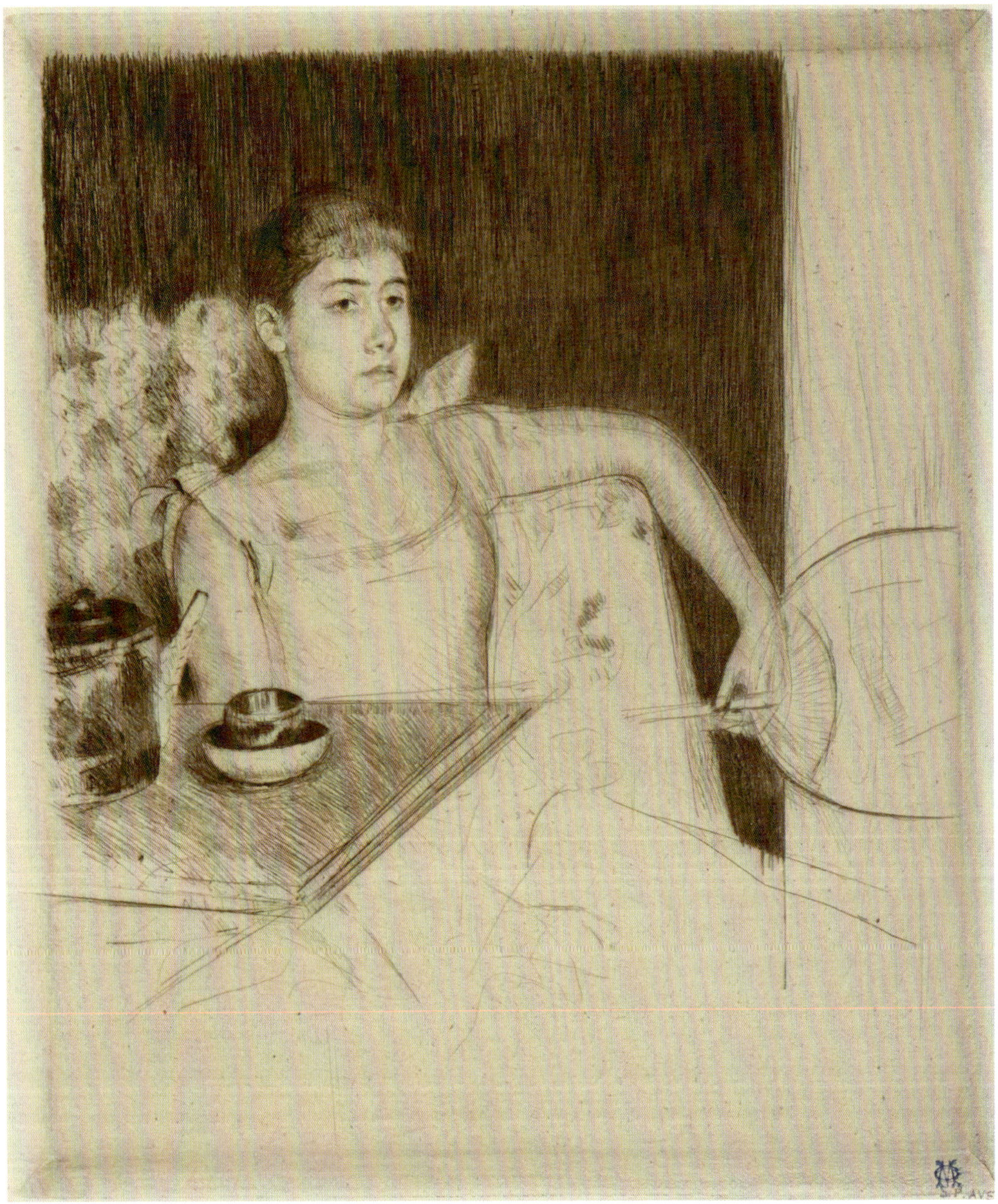

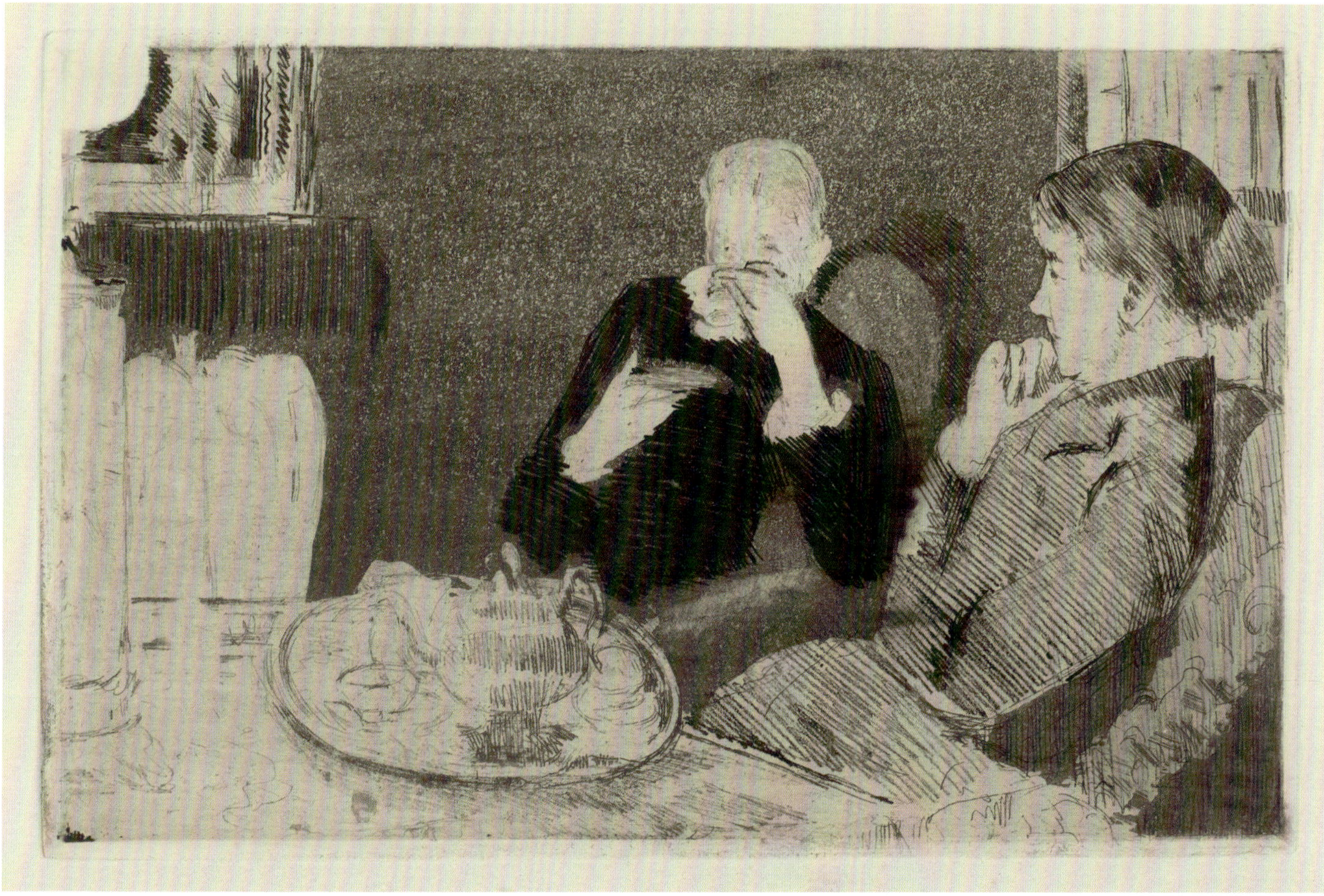

PLATE 59
Mary Cassatt
(American, 1844–1926)
Lydia and Her Mother at Tea
1882
Soft-ground etching and aquatint
on paper
Plate: 7 × 11 in. (17.8 × 27.9 cm)
Courtesy National Gallery of Art,
Washington, D.C.
1949.5.465

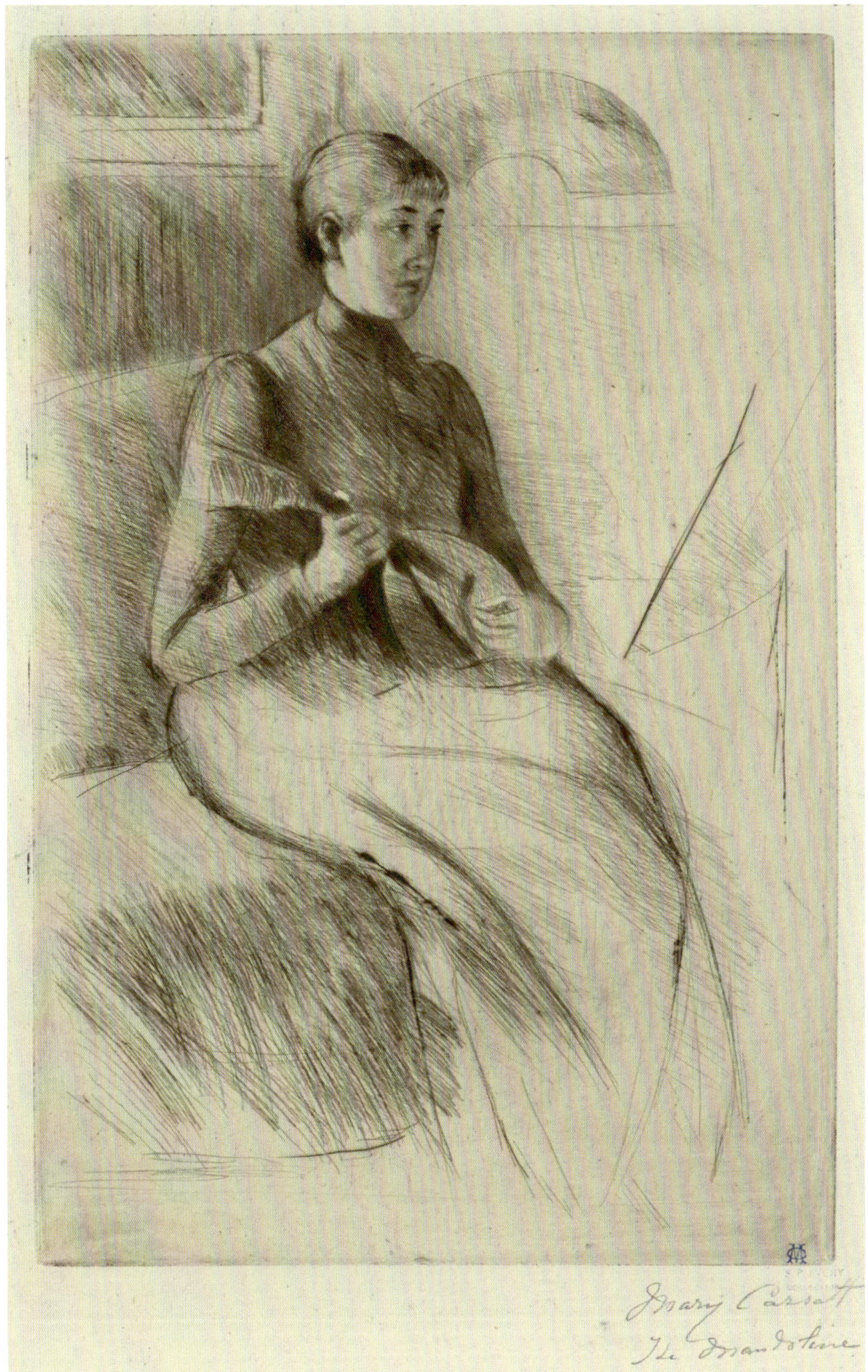

PLATE 60
Mary Cassatt
(American, 1844–1926)
The Mandolin Player
1889
Drypoint on paper
Image: 9 ⅛ × 6 ⅜ in. (23.2 × 16.2 cm)
Sheet: 14 9⁄16 × 9 11⁄16 in. (37 × 24.6 cm)
S. P. Avery Collection, Miriam and Ira D. Wallach Division of Art, Prints and Photographs, The New York Public Library, Astor, Lenox and Tilden Foundations

PLATE 61 (*facing page*)
Mary Cassatt
(American, 1844–1926)
Woman Bathing
1891
Color drypoint and aquatint on paper
Plate: 14 ⅜ × 10 ½ in. (36.5 × 26.8 cm)
Sheet: 17 ⅛ × 12 in. (43 × 31.5 cm)
Image courtesy of the Prints & Photographs Division, Library of Congress, LC-DIG-ppmsca-38331

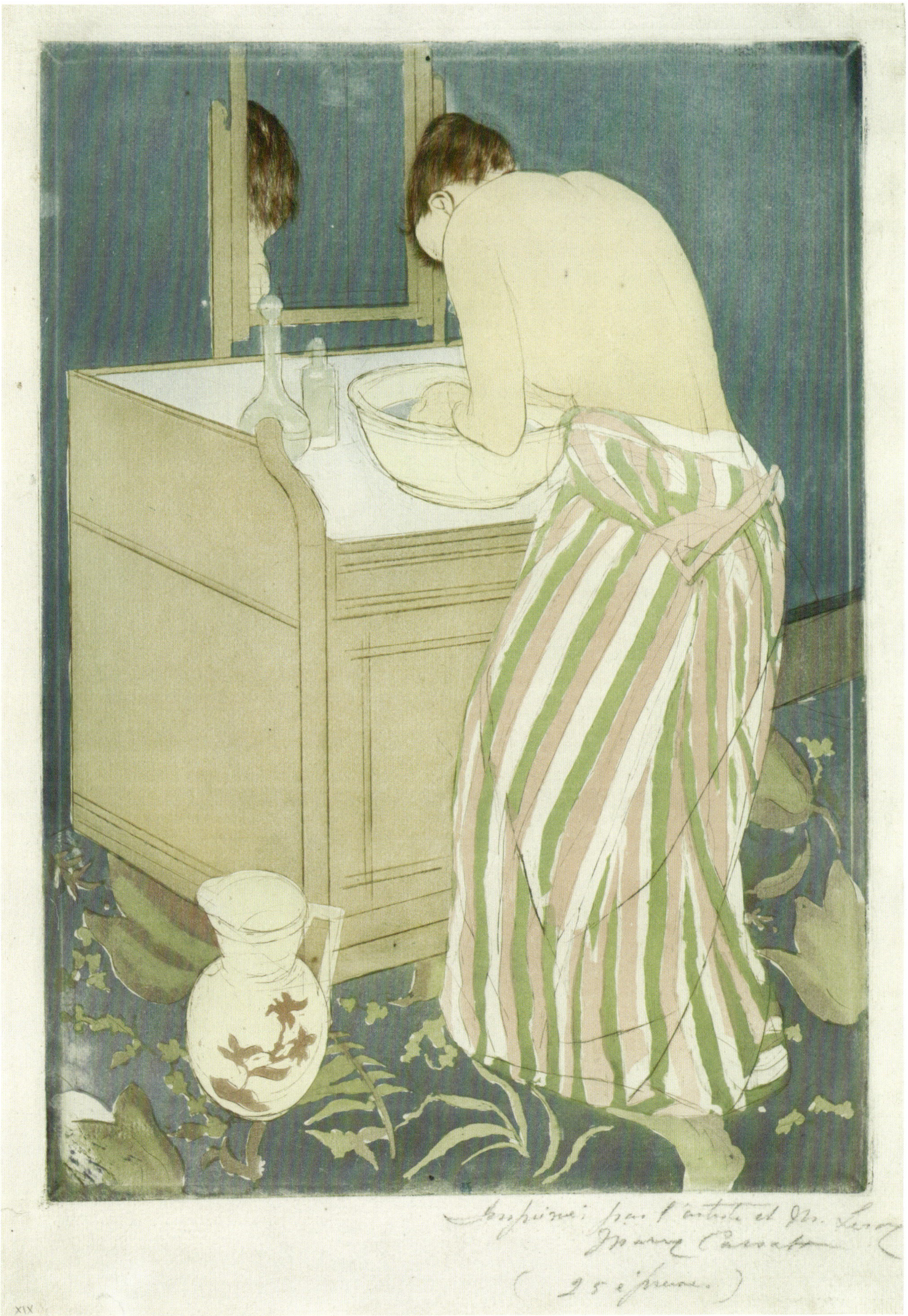
Imprimé par l'artiste et M. Leroy
Mary Cassatt
(25 épreuves)

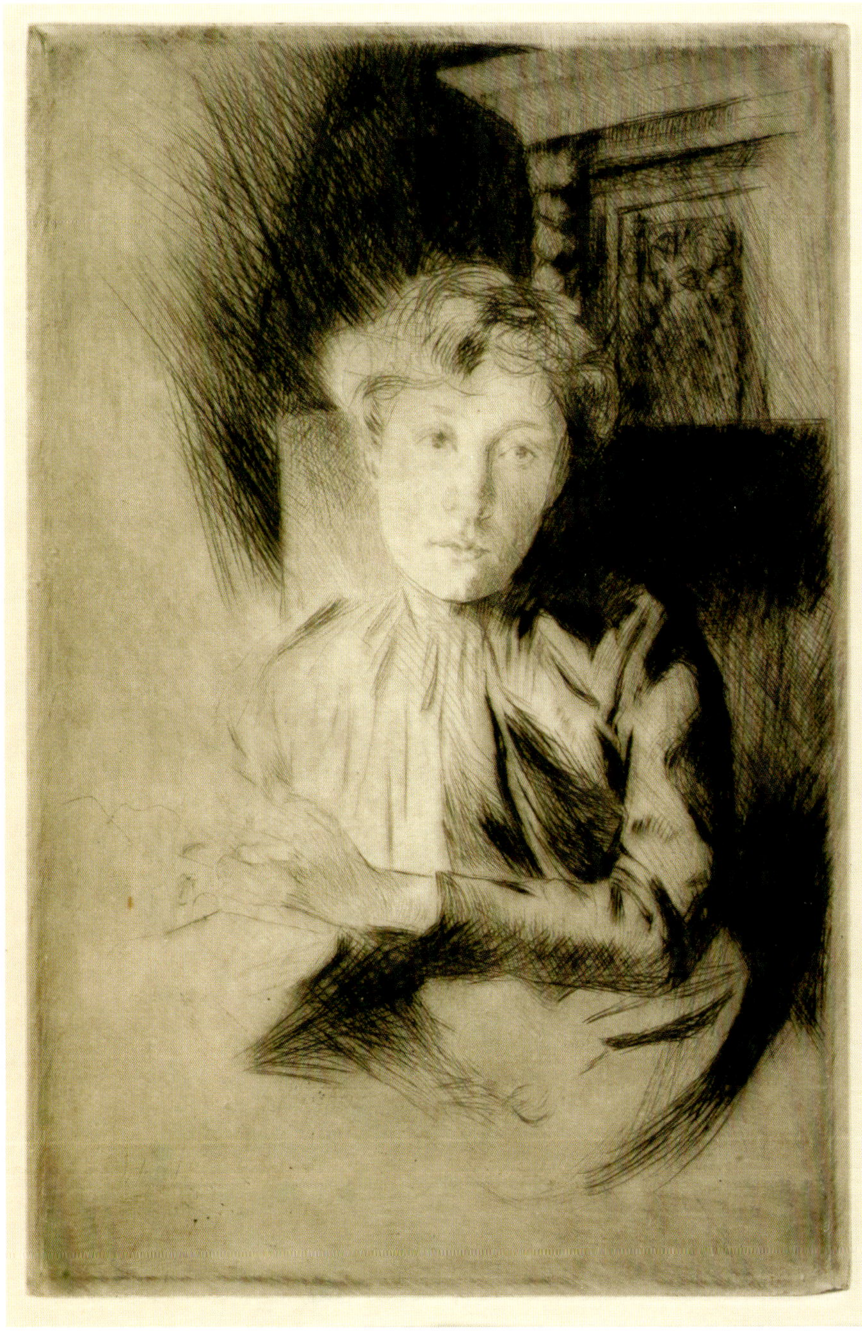

PLATE 62
J. Alden Weir
(American, 1852–1919)
By Candlelight
c. 1887–1893
Drypoint on paper
Plate: 9 ½ × 6 ⅜ in. (24 × 16.1 cm)
Smithsonian American Art Museum,
Gift of Brigham Young University
1972.84.11

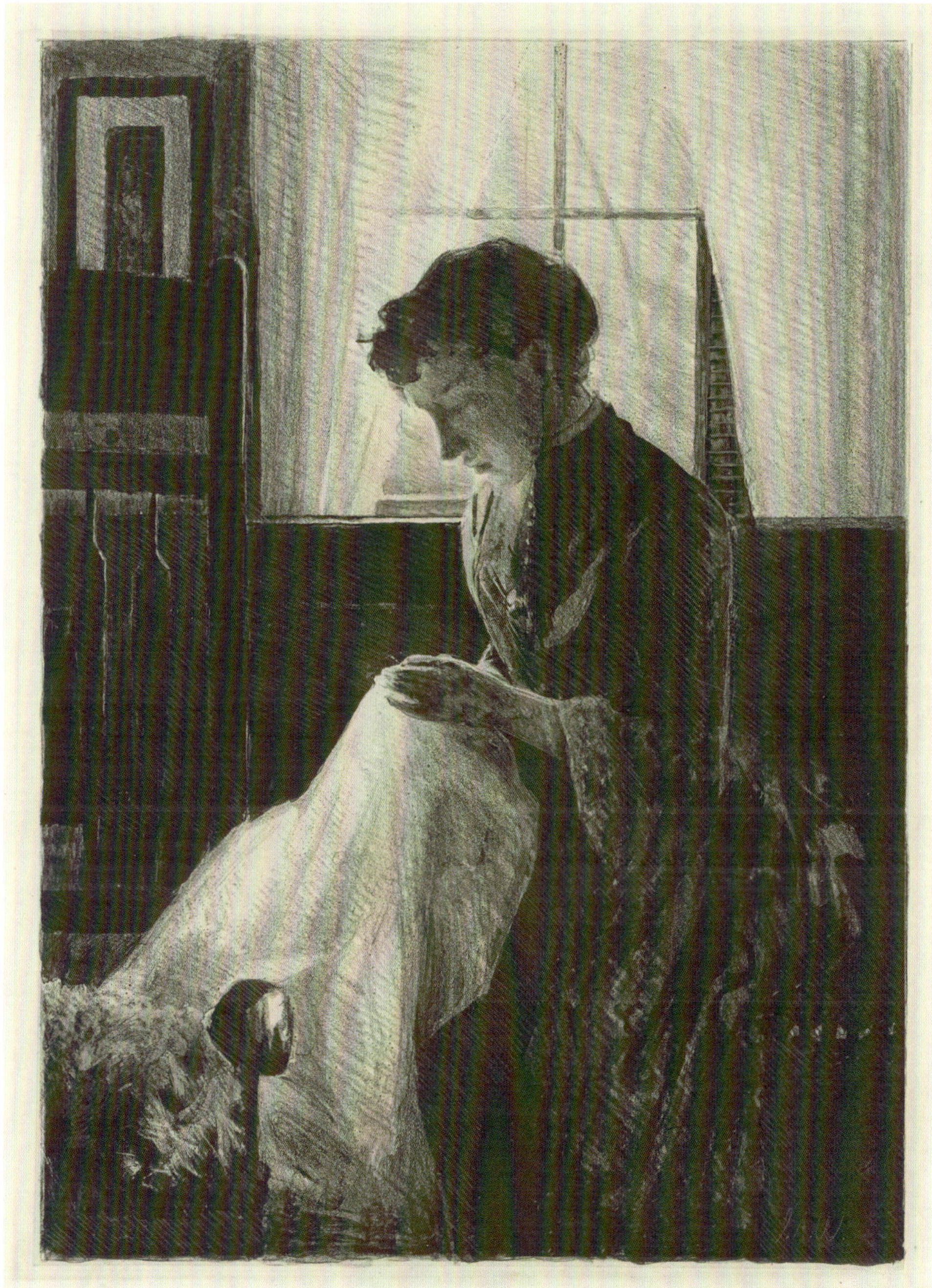

PLATE 63
J. Alden Weir
(American, 1852–1919)
A Woman Sewing (Profile Portrait of a Woman Sewing)
c. 1890
Lithograph on paper
Image: 12 3/8 × 8 7/8 in. (31.5 × 22.6 cm)
Sheet: 14 15/16 × 12 in. (38 × 30.5 cm)
S. P. Avery Collection, Print Collection, Miriam and Ira D. Wallach Division of Art, Prints and Photographs, The New York Public Library, Astor, Lenox and Tilden Foundations

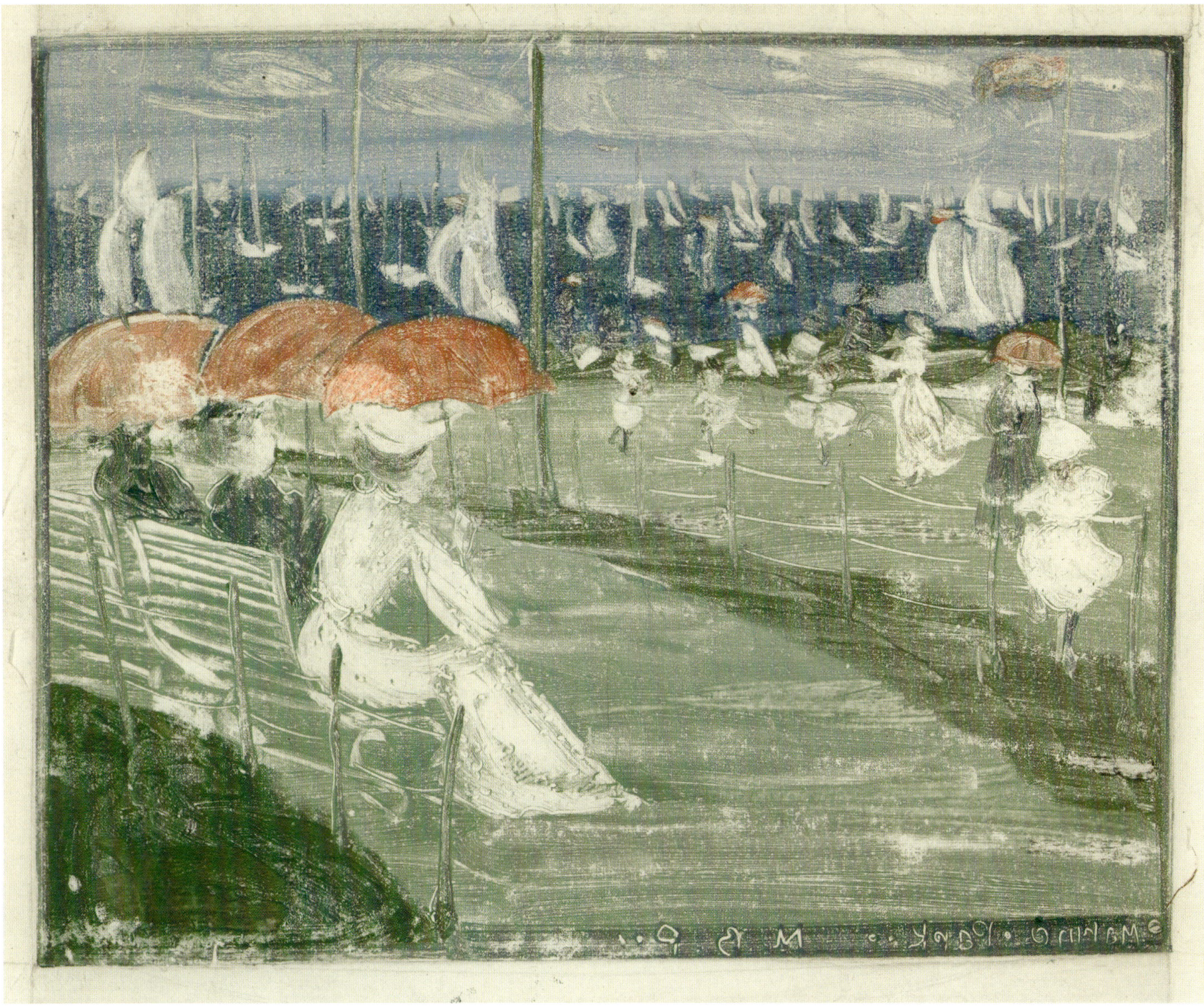

PLATE 64
Maurice Brazil Prendergast
(American, born in Canada, 1858–1924)
Marine Park, South Boston
c. 1895–1897
Monotype on paper with pencil additions
Sheet: 9 ⅞ × 12 ⅝ in. (25.1 × 32.1 cm)
Williams College Museum of Art,
Williamstown, MA, Gift of George and
Wilhelmina Batchelder
98.2

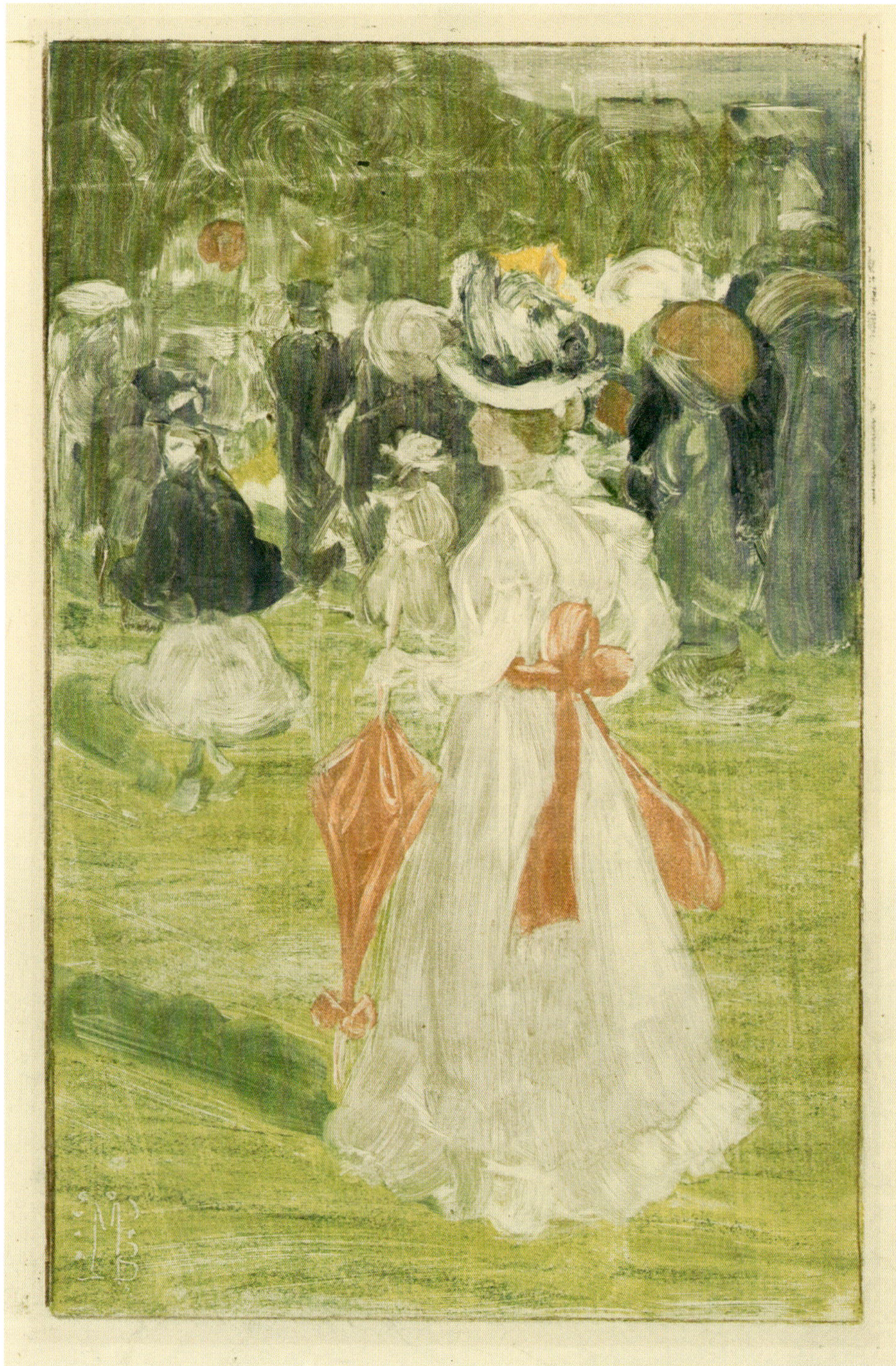

PLATE 65
Maurice Brazil Prendergast
(American, born in Canada, 1858–1924)
Franklin Park
c. 1895–1897
Monotype on paper with colored
pencil additions
10 ⅛ × 6 ⅝ in. (25.7 × 16.8 cm)
Williams College Museum of Art,
Williamstown, MA, Bequest of
Sophia W. Brumbaugh
M.2004.13.3

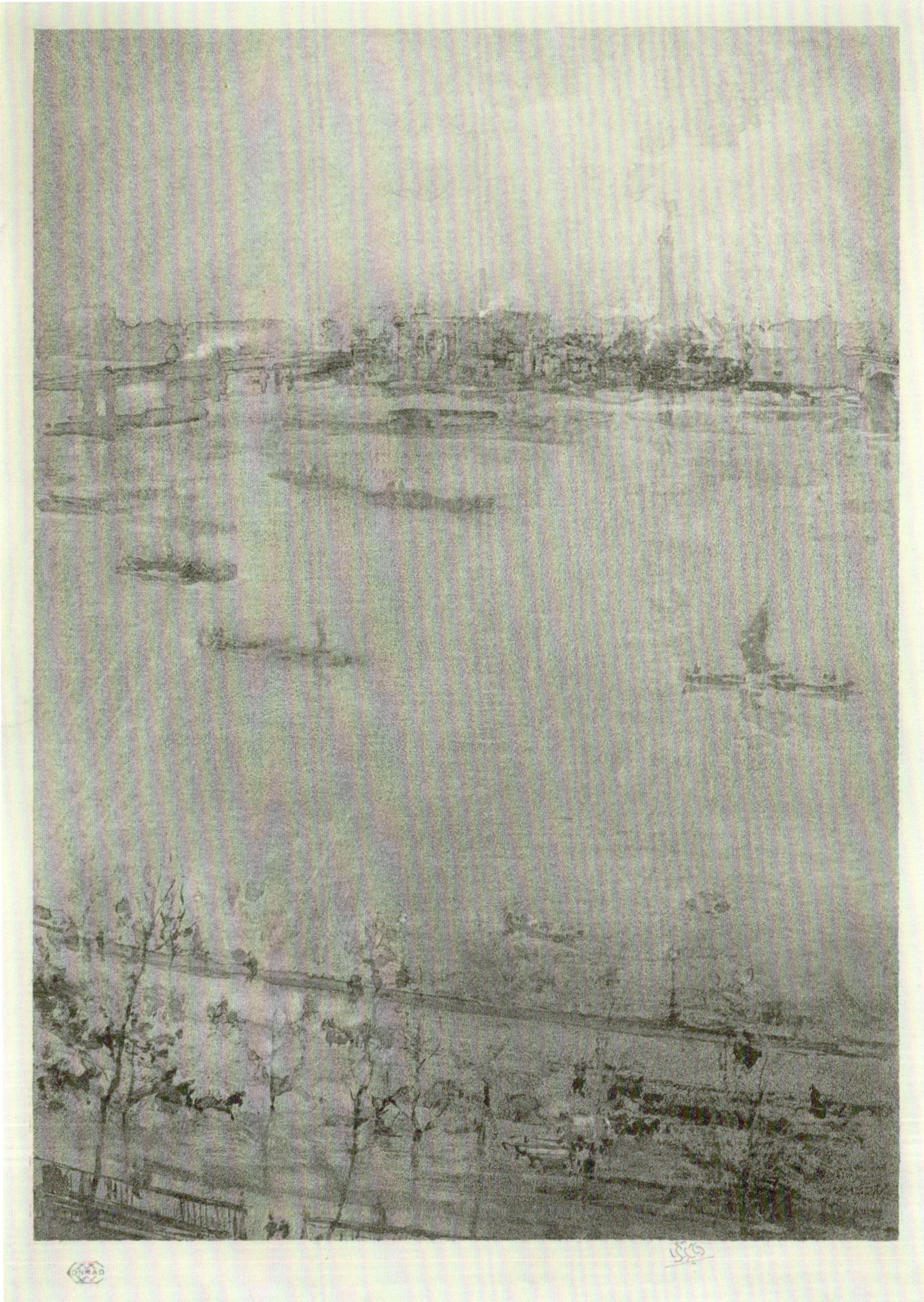

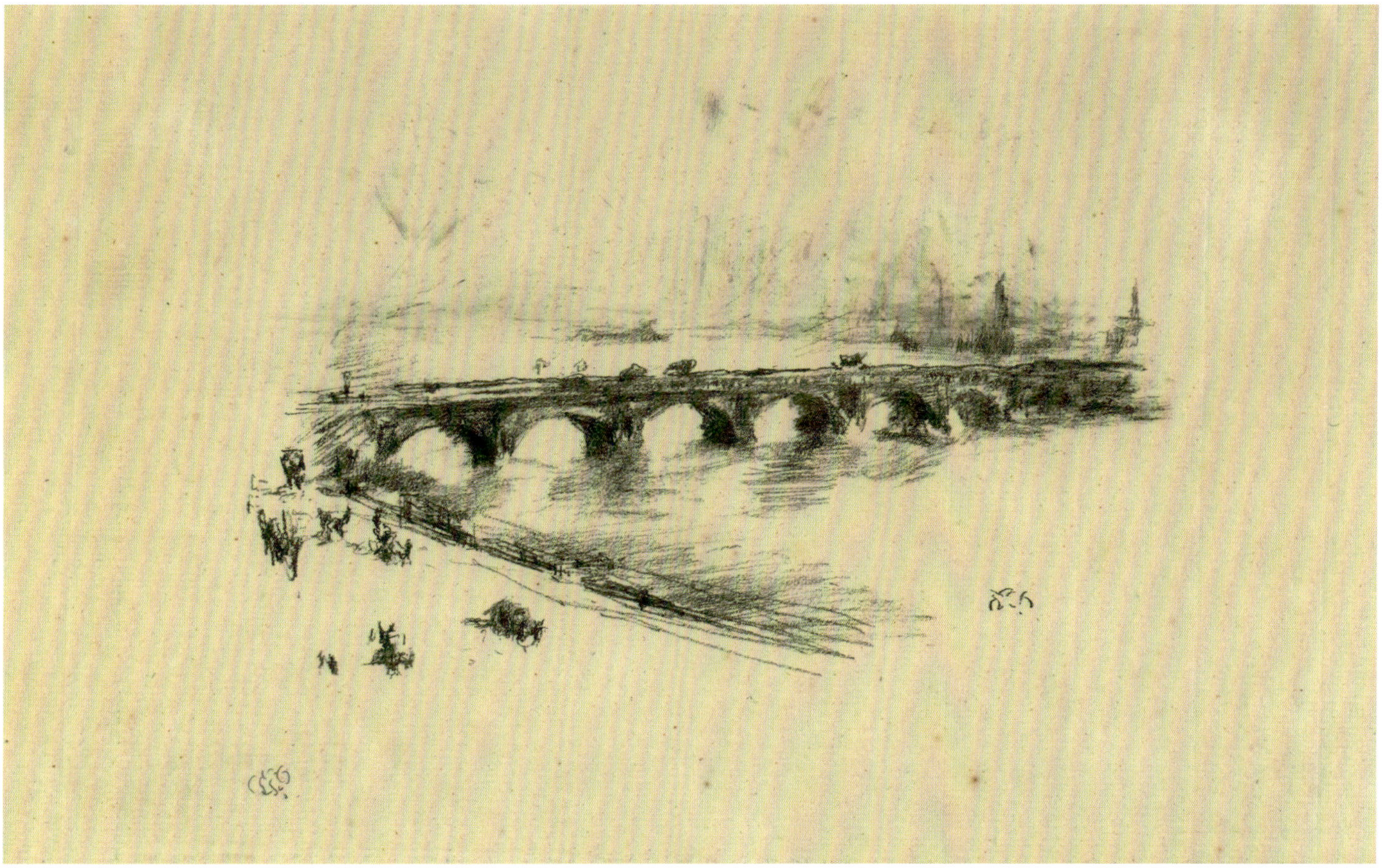

PLATE 66 (*facing page*)
James Abbott McNeill Whistler
(American, 1834–1903)
The Thames
1896
Lithotint with scraping on paper
Image: 10 7⁄16 × 7 3⁄8 in. (26.5 × 18.7 cm)
Sheet: 11 13⁄16 × 8 7⁄16 in. (30 × 21.4 cm)
The Baltimore Museum of Art: The Conrad Collection
BMA 1932.17.19
Photography by: Mitro Hood

PLATE 67
James Abbott McNeill Whistler
(American, 1834–1903)
[*Evening, Little Waterloo Bridge*]
1896
Lithograph on paper
Image: 4 7⁄8 × 7 1⁄2 in. (12.3 × 19.3 cm)
Sheet: 7 7⁄8 × 12 1⁄16 in. (19.9 × 30.7 cm)
Image courtesy of the Prints & Photographs Division, Library of Congress, LC-DIG-ppmsca-06828

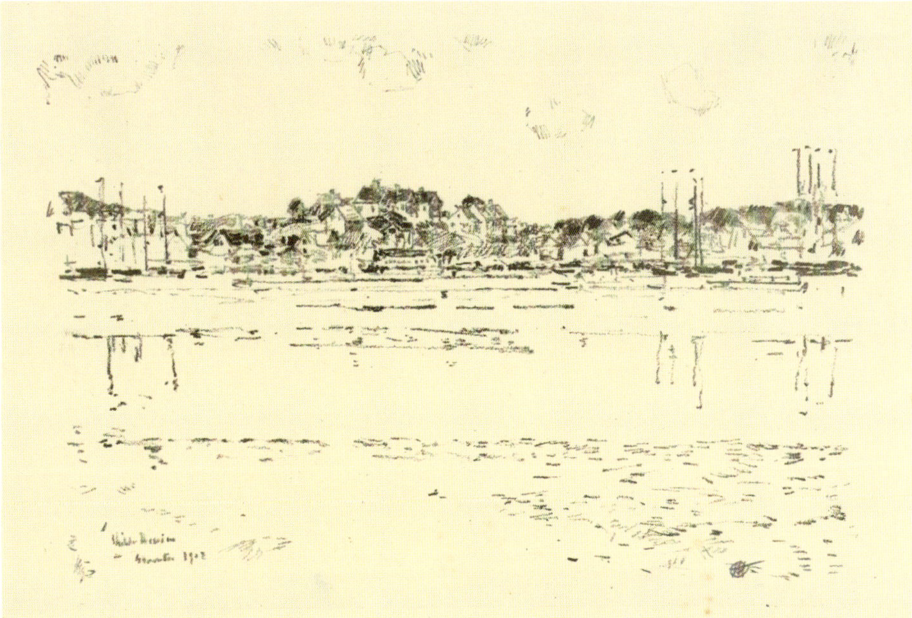

PLATE 68
Frederick Childe Hassam
(American, 1859–1935)
Inner Harbor (Gloucester)
1918
Lithograph on paper
7 7⁄16 × 11 ½ in. (18.9 × 29.2 cm)
Telfair Museums, Savannah, Georgia
Gift of Mrs. Childe Hassam through
Mr. Frank P. Crasto, Jr.
1940.13.16
Photo by David J. Kaminsky

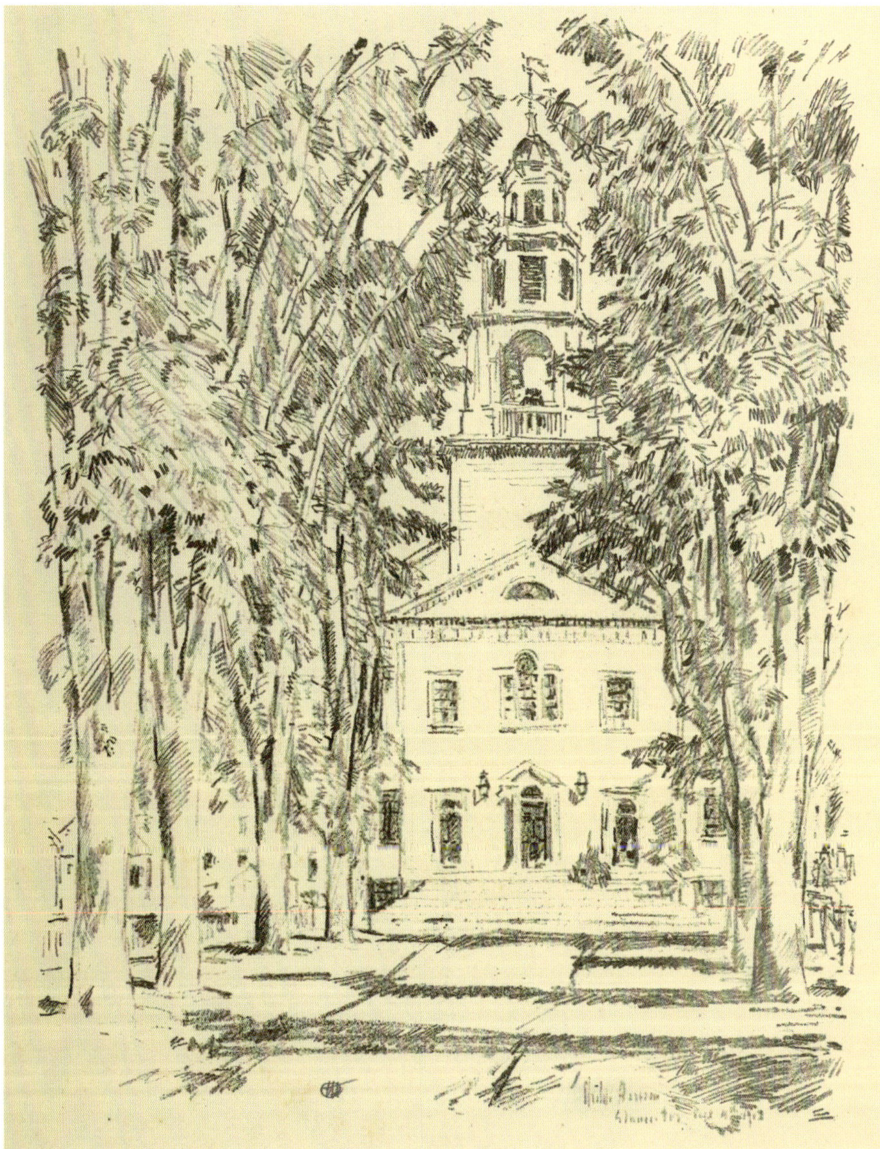

PLATE 69
Frederick Childe Hassam
(American, 1859–1935)
Colonial Church Gloucester
1918
Lithograph on paper
13 ¼ × 10 ⅛ in. (33.7 × 25.7 cm)
Telfair Museums, Savannah, Georgia
Gift of Mrs. Childe Hassam through
Mr. Frank P. Crasto, Jr.
1940.13.14
Photo by David J. Kaminsky

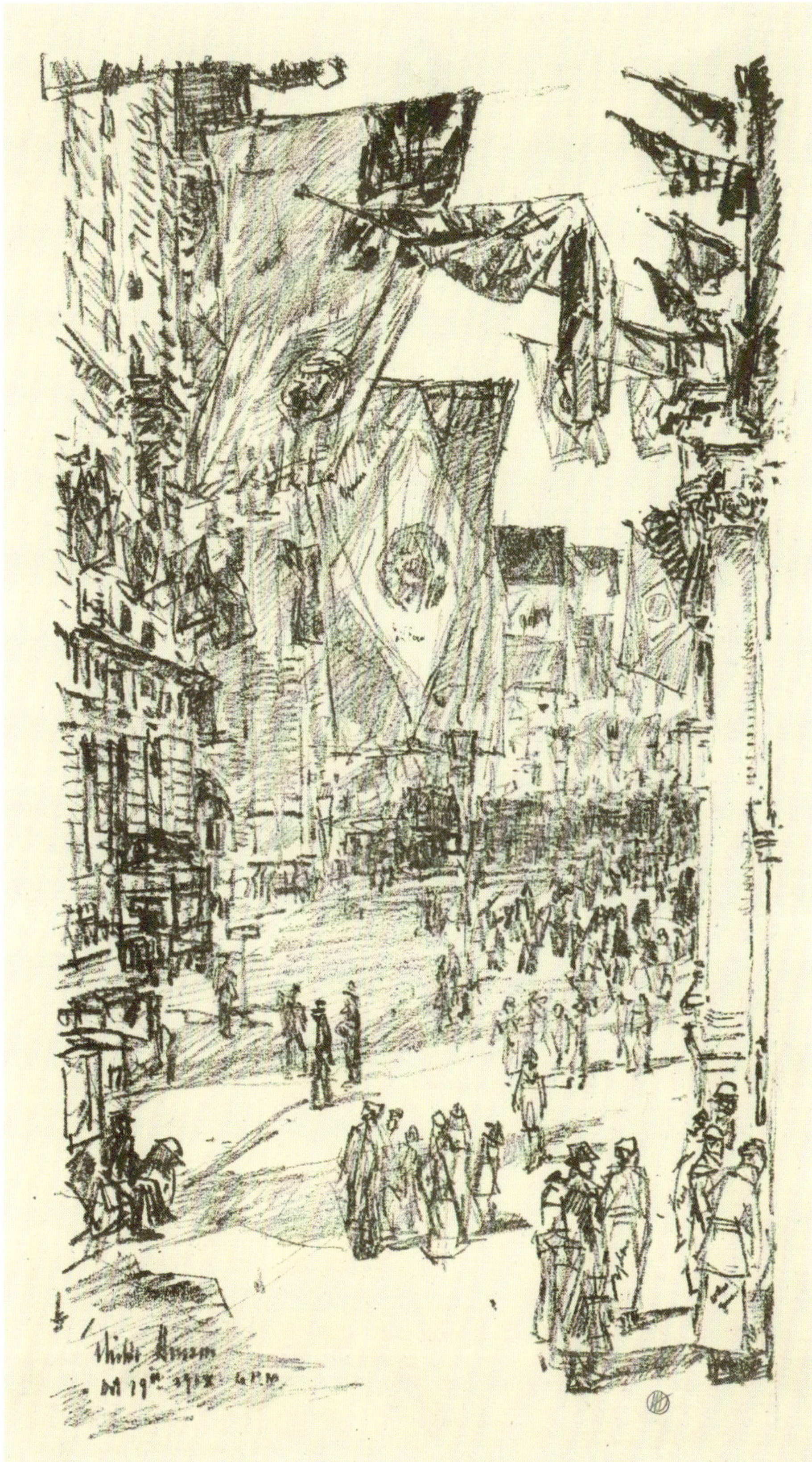

PLATE 70
Frederick Childe Hassam
(American, 1859–1935)
Avenue of the Allies
1918
Lithograph on paper
Image: 12 ⅝ × 7 ¹⁄₁₆ in. (32 × 18 cm)
Sheet: 16 ¹³⁄₁₆ × 11 ⁷⁄₁₆ in. (42.7 × 29 cm)
Print Collection, Miriam and Ira D. Wallach Division of Art, Prints and Photographs, The New York Public Library, Astor, Lenox and Tilden Foundations

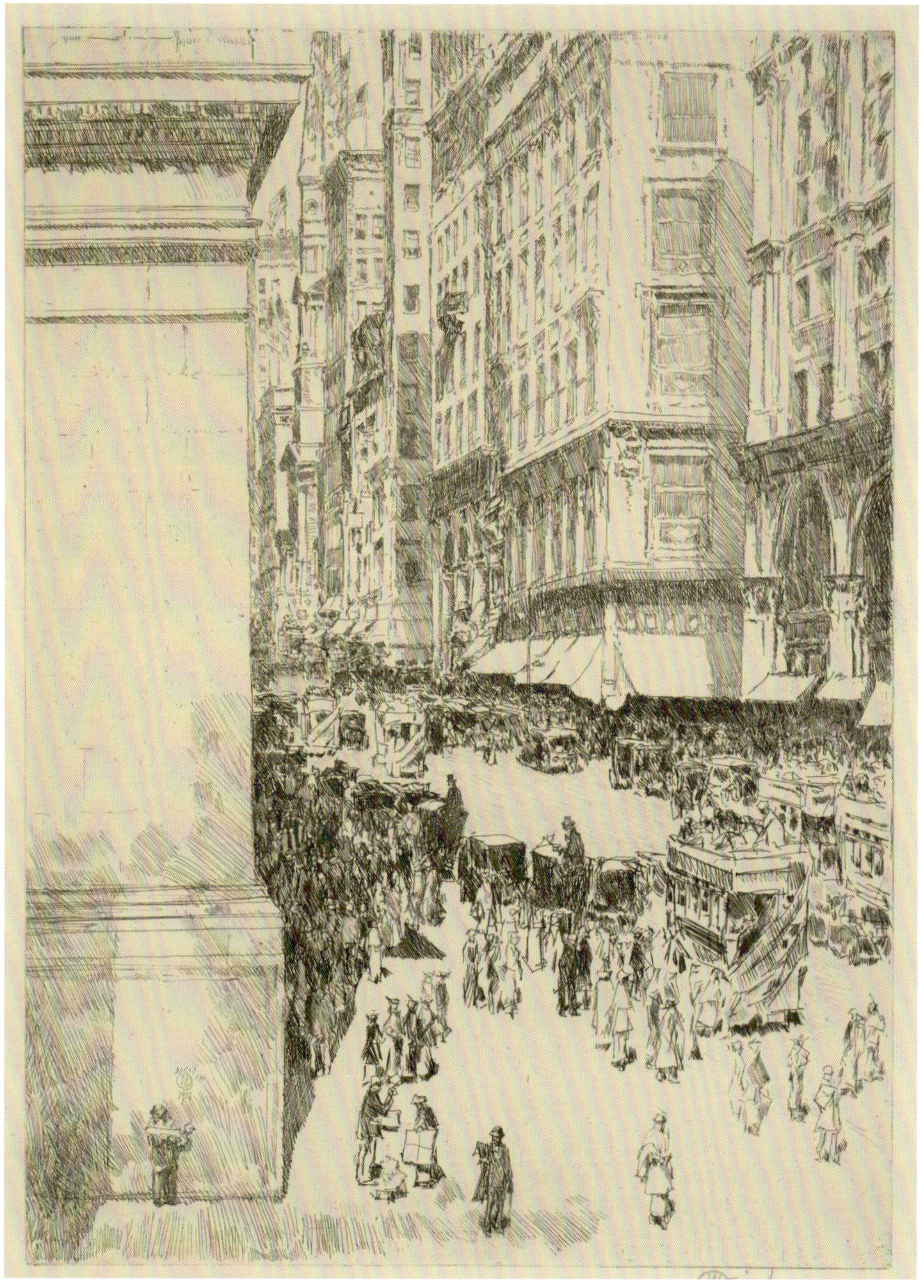

PLATE 71
Frederick Childe Hassam
(American, 1859–1935)
Fifth Avenue, Noon
1916
Etching on paper
Plate: 9 ⅞ × 7 ⅛ in. (25.3 × 18.3 cm)
Sheet: 12 ½ × 9 13⁄16 in. (31.8 × 25 cm)
Image courtesy of the Prints & Photographs Division, Library of Congress, LC-DIG-ppmsca 38333

PLATE 72
Frederick Childe Hassam
(American, 1859–1935)
Washington's Birthday (Fifth Avenue & 23rd Street), Flatiron Building, completed 1902, New York
1916
Etching on paper
Plate: 12 ¾ × 7 in. (32.4 × 17.8 cm)
Sheet: 16 ¼ × 9 ⅜ in. (41.3 × 23.8 cm)
Philadelphia Museum of Art, Pennsylvania, Gift of Bryant W. Langston, 1958
1958-149-31

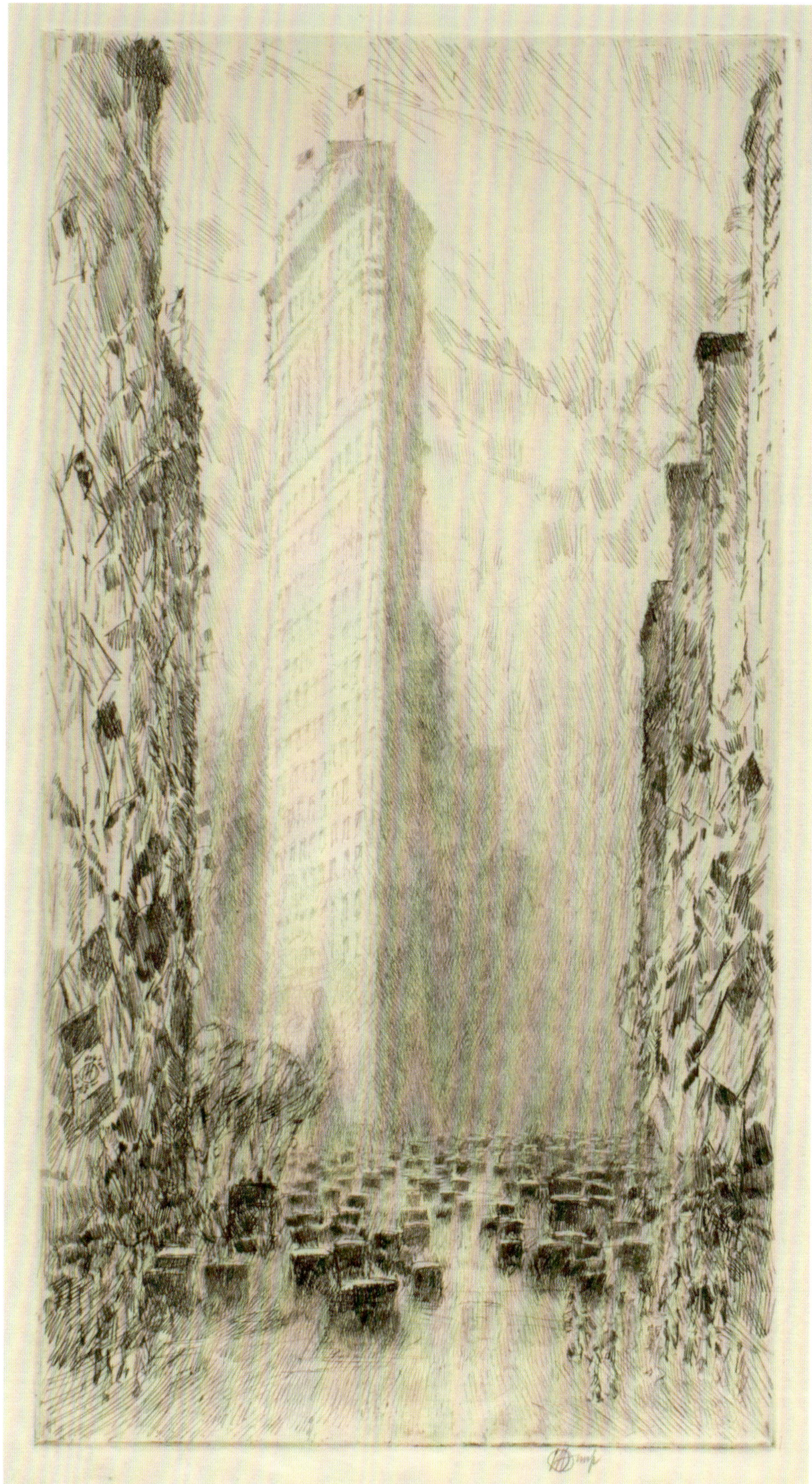

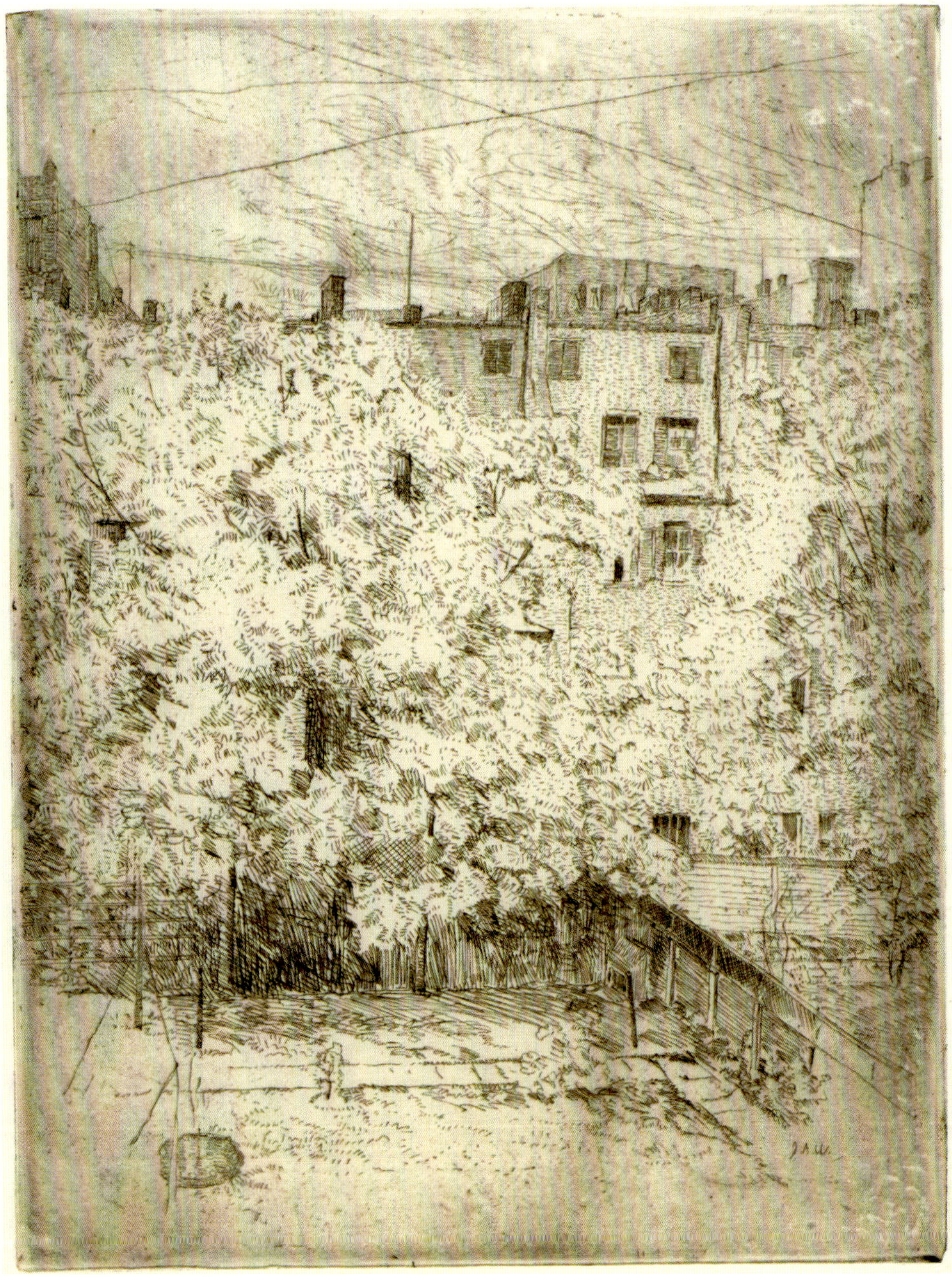

PLATE 73
J. Alden Weir
(American, 1852–1919)
My Back Yard no. 2
1890
Etching on paper
Plate: 7 ⅞ × 6 in. (20 × 15.2 cm)
Smithsonian American Art Museum, Gift of Brigham Young University
1972.84.70

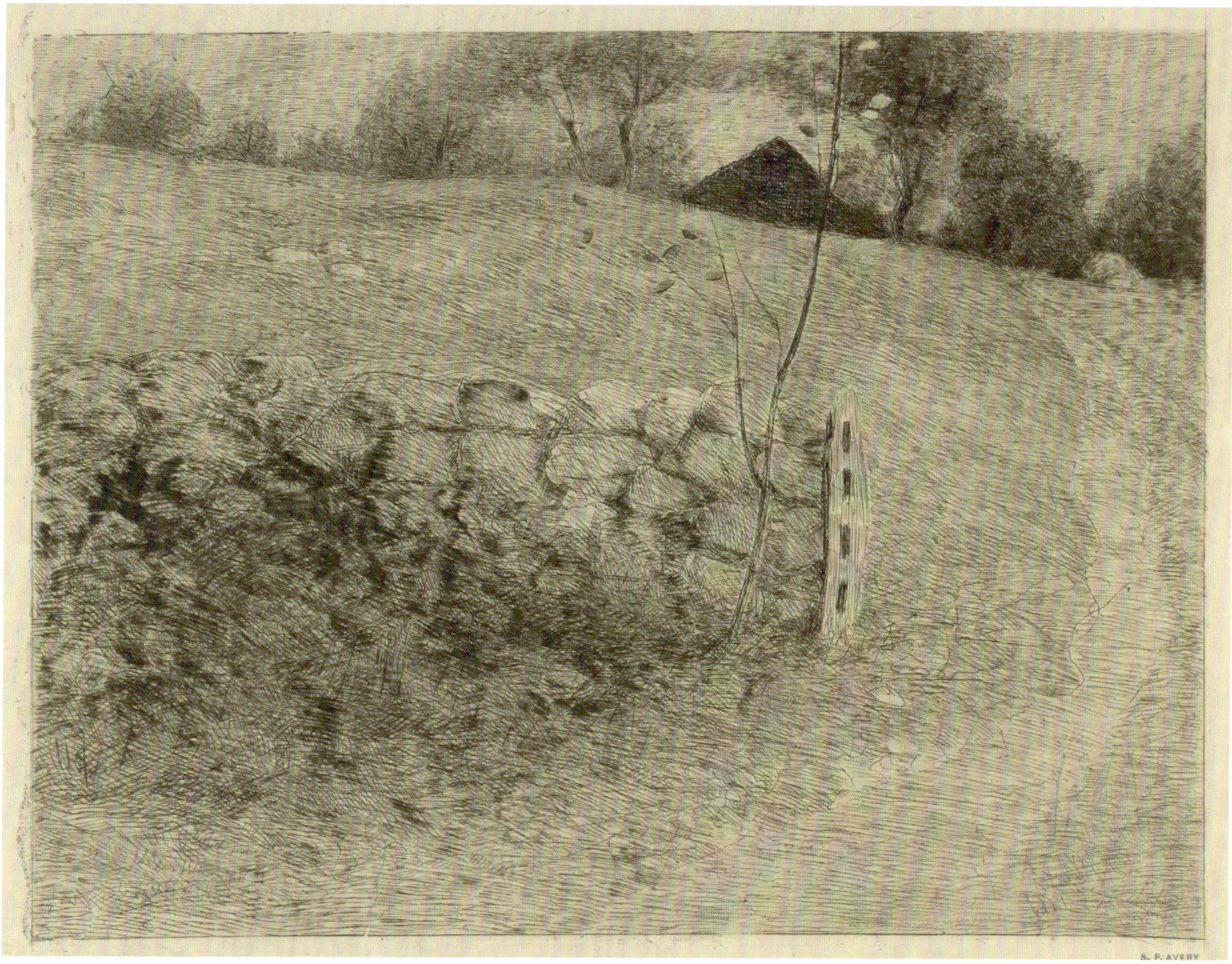

PLATE 74
J. Alden Weir
(American, 1852–1919)
The Barn Lot
1890
Etching and drypoint on paper
Image: 7 11/16 × 10 1/4 in. (19.5 × 26 cm)
Sheet: 12 5/8 × 17 11/16 in. (32 × 45 cm)
S. P. Avery Collection, Print Collection, Miriam and Ira D. Wallach Division of Art, Prints and Photographs, The New York Public Library, Astor, Lenox and Tilden Foundations

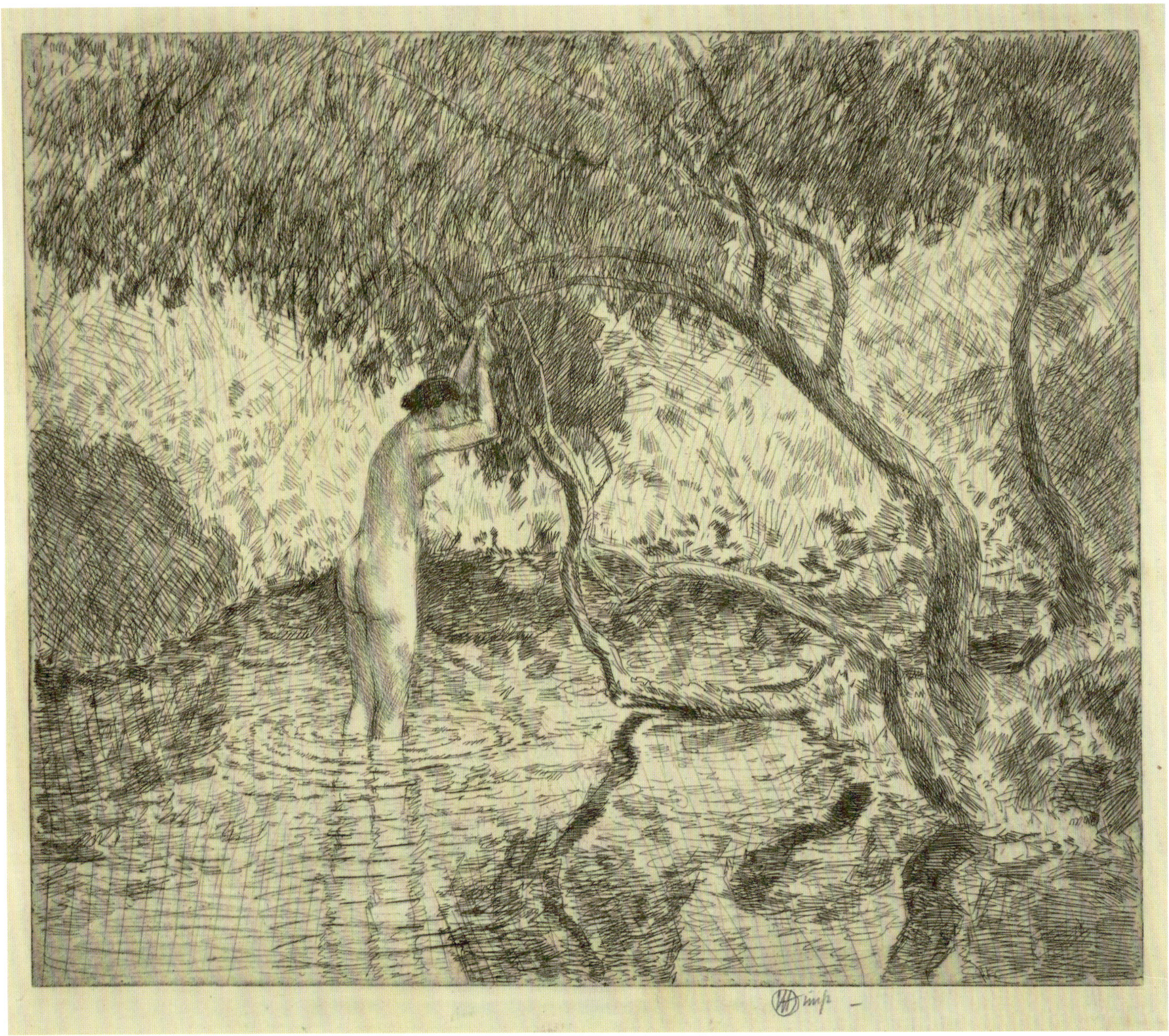

PLATE 75
Frederick Childe Hassam
(American, 1859–1935)
The Willow Pool
1917
Etching on paper
7 ⅜ × 8 ¹⁵⁄₁₆ in. (18.7 × 22.7 cm)
Telfair Museums, Savannah, Georgia
Gift of Mrs. Frederick Childe Hassam through Frank P. Crasto, Jr.
1940.13.12
Photo by David J. Kaminsky

PLATE 76 (*facing page*)
Frederick Childe Hassam
(American, 1859–1935)
The Steps
1915
Etching on paper
Plate: 10 ¾ × 7 ⅝ in. (27.8 × 19.5 cm)
Sheet: 13 ⅝ × 9 ½ in. (34.6 × 24.2 cm)
Image courtesy of the Prints & Photographs Division, Library of Congress, LC-DIG-ppmsca 38334

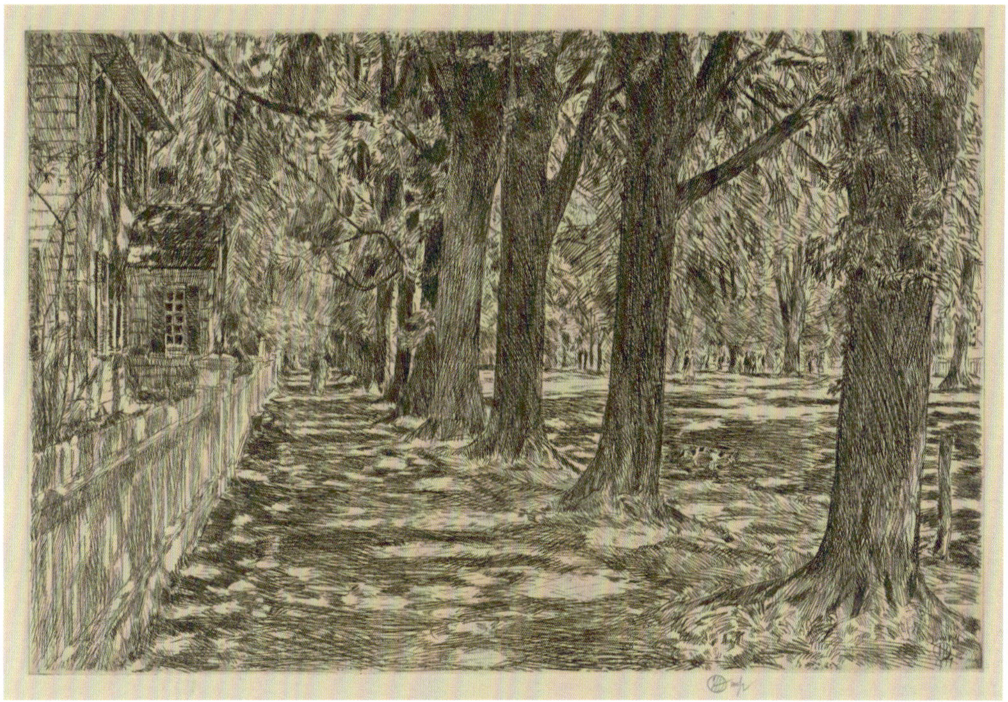

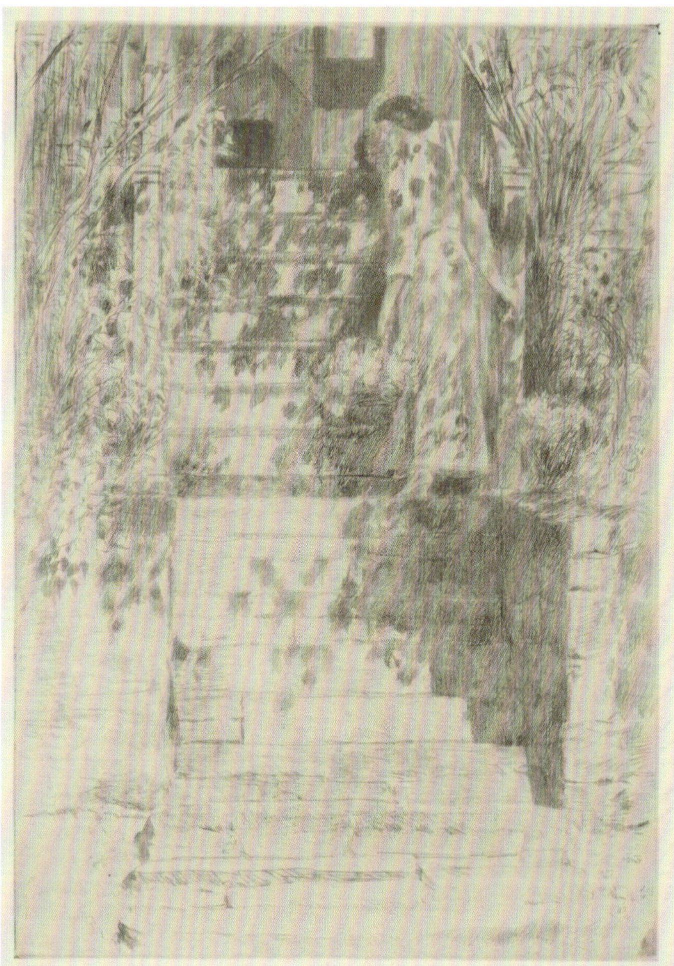

PLATE 77
Frederick Childe Hassam
(American, 1859–1935)
Easthampton
1917
Etching on paper
Image: 7 7⁄16 × 11 3⁄8 in. (18.9 × 28.9 cm)
Sheet: 9 13⁄16 × 13 3⁄4 in. (24.9 × 35 cm)
Print Collection, Miriam and Ira D. Wallach Division of Art, Prints and Photographs, The New York Public Library, Astor, Lenox and Tilden Foundations

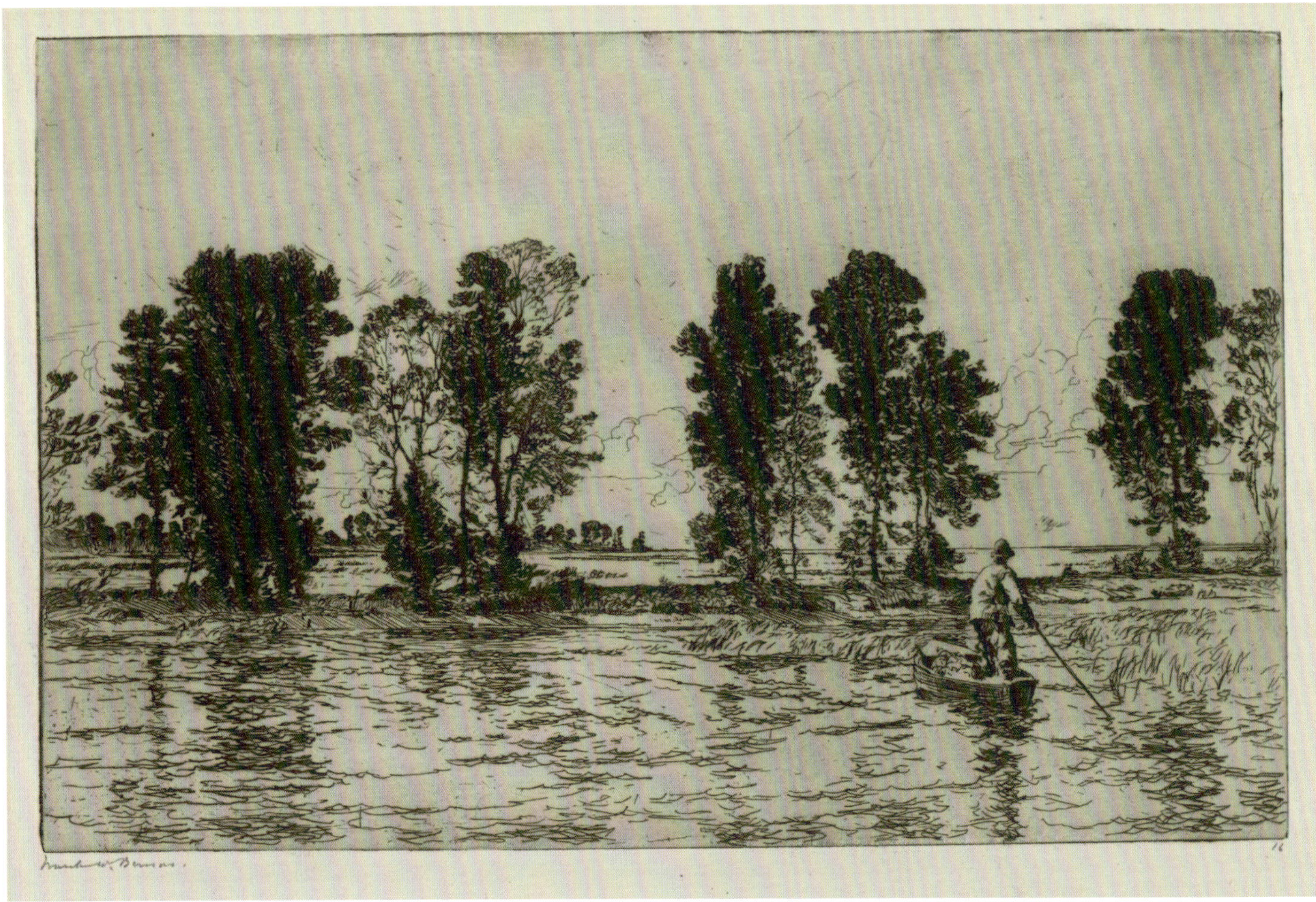

PLATE 78
Frank Benson
(American, 1862–1951)
[*Second Island Outlet*]
1916
Etching on paper
Plate: 8 ⅝ × 13 ⅝ in. (22.3 × 34.7 cm)
Sheet: 12 15⁄16 × 16 in. (32.8 × 40.6 cm)
Image courtesy of the Prints & Photographs Division, Library of Congress, LC-DIG-ppmsca-38330

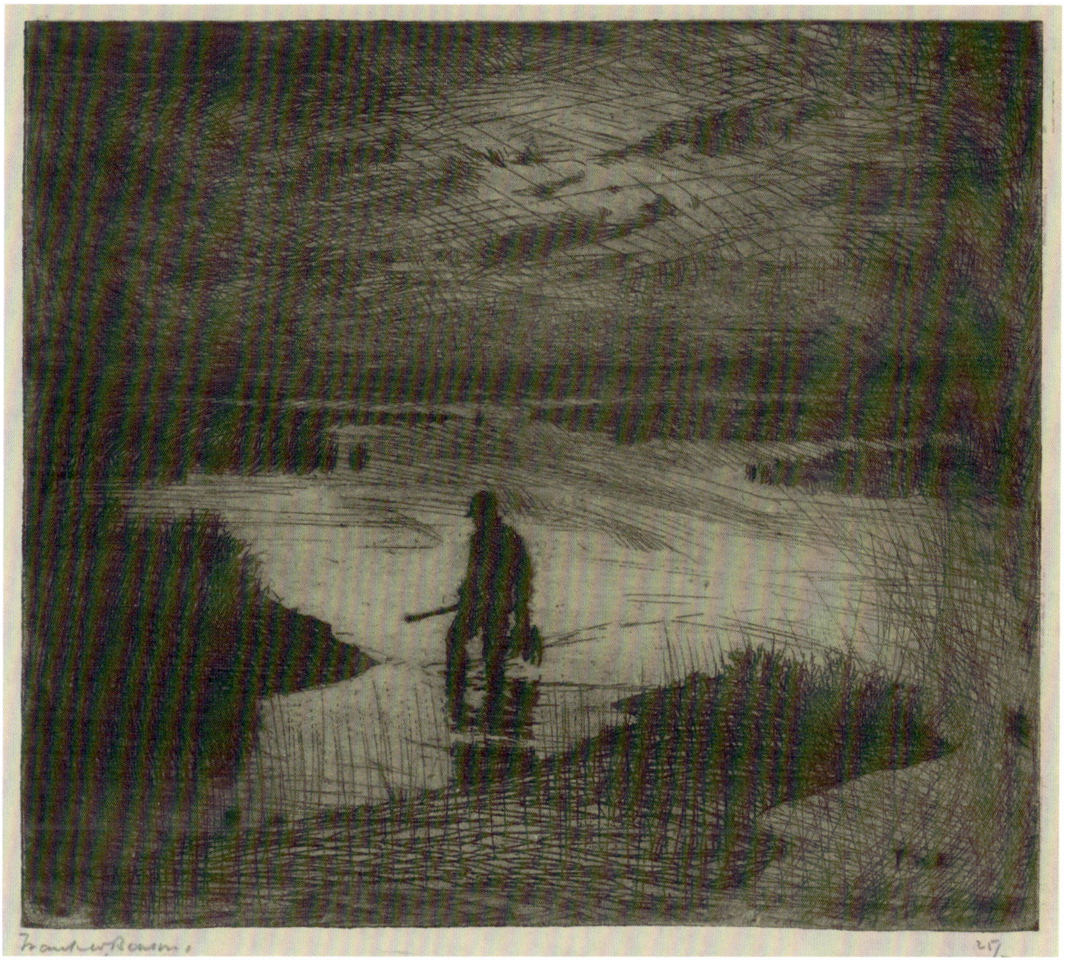

PLATE 79
Frank Benson
(American, 1862–1951)
[*Dusk*]
1914
Etching on paper
Plate: 9 ⅓ × 10 ⅞ in. (23.7 × 27.5 cm)
Sheet: 11 1/16 × 13 ⅞ in. (28.2 × 35.3 cm)
Image courtesy of the Prints & Photographs Division, Library of Congress, LC-DIG-ppmsca 38332

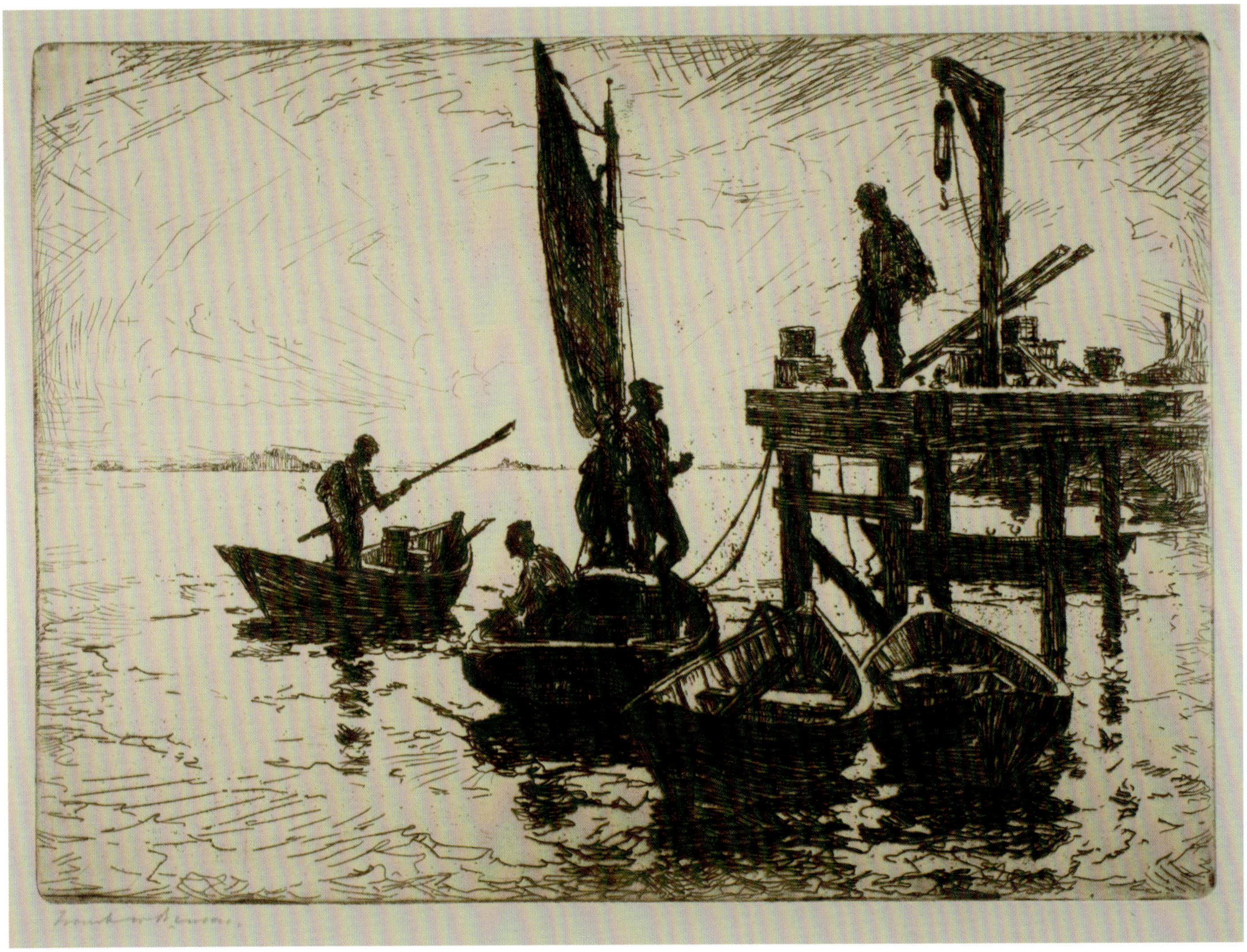

PLATE 80
Frank Benson
(American, 1862–1951)
Boats at Dawn
1920
Etching (zinc) on paper
Plate: 7 ¼ × 11 ¼ in. (18.4 × 28.6 cm)
Sheet: 11 ½ × 13 ¾ in. (29.2 × 34.9 cm)
Philadelphia Museum of Art, Pennsylvania,
The William S. Pilling Collection, 1933
1933-72-1041

PLATE 81
Frank Benson
(American, 1862–1951)
The Landing
1915
Etching on paper
Plate: 7 11/16 × 10 ¾ in. (19.5 × 27.3 cm)
Sheet: 10 5/16 × 14 ¼ in. (26.2 × 36.2 cm)
Philadelphia Museum of Art, Pennsylvania,
The William S. Pilling Collection, 1933
1933-72-1061

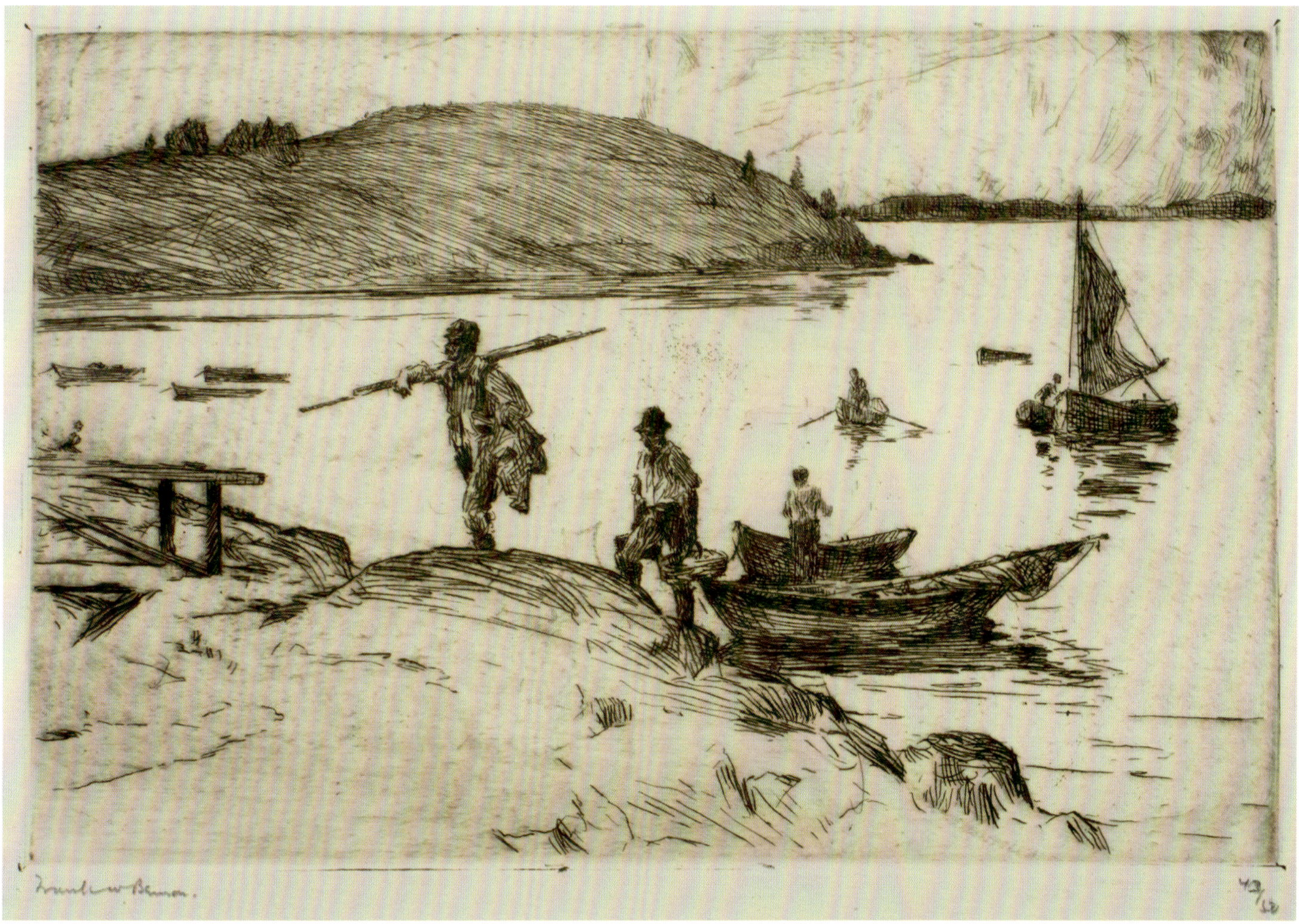

Contributors

Sophia Krzys Acord is Associate Director of the University of Florida Center for the Humanities and the Public Sphere and Lecturer in the Department of Sociology and Criminology and Law. Her past work, published in *Sociologie de l'art*, *Qualitative Sociology*, and *Artistic Practices,* examined curatorial practices in contemporary art. Her present research concerns the production of knowledge in the humanities, particularly the impact of digital technologies on engaging publics with scholarly work. Dr. Acord currently works in program development and evaluation to increase the profile of humanistic scholarship at the University of Florida and in the broader community.

Sean Patrick Adams is Associate Professor of History at the University of Florida, where he teaches courses in American capitalism and nineteenth-century U.S. history. His research interests include political economy, energy policy, and industrialization in the United States. His books include *Old Dominion, Industrial Commonwealth: Coal, Politics, and Economy in Antebellum America* (2004) and *Home Fires: How Americans Kept Warm in the Nineteenth Century* (2014). He has published articles recently in the *Journal of American History*, *Enterprise and Society*, *Business History,* and Common-place.org, as well as several chapters in published collections.

Melissa Lee Hyde is Professor of eighteenth- and nineteenth-century European art at the University of Florida. She is the author of numerous publications that focus on gender and visual culture in France. Her books include *Making Up the Rococo: François Boucher and His Critics* (2006) and several coedited volumes. Soon to be published is a book, coauthored with Mary D. Sheriff, titled *Women in French Art: Rococo to Romanticism, 1750–1830.* Hyde has held postdoctoral positions at the American Association of University Women and the Getty Research Institute and, more recently, has been a fellow at the Clark Art Institute and at the Institut national d'histoire de l'art, Paris.

Nancy Mowll Mathews recently retired as the Eugénie Prendergast Senior Curator of Nineteenth and Twentieth Century Art at the Williams College Museum of Art; she is currently Visiting Associate Professor at the Massachusetts College of Liberal Arts. Mathews received her Ph.D. from the Institute of Fine Arts, New York University, and was at Williams College from 1984 to 2012. In addition to directing the Prendergast Archive and Study Center at the college museum, she taught in the Williams College Art Department and Graduate Program in the History of Art. She is the coauthor of the Prendergast catalogue raisonné and is the author of books on Maurice and Charles Prendergast, Mary Cassatt, Paul Gauguin, and the relationship between art and early film.

Courtney A. McNeil is Curator of Fine Arts and Exhibitions for Telfair Museums in Savannah, Georgia, the oldest public art museum in the South. At the Telfair she has served as lead curator for numerous exhibitions, including *Spanish Sojourns: Robert Henri and the Spirit of Spain*; *Dan Winters's America: Icons and Ingenuity*; and *Beyond Whistler: Modern and Contemporary Prints from the Telfair's Collection*. Before coming to the Telfair, she was employed at Childs Gallery in Boston, where she specialized in American and European prints and nineteenth- and early-twentieth-century American painting. She holds a B.A. from Georgetown University and an M.A. from the Courtauld Institute of Art in London.

Carol J. Murphy is Professor of French in the Department of Languages, Literatures and Cultures at the University of Florida, and founding Director of the France-Florida Research Institute (2002–2012). Her fields of specialization are twentieth- and twenty-first-century French fiction and critical theory. In addition to book-length studies on Marguerite Duras and Julien Gracq and a translation of an essay on art by the writer-editor Jean Paulhan, she has written numerous articles on contemporary cultural production in France. Her course "Text and Image," offered to both undergraduate and graduate students, examines the intersection of modernist currents (Impressionism, Cubism, Futurism, Surrealism) in French literature and the plastic arts.

Louise M. Newman is a specialist in U.S. women's history, and Associate Professor of U.S. history at the University of Florida, where she has taught for the past twenty years. She is the author of *White Women's Rights: The Racial Origins of Feminism in the United States* (1999), as well as editor of *Men's Ideas/Women's Realities: Popular Science, 1870–1915* (1985). She has written articles on the history of women's rights, race, and imperialism in the nineteenth century and on the history of second-wave feminism in the twentieth century.

DULCE M. ROMÁN is Curator of Modern Art and Curatorial Chair at the Samuel P. Harn Museum of Art, University of Florida. She is responsible for the development and management of the Harn's collection of modern art from the United States, Latin America, and Europe. Since joining the Harn staff she has curated more than twenty exhibitions, including the current exhibition, *Monet and American Impressionism*. Before coming to the Harn, she served as a researcher of Spanish art at the Frick Collection and in the department of European paintings at the Metropolitan Museum of Art. She holds a B.A. in psychology from Harvard University and M.A. and Master of Philosophy degrees in art history from Columbia University.

ERIC J. SEGAL is Education Curator of Academic Programs at the Samuel P. Harn Museum of Art. He earned M.A. and Ph.D. degrees in American art history from the University of California, Los Angeles. Prior to joining the Harn staff, he served as Assistant Professor of art history at the University of Florida. His teaching has included museum courses as well as undergraduate and graduate courses in the history of American and African American art, illustration, and museum history and theory. He has published on nineteenth- and twentieth-century American art and illustration, and he lectures on American art and museum education.

STEPHANIE A. SMITH is Associate Chair and Undergraduate Coordinator of English at the University of Florida. She received her Ph.D. from Berkeley and has been at the University of Florida since 1990. She is the author of eight books, two young-adult novels, two books of criticism, and four novels, including the *Warpaint* trilogy; she has won multiple fiction residencies at the Noepe Center for the Literary Arts, Hedgebrook, Norcroft, Provincetown, and Dorland and was a 1998 Visiting NEH Scholar at UCLA. Examining the intersections of science, literature, race, and gender, her essays, short stories, and reviews have appeared in numerous publications. Currently, she is finishing a critical book and a new novel, *Strange Grace*.

GAYLE ZACHMANN is Associate Professor of French Studies at the University of Florida and Affiliate Faculty in the Center for European Studies and the Center for Jewish Studies. She serves as North American editor of the journal *Romance Studies*, and her publications include *Frameworks for Mallarmé: The "Photo" and the "Graphic" of an Interdisciplinary Aesthetic* (2008), a special number of the *South Central Review* titled "Cultural Production in Nineteenth-Century France," and articles on French avant-garde writers and artists such as Stéphane Mallarmé, Villiers de L'Isle-Adam, Marcel Schwob, Claude Cahun, and Lise Deharme.